RAY LOWRY

INK

RAY LOWRY – INK

Drunk at the drawing board. Cartoons and strips from a deranged mind.

(Follow up: Drunk at the drawing board, again.)

First Published in Great Britain in 1998 by
The Do-Not Press
PO Box 4215
London SE23 2QD

A paperback original.

ISBN 1 899344 21 7

British Library Cataloguing in Publication Data. A catalogue record for this book is available from the British Library.

h g f e d c b a

Printed and bound in Great Britain by The Guernsey Press Co Ltd.

Ray Lowry writes his own biography...

"Ray Lowry's cartoons and illustrations appeared in the underground press of the late 1960s, before he rose to greater obscurity with regular appearances in Punch, Private Eye and Mayfair (the magazine).

For many years he was a weekly cartoonist for the NME, contributing cartoons, strips, illustrations and begging letters before becoming irredeemably passé in the 1980s.

Since then he was worked for the Guardian, Observer, Spectator, the Oldie and Loaded.

He has recently illustrated a harrowing account of life on the road with The Clash, designed the cover of Elvis – The Novel for The Do-Not Press and for a while contributed a weekly cartoon to The Big Issue from his cardboard box on the Thames Embankment. He also illustrates the rock music section of Tatler magazine and is one third of the infamous West Texas Triangle.

There are a number of single frame cartoons scattered throughout INK.
A lot of old favourites from the likes of NME, Punch and Private Eye,
and a bunch of previously unseen drawings.

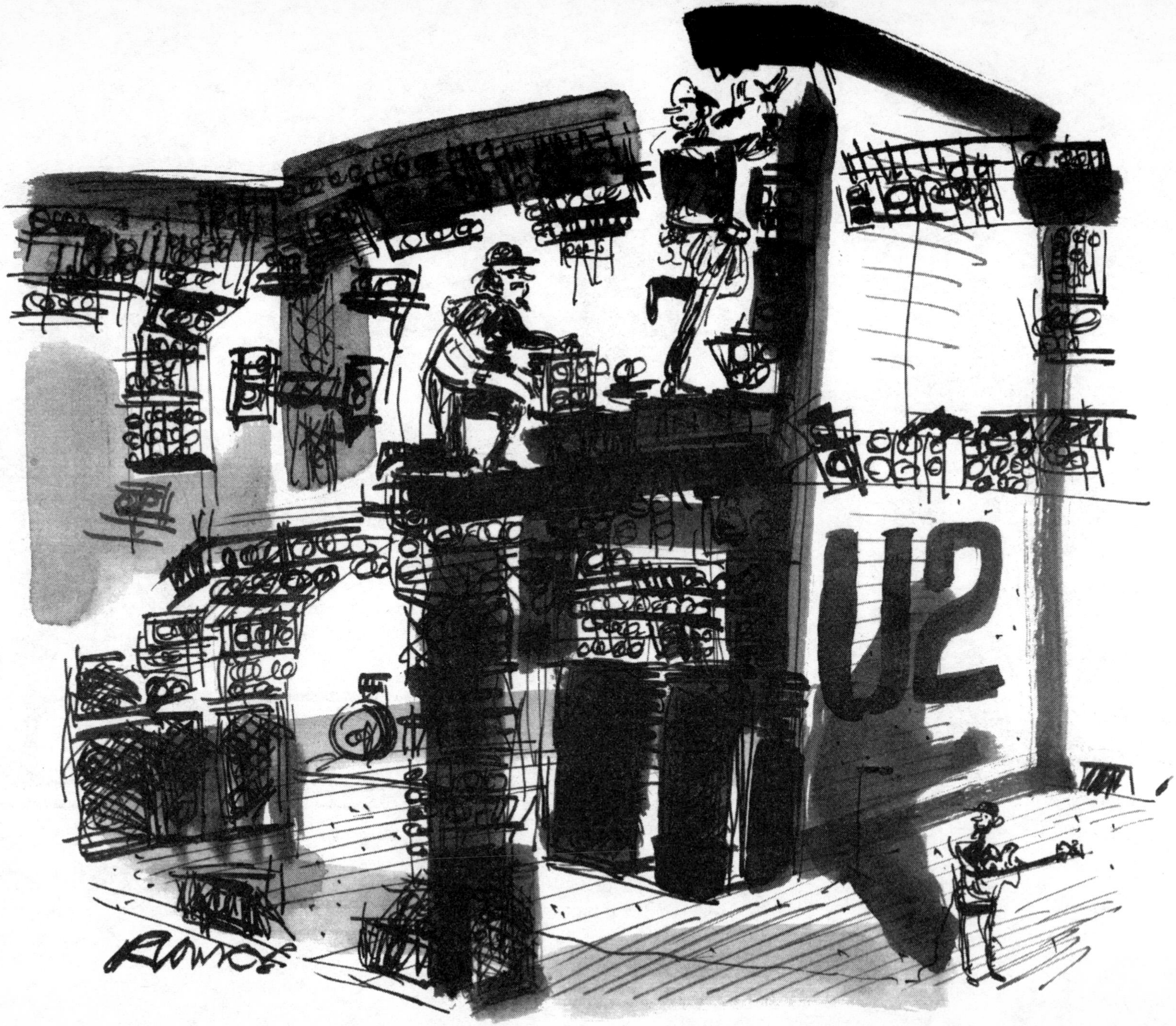
U2

"This was bound to happen sooner or later. You're dismantling the rig while I'm still putting it up!"

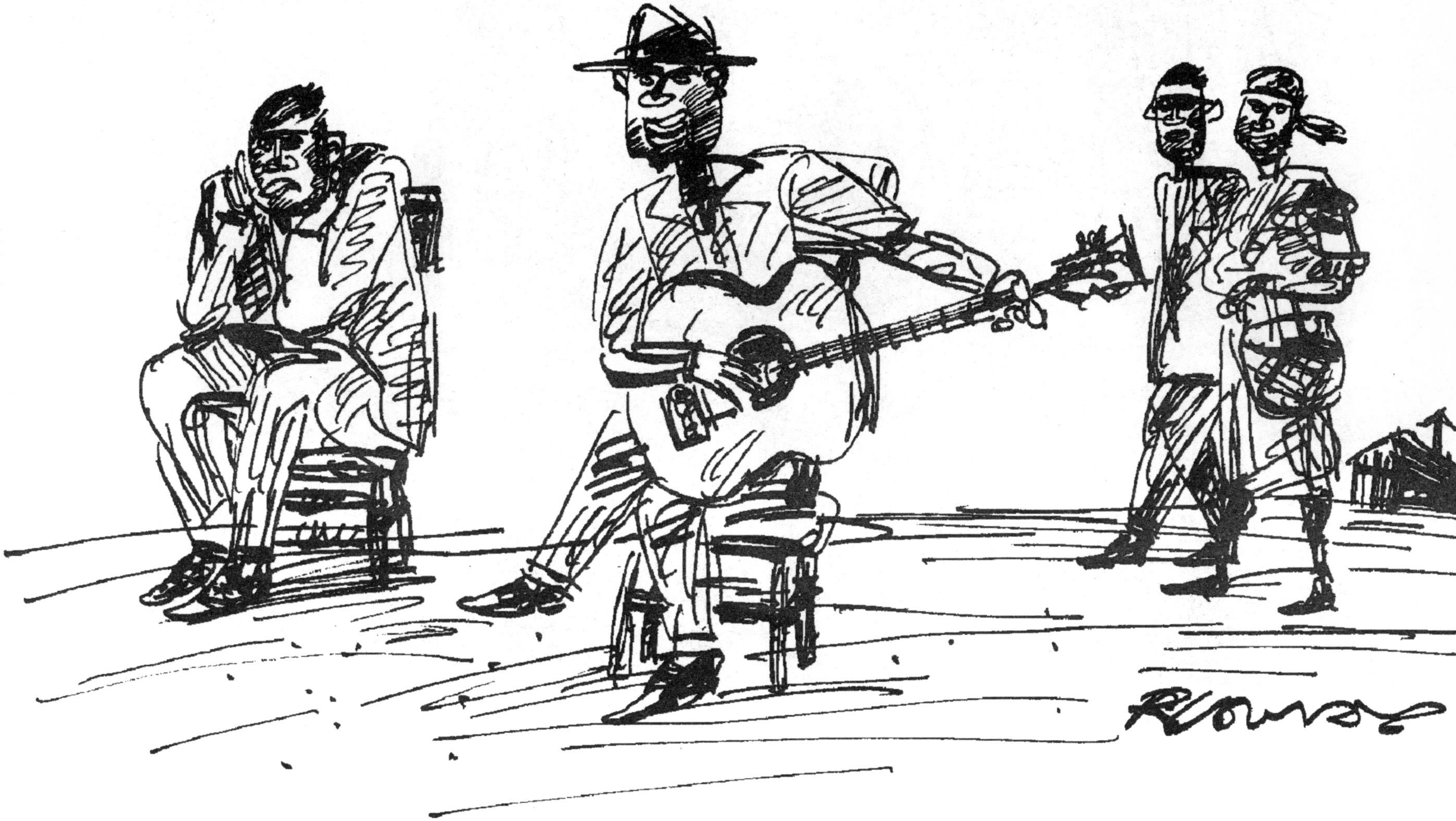

"Since he became a recording star he employs that little man to have the blues for him."

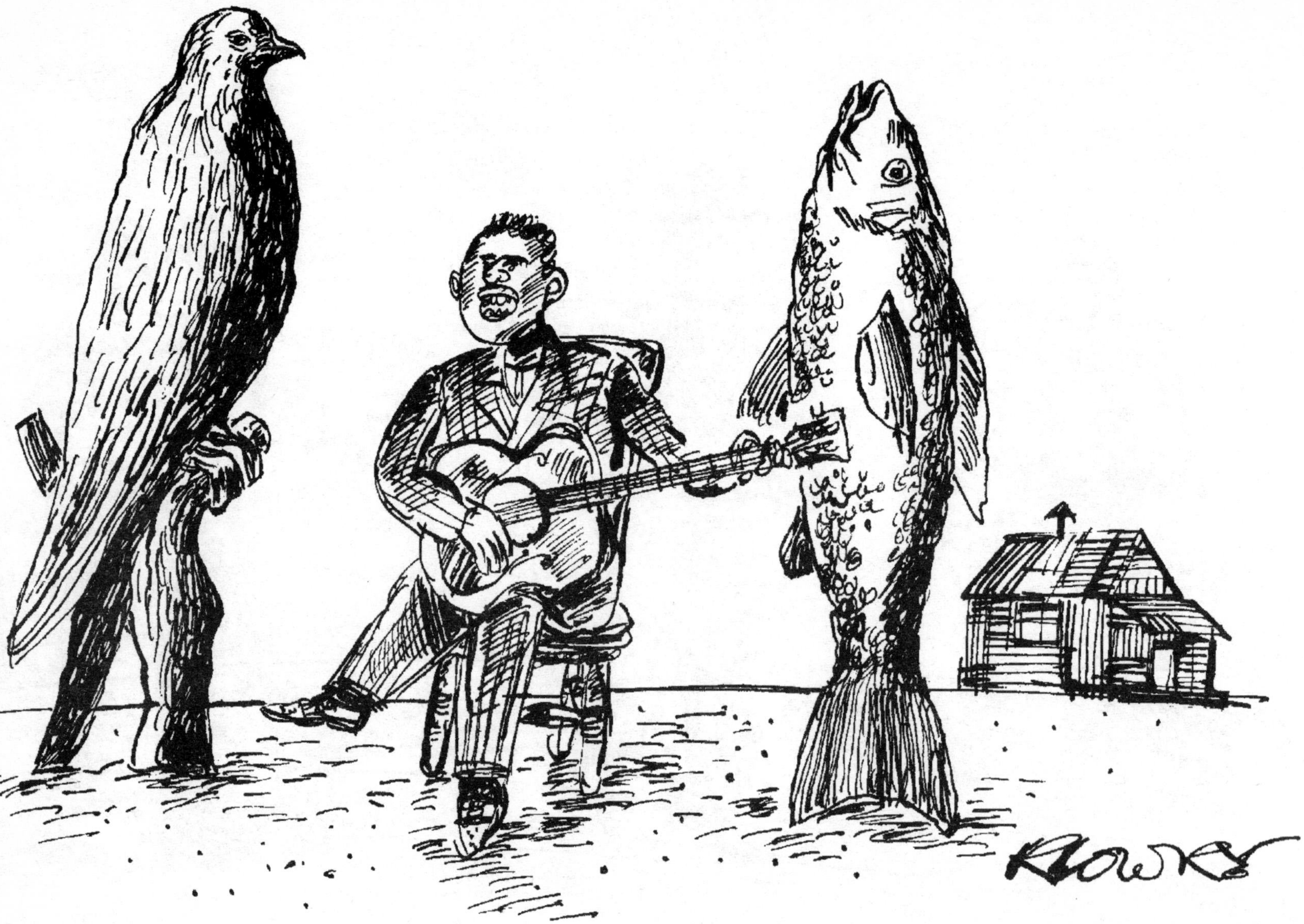

"Woke up this mornin' – got the surrealist blues!"

IF ALLEN GINSBERG had gone into fast food…

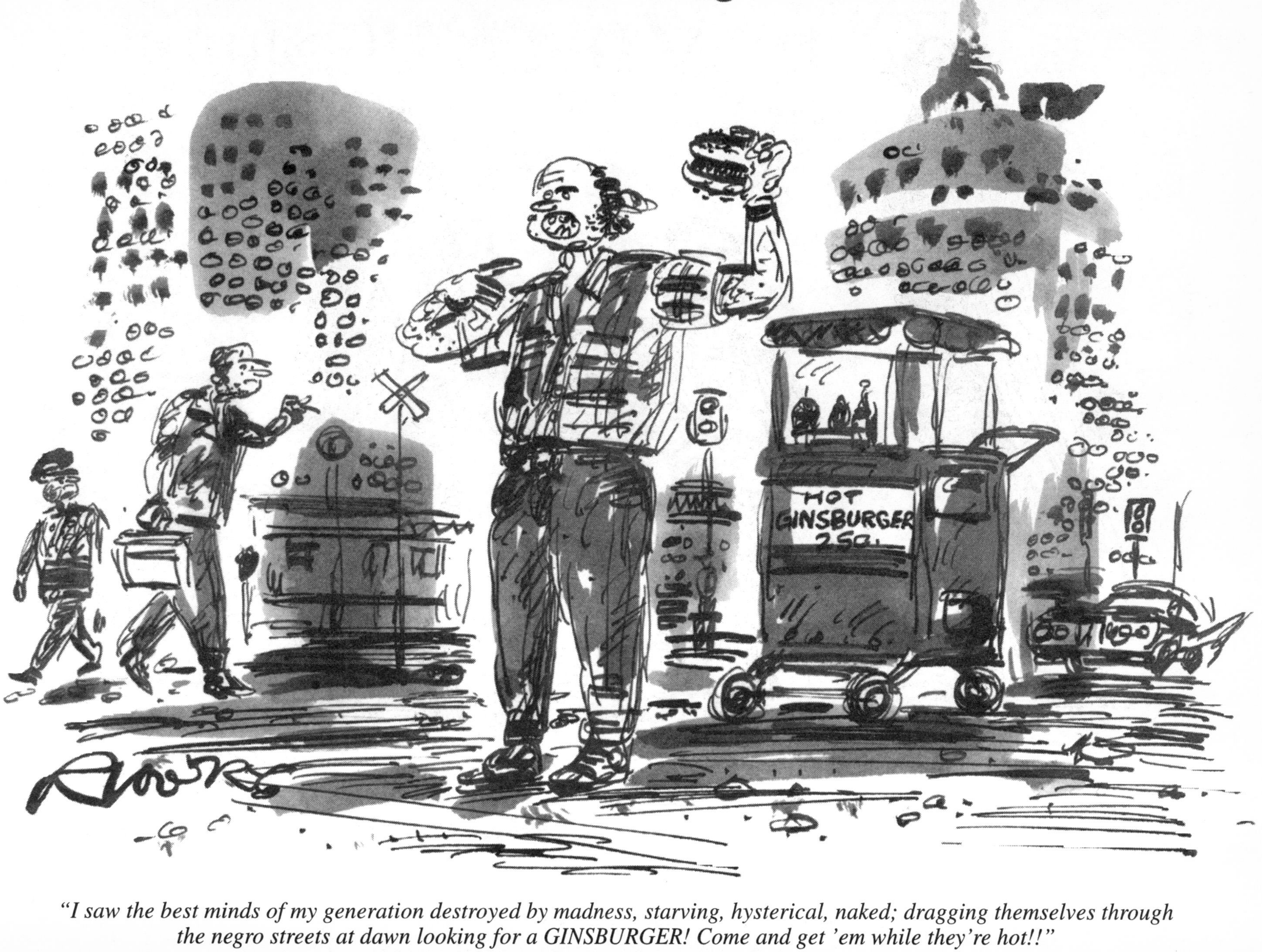
HOT
GINSBURGER
25¢.

"I saw the best minds of my generation destroyed by madness, starving, hysterical, naked; dragging themselves through the negro streets at dawn looking for a GINSBURGER! Come and get 'em while they're hot!!"

IF GENE VINCENT HAD LIVED…

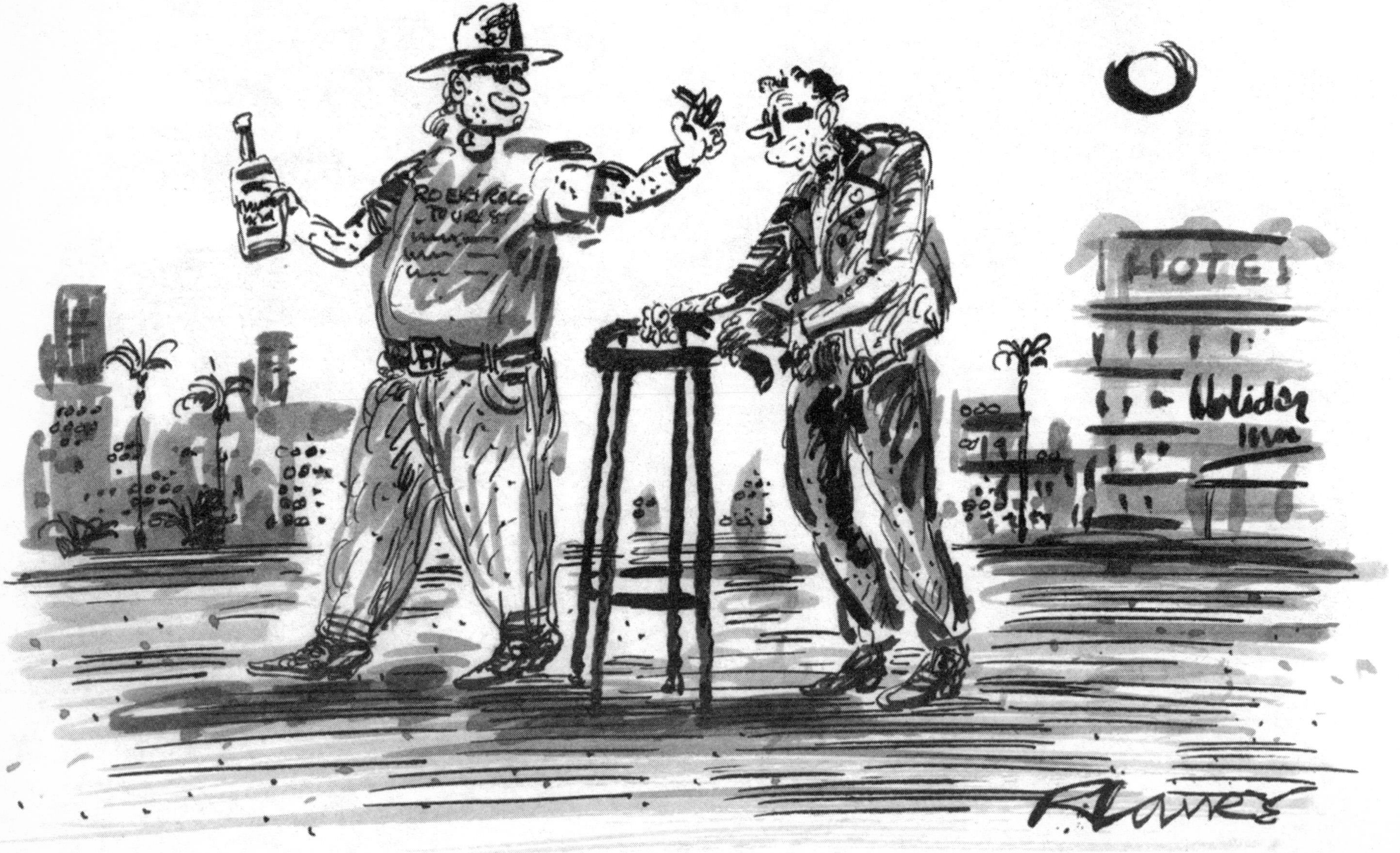
HOTEL
Holiday Inn

"The kids'll love it, Gene – a black leather zimmer!"

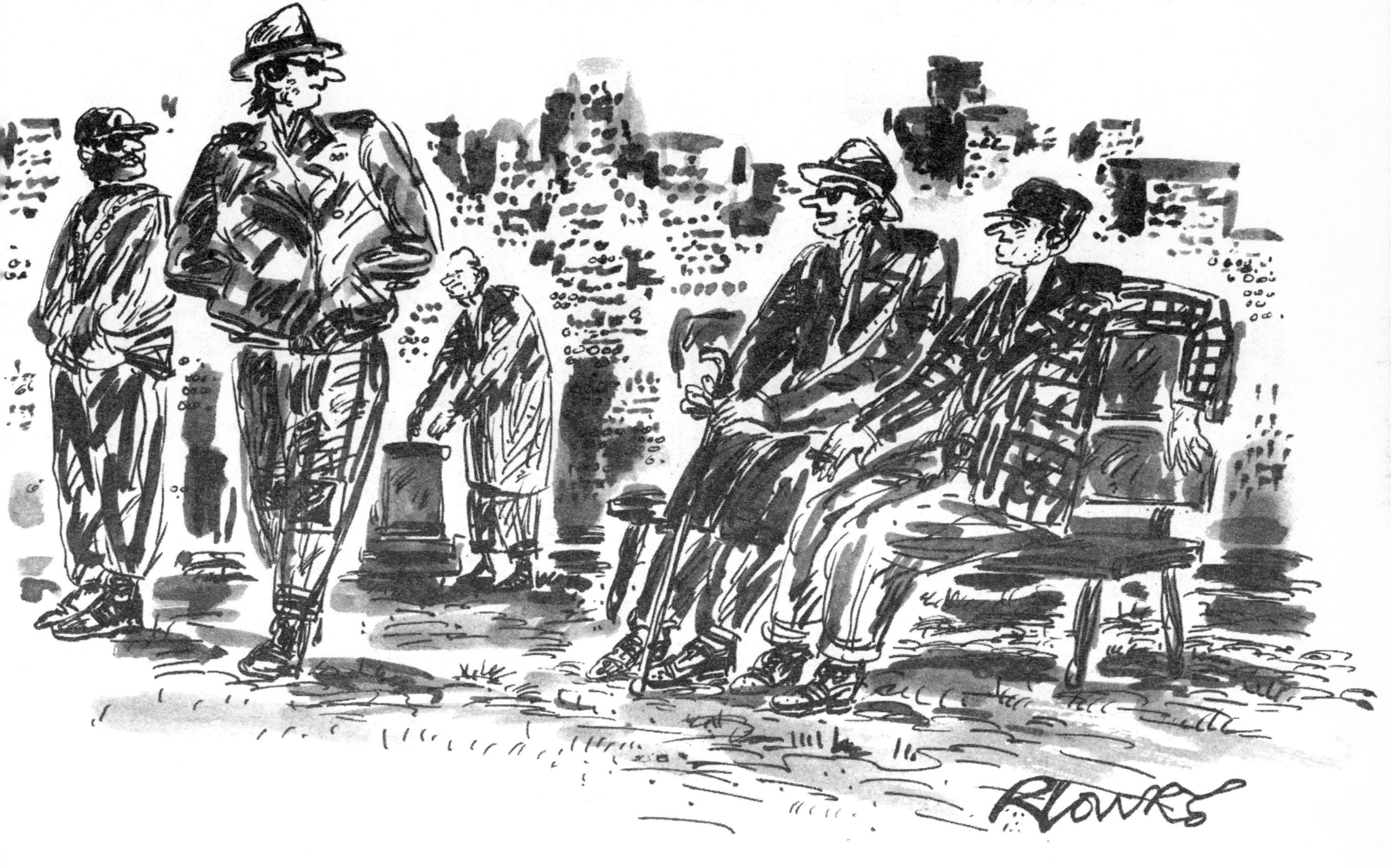

FLOWERS

"We're waiting for the man, as well. The man with the zimmers."

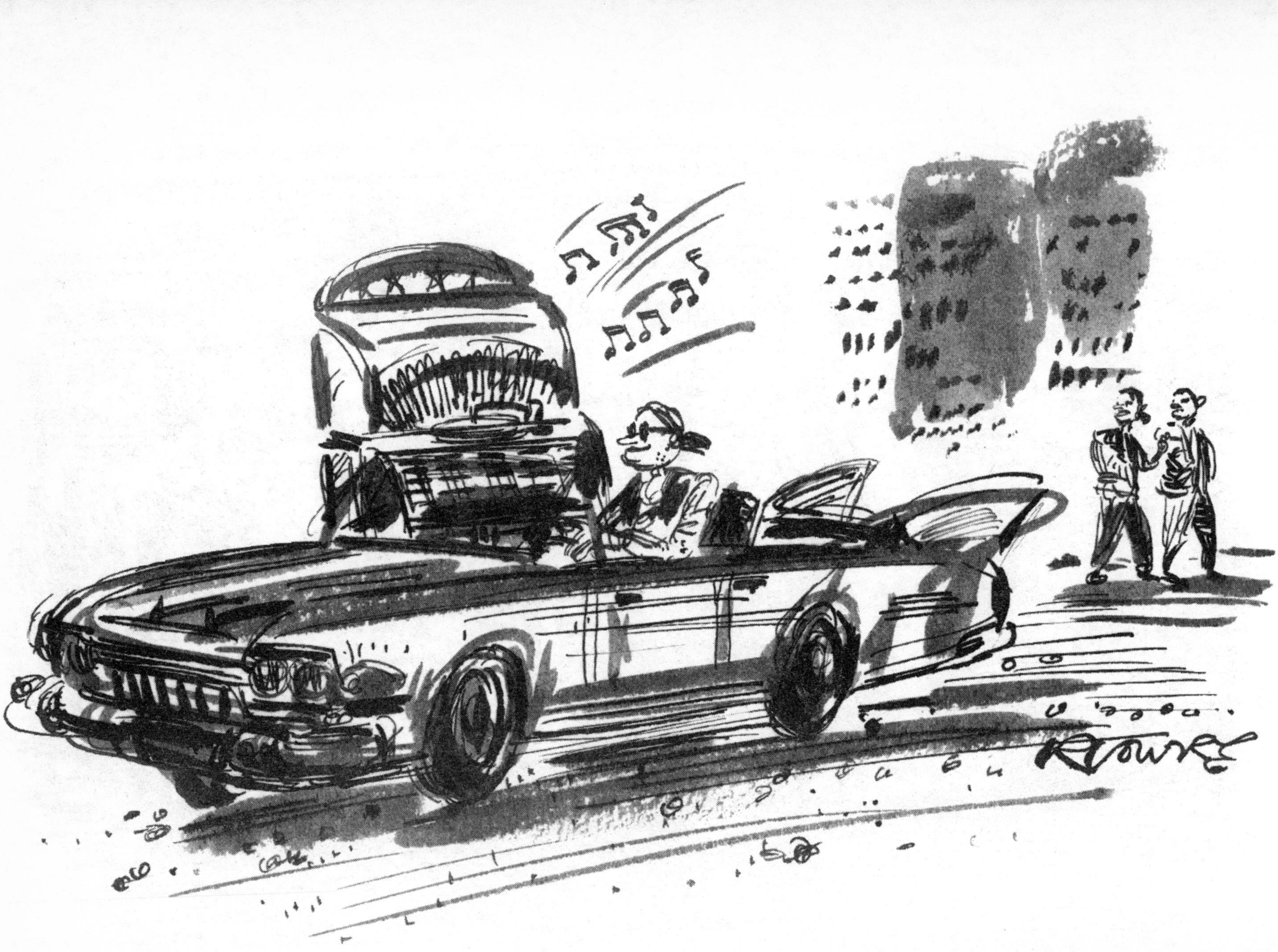

"Bloody nouveau riche – an in-car jukebox!"

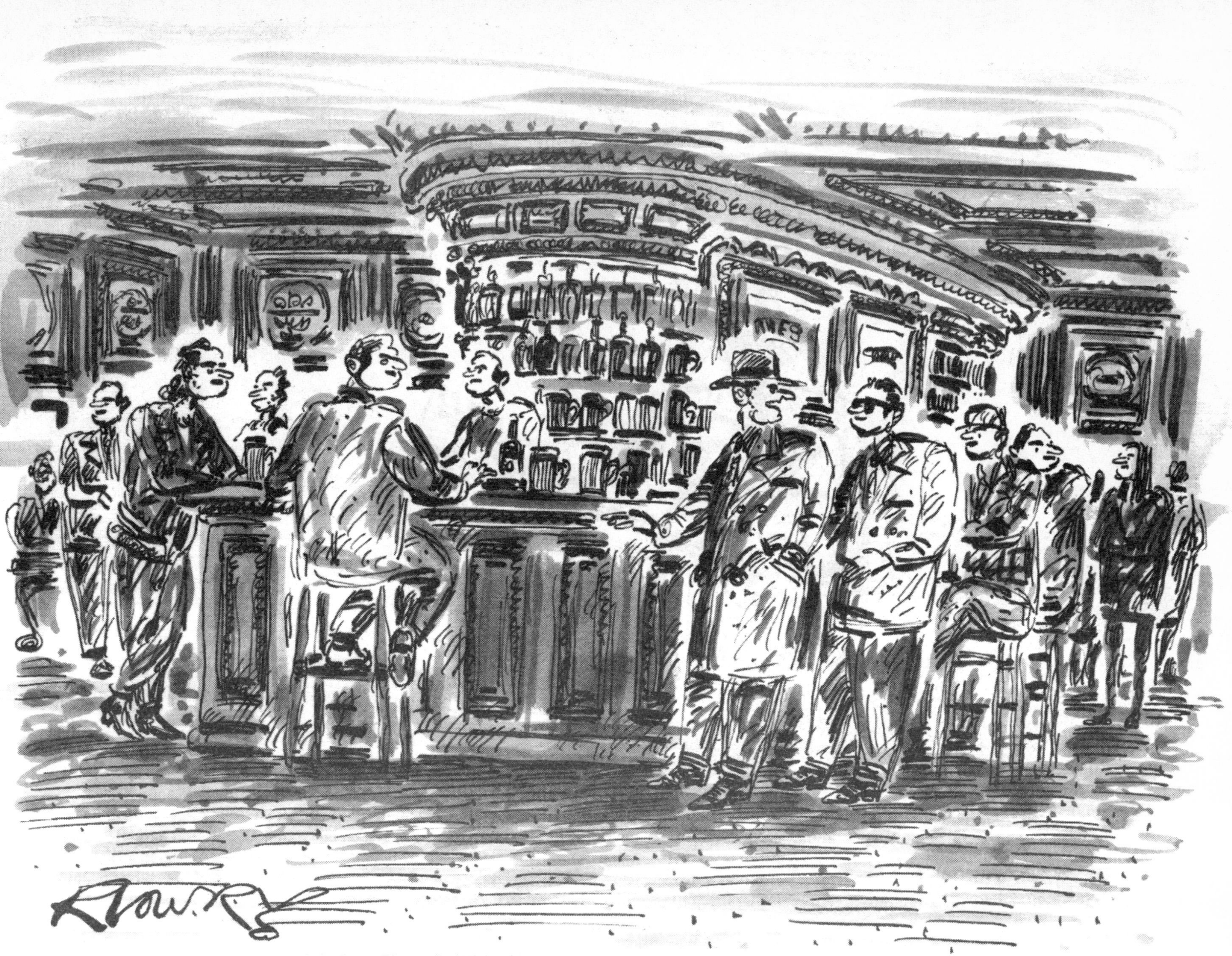

"This is the exact spot where I discovered the meaninglessness of life."

Can A Bluesman sing the Punks?

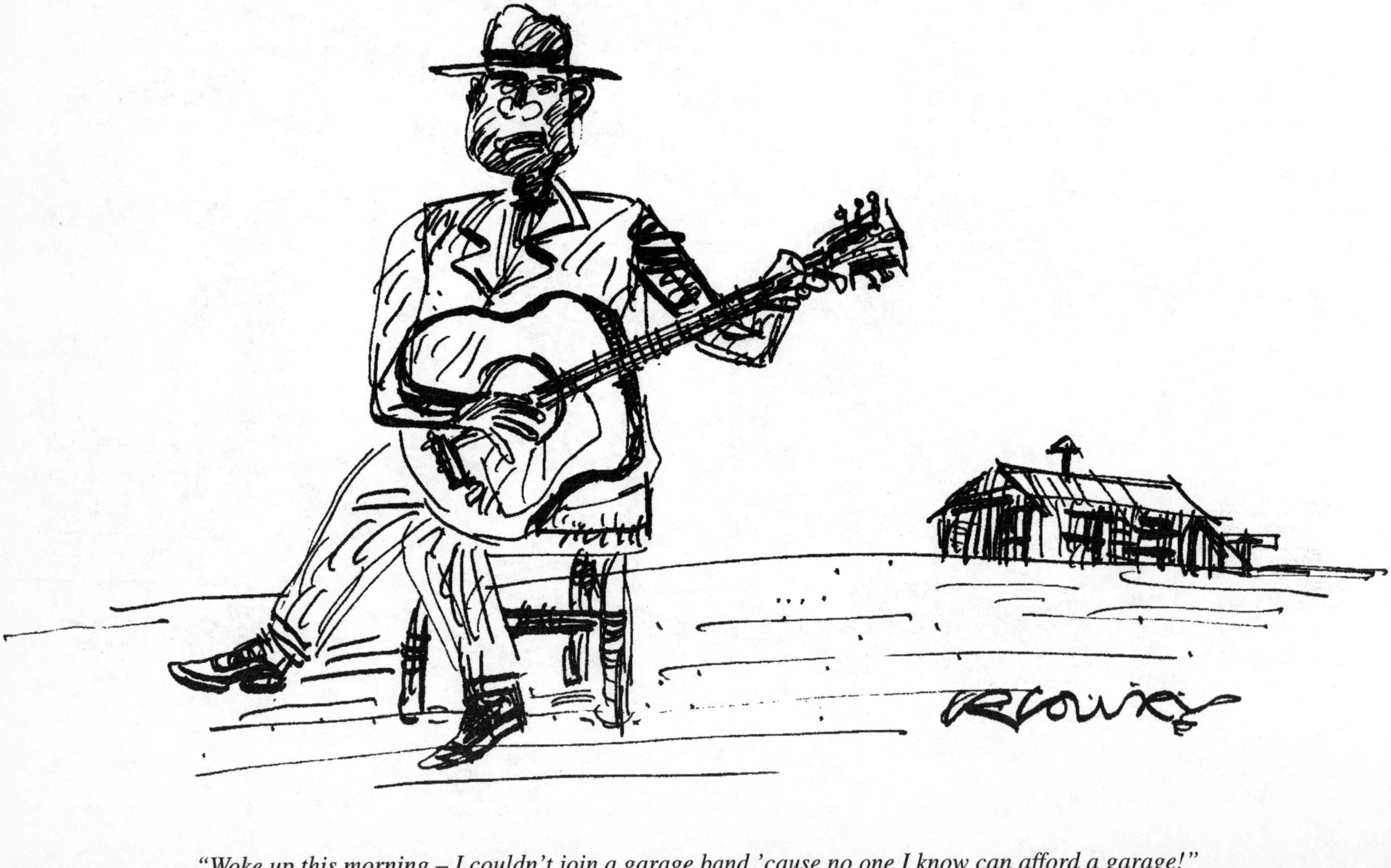

"Woke up this morning – I couldn't join a garage band 'cause no one I know can afford a garage!"

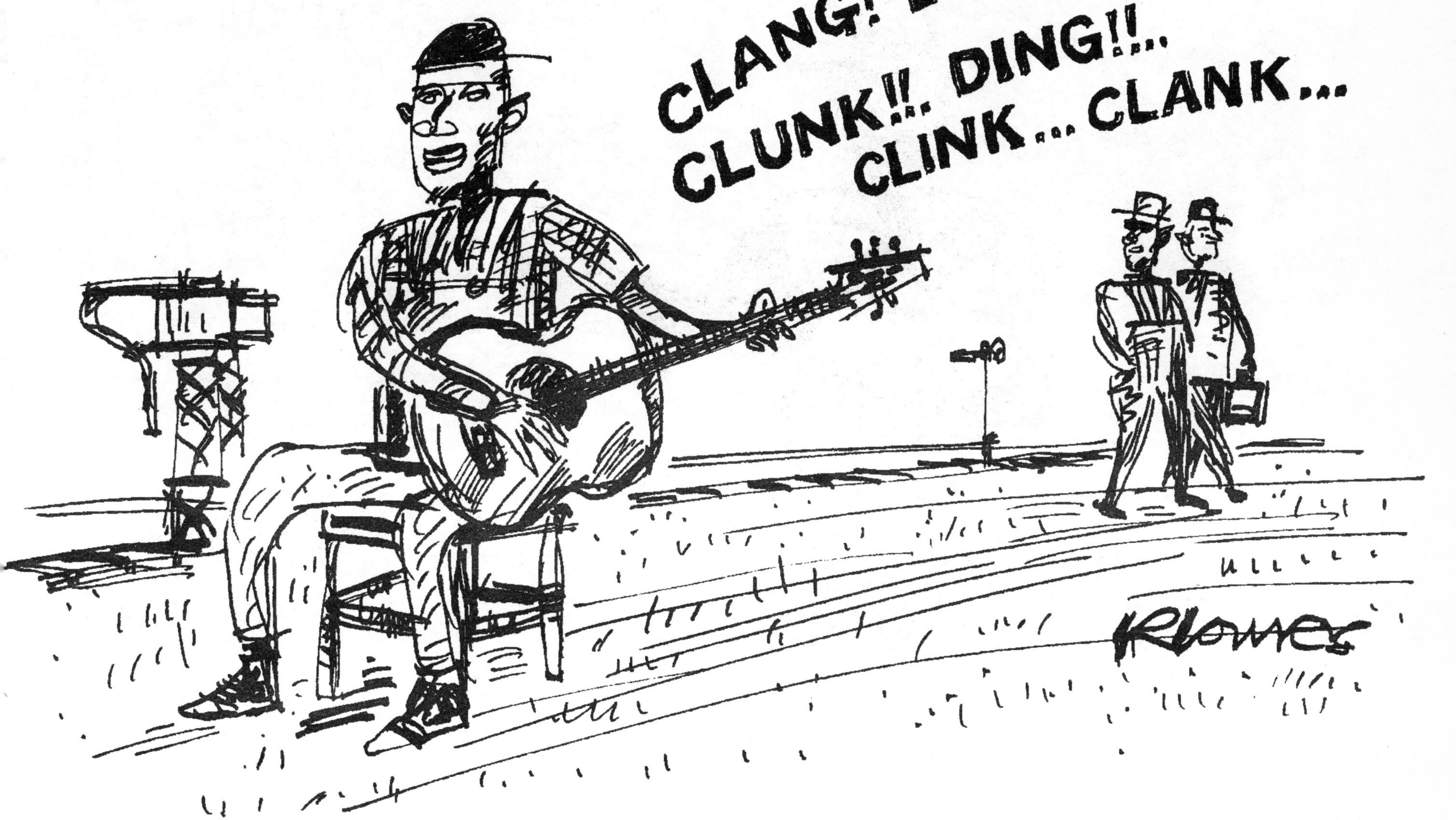
CLANG! BOING!!!
CLUNK!!... DING!!...
CLINK... CLANK...
KLOWES

"That's Johnny B. Goode. He plays that guitar just like ringing a bell. Unfortunately."

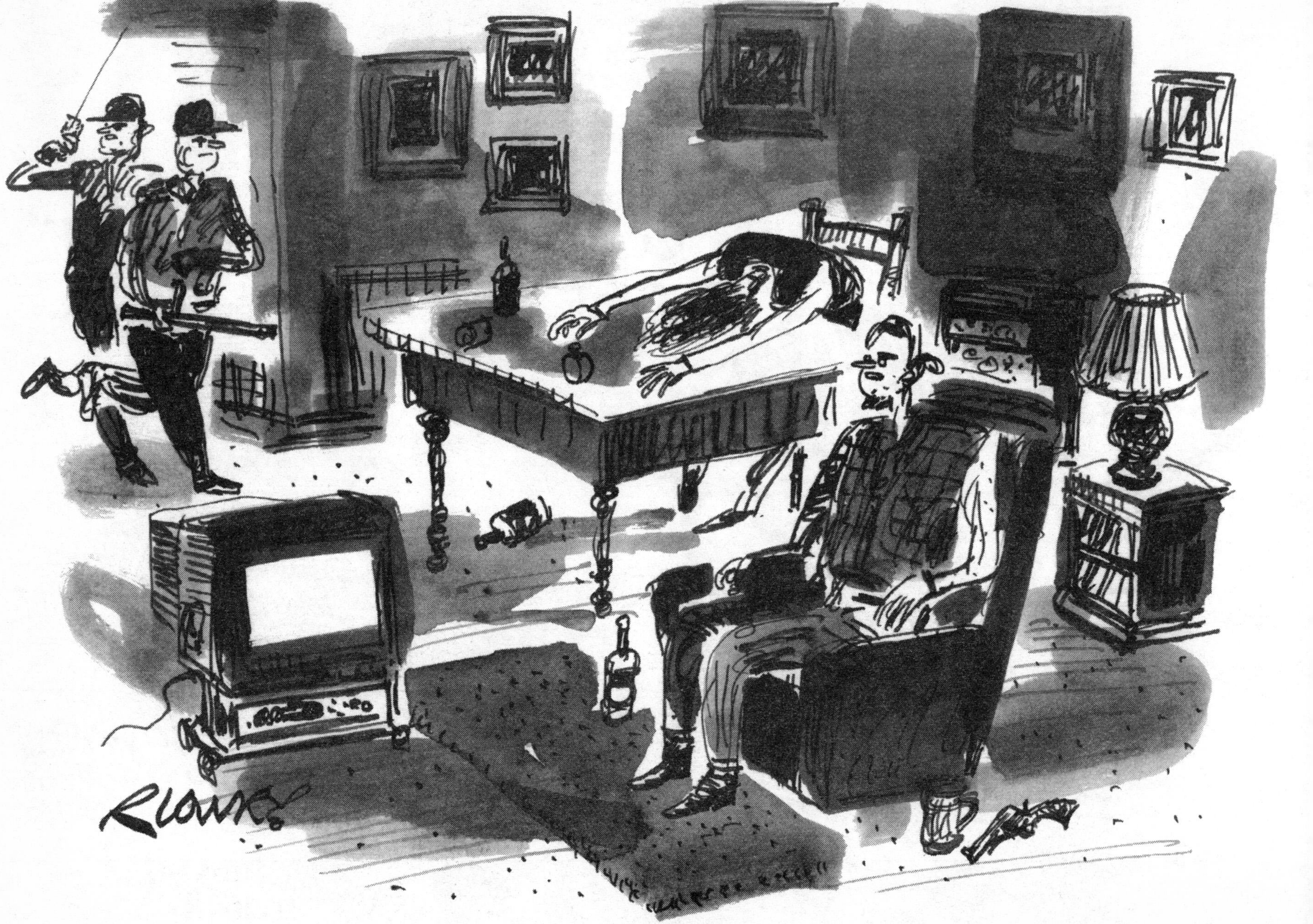

"She died of natural causes – I shot her!"

THAT STRUMMER/JONES REUNION ...

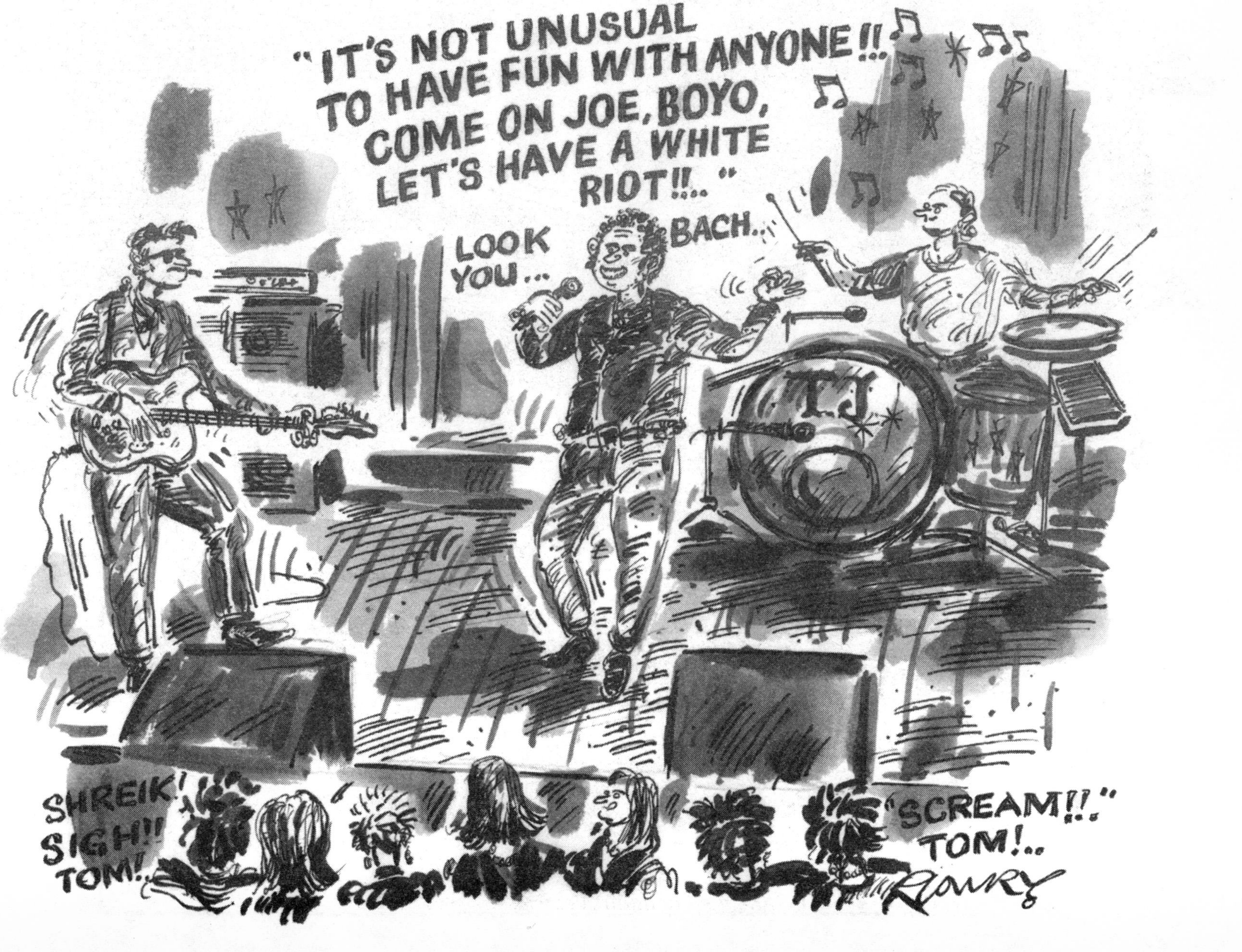
"IT'S NOT UNUSUAL TO HAVE FUN WITH ANYONE!!.. COME ON JOE, BOYO, LET'S HAVE A WHITE RIOT!!.."
LOOK YOU...
BACH..
TJ
SHREIK! SIGH!! TOM!..
"SCREAM!!." TOM!..
RLOWRY

The Black Man's burden...

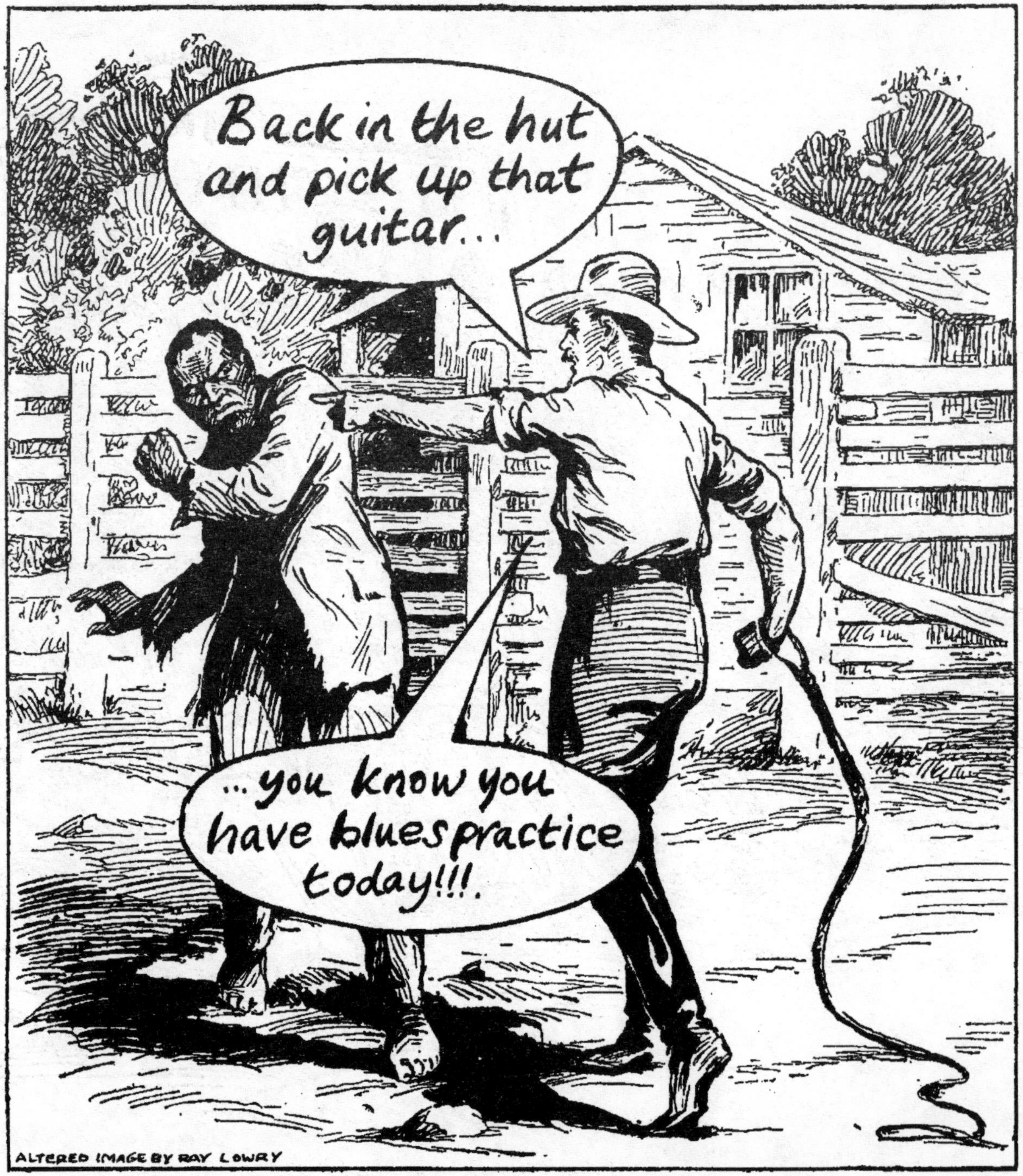
Back in the hut and pick up that guitar...
...you know you have bluespractice today!!!.
ALTERED IMAGE BY RAY LOWRY

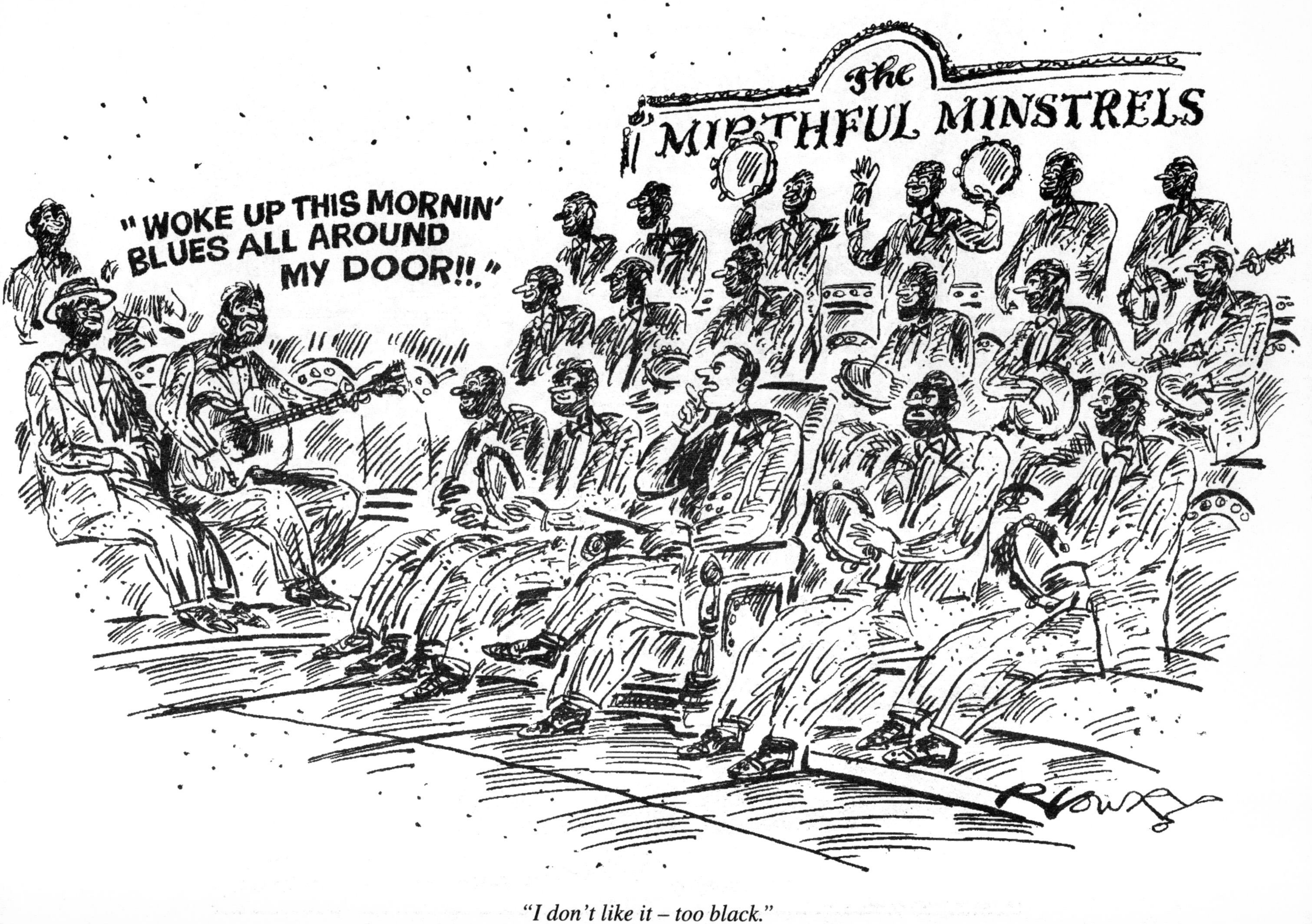

"WOKE UP THIS MORNIN' BLUES ALL AROUND MY DOOR!!,"
The MIRTHFUL MINSTRELS

"I don't like it – too black."

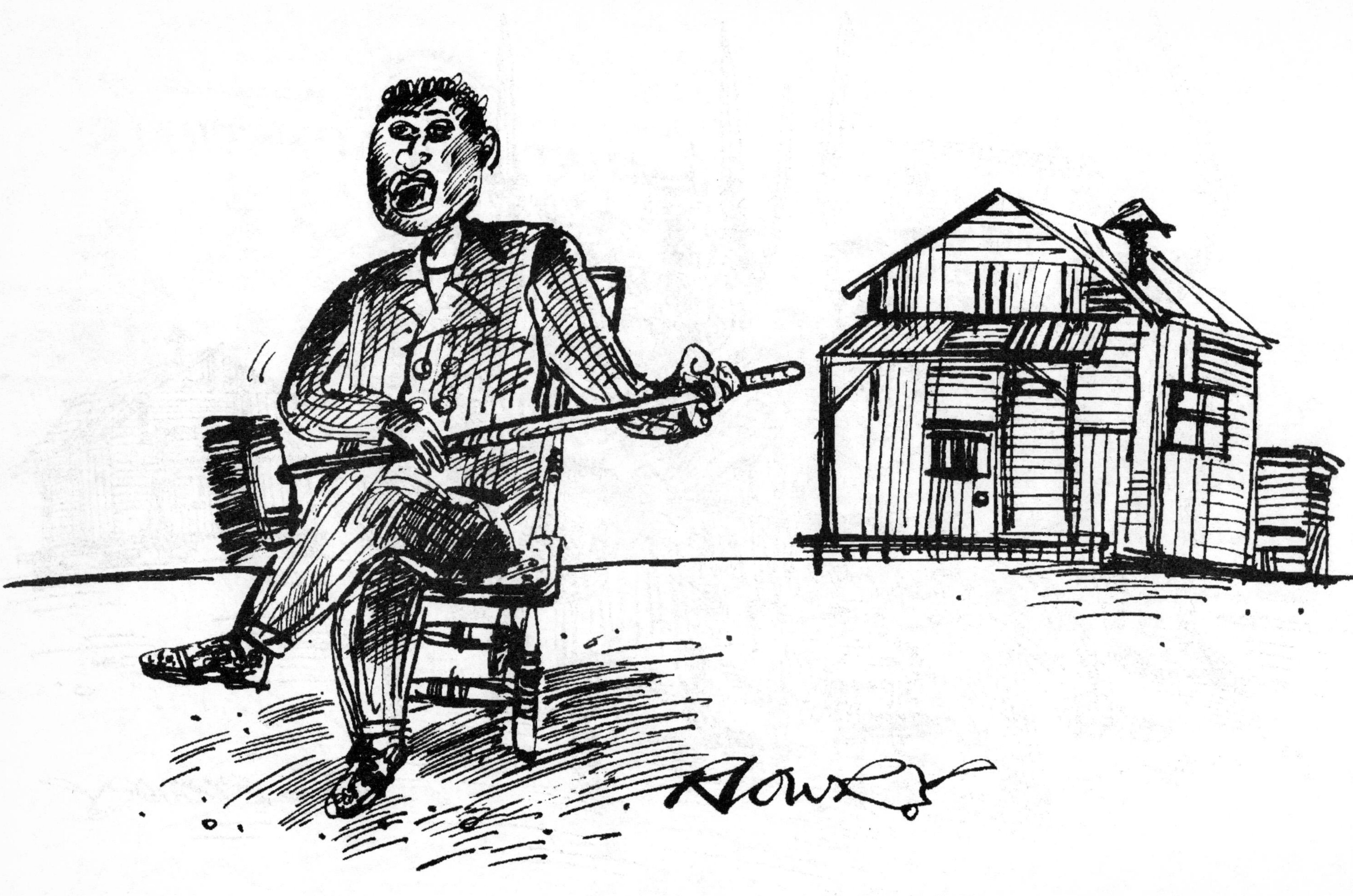

"Woke up this mornin' – couldn't even afford a guitar!"

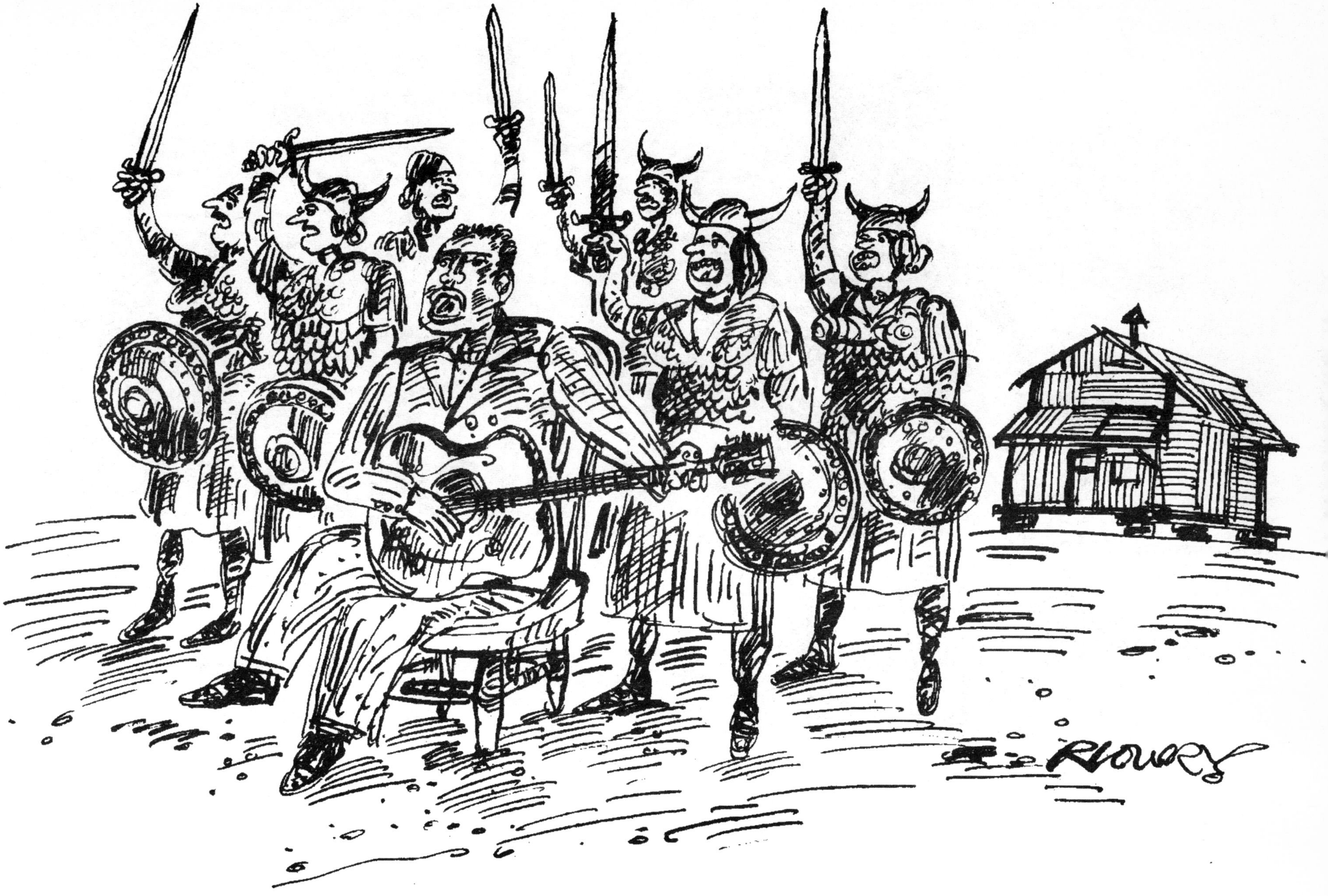
RLOWRY

"Woke up this mornin' – got the Wagnerian blues!"

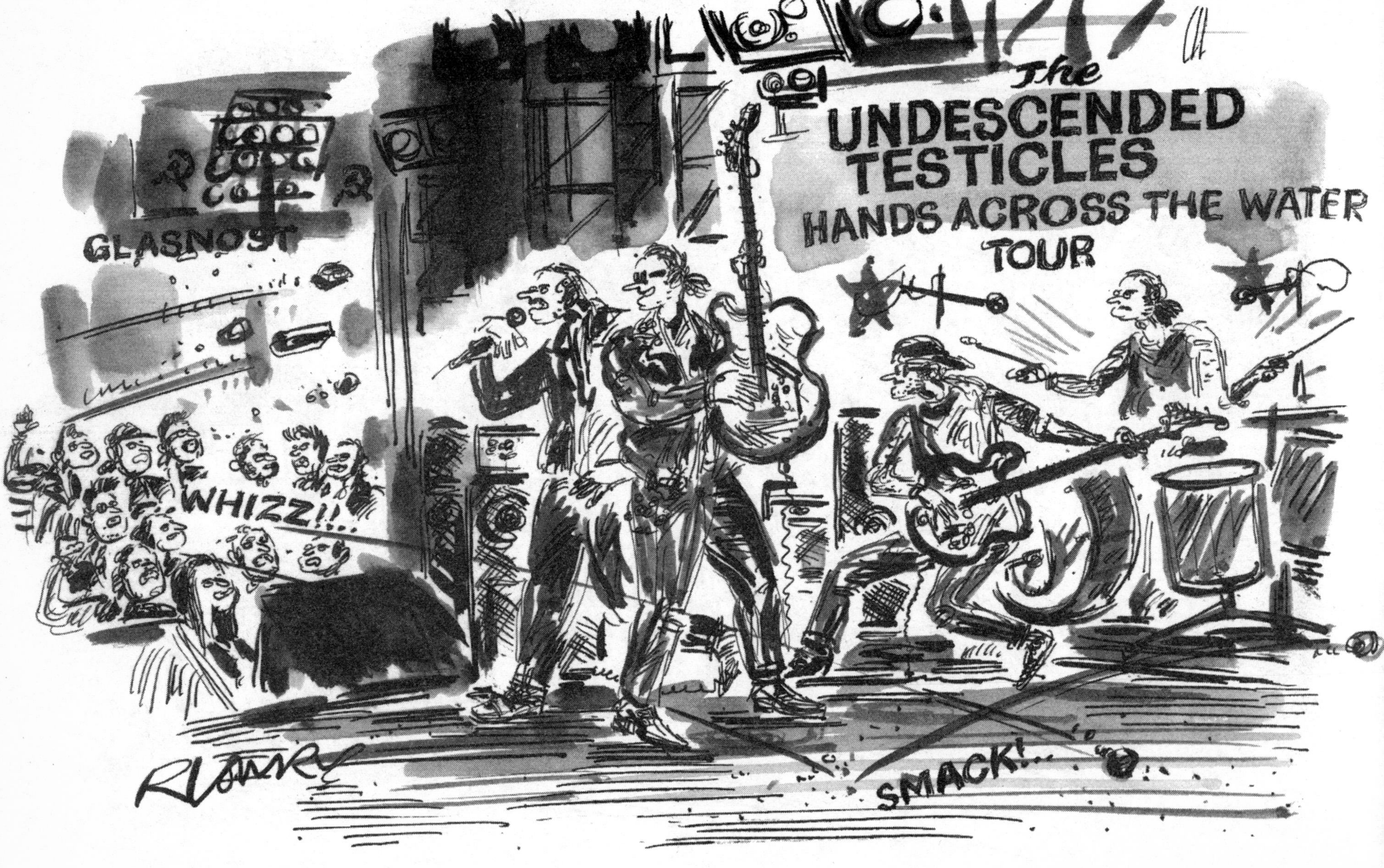
The
UNDESCENDED
TESTICLES
HANDS ACROSS THE WATER
TOUR
GLASNOST
WHIZZ!!
SMACK!..

"This must be our most ideologically sound gig ever. Those are genuine pieces of the Berlin Wall they're hurling at us!"

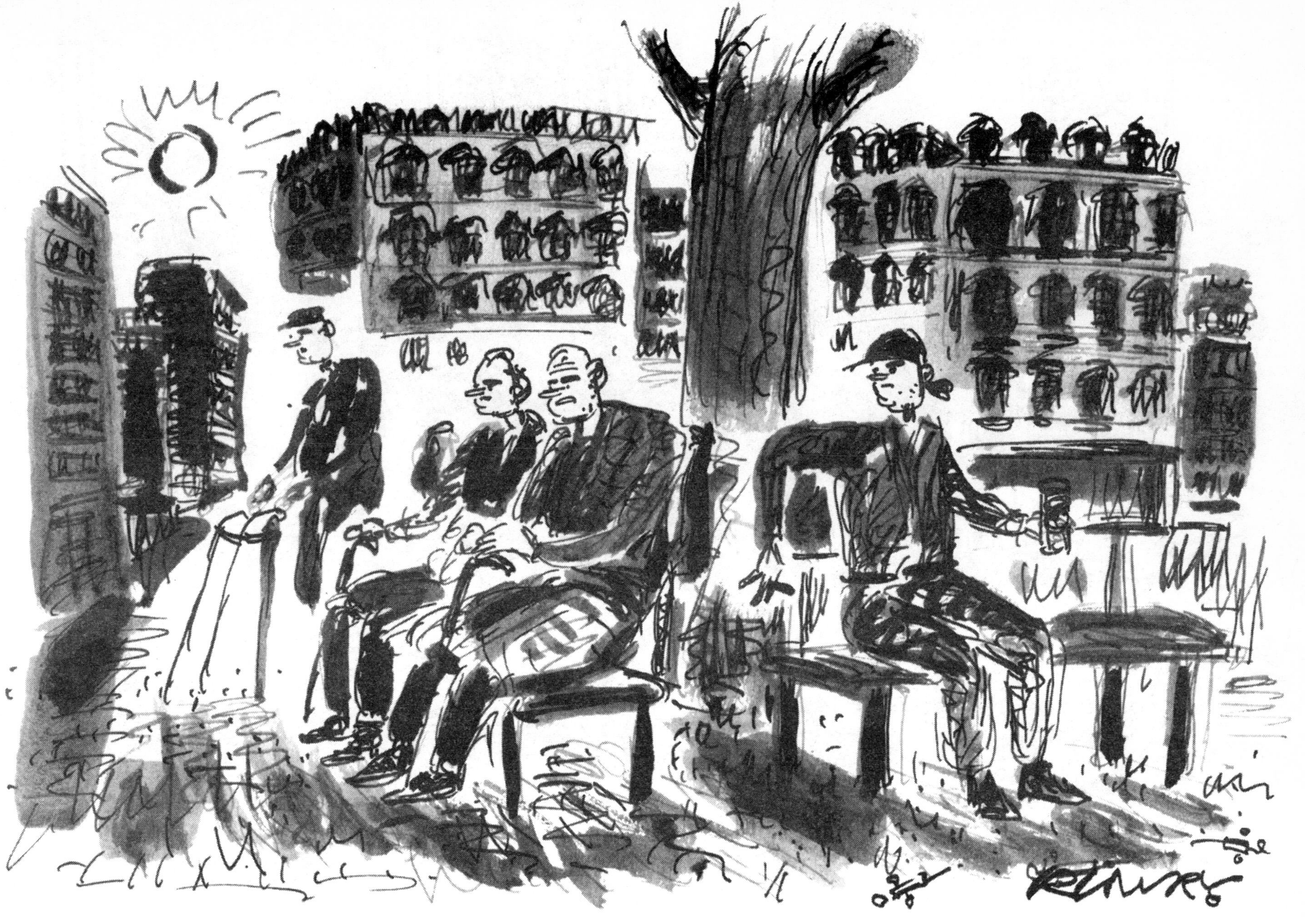

"We're all on the big H, of course. Horlicks."

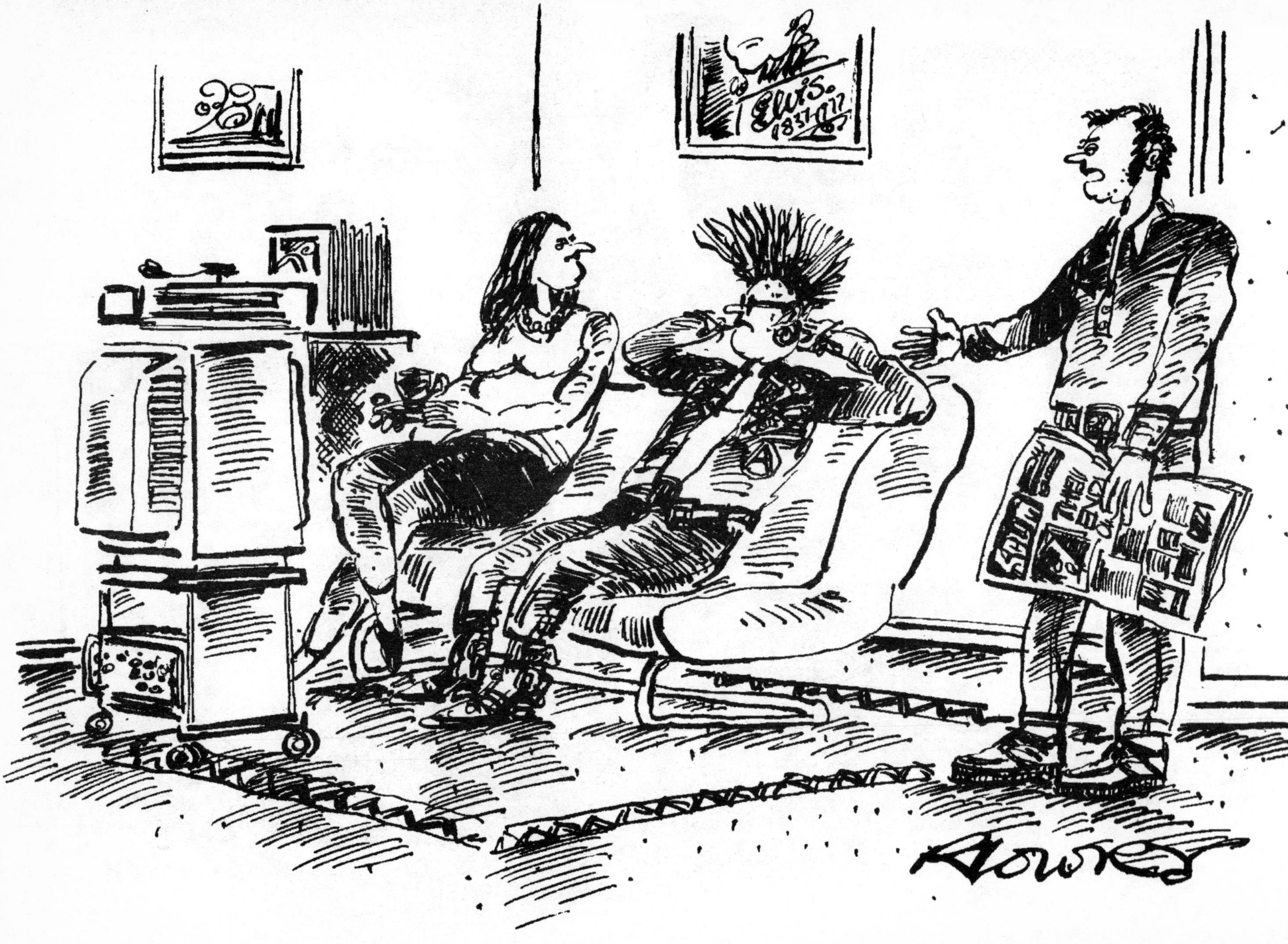
Elvis

"So what does HE know about being a crazy mixed up kid? I was a crazy mixed up kid before he was even born!"

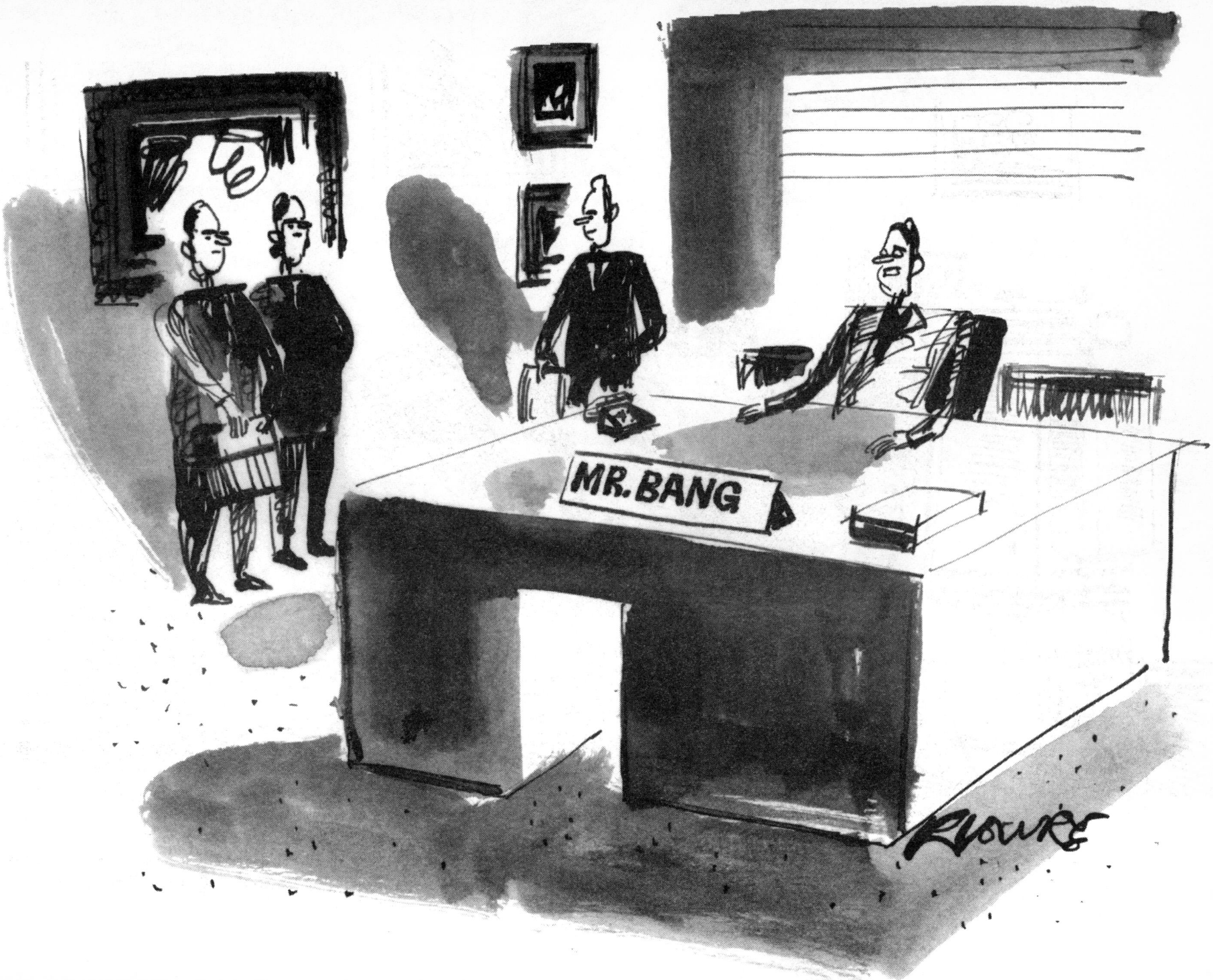
MR. BANG

"I'm sorry Mr Crash, Mr Wallop – but I've decided to go with Olufsen here."

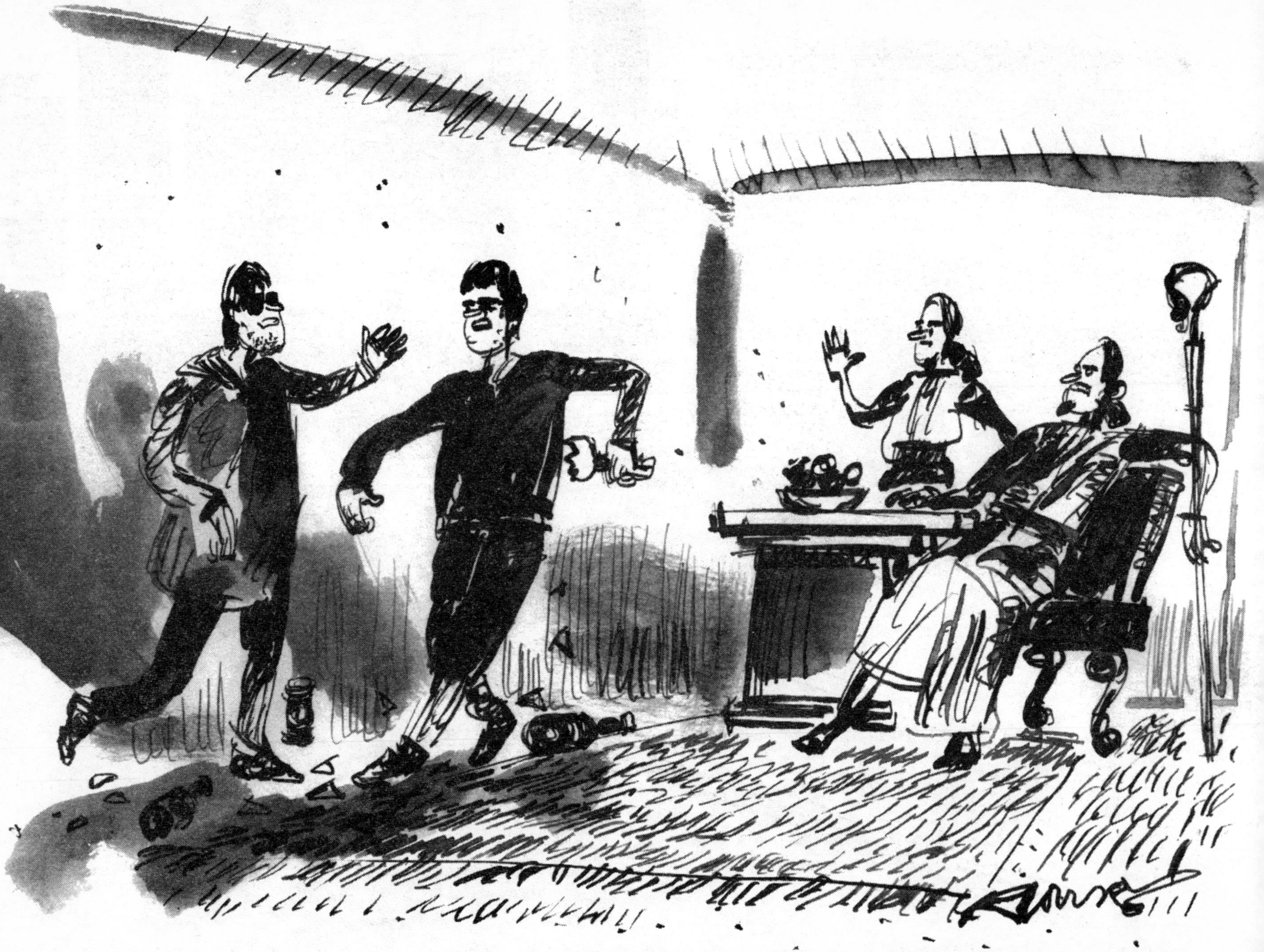

"It was bad enough when we just had Cain and Abel, but since Noel and Liam came along…!!"

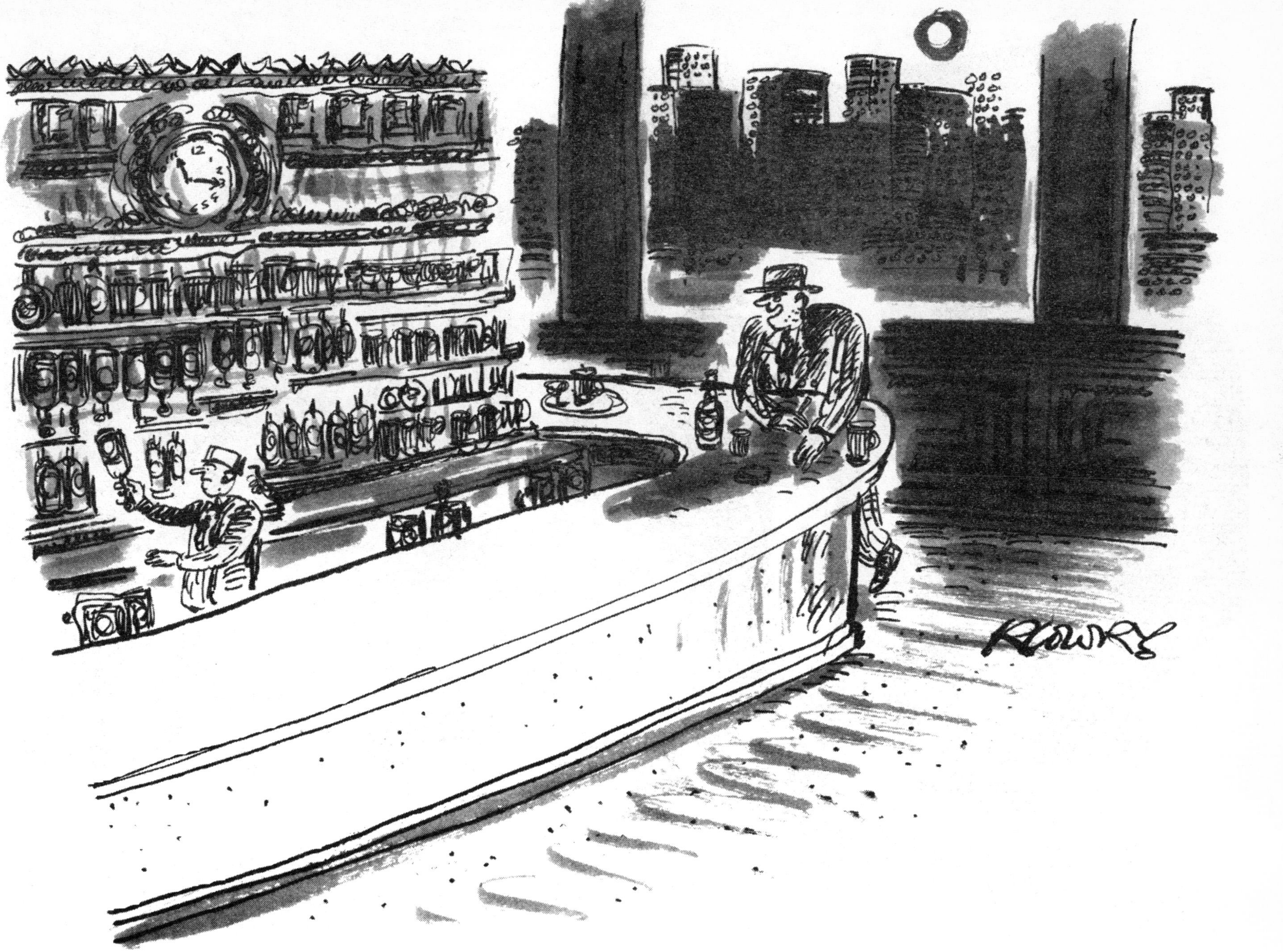

"I like to take my time and approach the traditional Saturday night celebrations on a relaxed and insouciant manner. That's why I start drinking on Saturday mornings."

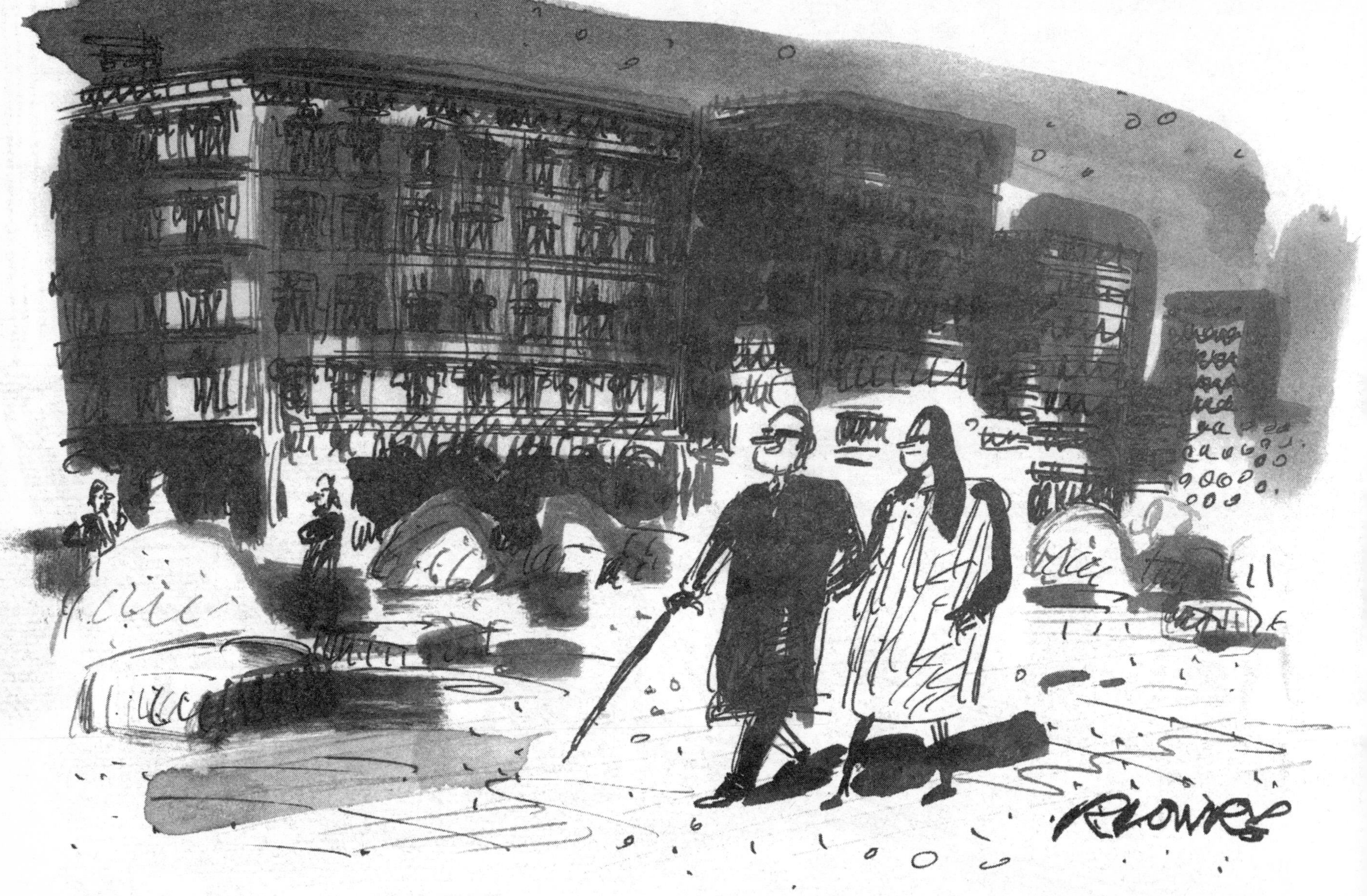

"Doesn't the snow give everything such a picturesque, white covering? The drunks collapsed in the gutter, the homeless in their cardboard boxes..."

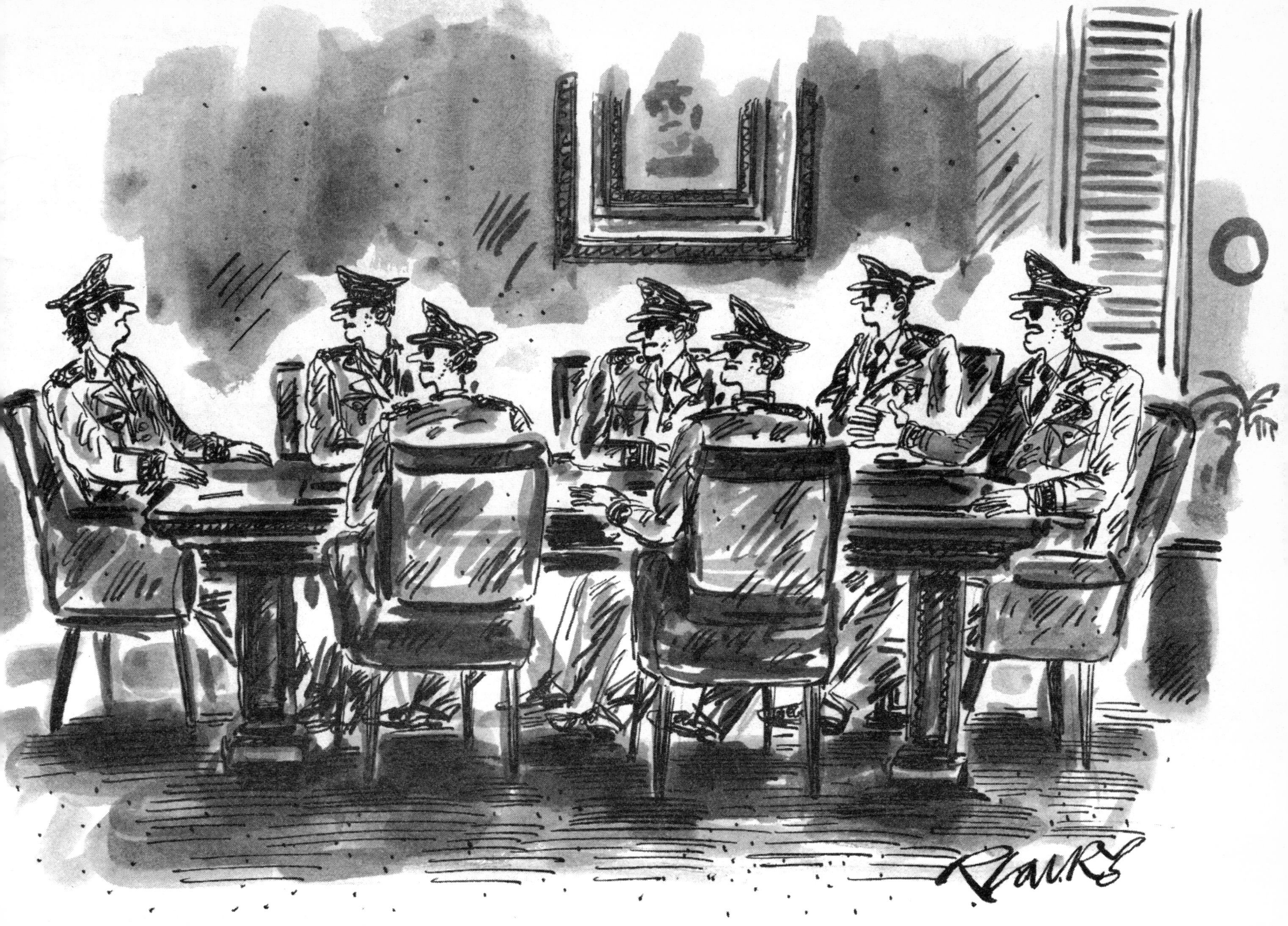

"The other Colonels and I suspect you of being Roy Orbison... "

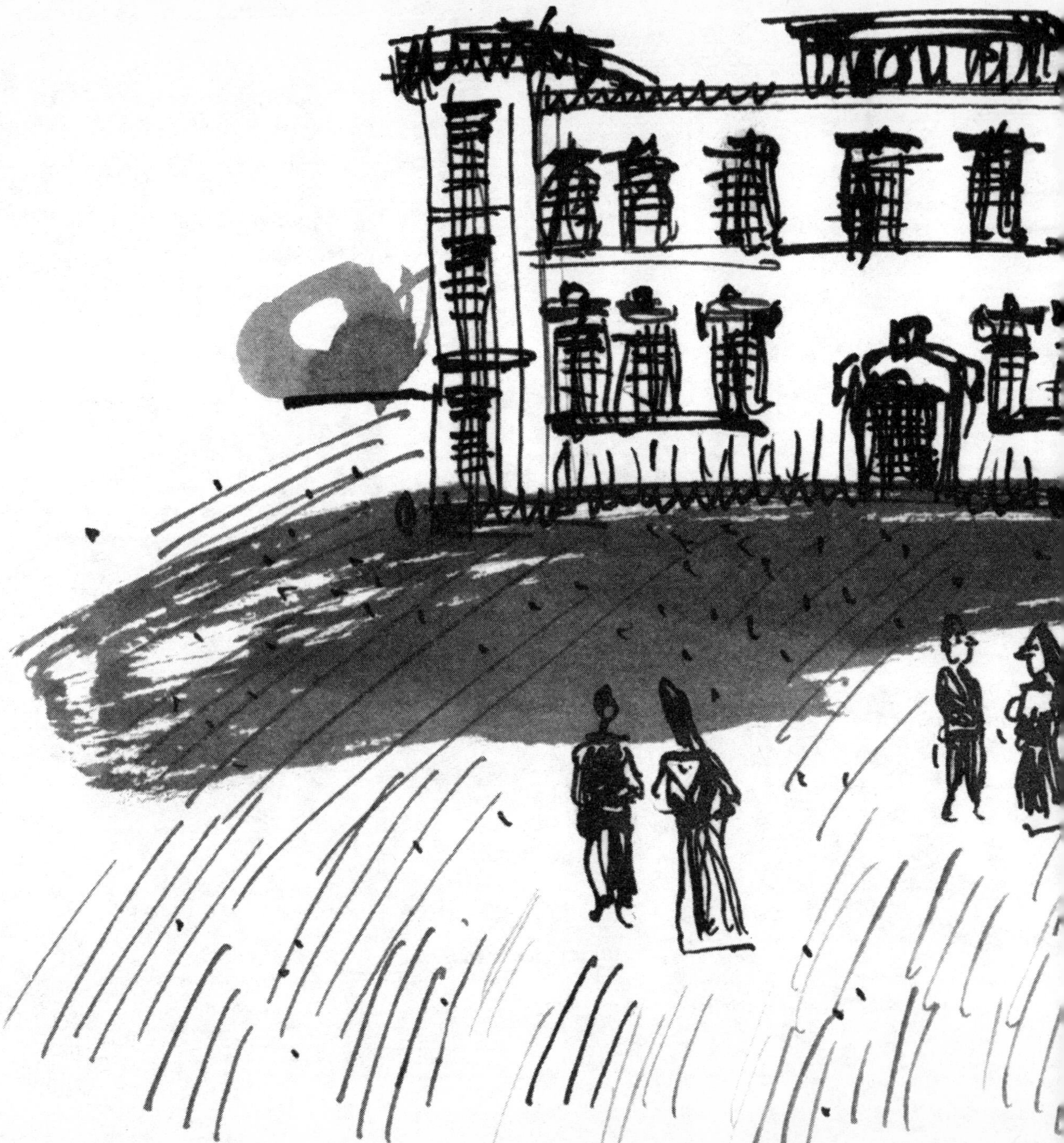

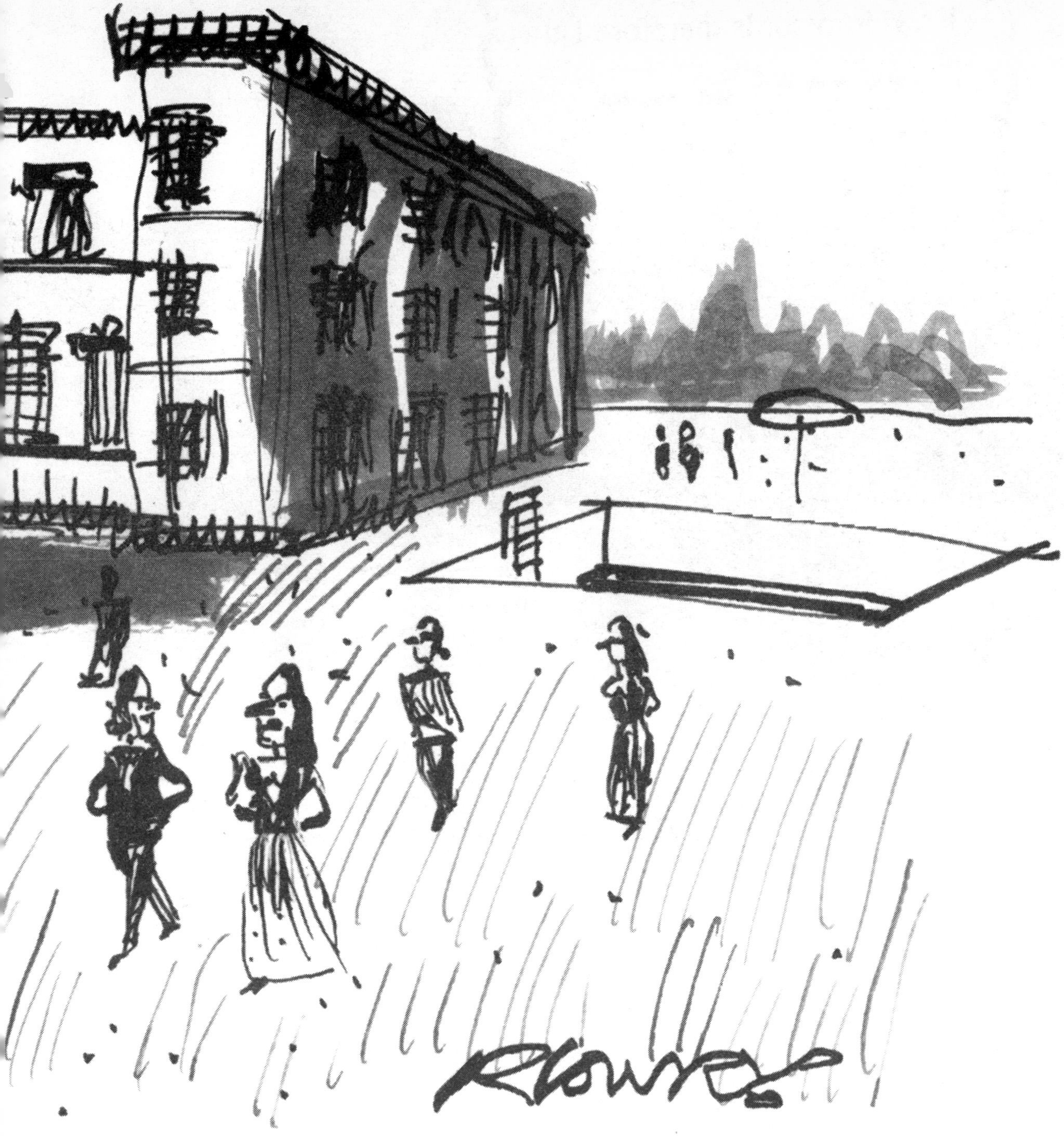

"Terrific party Simon – but don't you think the dead Rolling Stone in the pool dates us?"

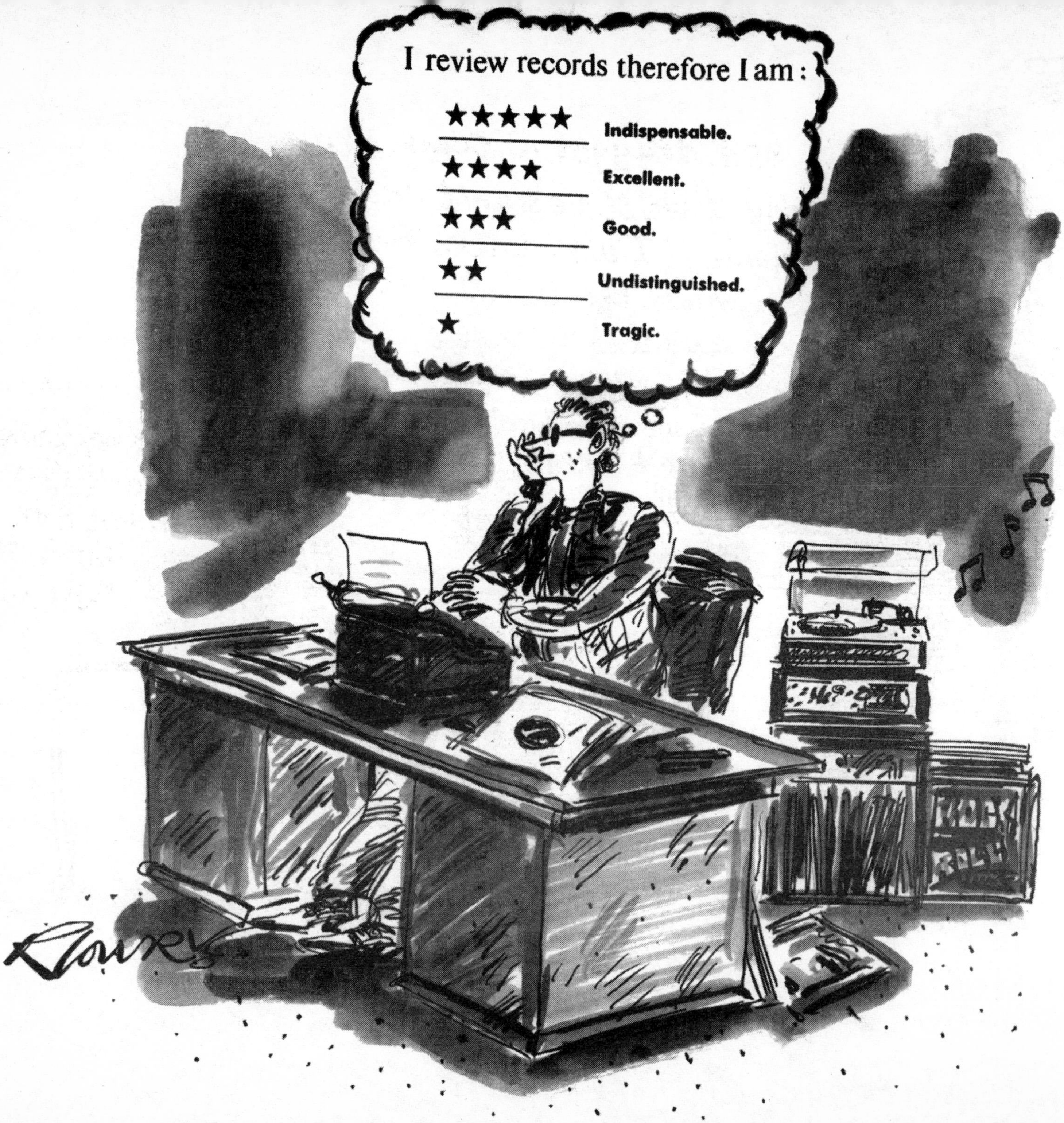

I review records therefore I am :
★★★★★ Indispensable.
★★★★ Excellent.
★★★ Good.
★★ Undistinguished.
★ Tragic.

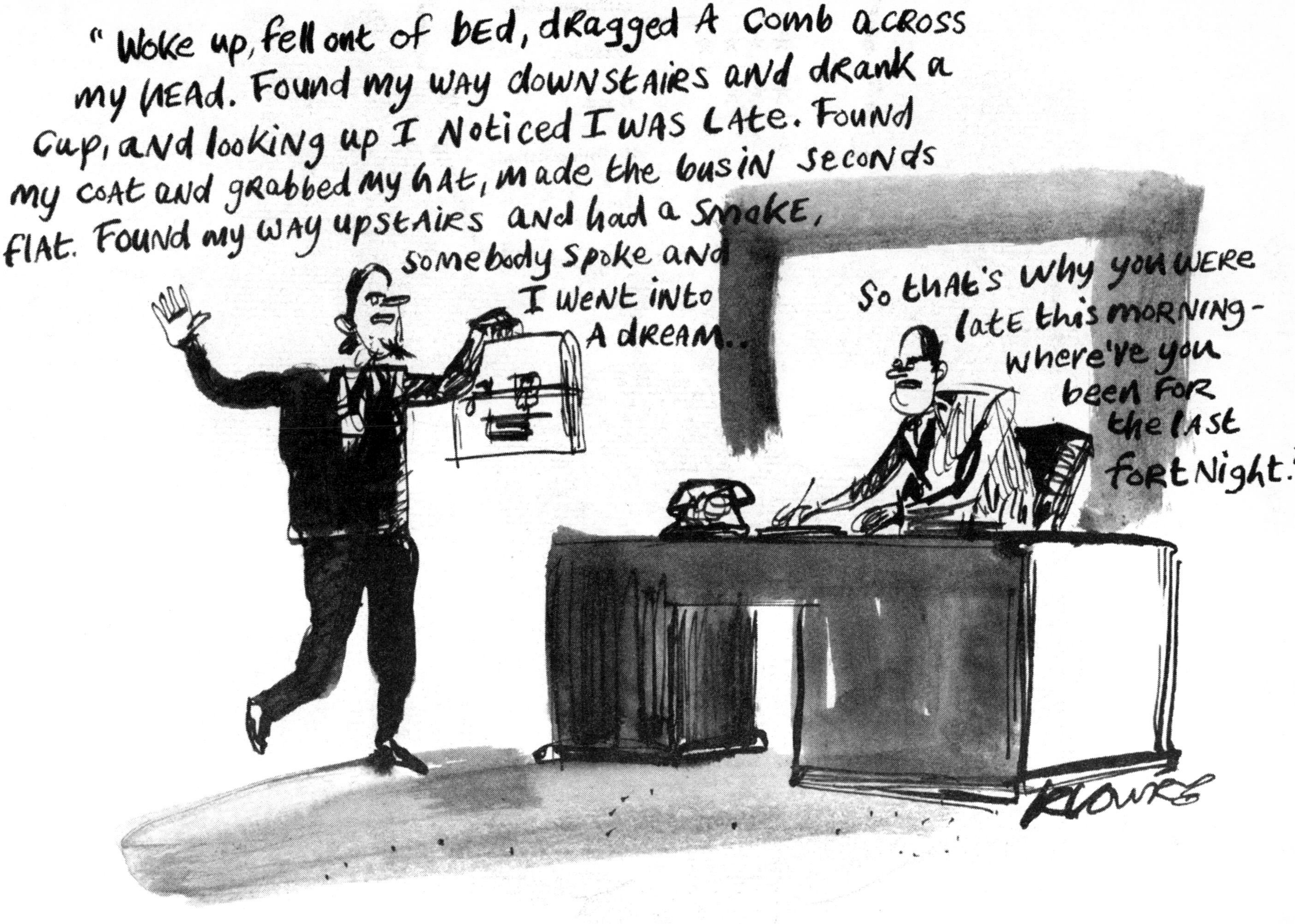
"Woke up, fell out of bed, dragged a comb across my head. Found my way downstairs and drank a cup, and looking up I noticed I was late. Found my coat and grabbed my hat, made the bus in seconds flat. Found my way upstairs and had a smoke, somebody spoke and I went into a dream..
So that's why you were late this morning - where've you been for the last fortnight?

These strips are the highlights of a series that ran briefly in Punch sometime in the late nineteen eighties titled Chartism. The familiar obsessions, I think…

METALLL!!!!..
WE'RE ON A HIGHWAY TO HELL WITH THE HAMMER DOWN, BOY!! LIKE, R.P.M..!!!..
WE'VE RIDDEN THE RAINBOW STRAIGHT TO THE STEEL GLOVED GRIP ON THE THROBBING HEART OF THE BLOODY CORPSE OF MIGHTY METAL!
WITH ONE FIST DOWN THE THROAT OF ROCK AND ROLL AND THE OTHER ONE SHOVED UP THE SKIRT OF REALITY!.
IT'S A MAN'S LIFE!!.
THERE'S ONLY ONE DRAWBACK, REALLY..
YOU HAVE TO GO OUT THERE & SING THIS BLOODY ARRANT NONSENSE EVERY NIGHT!!!
WE'RE ON A HIGHWAY TO HELL WITH THE HAMMER DOWN!!! ♫ WE'VE RIDDEN THE RAINBOW STRAIGHT TO THE THROBBING HEART.
NEXT
ON A HIGHWAY TO HELL WITH THE HAMMER DOWN - FROM OUR MOTORING CORRESPONDENT.

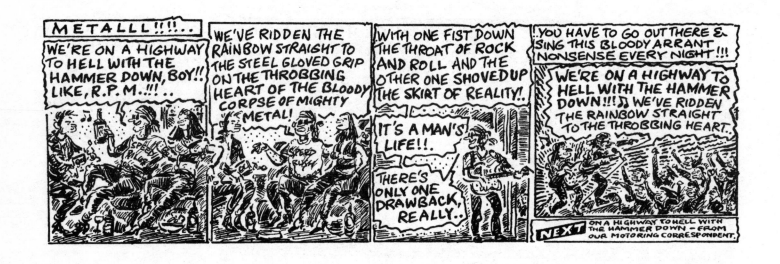

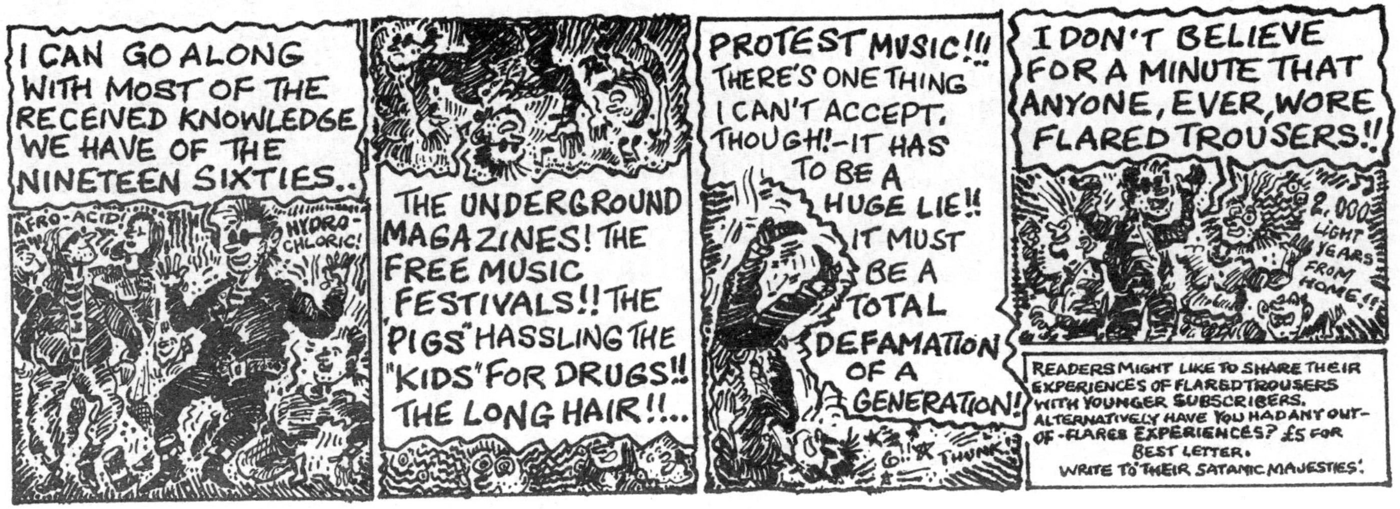
I CAN GO ALONG WITH MOST OF THE RECEIVED KNOWLEDGE WE HAVE OF THE NINETEEN SIXTIES..
AFRO-ACID!
HYDRO-CHLORIC!
THE UNDERGROUND MAGAZINES! THE FREE MUSIC FESTIVALS!! THE "PIGS" HASSLING THE "KIDS" FOR DRUGS!! THE LONG HAIR!!...
PROTEST MUSIC!!! THERE'S ONE THING I CAN'T ACCEPT, THOUGH!-IT HAS TO BE A HUGE LIE!! IT MUST BE A TOTAL DEFAMATION OF A GENERATION!
THUNK!!
I DON'T BELIEVE FOR A MINUTE THAT ANYONE, EVER, WORE FLARED TROUSERS!!
2,000 LIGHT YEARS FROM HOME!!
READERS MIGHT LIKE TO SHARE THEIR EXPERIENCES OF FLARED TROUSERS WITH YOUNGER SUBSCRIBERS. ALTERNATIVELY HAVE YOU HAD ANY OUT-OF-FLARES EXPERIENCES? £5 FOR BEST LETTER.
WRITE TO 'THEIR SATANIC MAJESTIES'.

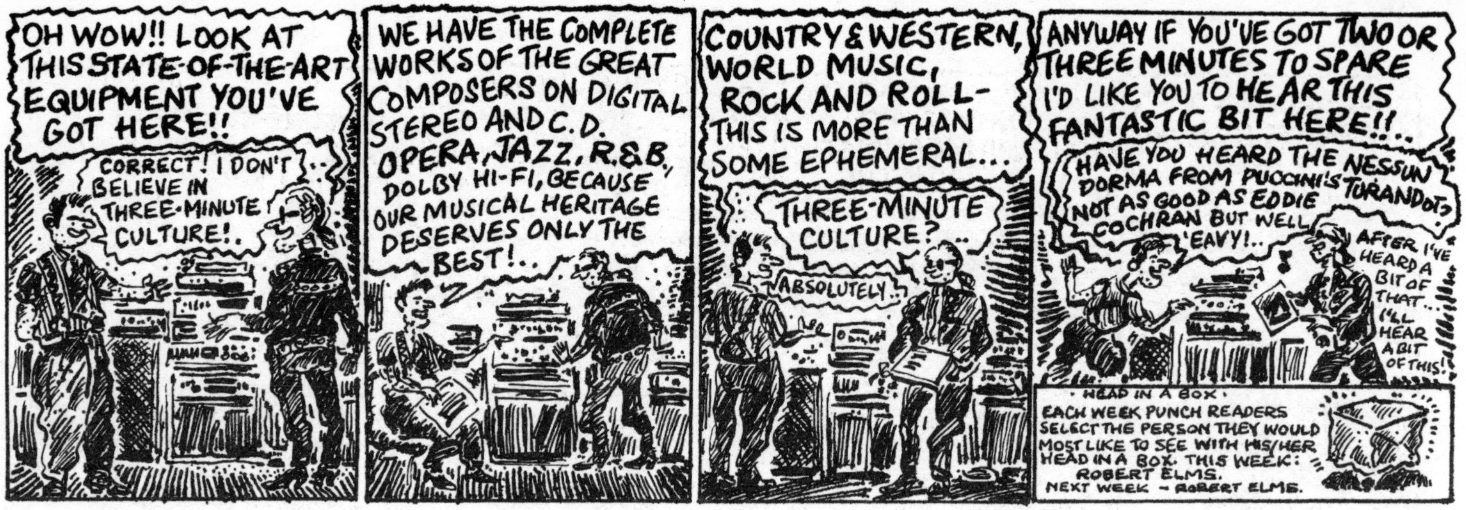
OH WOW!! LOOK AT THIS STATE-OF-THE-ART EQUIPMENT YOU'VE GOT HERE!!
CORRECT! I DON'T BELIEVE IN THREE-MINUTE CULTURE!..
WE HAVE THE COMPLETE WORKS OF THE GREAT COMPOSERS ON DIGITAL STEREO AND C.D. OPERA, JAZZ, R.&B., DOLBY HI-FI, BECAUSE OUR MUSICAL HERITAGE DESERVES ONLY THE BEST!..
COUNTRY & WESTERN, WORLD MUSIC, ROCK AND ROLL- THIS IS MORE THAN SOME EPHEMERAL...
THREE-MINUTE CULTURE?..
ABSOLUTELY..
ANYWAY IF YOU'VE GOT TWO OR THREE MINUTES TO SPARE I'D LIKE YOU TO HEAR THIS FANTASTIC BIT HERE!!..
HAVE YOU HEARD THE NESSUN DORMA FROM PUCCINI'S TURANDOT? NOT AS GOOD AS EDDIE COCHRAN BUT WELL 'EAVY!..
AFTER I'VE HEARD A BIT OF THAT.. I'LL HEAR A BIT OF THIS!
HEAD IN A BOX
EACH WEEK PUNCH READERS SELECT THE PERSON THEY WOULD MOST LIKE TO SEE WITH HIS/HER HEAD IN A BOX. THIS WEEK: ROBERT ELMS.
NEXT WEEK - ROBERT ELMS.

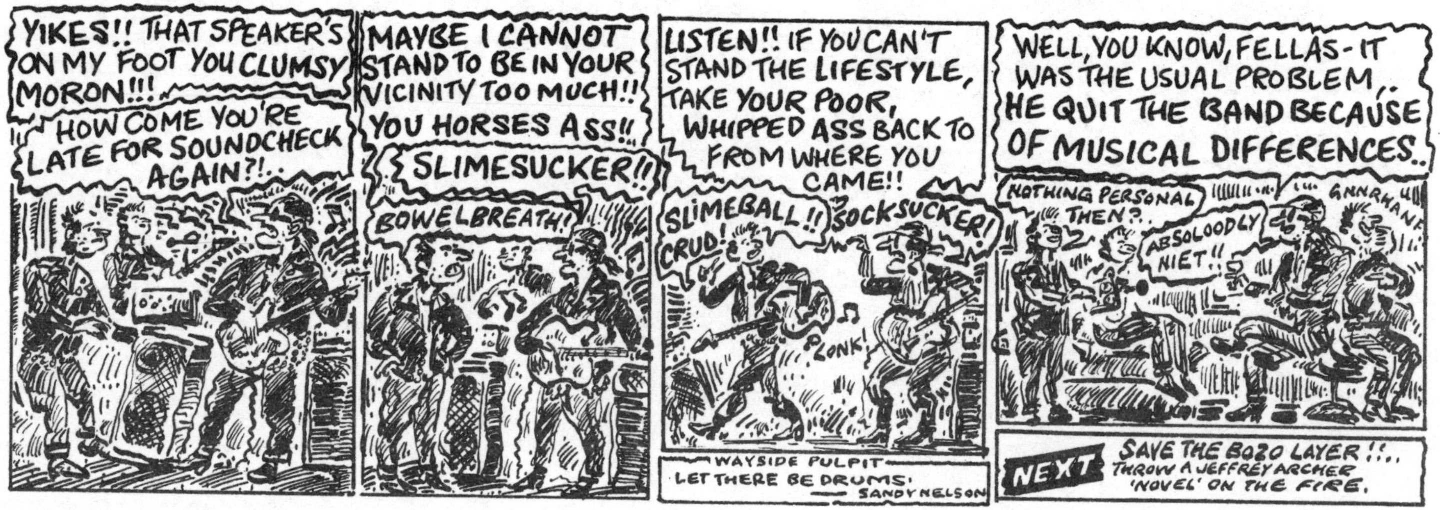
YIKES!! THAT SPEAKER'S ON MY FOOT YOU CLUMSY MORON!!!
HOW COME YOU'RE LATE FOR SOUNDCHECK AGAIN?!..
MAYBE I CANNOT STAND TO BE IN YOUR VICINITY TOO MUCH!! YOU HORSES ASS!!
SLIMESUCKER!!
BOWELBREATH!
LISTEN!! IF YOU CAN'T STAND THE LIFESTYLE, TAKE YOUR POOR, WHIPPED ASS BACK TO FROM WHERE YOU CAME!!
SLIMEBALL!!
SOCKSUCKER!
CRUD!
ZONK!
WELL, YOU KNOW, FELLAS- IT WAS THE USUAL PROBLEM,. HE QUIT THE BAND BECAUSE OF MUSICAL DIFFERENCES..
NOTHING PERSONAL THEN?..
ABSOLOODLY NIET!!
GNNRHANF
WAYSIDE PULPIT
LET THERE BE DRUMS.
— SANDY NELSON
NEXT
SAVE THE BOZO LAYER!!.. THROW A JEFFREY ARCHER 'NOVEL' ON THE FIRE.

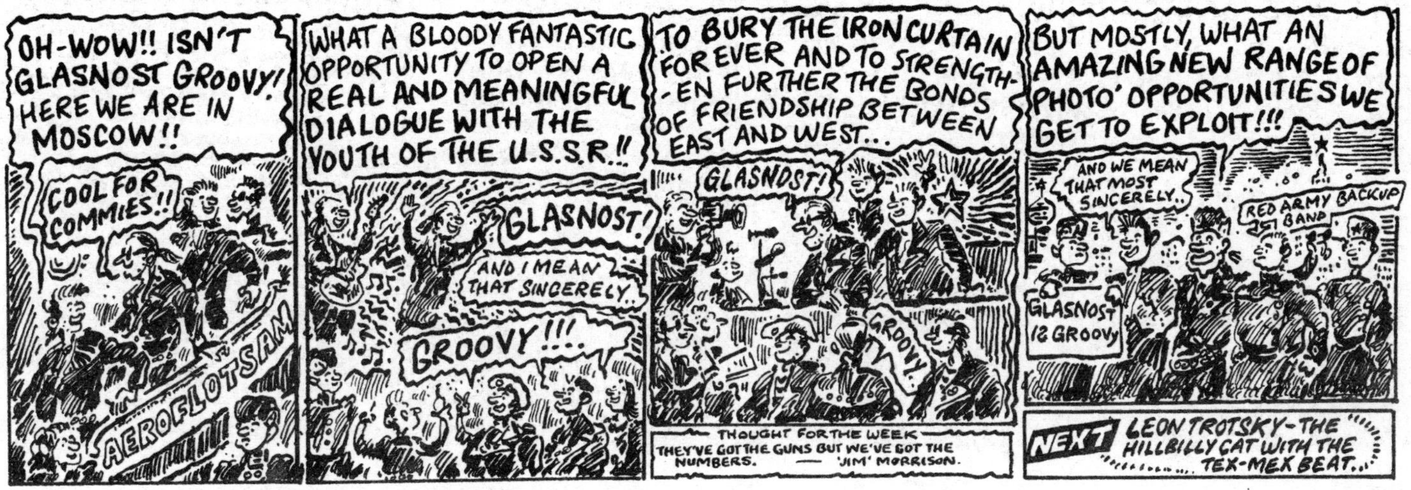
OH-WOW!! ISN'T GLASNOST GROOVY! HERE WE ARE IN MOSCOW!!
COOL FOR COMMIES!!
AEROFLOTSAM
WHAT A BLOODY FANTASTIC OPPORTUNITY TO OPEN A REAL AND MEANINGFUL DIALOGUE WITH THE YOUTH OF THE U.S.S.R.!!
GLASNOST!
AND I MEAN THAT SINCERELY.
GROOVY!!!..
TO BURY THE IRON CURTAIN FOR EVER AND TO STRENGTH-EN FURTHER THE BONDS OF FRIENDSHIP BETWEEN EAST AND WEST...
GLASNOST!
GROOVY
THOUGHT FOR THE WEEK
THEY'VE GOT THE GUNS BUT WE'VE GOT THE NUMBERS. — 'JIM' MORRISON.
BUT MOSTLY, WHAT AN AMAZING NEW RANGE OF PHOTO' OPPORTUNITIES WE GET TO EXPLOIT!!!
AND WE MEAN THAT MOST SINCERELY..
RED ARMY BACKUP BAND
GLASNOST IS GROOVY
NEXT LEON TROTSKY - THE HILLBILLY CAT WITH THE TEX-MEX BEAT..

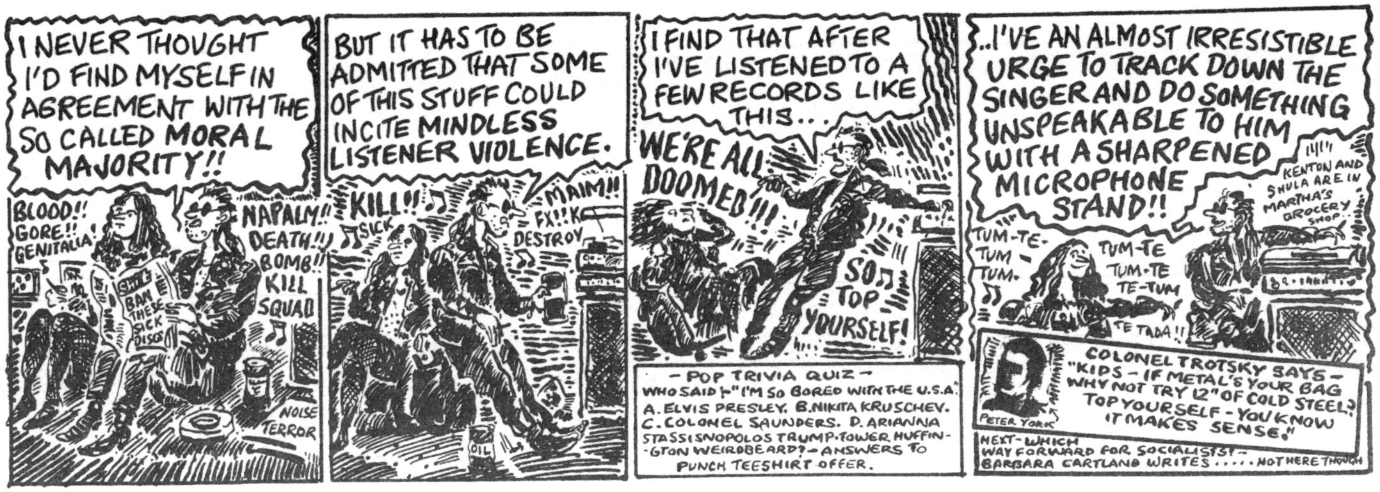
I NEVER THOUGHT I'D FIND MYSELF IN AGREEMENT WITH THE SO CALLED MORAL MAJORITY!!
BLOOD!! GORE!! GENITALIA!
NAPALM!! DEATH!! BOMB!! KILL SQUAD
BAN THESE SICK DISCS
NOISE TERROR
BUT IT HAS TO BE ADMITTED THAT SOME OF THIS STUFF COULD INCITE MINDLESS LISTENER VIOLENCE.
KILL!!
SICK
MAIM!!
F%!!K
DESTROY
OIL
I FIND THAT AFTER I'VE LISTENED TO A FEW RECORDS LIKE THIS...
WE'RE ALL DOOMED!!!
SO TOP YOURSELF!
- POP TRIVIA QUIZ -
WHO SAID :- "I'M SO BORED WITH THE U.S.A."
A. ELVIS PRESLEY. B. NIKITA KRUSCHEV. C. COLONEL SAUNDERS. D. ARIANNA STASSISNOPOLOS TRUMP-TOWER HUFFIN-GTON WEIRDBEARD? - ANSWERS TO PUNCH TEESHIRT OFFER.
..I'VE AN ALMOST IRRESISTIBLE URGE TO TRACK DOWN THE SINGER AND DO SOMETHING UNSPEAKABLE TO HIM WITH A SHARPENED MICROPHONE STAND!!
KENTON AND SHULA ARE IN MARTHA'S GROCERY SHOP
TUM-TE-TUM TUM.
TUM-TE TUM-TE TE-TUM
TE TADA!!
PETER YORK
COLONEL TROTSKY SAYS - "KIDS - IF METAL'S YOUR BAG WHY NOT TRY 12" OF COLD STEEL? TOP YOURSELF - YOU KNOW IT MAKES SENSE."
NEXT - WHICH WAY FORWARD FOR SOCIALISTS? - BARBARA CARTLAND WRITES ..... NOT HERE THOUGH

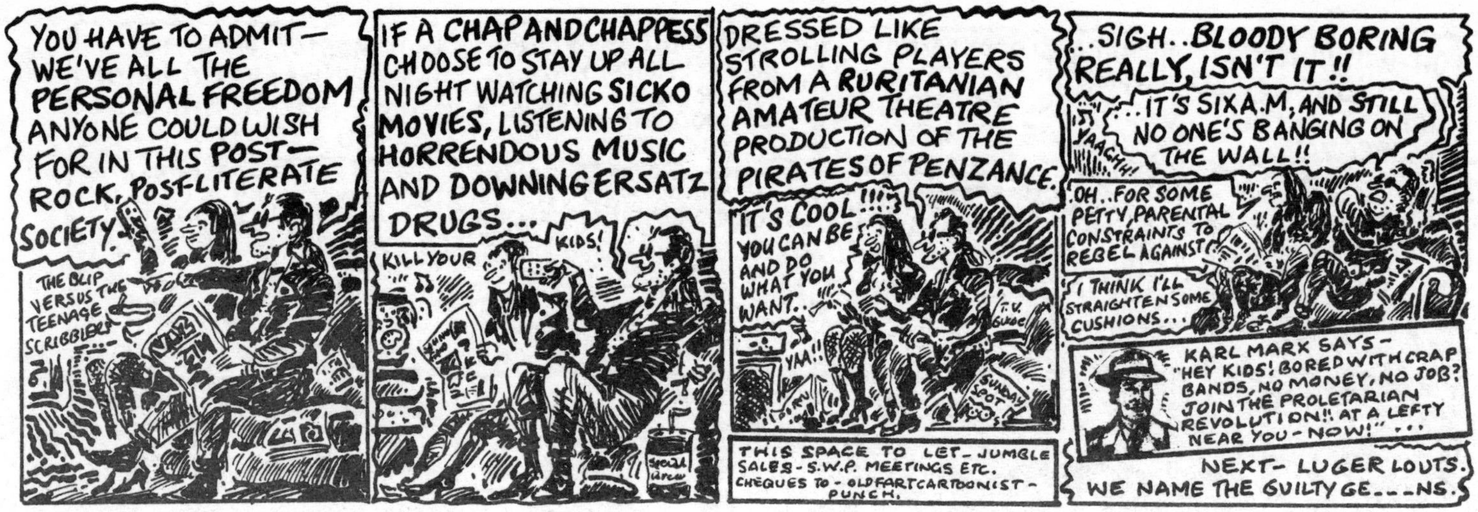
YOU HAVE TO ADMIT— WE'VE ALL THE PERSONAL FREEDOM ANYONE COULD WISH FOR IN THIS POST-ROCK, POST-LITERATE SOCIETY.
THE BLIP VERSUS THE TEENAGE SCRIBBLERS
IF A CHAP AND CHAPPESS CHOOSE TO STAY UP ALL NIGHT WATCHING SICKO MOVIES, LISTENING TO HORRENDOUS MUSIC AND DOWNING ERSATZ DRUGS...
KILL YOUR
KIDS!
DRESSED LIKE STROLLING PLAYERS FROM A RURITANIAN AMATEUR THEATRE PRODUCTION OF THE PIRATES OF PENZANCE.
IT'S COOL!!! YOU CAN BE AND DO WHAT YOU WANT...
YAA!!
T.V. GUIDE
SUNDAY SPOT
THIS SPACE TO LET - JUMBLE SALES - S.W.P. MEETINGS ETC. CHEQUES TO - OLDFARTCARTOONIST - PUNCH.
...SIGH.. BLOODY BORING REALLY, ISN'T IT!!
YAAGH!!
...IT'S SIX A.M. AND STILL NO ONE'S BANGING ON THE WALL!!
OH.. FOR SOME PETTY, PARENTAL CONSTRAINTS TO REBEL AGAINST!
I THINK I'LL STRAIGHTEN SOME CUSHIONS...
KARL MARX SAYS - "HEY KIDS! BORED WITH CRAP BANDS, NO MONEY, NO JOB? JOIN THE PROLETARIAN REVOLUTION!! AT A LEFTY NEAR YOU - NOW!" ...
NEXT - LUGER LOUTS. WE NAME THE GUILTY GE---NS.

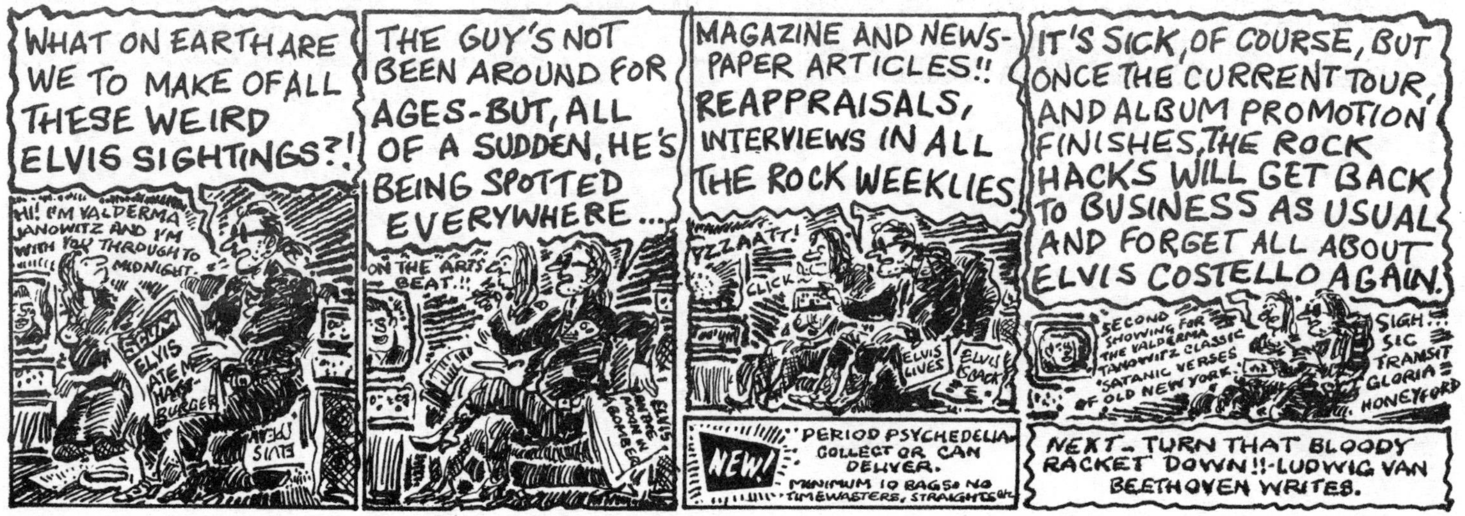
WHAT ON EARTH ARE WE TO MAKE OF ALL THESE WEIRD ELVIS SIGHTINGS?!
HI! I'M VALDERMA JANOWITZ AND I'M WITH YOU THROUGH TO MIDNIGHT.
ELVIS ATE A HAMBURGER
THE GUY'S NOT BEEN AROUND FOR AGES - BUT, ALL OF A SUDDEN, HE'S BEING SPOTTED EVERYWHERE...
ON THE ARTS BEAT!!
MAGAZINE AND NEWSPAPER ARTICLES!! REAPPRAISALS, INTERVIEWS IN ALL THE ROCK WEEKLIES.
YZZAATT!
CLICK
ELVIS LIVES
ELVIS BACK
NEW!
PERIOD PSYCHEDELIA COLLECT OR CAN DELIVER. MINIMUM 10 BAGS. NO TIMEWASTERS, STRAIGHTS etc.
IT'S SICK, OF COURSE, BUT ONCE THE 'CURRENT TOUR, AND ALBUM PROMOTION' FINISHES, THE ROCK HACKS WILL GET BACK TO BUSINESS AS USUAL AND FORGET ALL ABOUT ELVIS COSTELLO AGAIN.
SECOND SHOWING FOR THE VALDERMA JANOWITZ CLASSIC "SATANIC VERSES OF OLD NEW YORK."
SIGH... SIC TRANSIT GLORIA = HONEYFORD
NEXT - TURN THAT BLOODY RACKET DOWN!! - LUDWIG VAN BEETHOVEN WRITES.

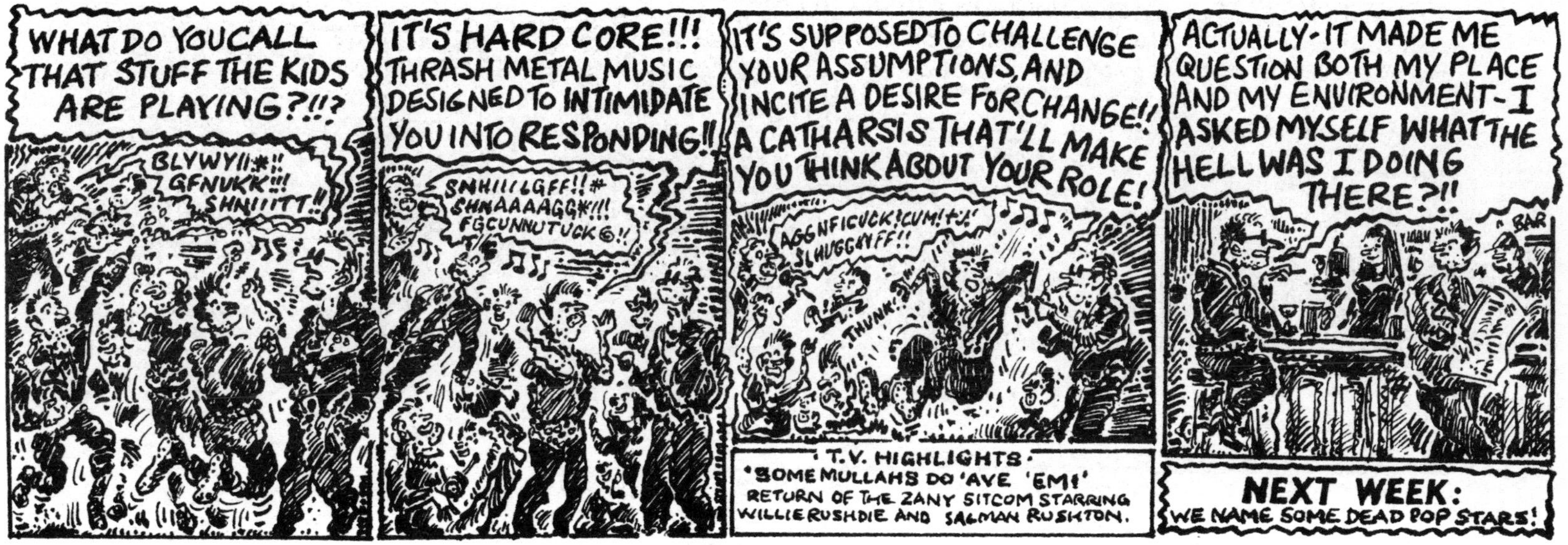
WHAT DO YOU CALL THAT STUFF THE KIDS ARE PLAYING?!!?
BLYWYII!*!! GFNUKK!!! SHNIIIITT!!
IT'S HARD CORE!!! THRASH METAL MUSIC DESIGNED TO INTIMIDATE YOU INTO RESPONDING!!
SNHIIILGFF!!# SHNAAAAAGG*!!! FGCUNNUTUCK©!!
IT'S SUPPOSED TO CHALLENGE YOUR ASSUMPTIONS, AND INCITE A DESIRE FOR CHANGE!! A CATHARSIS THAT'LL MAKE YOU THINK ABOUT YOUR ROLE!
AGGNFICUCK!CUM!+! SLHUGGNFF!!
THUNK!
T.V. HIGHLIGHTS
'SOME MULLAHS DO 'AVE 'EM!'
RETURN OF THE ZANY SITCOM STARRING WILLIE RUSHDIE AND SALMAN RUSHTON.
ACTUALLY - IT MADE ME QUESTION BOTH MY PLACE AND MY ENVIRONMENT - I ASKED MYSELF WHAT THE HELL WAS I DOING THERE?!!
BAR
NEXT WEEK:
WE NAME SOME DEAD POP STARS!

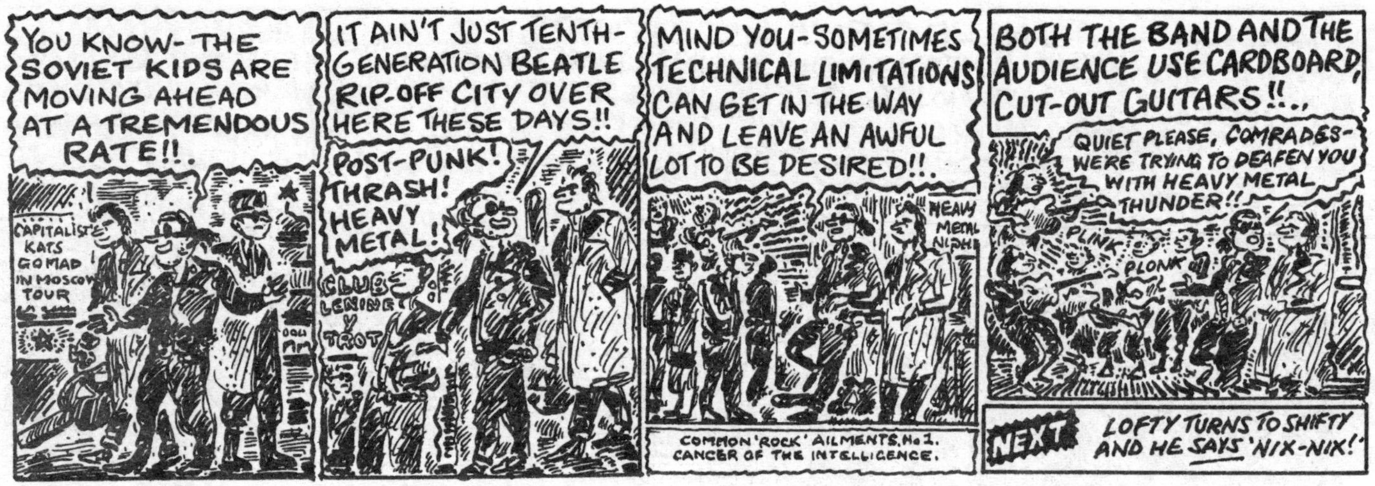
YOU KNOW- THE SOVIET KIDS ARE MOVING AHEAD AT A TREMENDOUS RATE!!.
CAPITALIST KATS GO MAD IN MOSCOW TOUR
IT AIN'T JUST TENTH-GENERATION BEATLE RIP-OFF CITY OVER HERE THESE DAYS!!
POST-PUNK! THRASH! HEAVY METAL!
CLUB LENINE Y TROT
MIND YOU - SOMETIMES TECHNICAL LIMITATIONS CAN GET IN THE WAY AND LEAVE AN AWFUL LOT TO BE DESIRED!!.
HEAVY METAL NIGHT
COMMON 'ROCK' AILMENTS. No 1.
CANCER OF THE INTELLIGENCE.
BOTH THE BAND AND THE AUDIENCE USE CARDBOARD, CUT-OUT GUITARS!!..
QUIET PLEASE, COMRADES- WE'RE TRYING TO DEAFEN YOU WITH HEAVY METAL THUNDER!!
PLINK
PLONK
NEXT
LOFTY TURNS TO SHIFTY AND HE SAYS 'NIX-NIX!'

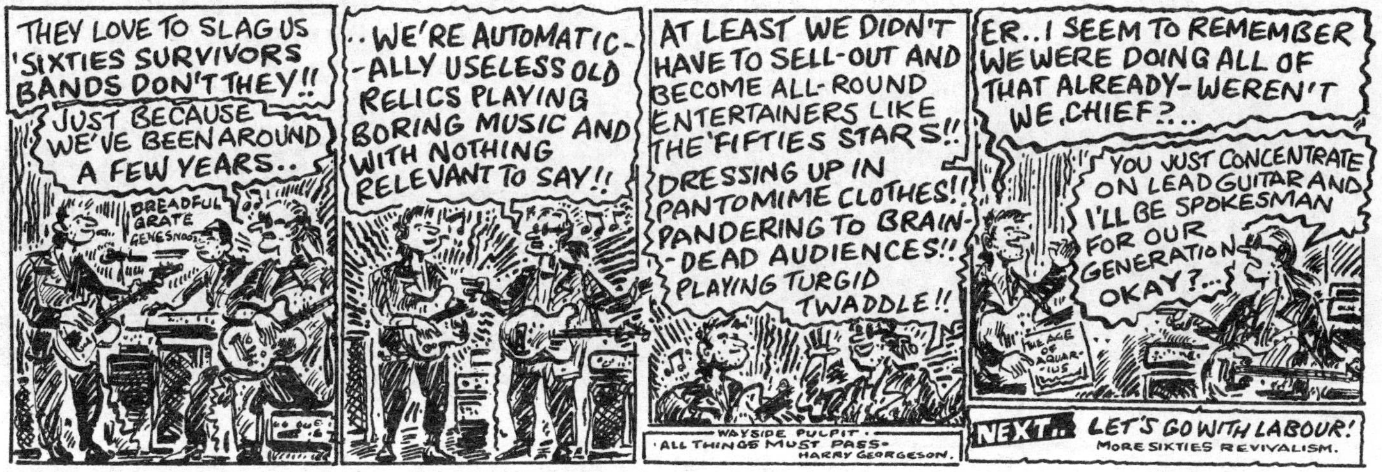
THEY LOVE TO SLAG US 'SIXTIES SURVIVORS BANDS DON'T THEY!!
JUST BECAUSE WE'VE BEEN AROUND A FEW YEARS..
DREADFUL GRATE
..WE'RE AUTOMATIC-ALLY USELESS OLD RELICS PLAYING BORING MUSIC AND WITH NOTHING RELEVANT TO SAY!!
AT LEAST WE DIDN'T HAVE TO SELL-OUT AND BECOME ALL-ROUND ENTERTAINERS LIKE THE 'FIFTIES STARS!!
DRESSING UP IN PANTOMIME CLOTHES!! PANDERING TO BRAIN-DEAD AUDIENCES!! PLAYING TURGID TWADDLE!!
WAYSIDE PULPIT · 'ALL THINGS MUST PASS' HARRY GEORGESON.
ER.. I SEEM TO REMEMBER WE WERE DOING ALL OF THAT ALREADY—WEREN'T WE, CHIEF?...
YOU JUST CONCENTRATE ON LEAD GUITAR AND I'LL BE SPOKESMAN FOR OUR GENERATION.. OKAY?...
NEXT.. LET'S GO WITH LABOUR! MORE SIXTIES REVIVALISM.

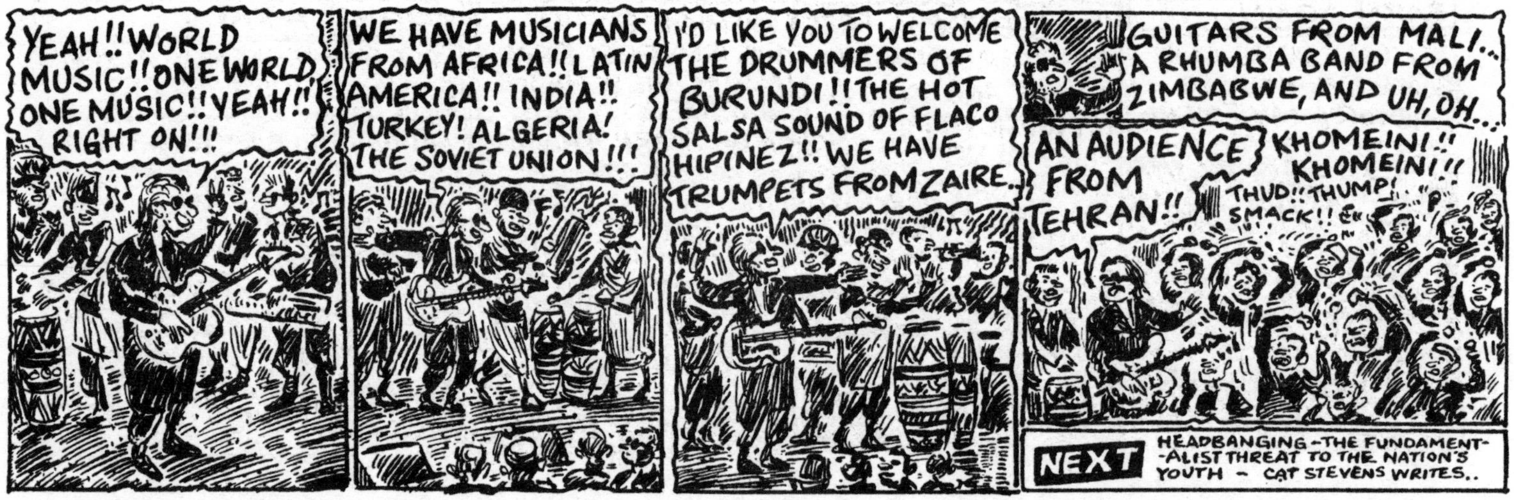
YEAH!! WORLD MUSIC!! ONE WORLD, ONE MUSIC!! YEAH!! RIGHT ON!!!
WE HAVE MUSICIANS FROM AFRICA!! LATIN AMERICA!! INDIA!! TURKEY! ALGERIA! THE SOVIET UNION!!!
I'D LIKE YOU TO WELCOME THE DRUMMERS OF BURUNDI!! THE HOT SALSA SOUND OF FLACO HIPINEZ!! WE HAVE TRUMPETS FROM ZAIRE..
GUITARS FROM MALI... A RHUMBA BAND FROM ZIMBABWE, AND UH, OH...
AN AUDIENCE FROM TEHRAN!!
KHOMEINI!! KHOMEINI!!
THUD!! THUMP! SMACK!!
NEXT
HEADBANGING - THE FUNDAMENT-ALIST THREAT TO THE NATION'S YOUTH - CAT STEVENS WRITES..

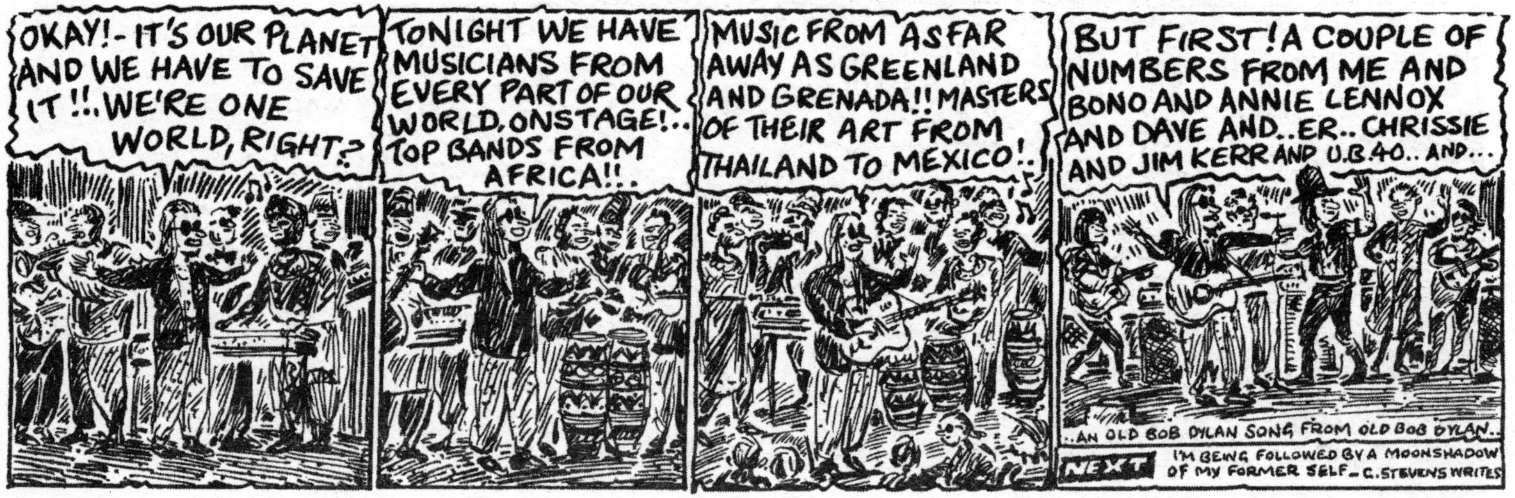
OKAY! - IT'S OUR PLANET AND WE HAVE TO SAVE IT!!. WE'RE ONE WORLD, RIGHT?
TONIGHT WE HAVE MUSICIANS FROM EVERY PART OF OUR WORLD, ONSTAGE!.. TOP BANDS FROM AFRICA!!.
MUSIC FROM AS FAR AWAY AS GREENLAND AND GRENADA!! MASTERS OF THEIR ART FROM THAILAND TO MEXICO!.
BUT FIRST! A COUPLE OF NUMBERS FROM ME AND BONO AND ANNIE LENNOX AND DAVE AND.. ER.. CHRISSIE AND JIM KERR AND U.B.40.. AND...
..AN OLD BOB DYLAN SONG FROM OLD BOB DYLAN..
NEXT
I'M BEING FOLLOWED BY A MOONSHADOW OF MY FORMER SELF - C. STEVENS WRITES

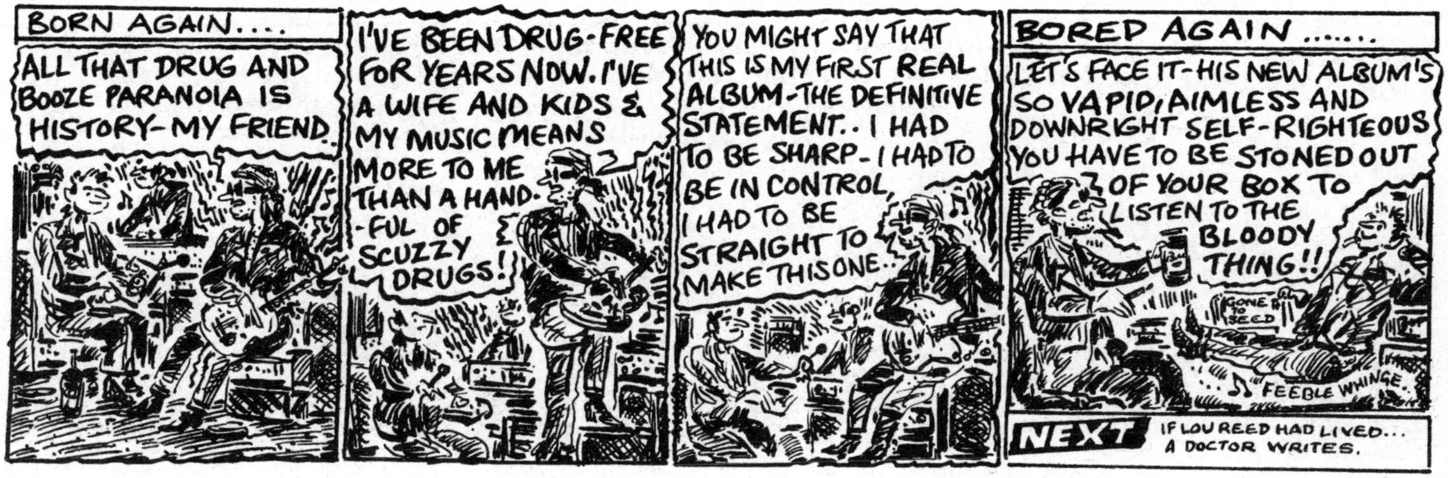
BORN AGAIN....
ALL THAT DRUG AND BOOZE PARANOIA IS HISTORY- MY FRIEND.
I'VE BEEN DRUG-FREE FOR YEARS NOW. I'VE A WIFE AND KIDS & MY MUSIC MEANS MORE TO ME THAN A HAND-FUL OF SCUZZY DRUGS!
YOU MIGHT SAY THAT THIS IS MY FIRST REAL ALBUM-THE DEFINITIVE STATEMENT.. I HAD TO BE SHARP- I HAD TO BE IN CONTROL, I HAD TO BE STRAIGHT TO MAKE THIS ONE..
BORED AGAIN.......
LET'S FACE IT- HIS NEW ALBUM'S SO VAPID, AIMLESS AND DOWNRIGHT SELF-RIGHTEOUS YOU HAVE TO BE STONED OUT OF YOUR BOX TO LISTEN TO THE BLOODY THING!!
GONE TO SEED
"FEEBLE WHINGE."
NEXT
IF LOU REED HAD LIVED... A DOCTOR WRITES.

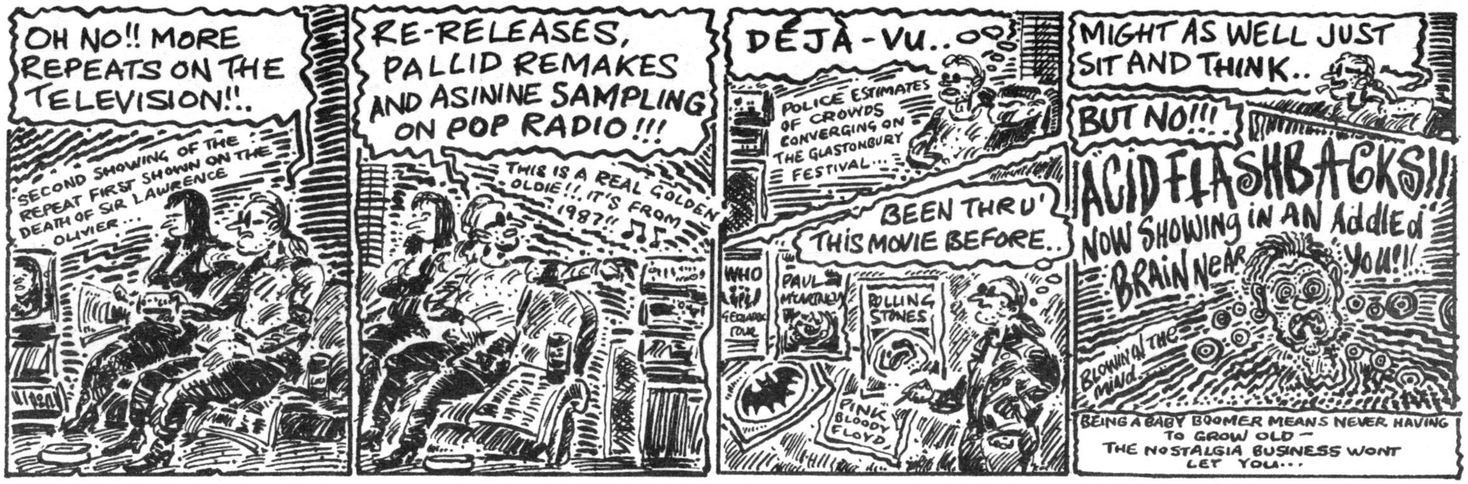
OH NO!! MORE REPEATS ON THE TELEVISION!!..
SECOND SHOWING OF THE REPEAT FIRST SHOWN ON THE DEATH OF SIR LAWRENCE OLIVIER...
RE-RELEASES, PALLID REMAKES AND ASININE SAMPLING ON POP RADIO!!!
THIS IS A REAL GOLDEN OLDIE!! IT'S FROM 1987!!
DÉJÀ-VU..
POLICE ESTIMATES OF CROWDS CONVERGING ON THE GLASTONBURY FESTIVAL...
BEEN THRU' THIS MOVIE BEFORE..
WHO
PAUL McCARTNEY
ROLLING STONES
PINK BLOODY FLOYD
MIGHT AS WELL JUST SIT AND THINK..
BUT NO!!!....
ACID FLASHBACKS!!!
NOW SHOWING IN AN Addled BRAIN NeAR YOU!!!
BLOWIN' IN THE MIND..
BEING A BABY BOOMER MEANS NEVER HAVING TO GROW OLD - THE NOSTALGIA BUSINESS WONT LET YOU...

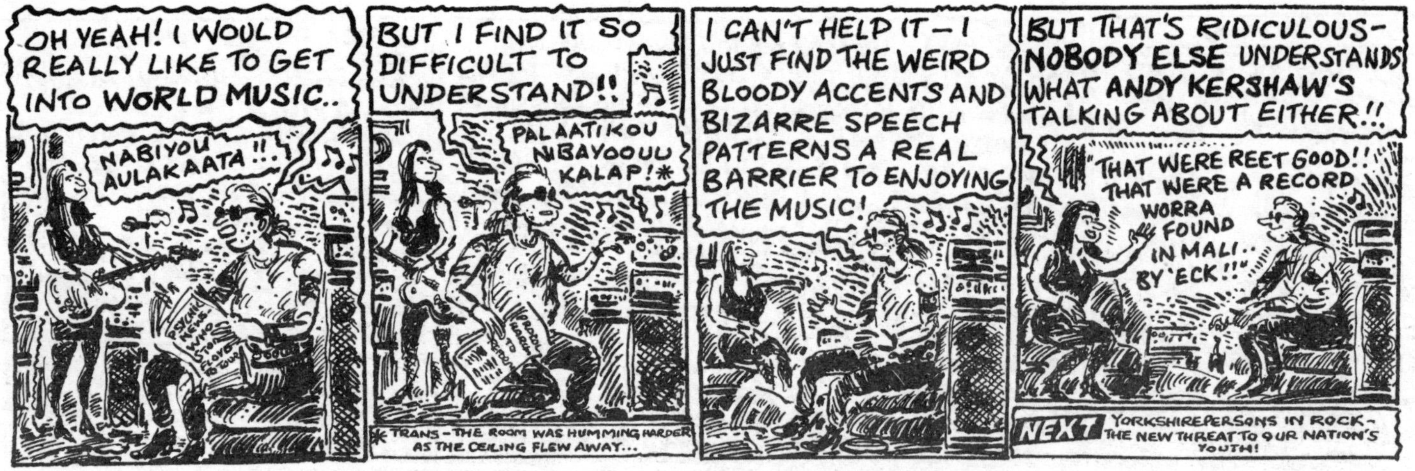
OH YEAH! I WOULD REALLY LIKE TO GET INTO WORLD MUSIC..
NABIYOU AULAKAATA!!..
BUT I FIND IT SO DIFFICULT TO UNDERSTAND!!
PALAATIKOU NIBAYOOUU KALAP!*
* TRANS — THE ROOM WAS HUMMING HARDER AS THE CEILING FLEW AWAY...
I CAN'T HELP IT — I JUST FIND THE WEIRD BLOODY ACCENTS AND BIZARRE SPEECH PATTERNS A REAL BARRIER TO ENJOYING THE MUSIC!
BUT THAT'S RIDICULOUS— NOBODY ELSE UNDERSTANDS WHAT ANDY KERSHAW'S TALKING ABOUT EITHER!!
"THAT WERE REET GOOD!! THAT WERE A RECORD WORRA FOUND IN MALI.. BY 'ECK!!"
NEXT YORKSHIREPERSONS IN ROCK — THE NEW THREAT TO OUR NATION'S YOUTH!

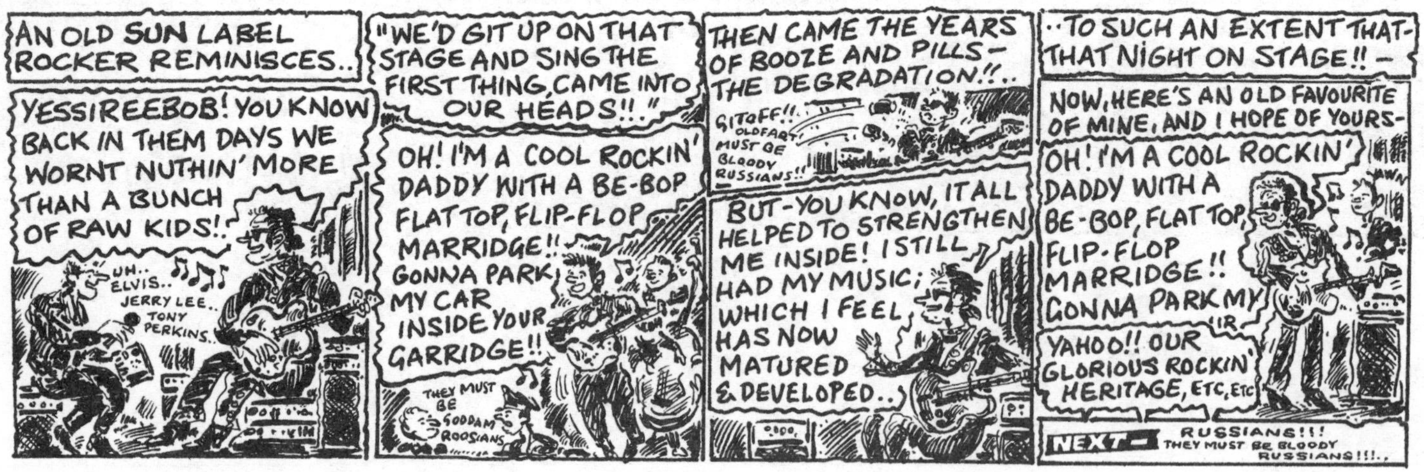
AN OLD SUN LABEL ROCKER REMINISCES..
YESSIREEBOB! YOU KNOW BACK IN THEM DAYS WE WORNT NUTHIN' MORE THAN A BUNCH OF RAW KIDS!..
UH.. ELVIS.. JERRY LEE.. TONY PERKINS..
"WE'D GIT UP ON THAT STAGE AND SING THE FIRST THING CAME INTO OUR HEADS!!"
OH! I'M A COOL ROCKIN' DADDY WITH A BE-BOP FLAT TOP, FLIP-FLOP MARRIDGE!! GONNA PARK MY CAR INSIDE YOUR GARRIDGE!!
THEY MUST BE GODDAM ROOSIANS
THEN CAME THE YEARS OF BOOZE AND PILLS— THE DEGRADATION!!..
GITOFF!! OLDFART MUST BE BLOODY RUSSIANS!!
BUT — YOU KNOW, IT ALL HELPED TO STRENGTHEN ME INSIDE! I STILL HAD MY MUSIC; WHICH I FEEL HAS NOW MATURED & DEVELOPED..
..TO SUCH AN EXTENT THAT THAT NIGHT ON STAGE!! —
NOW, HERE'S AN OLD FAVOURITE OF MINE, AND I HOPE OF YOURS—
OH! I'M A COOL ROCKIN' DADDY WITH A BE-BOP, FLAT TOP, FLIP-FLOP MARRIDGE!! GONNA PARK MY
YAHOO!! OUR GLORIOUS ROCKIN' HERITAGE, ETC, ETC
NEXT — RUSSIANS!!! THEY MUST BE BLOODY RUSSIANS!!!..

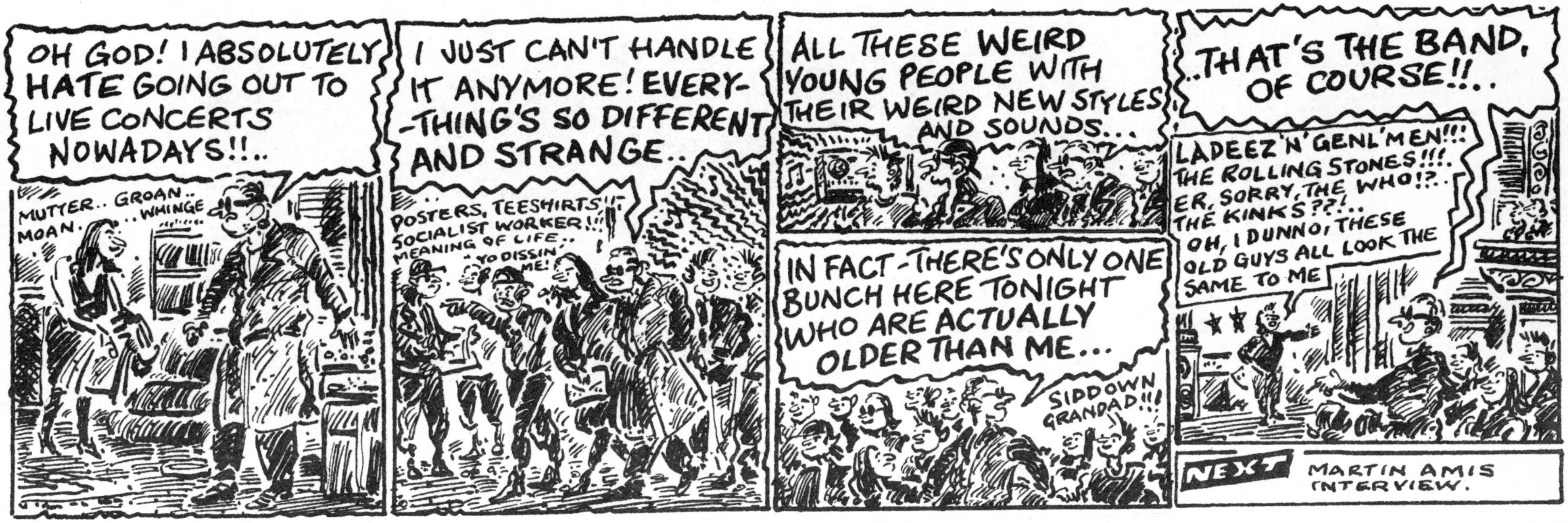
OH GOD! I ABSOLUTELY HATE GOING OUT TO LIVE CONCERTS NOWADAYS!!..
MUTTER.. GROAN.. MOAN.. ..WHINGE
I JUST CAN'T HANDLE IT ANYMORE! EVERY-THING'S SO DIFFERENT AND STRANGE..
..POSTERS, TEESHIRTS!! SOCIALIST WORKER!!! MEANING OF LIFE..
YO DISSIN' ME!
ALL THESE WEIRD YOUNG PEOPLE WITH THEIR WEIRD NEW STYLES AND SOUNDS...
IN FACT - THERE'S ONLY ONE BUNCH HERE TONIGHT WHO ARE ACTUALLY OLDER THAN ME...
SIDDOWN GRANDAD!!!
..THAT'S THE BAND, OF COURSE!!..
LADEEZ 'N' GENL'MEN!!! THE ROLLING STONES!!!.. ER, SORRY, THE WHO!?.. THE KINKS??!..
OH, I DUNNO, THESE OLD GUYS ALL LOOK THE SAME TO ME
NEXT
MARTIN AMIS INTERVIEW.

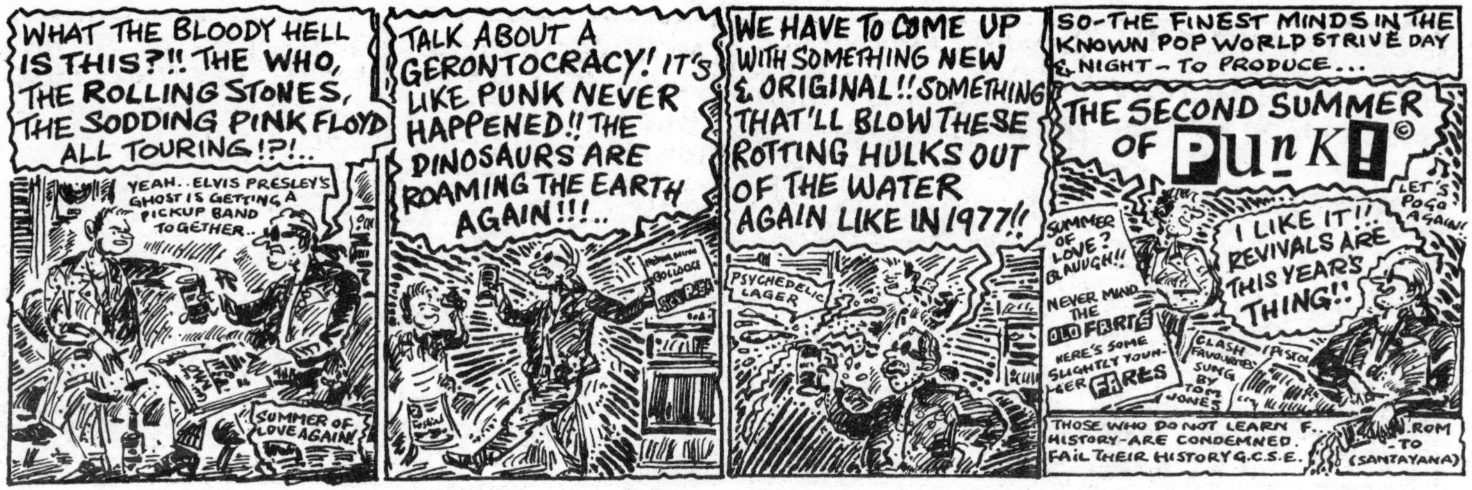
WHAT THE BLOODY HELL IS THIS?!! THE WHO, THE ROLLING STONES, THE SODDING PINK FLOYD ALL TOURING!?!..
YEAH.. ELVIS PRESLEY'S GHOST IS GETTING A PICKUP BAND TOGETHER..
SUMMER OF LOVE AGAIN!
TALK ABOUT A GERONTOCRACY! IT'S LIKE PUNK NEVER HAPPENED!! THE DINOSAURS ARE ROAMING THE EARTH AGAIN!!!..
WE HAVE TO COME UP WITH SOMETHING NEW & ORIGINAL!! SOMETHING THAT'LL BLOW THESE ROTTING HULKS OUT OF THE WATER AGAIN LIKE IN 1977!!
PSYCHEDELIC LAGER
SO-THE FINEST MINDS IN THE KNOWN POP WORLD STRIVE DAY & NIGHT - TO PRODUCE...
THE SECOND SUMMER OF PUnK!©
LET'S POGO AGAIN!
SUMMER OF LOVE? BLAUUGH!!
NEVER MIND THE OLD FARTS
HERE'S SOME SLIGHTLY YOUNGER FARTS
CLASH FAVOURITES SUNG BY TOM JONES
I LIKE IT!! REVIVALS ARE THIS YEAR'S THING!!
THOSE WHO DO NOT LEARN F... .ROM HISTORY-ARE CONDEMNED. -TO FAIL THEIR HISTORY G.C.S.E. (SANTAYANA)

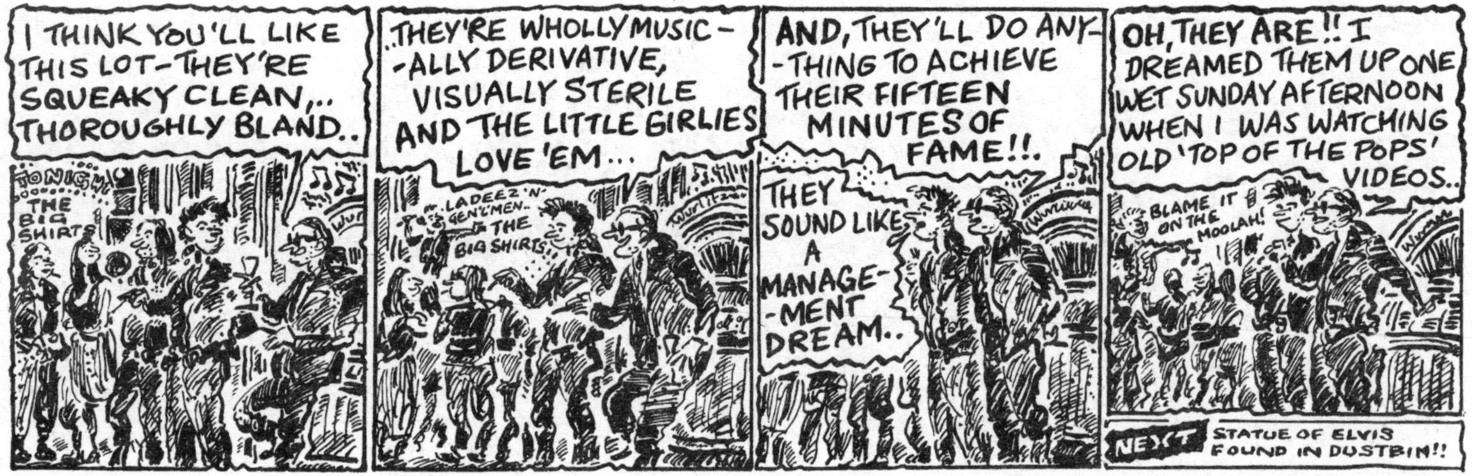
I THINK YOU'LL LIKE THIS LOT-THEY'RE SQUEAKY CLEAN,.. THOROUGHLY BLAND..
TONIGHT THE BIG SHIRTS
THEY'RE WHOLLY MUSIC--ALLY DERIVATIVE, VISUALLY STERILE AND THE LITTLE GIRLIES LOVE 'EM...
LADEEZ 'N' GEN'LMEN.. THE BIG SHIRTS
AND, THEY'LL DO ANY--THING TO ACHIEVE THEIR FIFTEEN MINUTES OF FAME!!.
THEY SOUND LIKE A MANAGE--MENT DREAM..
OH, THEY ARE!! I DREAMED THEM UP ONE WET SUNDAY AFTERNOON WHEN I WAS WATCHING OLD 'TOP OF THE POPS' VIDEOS..
BLAME IT ON THE MOOLAH!
NEXT STATUE OF ELVIS FOUND IN DUSTBIN!!

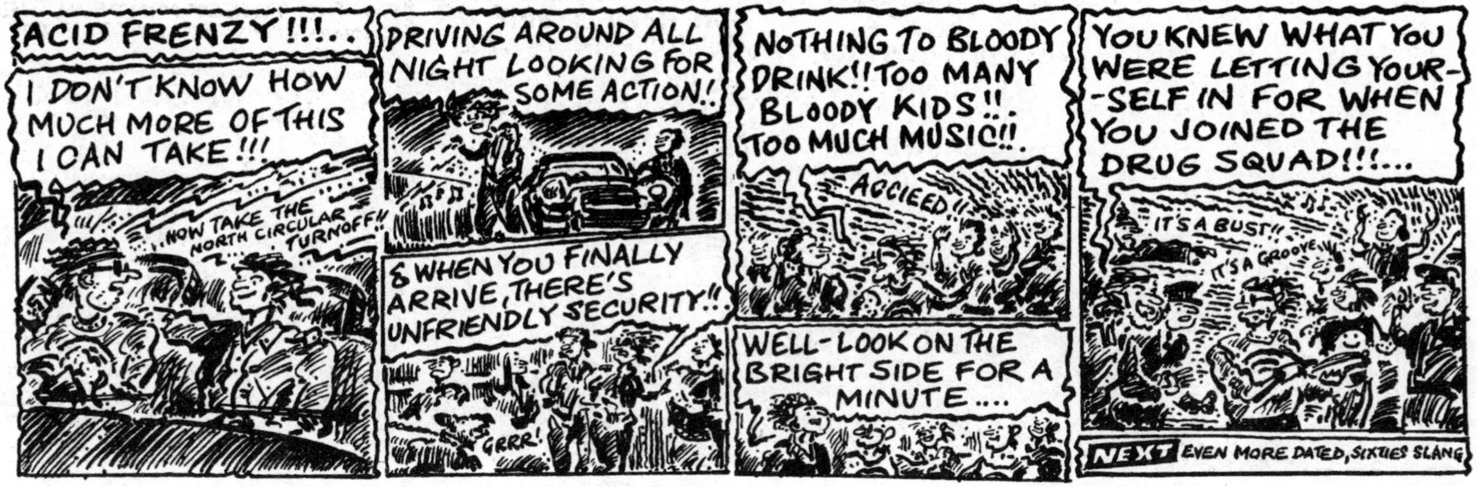
ACID FRENZY!!!..
I DON'T KNOW HOW MUCH MORE OF THIS I CAN TAKE!!!
..NOW TAKE THE NORTH CIRCULAR TURNOFF!!
DRIVING AROUND ALL NIGHT LOOKING FOR SOME ACTION!
& WHEN YOU FINALLY ARRIVE, THERE'S UNFRIENDLY SECURITY!!
GRRR!
NOTHING TO BLOODY DRINK!! TOO MANY BLOODY KIDS!!.. TOO MUCH MUSIC!!.
ACCIEED!!
WELL-LOOK ON THE BRIGHT SIDE FOR A MINUTE....
YOU KNEW WHAT YOU WERE LETTING YOUR--SELF IN FOR WHEN YOU JOINED THE DRUG SQUAD!!!...
IT'S A BUST!!
IT'S A GROOVE
NEXT EVEN MORE DATED, SIXTIES SLANG

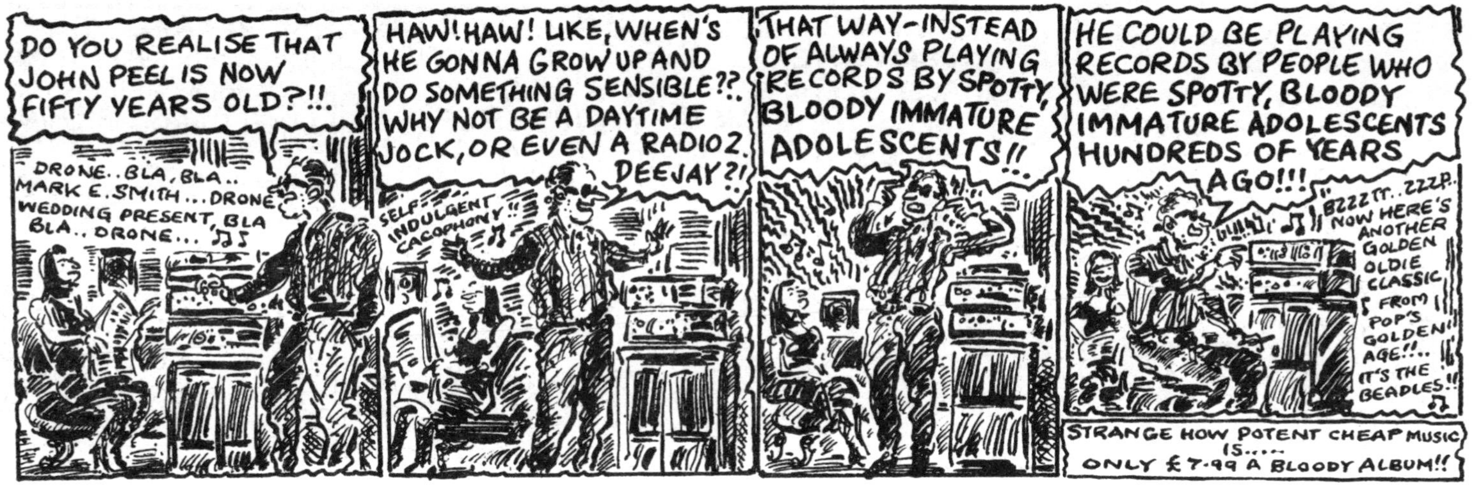
DO YOU REALISE THAT JOHN PEEL IS NOW FIFTY YEARS OLD?!!.
DRONE..BLA, BLA.. MARK E. SMITH...DRONE WEDDING PRESENT, BLA BLA..DRONE...
HAW! HAW! LIKE, WHEN'S HE GONNA GROW UP AND DO SOMETHING SENSIBLE??. WHY NOT BE A DAYTIME JOCK, OR EVEN A RADIO 2 DEEJAY?!
SELF INDULGENT CACOPHONY!!
THAT WAY-INSTEAD OF ALWAYS PLAYING RECORDS BY SPOTTY, BLOODY IMMATURE ADOLESCENTS!!..
HE COULD BE PLAYING RECORDS BY PEOPLE WHO WERE SPOTTY, BLOODY IMMATURE ADOLESCENTS HUNDREDS OF YEARS AGO!!!
BZZZTT..ZZZP. NOW HERE'S ANOTHER GOLDEN OLDIE CLASSIC FROM POP'S GOLDEN AGE!!.. IT'S THE BEADLES!!
STRANGE HOW POTENT CHEAP MUSIC IS..... ONLY £7.99 A BLOODY ALBUM!!

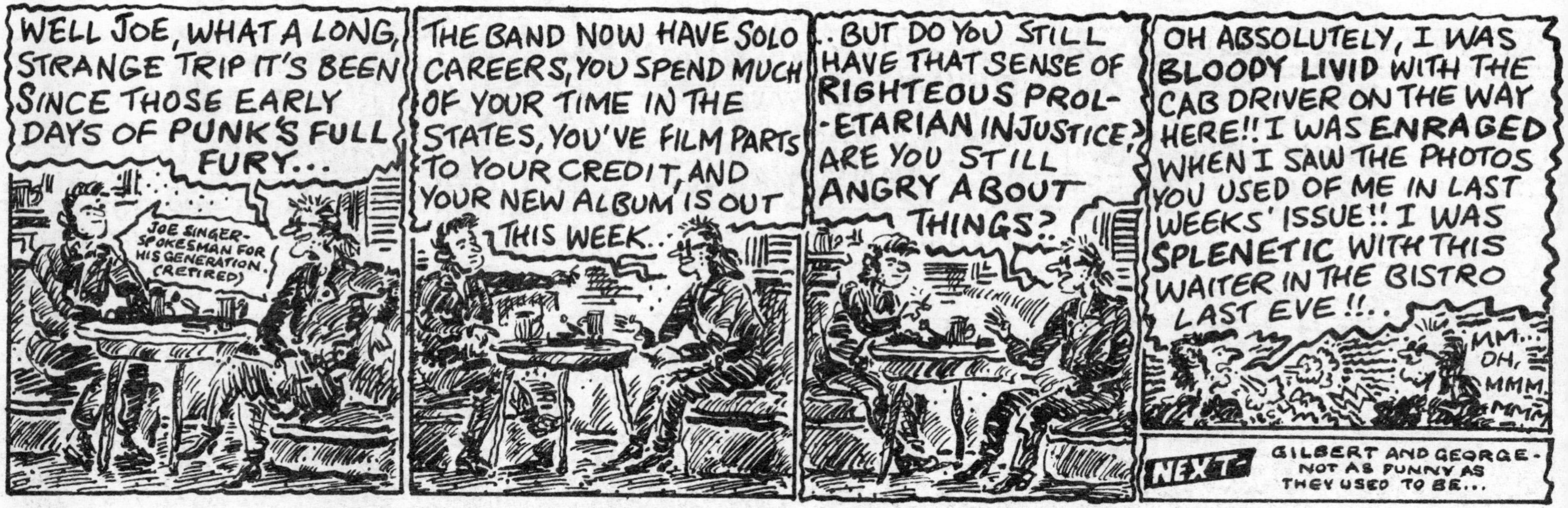
WELL JOE, WHAT A LONG, STRANGE TRIP IT'S BEEN SINCE THOSE EARLY DAYS OF PUNK'S FULL FURY...
JOE SINGER- SPOKESMAN FOR HIS GENERATION. (RETIRED)
THE BAND NOW HAVE SOLO CAREERS, YOU SPEND MUCH OF YOUR TIME IN THE STATES, YOU'VE FILM PARTS TO YOUR CREDIT, AND YOUR NEW ALBUM IS OUT THIS WEEK..
..BUT DO YOU STILL HAVE THAT SENSE OF RIGHTEOUS PROL-ETARIAN INJUSTICE, ARE YOU STILL ANGRY ABOUT THINGS?
OH ABSOLUTELY, I WAS BLOODY LIVID WITH THE CAB DRIVER ON THE WAY HERE!! I WAS ENRAGED WHEN I SAW THE PHOTOS YOU USED OF ME IN LAST WEEKS' ISSUE!! I WAS SPLENETIC WITH THIS WAITER IN THE BISTRO LAST EVE !!..
MM.. OH, MMM. MMM
NEXT- GILBERT AND GEORGE - NOT AS FUNNY AS THEY USED TO BE...

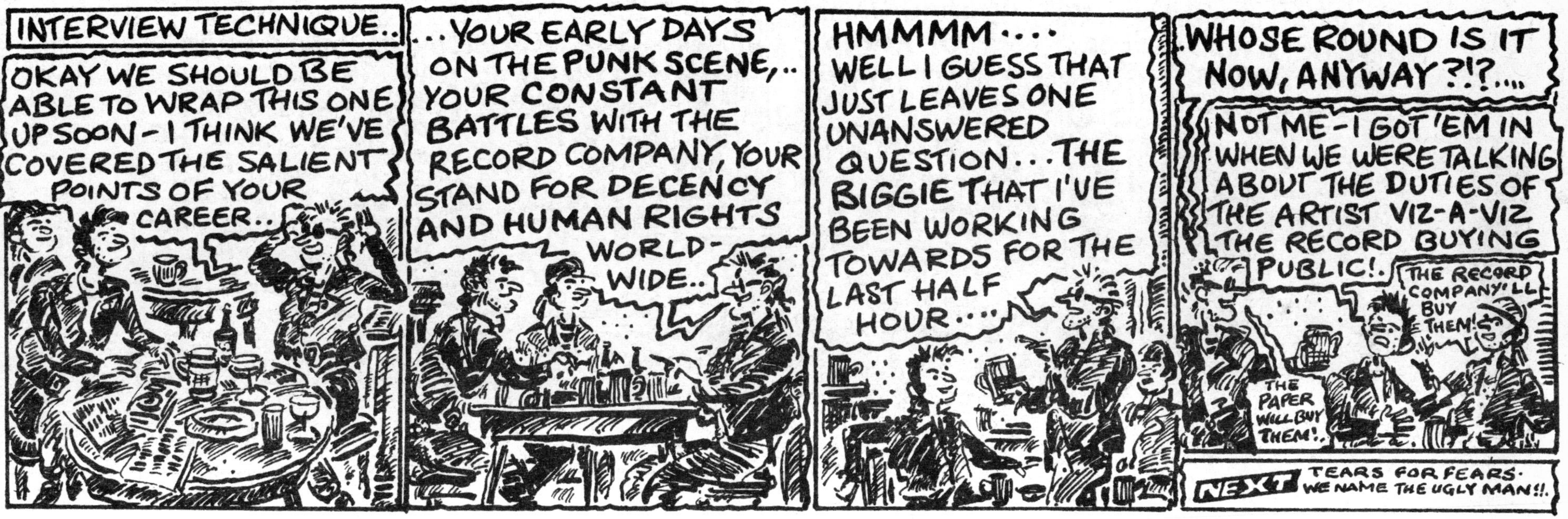
INTERVIEW TECHNIQUE..
OKAY WE SHOULD BE ABLE TO WRAP THIS ONE UP SOON - I THINK WE'VE COVERED THE SALIENT POINTS OF YOUR CAREER..
...YOUR EARLY DAYS ON THE PUNK SCENE,.. YOUR CONSTANT BATTLES WITH THE RECORD COMPANY, YOUR STAND FOR DECENCY AND HUMAN RIGHTS WORLD-WIDE..
HMMMM.... WELL I GUESS THAT JUST LEAVES ONE UNANSWERED QUESTION... THE BIGGIE THAT I'VE BEEN WORKING TOWARDS FOR THE LAST HALF HOUR....
.WHOSE ROUND IS IT NOW, ANYWAY?!?....
NOT ME - I GOT 'EM IN WHEN WE WERE TALKING ABOUT THE DUTIES OF THE ARTIST VIZ-A-VIZ THE RECORD BUYING PUBLIC!.
THE RECORD COMPANY'LL BUY THEM!
THE PAPER WILL BUY THEM!.
NEXT TEARS FOR FEARS. WE NAME THE UGLY MAN!!.

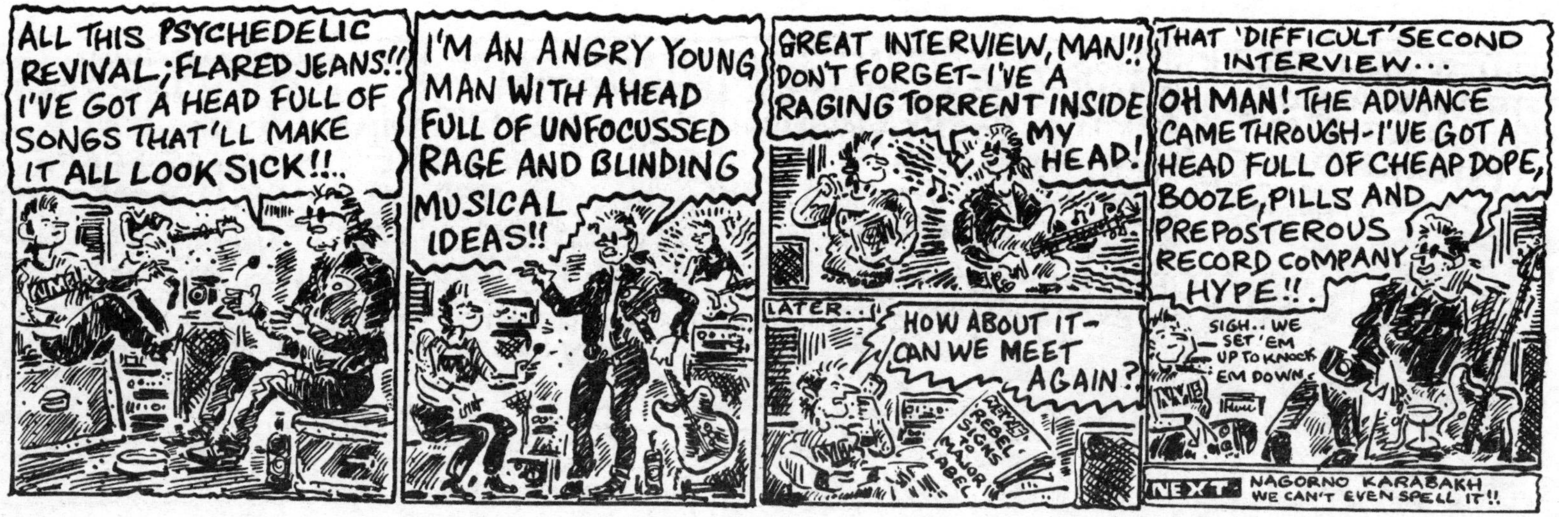
ALL THIS PSYCHEDELIC REVIVAL; FLARED JEANS!! I'VE GOT A HEAD FULL OF SONGS THAT'LL MAKE IT ALL LOOK SICK!!..
I'M AN ANGRY YOUNG MAN WITH A HEAD FULL OF UNFOCUSSED RAGE AND BLINDING MUSICAL IDEAS!!
GREAT INTERVIEW, MAN!! DON'T FORGET- I'VE A RAGING TORRENT INSIDE MY HEAD!
LATER...
HOW ABOUT IT- CAN WE MEET AGAIN?
REBEL SIGNS TO MAJOR LABEL
THAT 'DIFFICULT' SECOND INTERVIEW...
OH MAN! THE ADVANCE CAME THROUGH - I'VE GOT A HEAD FULL OF CHEAP DOPE, BOOZE, PILLS AND PREPOSTEROUS RECORD COMPANY HYPE!!
SIGH.. WE SET 'EM UP TO KNOCK 'EM DOWN..
NEXT: NAGORNO KARABAKH WE CAN'T EVEN SPELL IT!!

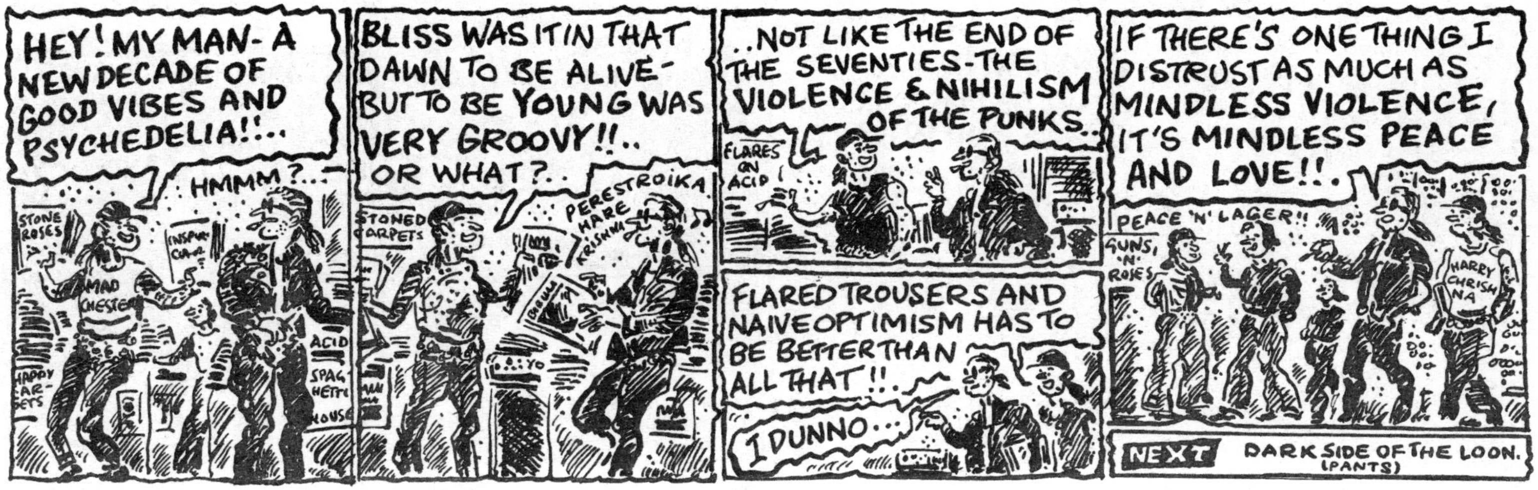

HEY! MY MAN- A NEW DECADE OF GOOD VIBES AND PSYCHEDELIA!!..
HMMM?..
STONE ROSES
MAD CHESTER
ACID SPAGHETTI HOUSE
BLISS WAS IT IN THAT DAWN TO BE ALIVE- BUT TO BE YOUNG WAS VERY GROOVY!!.. OR WHAT?..
STONED CARPETS
PERESTROIKA HARE KRISHNA
..NOT LIKE THE END OF THE SEVENTIES-THE VIOLENCE & NIHILISM OF THE PUNKS..
FLARES ON ACID
FLARED TROUSERS AND NAIVE OPTIMISM HAS TO BE BETTER THAN ALL THAT!!..
I DUNNO...
IF THERE'S ONE THING I DISTRUST AS MUCH AS MINDLESS VIOLENCE, IT'S MINDLESS PEACE AND LOVE!!.
PEACE 'N' LAGER!!
GUNS 'N' ROSES
HARRY CHRISHNA
NEXT
DARK SIDE OF THE LOON. (PANTS)

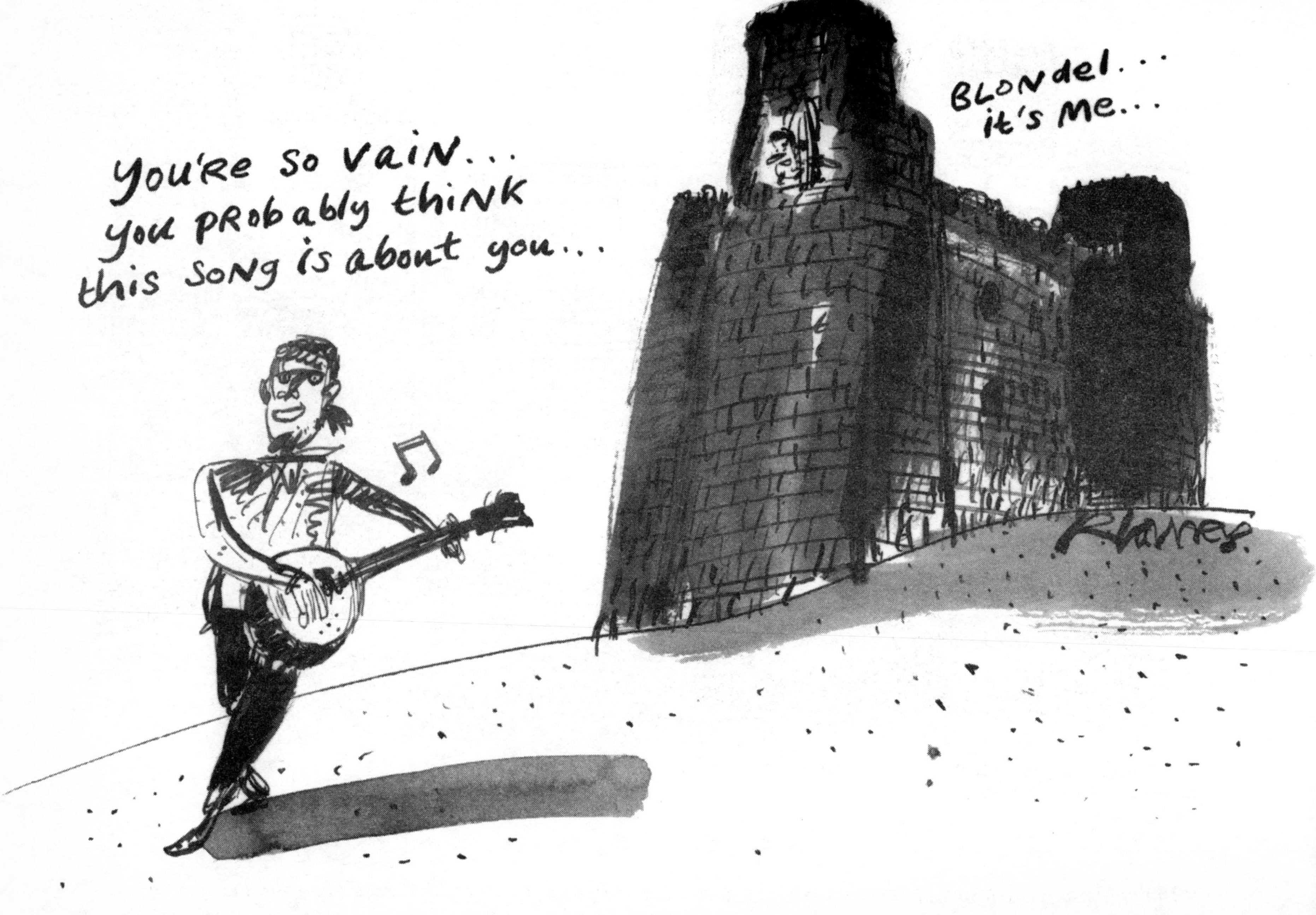
You're so vain...
you probably think
this song is about you...
BLONdel...
it's me...

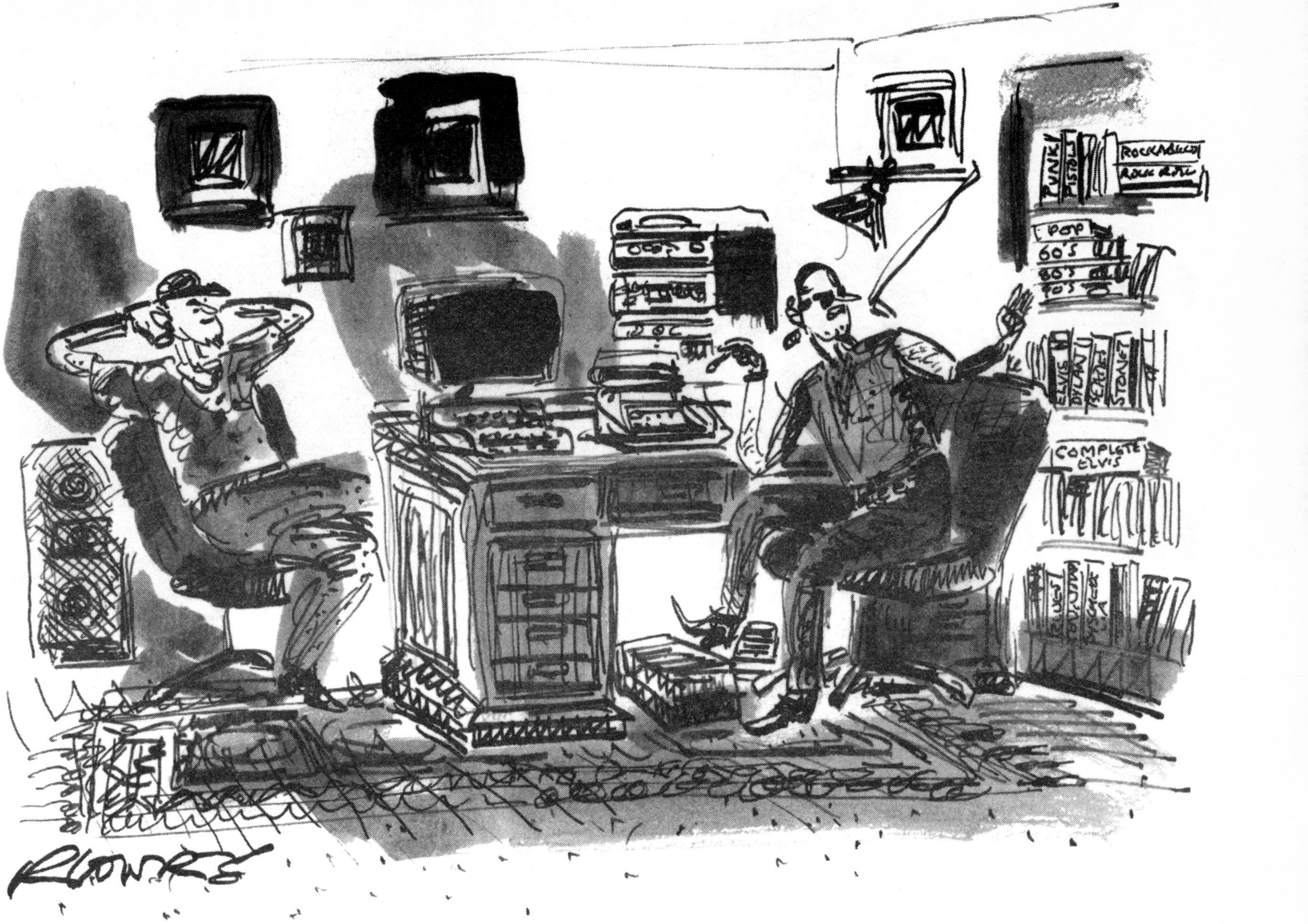
PUNK
ROCKABILLY
POP
60's
80's
70's
ELVIS
DYLAN
STONES
COMPLETE ELVIS

"I'm going to write a sort of personal odyssey. A searing, tripped out journey to the wild heart of the rock 'n' roll dream! As soon as I've thoroughly researched my sources here, of course."

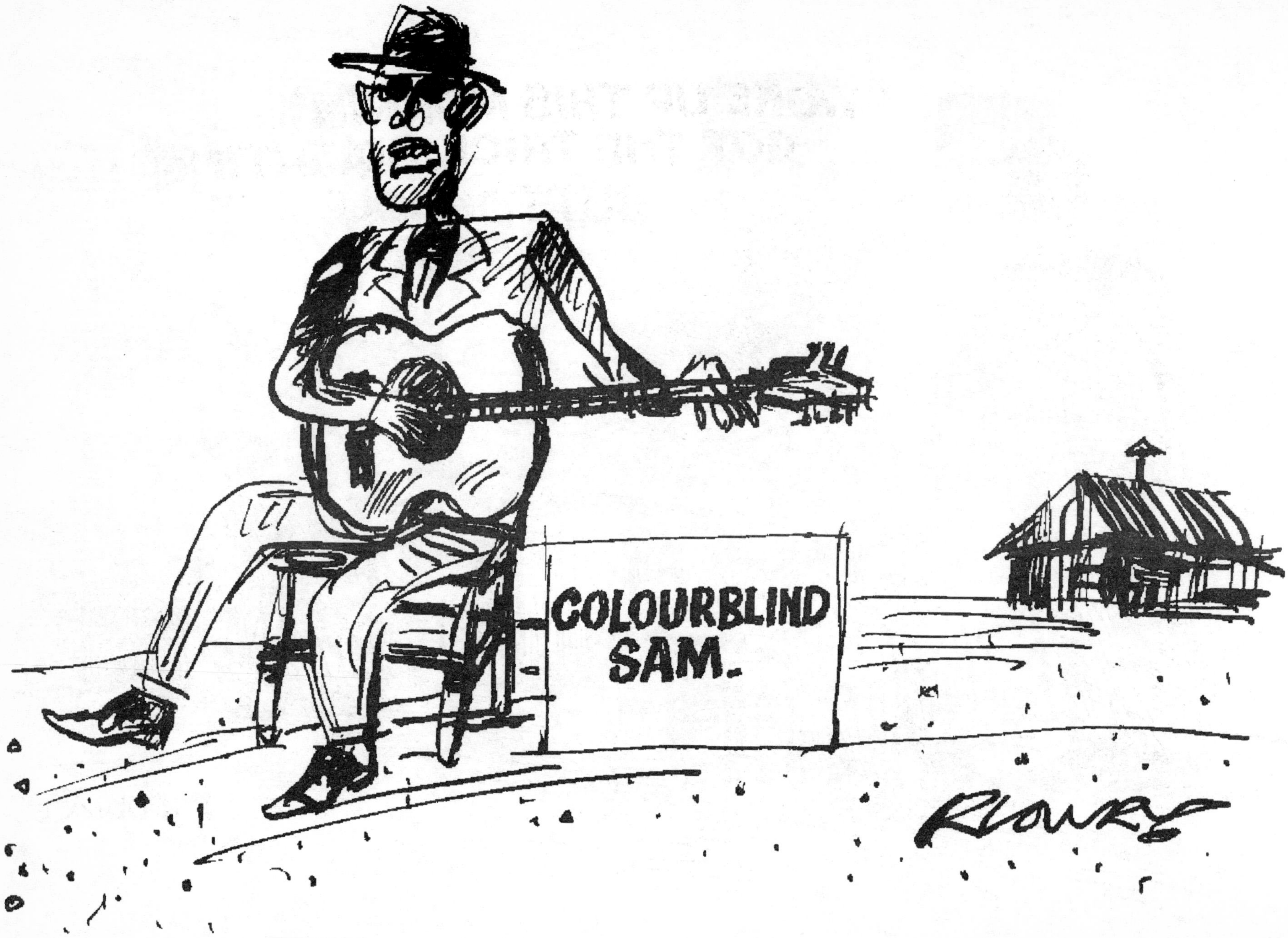
COLOURBLIND
SAM.
RLOWRY

"Woke up this morning – dammit I had the greens!"

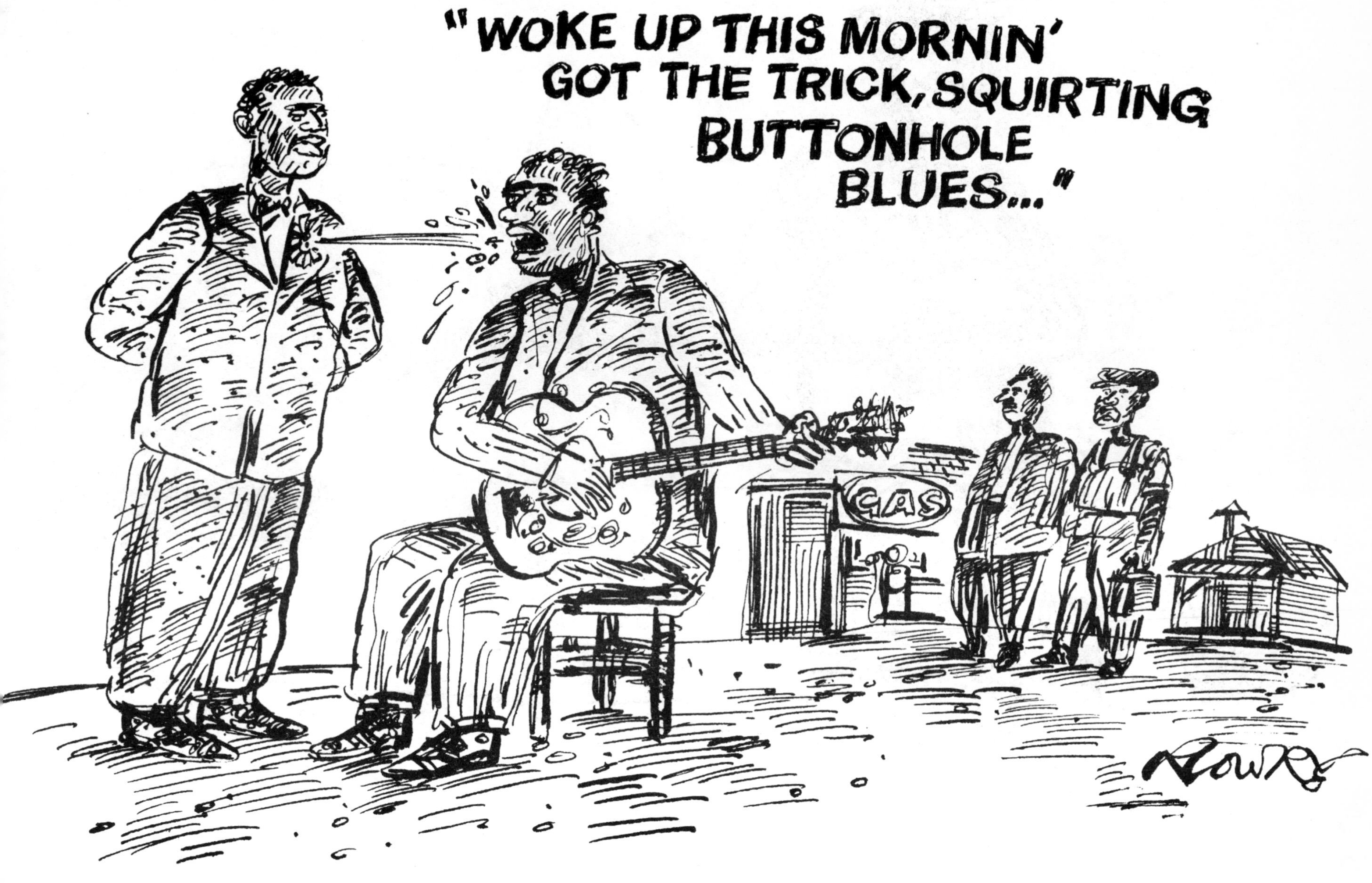
"WOKE UP THIS MORNIN'
GOT THE TRICK, SQUIRTING
BUTTONHOLE
BLUES..."
GAS

"He's really getting desperate for subject material since his records started selling successfully."

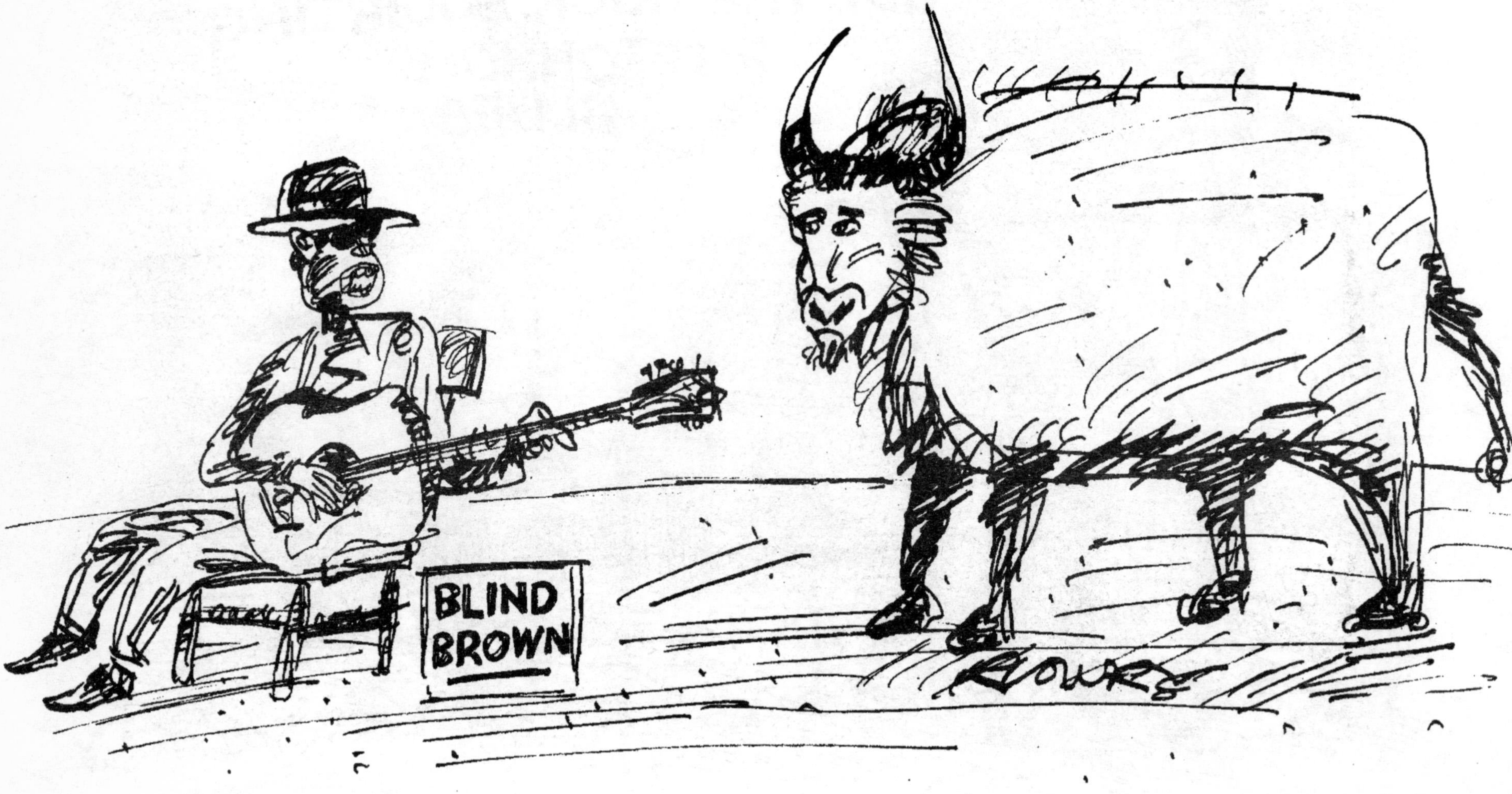
BLIND
BROWN

"You ain't nothin' but a hound dog!"

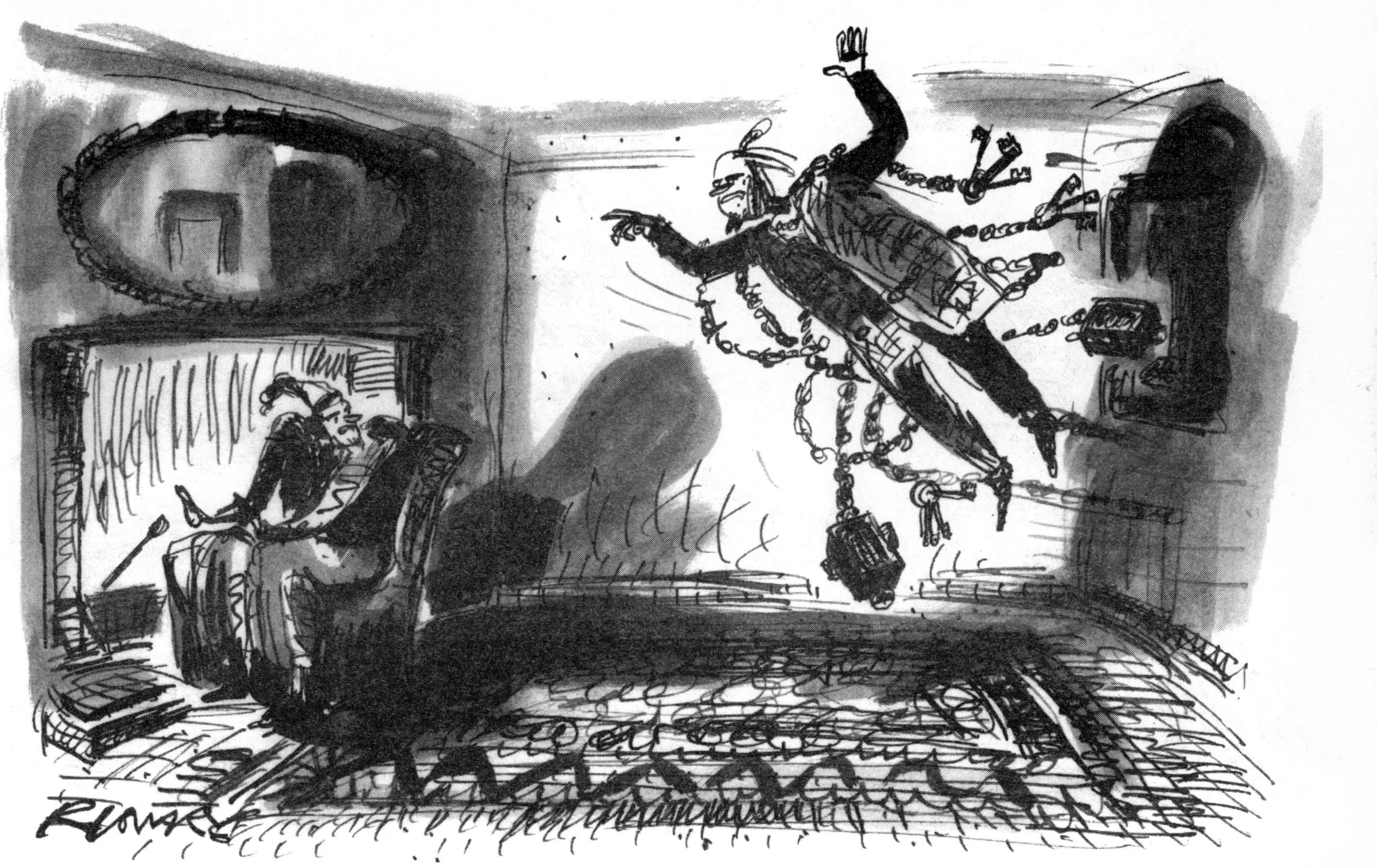

"Don't panic, Scrooge. It's only me, Jacob Marley – the grandfather of grunge!"

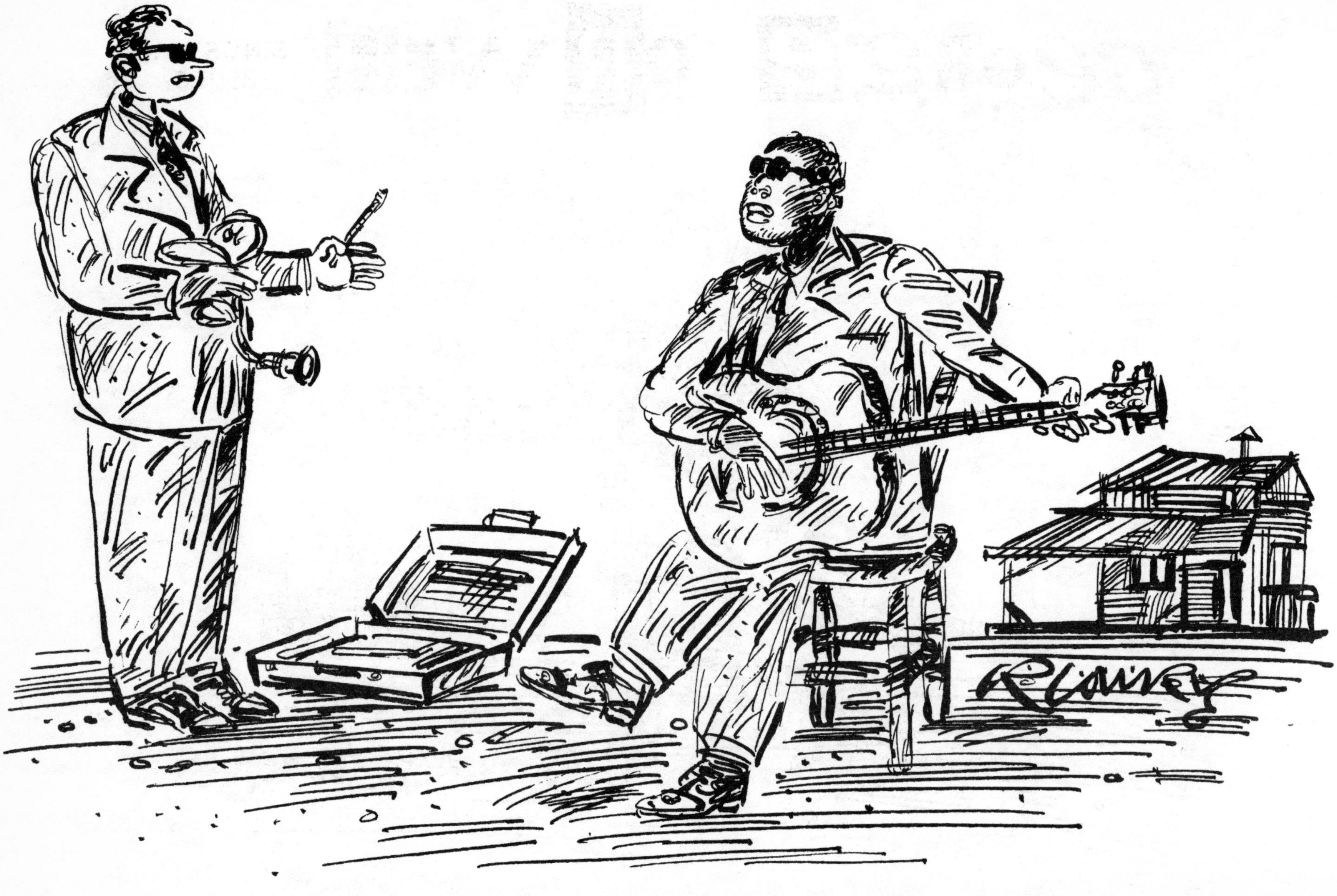

"Bad news, I'm afraid – there ain't no cure for the Summertime Blues!"

SINGS THE
BLUES.

"Woke up this morning – it was a bright cold day in April, and the clocks were striking thirteen!"

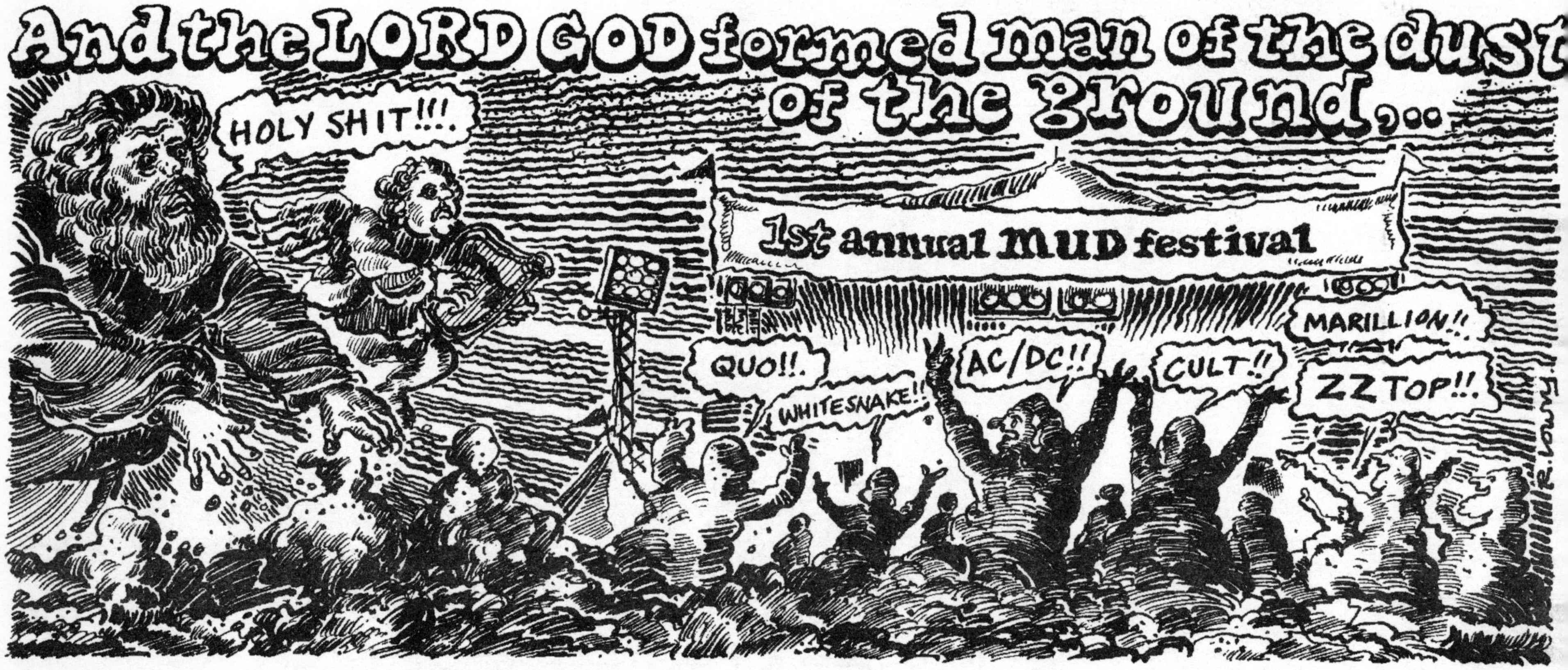
And the LORD GOD formed man of the dust of the ground,..
HOLY SHIT!!!.
1st annual MUD festival
QUO!!.
WHITESNAKE!!
AC/DC!!
CULT!!
MARILLION!!
ZZ TOP!!
R. Lowry

HITLER..THE ROCK'N' ROLL YEARS

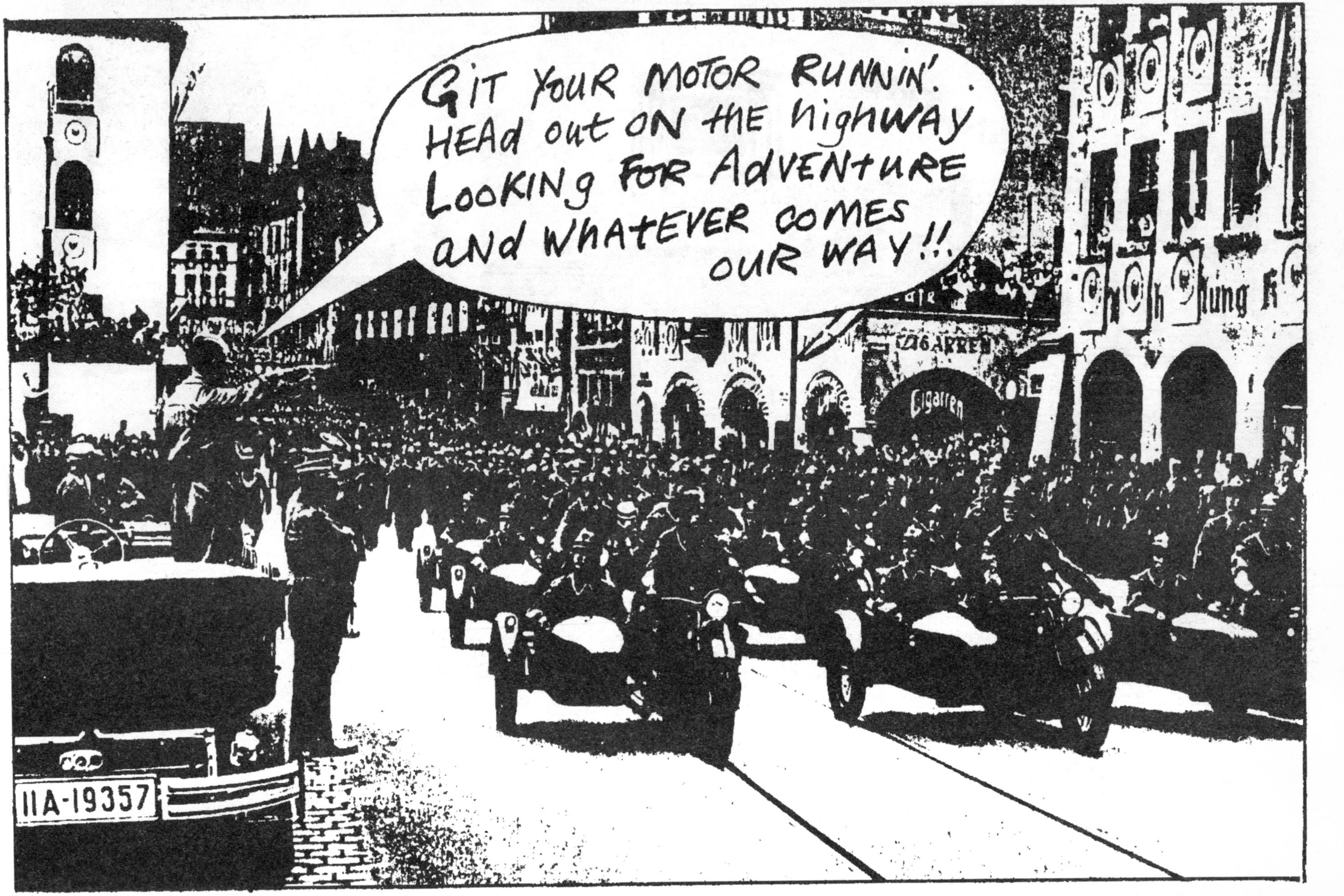
GIT YOUR MOTOR RUNNIN'. HEAD OUT ON THE HIGHWAY LOOKING FOR ADVENTURE AND WHATEVER COMES OUR WAY!!
CIGARREN
Cigarren
IIA-19357

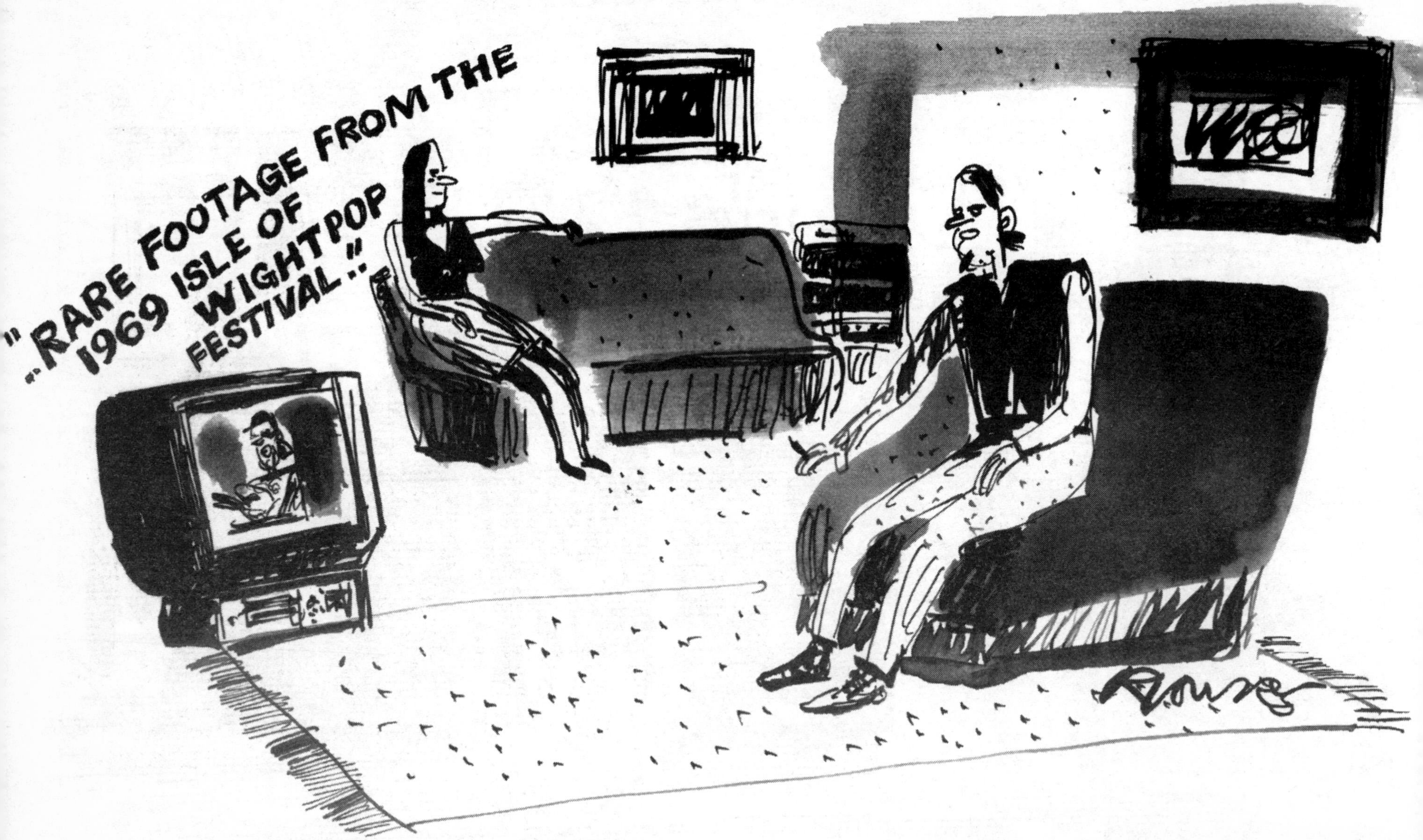
"RARE FOOTAGE FROM THE 1969 ISLE OF WIGHT POP FESTIVAL.."
Rowse

"I don't remember any of this – I must have been there!"

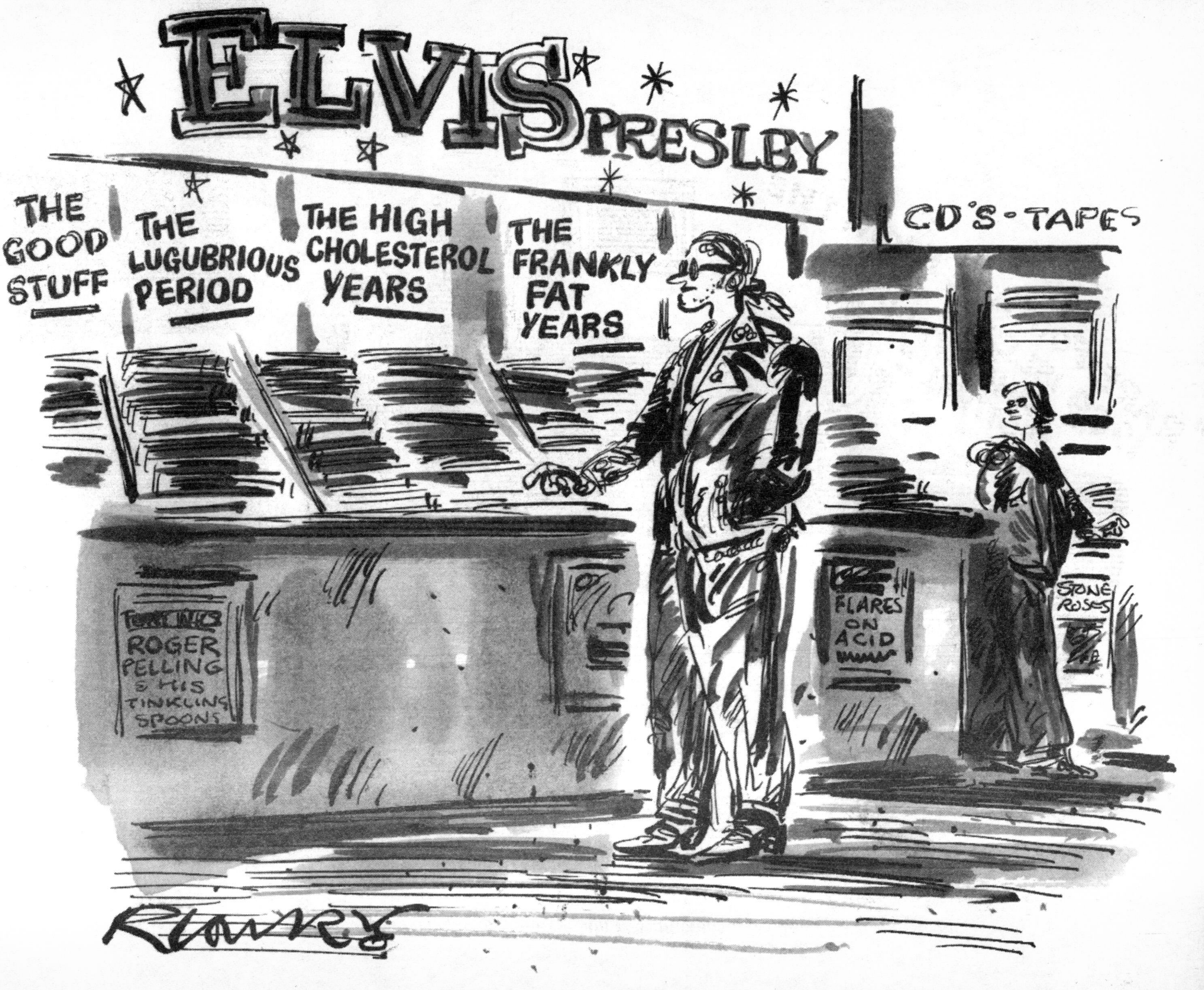
ELVIS PRESLEY
THE GOOD STUFF
THE LUGUBRIOUS PERIOD
THE HIGH CHOLESTEROL YEARS
THE FRANKLY FAT YEARS
CD'S - TAPES
ROGER PELLING & HIS TINKLING SPOONS
FLARES ON ACID
STONE ROSES

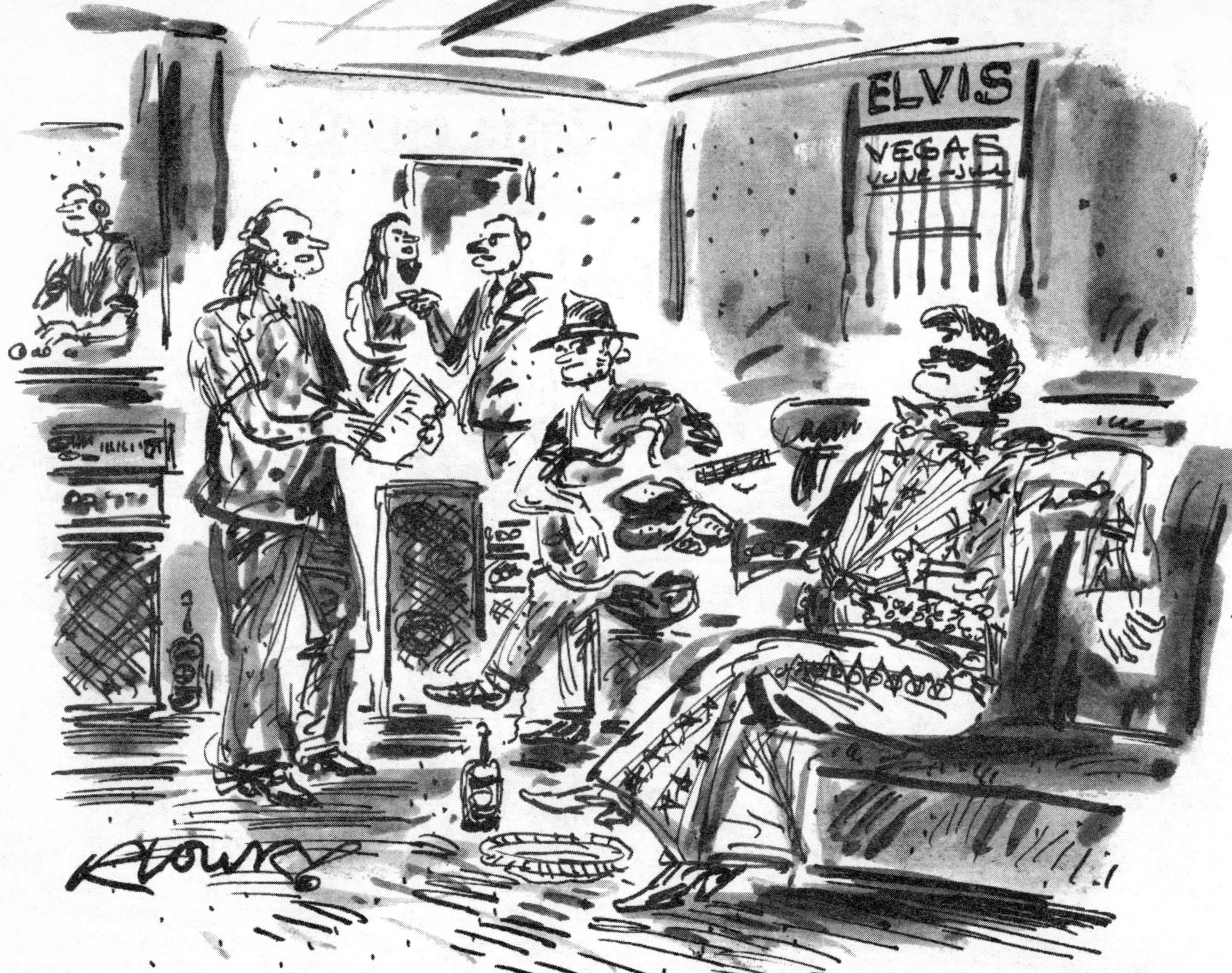
ELVIS
VEGAS

"When no one else can understand me – When everything I do is wrong – You give me hope and consolation – You give me cheeseburgers. *Well, apart from anything else, Elvis, it doesn't scan!*"

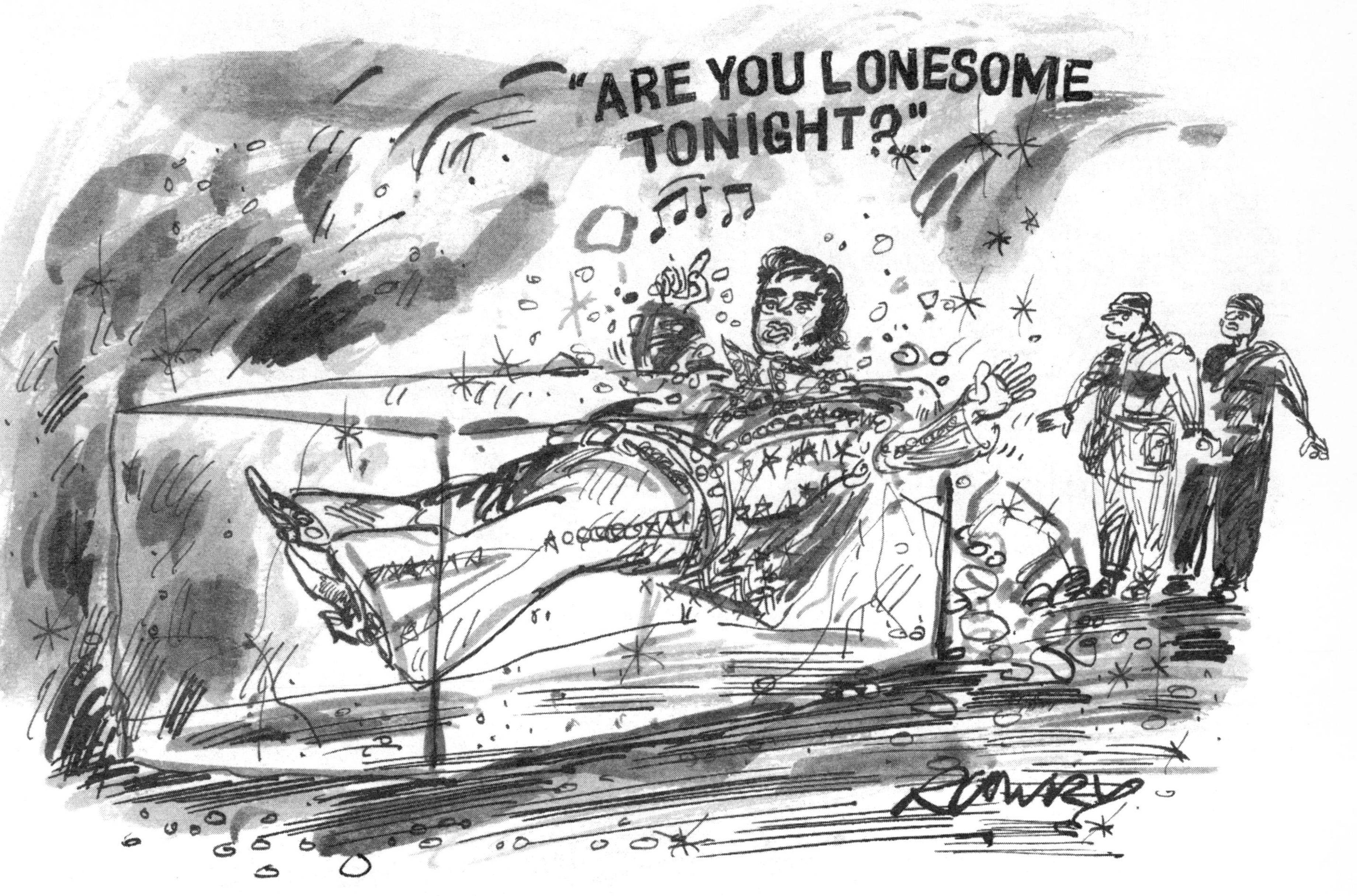
"ARE YOU LONESOME TONIGHT?"

"Apparently he's been suspended all along in that block of ice, waiting for the flares revival!"

JIM MORRISON – he tried to make love to the love generation…

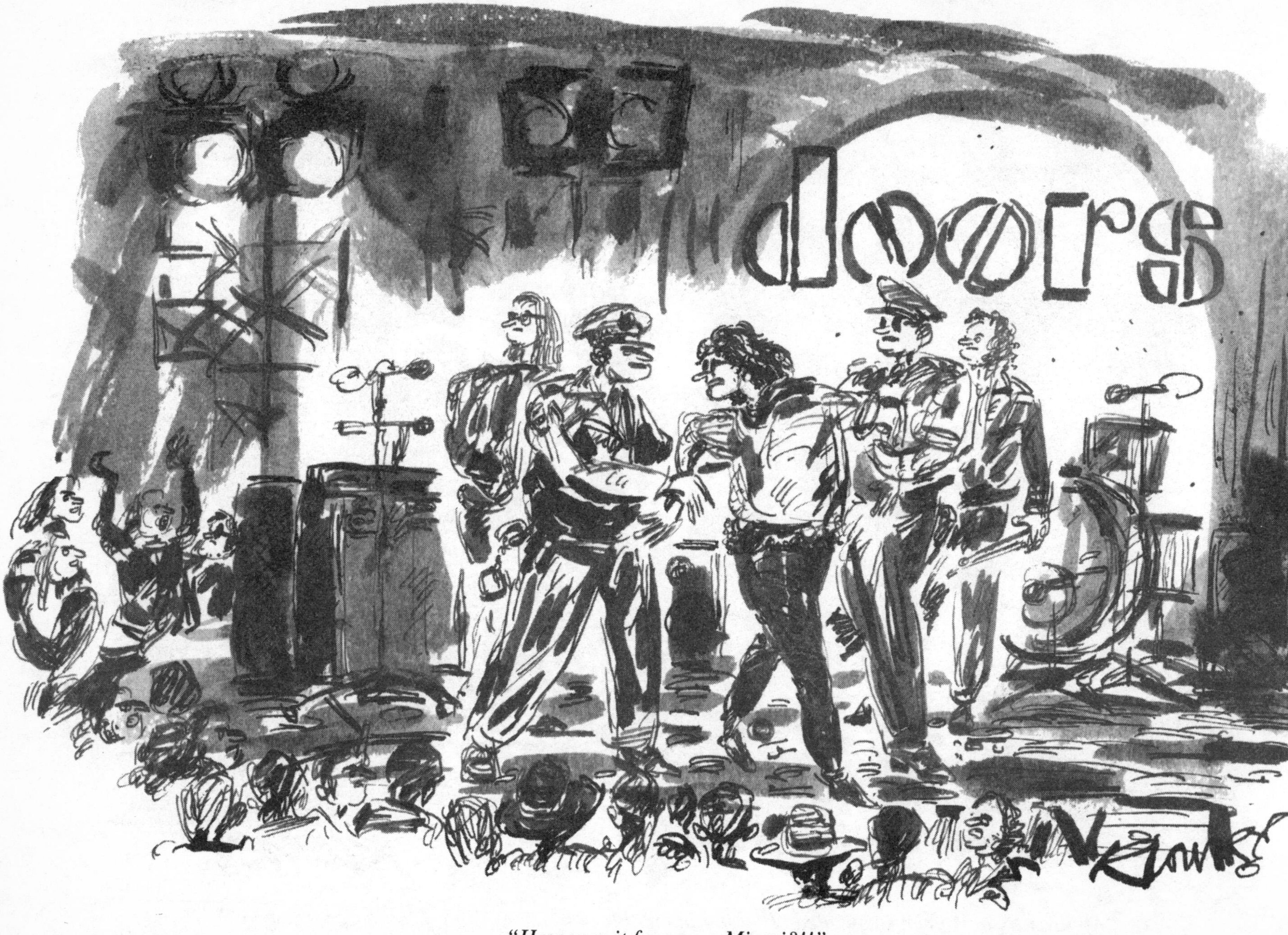
doors

"How was it for you – Miami?!!"

Heavy Metal sings the blues...

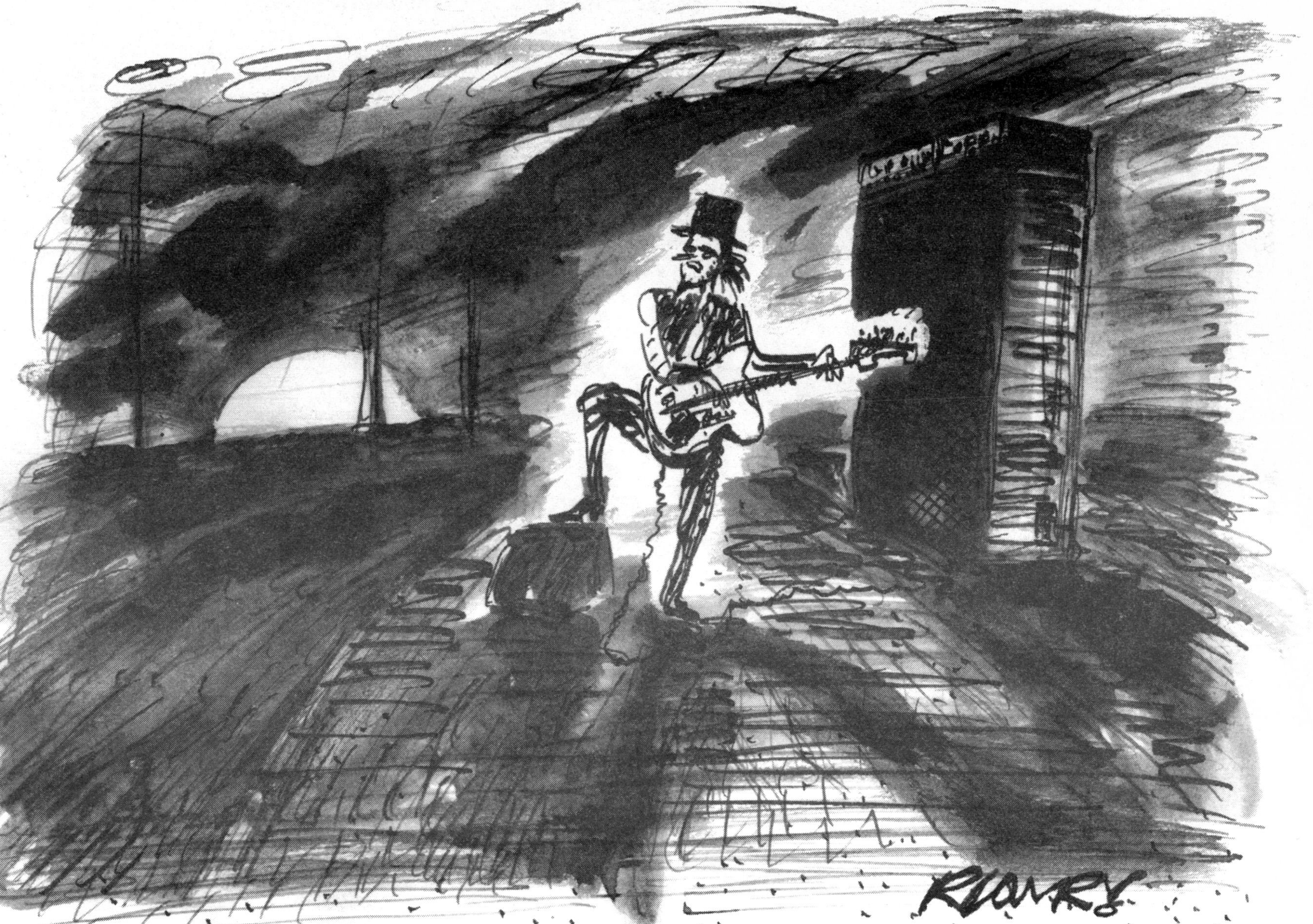

"I went down to the crossroads – there was nowhere to plug in the amps. Dammit, there wasn't even an audience!"

BOB DYLAN & VAN THE MAN SWING THE STANDARDS.

(ROCK'S MESSERS 'APPROACHABLE')

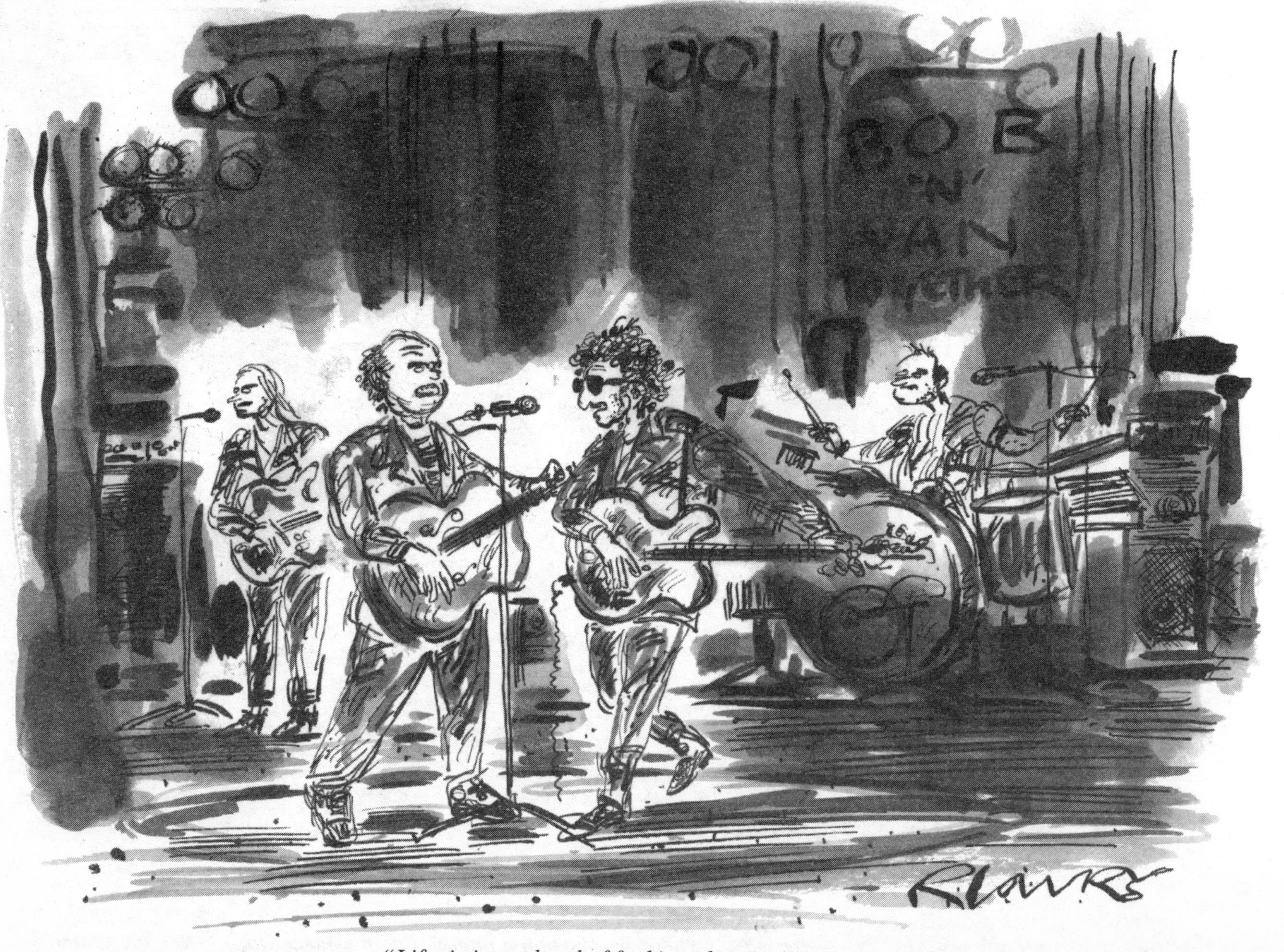
BOB 'N' VAN TOGETHER

"Life, is just a bowl of fucking cherries!"

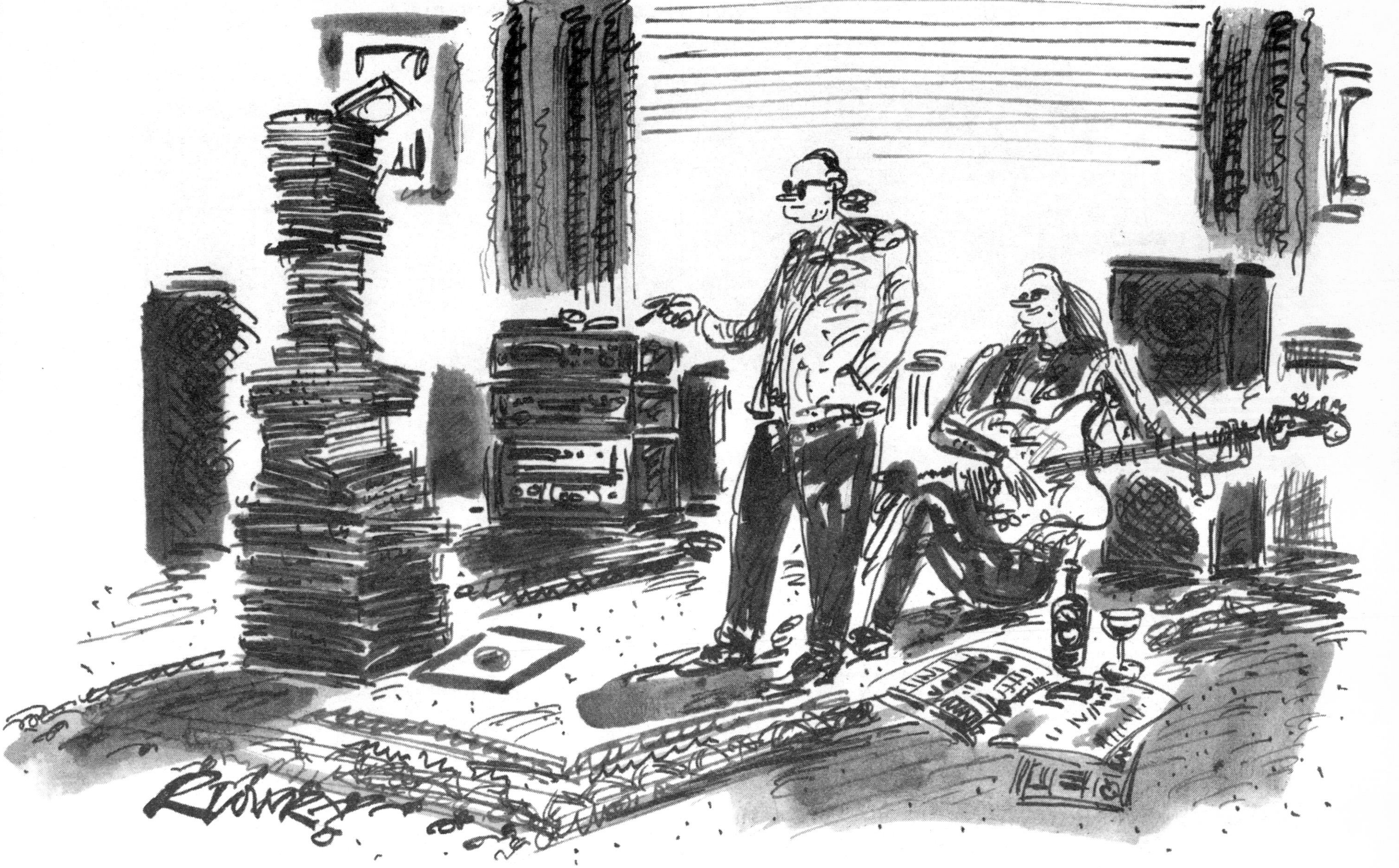

"It's my new, rationalised storage system. The CDs are stacked on top of my tapes, which balance on top of the redundant vinyl collection, that's gathering dust on a pile of old 78s I've had for years..."

rOCk and ROLL THE CORPORATE YEARS…

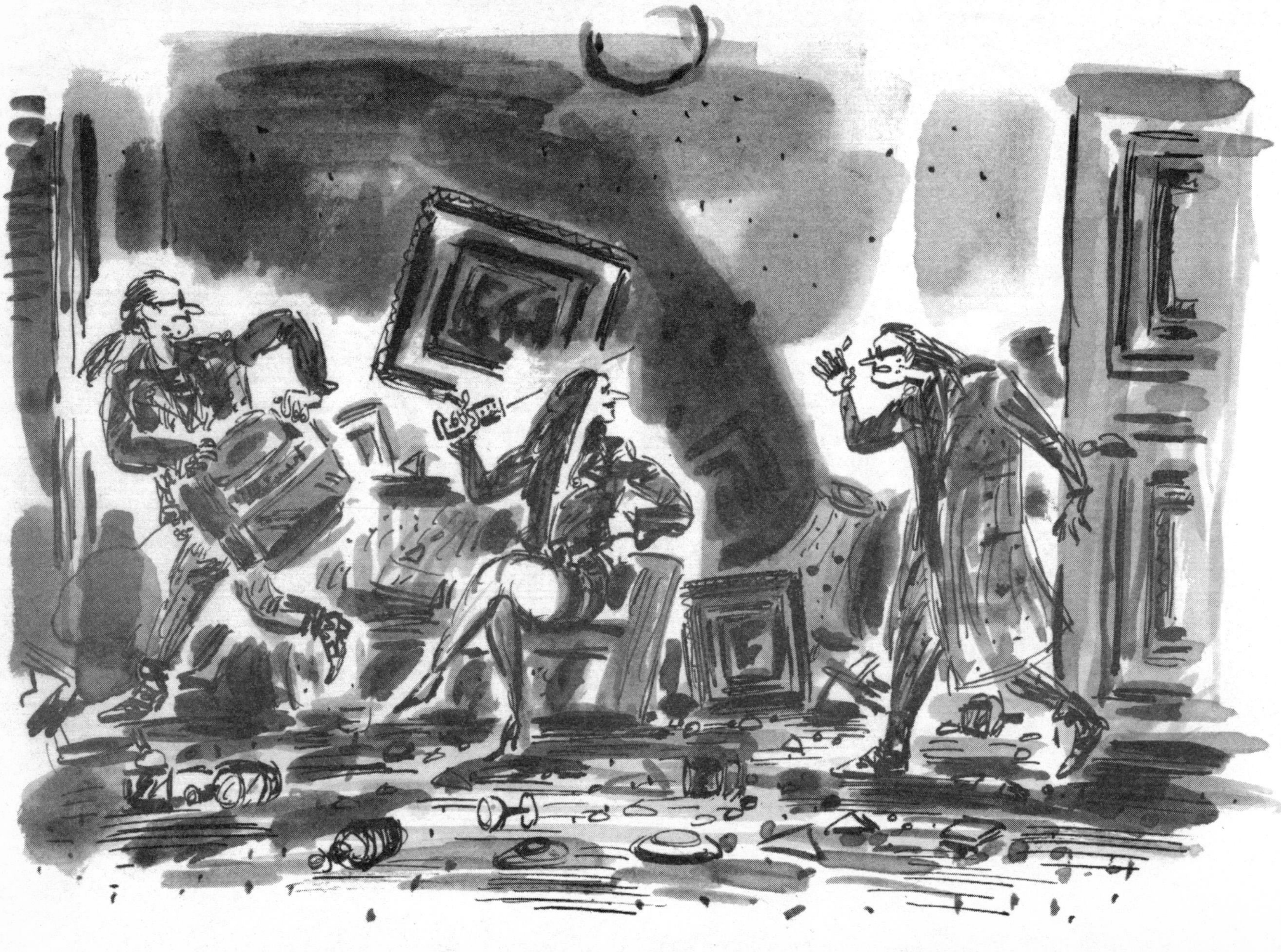

"What the hell are you wrecking your room for? We own the hotel chain!"

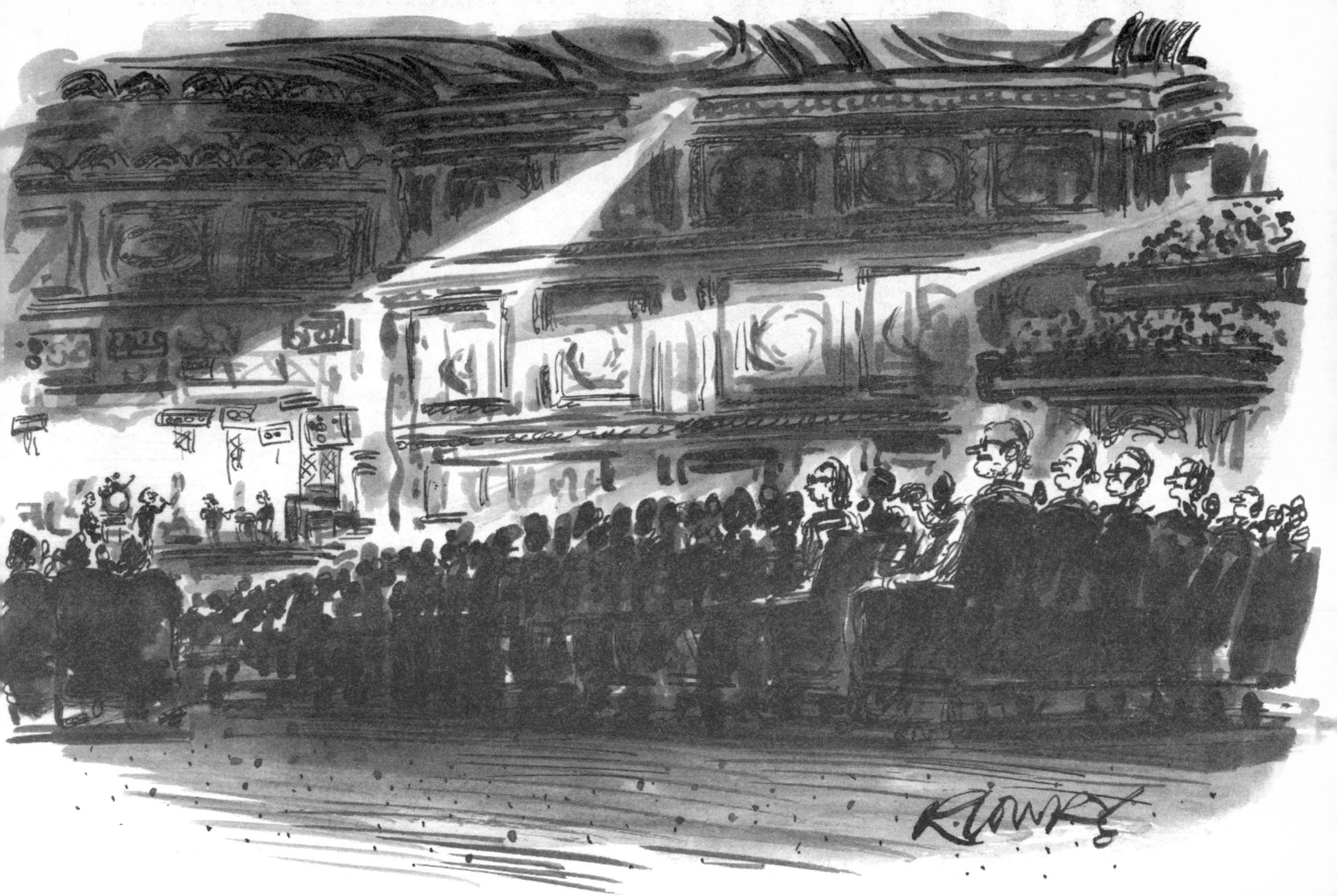

"This song's about a subject that means an awful lot to me and I hope that it does to you, too. It's about fish-farming in Scotland."

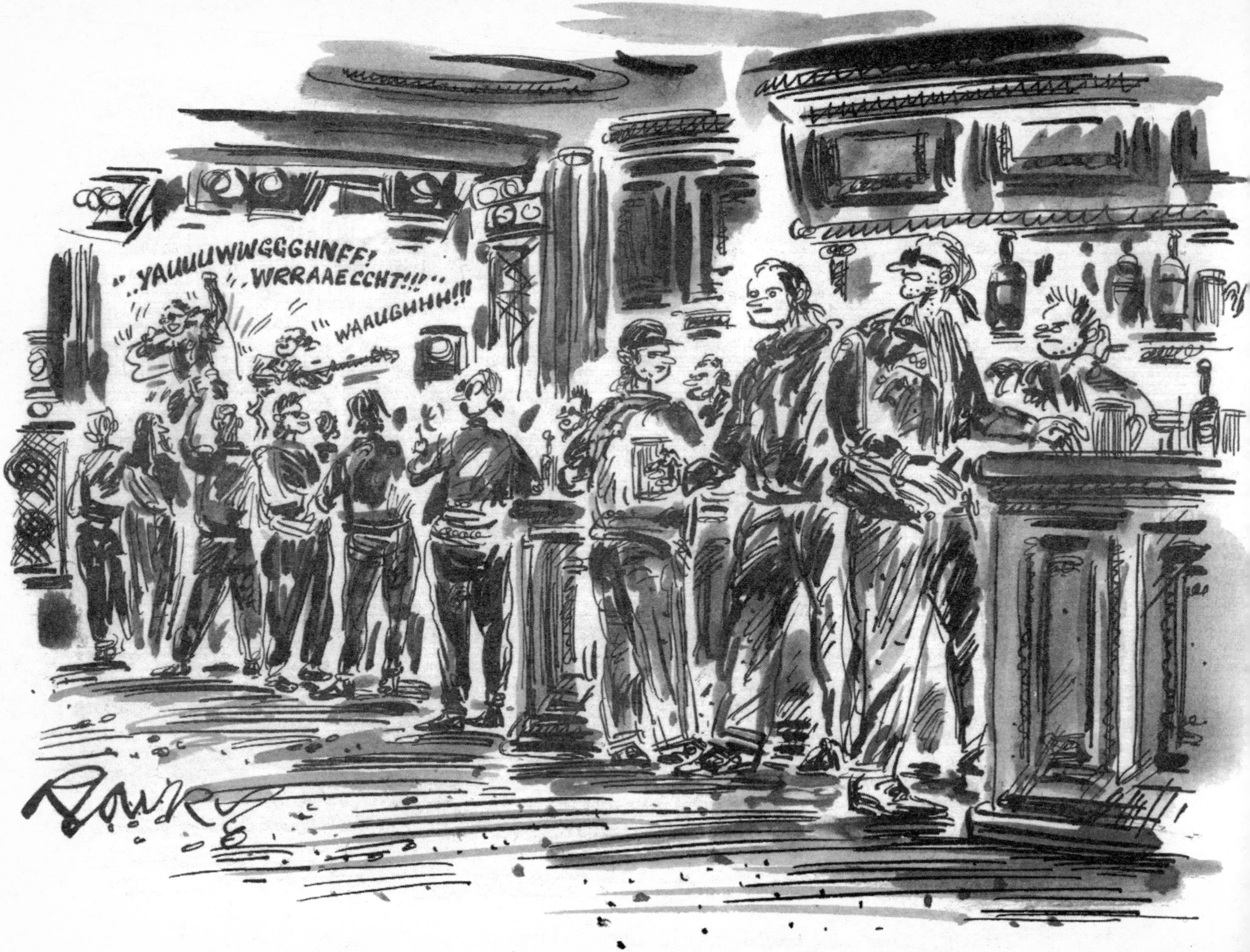
..YAUUUWWGGGGHNFF!
..WRRAAECCHT!!!..
WAAUGHHH!!!

"If music be the food of love, I think somebody's throwing up over there on the stage."

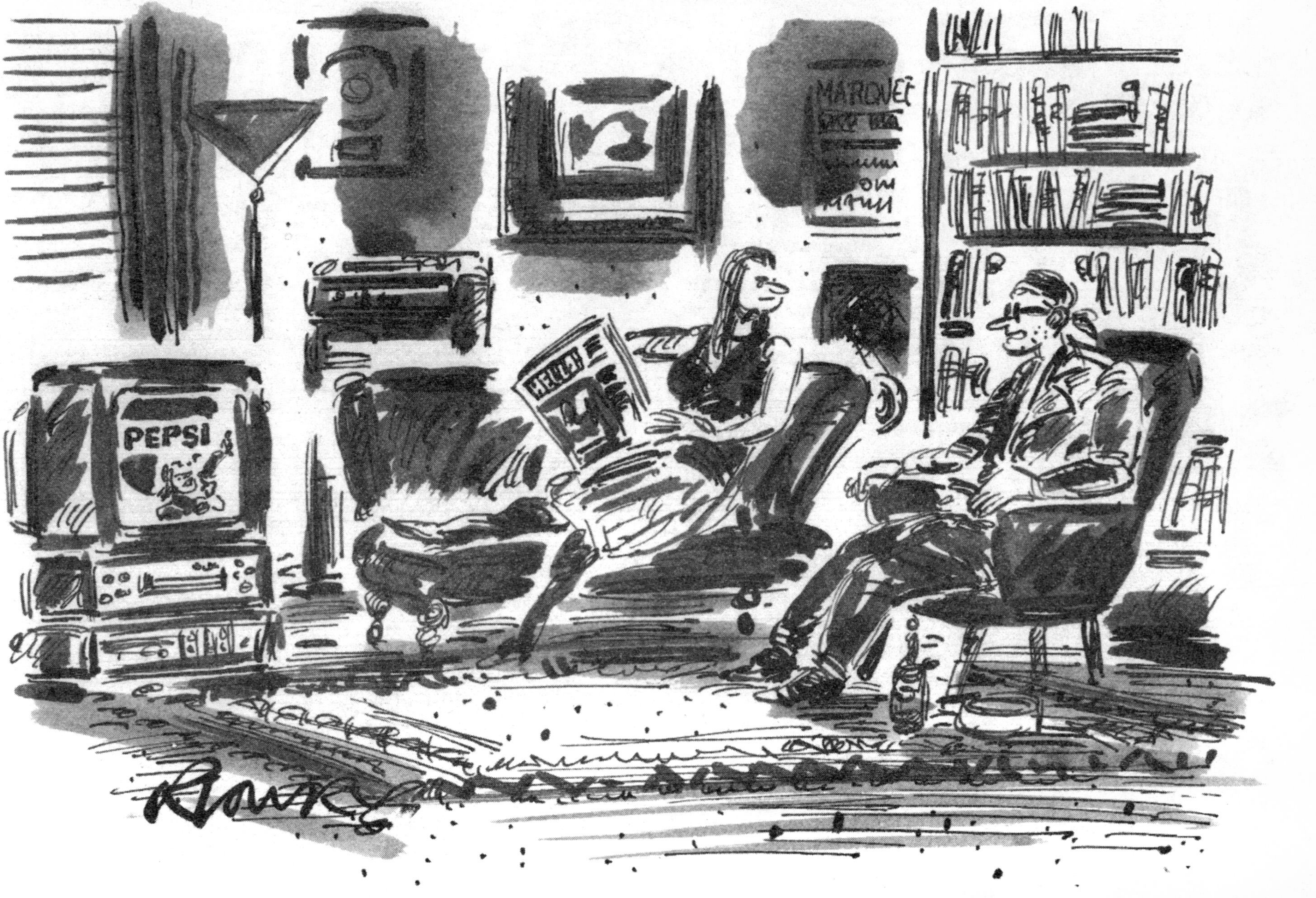
PEPSI

"I sold my soul to rock 'n' roll before it sold its *soul to the major multi-nationals."*

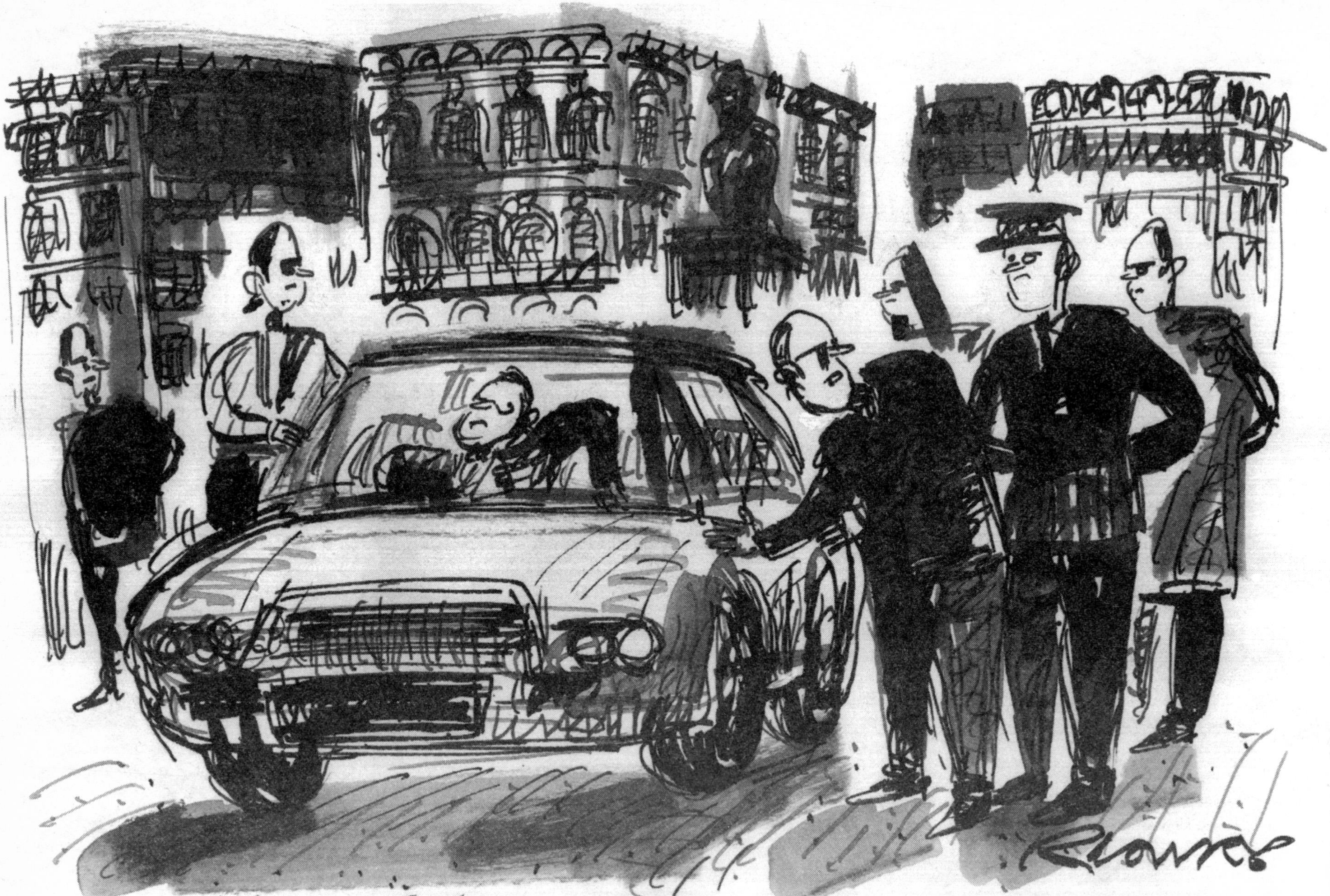

"It's a strange case of nature imitating art – he blew his mind out in a car, he didn't notice that the lights had changed.."

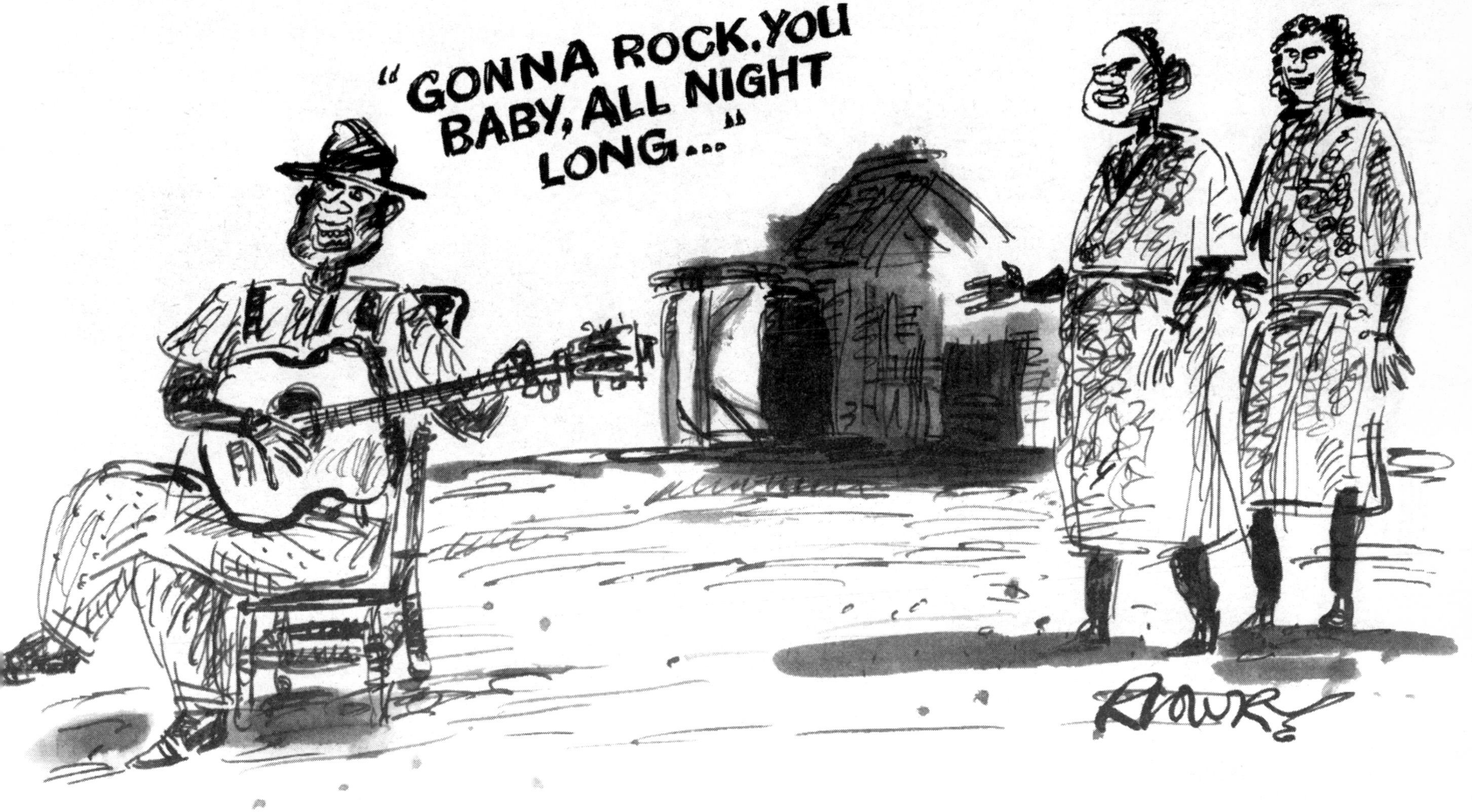
"GONNA ROCK YOU BABY, ALL NIGHT LONG..."

"He's a thirty minute man, all right – it takes him twenty-five minutes to get his trousers off."

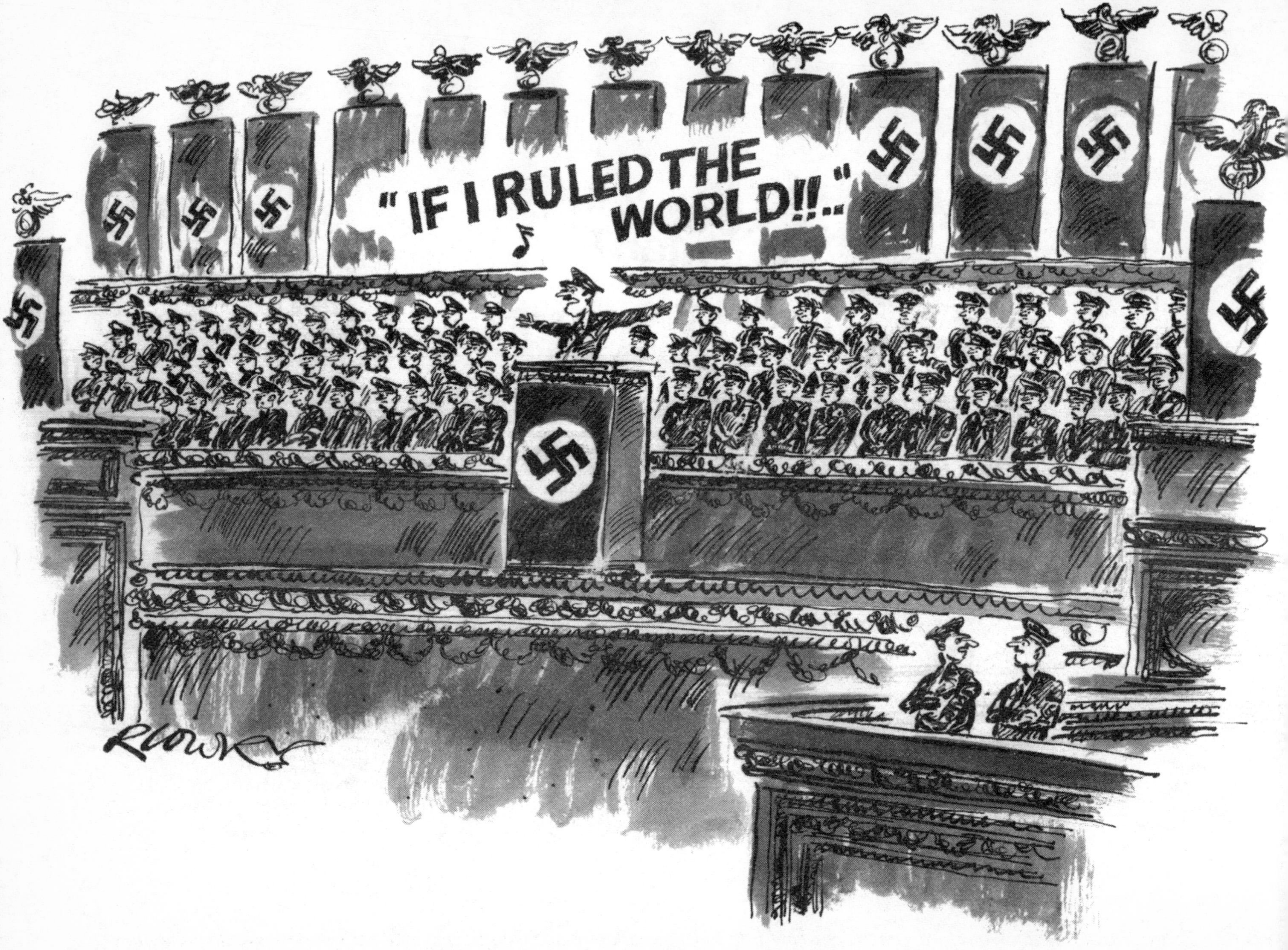

"IF I RULED THE WORLD!!.."

"It seems the Führer's decided to enter himself for this year's Eurovision Song Contest."

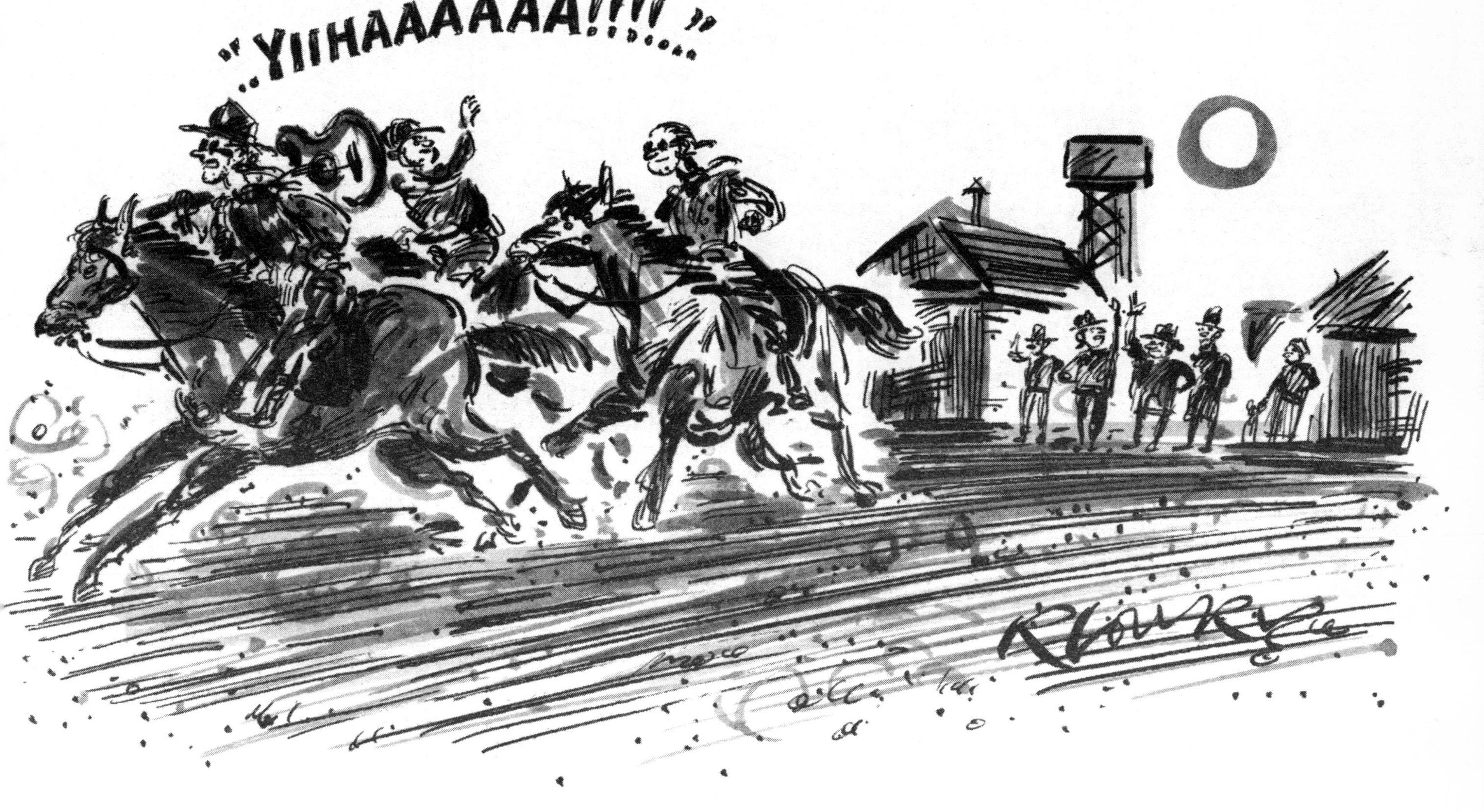
"..YIIHAAAAAAA!!!!.."

"That was the Hank Wangford gang. They ride into town a-whoopin' and a-hollerin', make a sympathetic documentary about the roots of indigenous musical culture and then ride out again..."

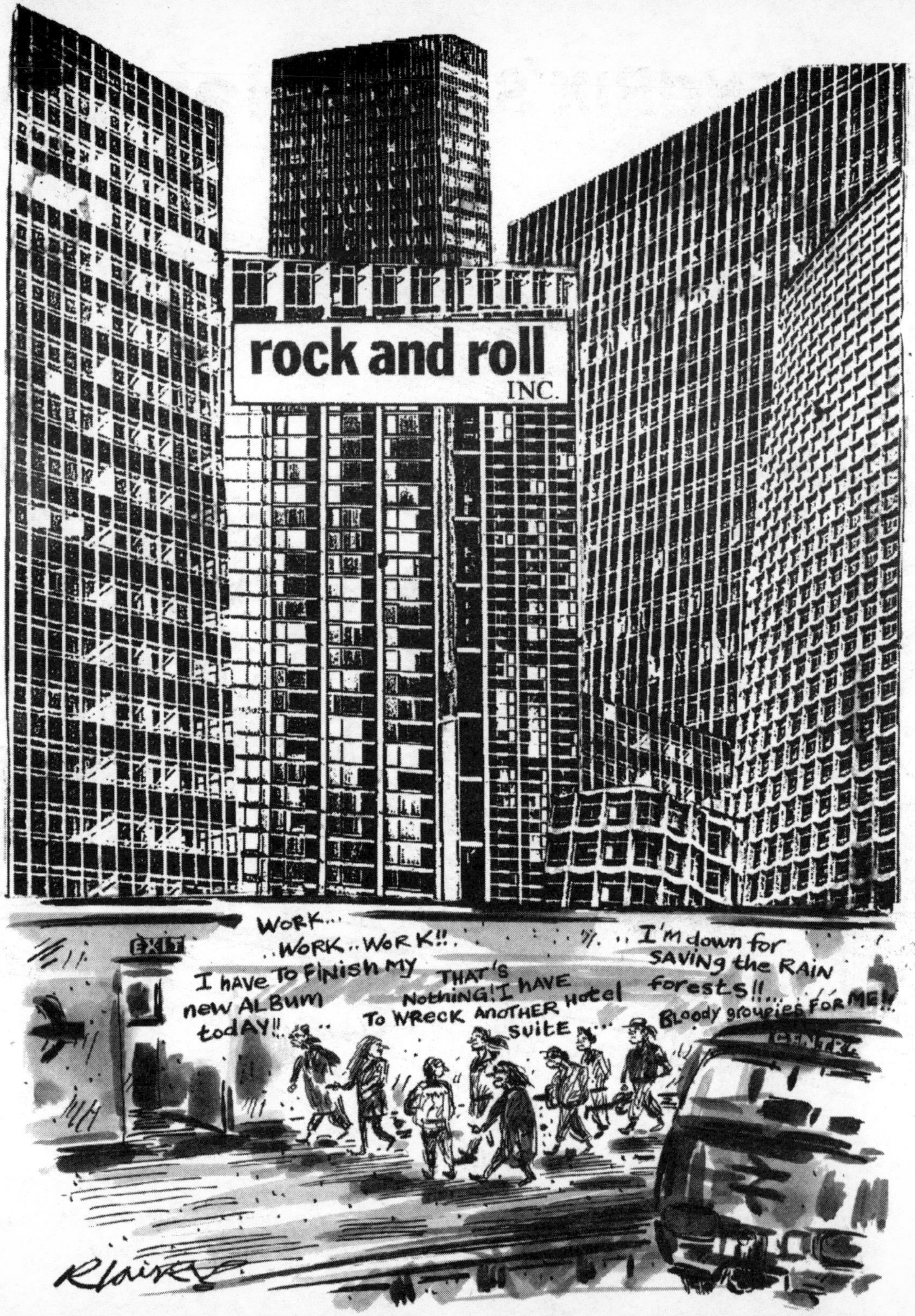
rock and roll INC.
EXIT
WORK... ..WORK..WORK!!
I have To FINISH my new ALBUM todAY!!
THAT'S Nothing! I HAVE To WRECK ANOTHER Hotel SUITE...
..I'm down for SAVING the RAIN forests!!...
Bloody groupies FOR ME!!
RLairK

JIMI HENDRIX'S BAD HAIR DAY....

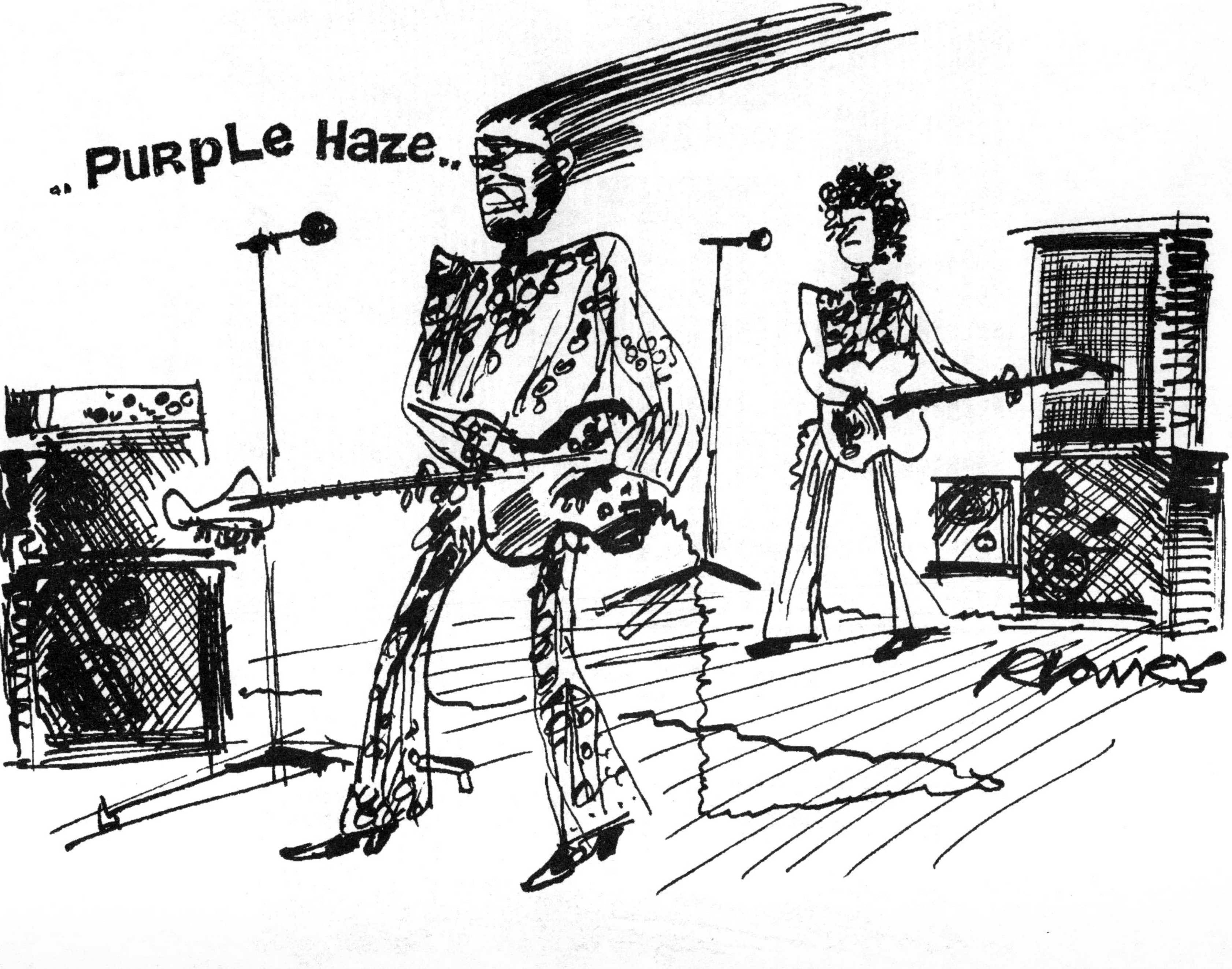
..PURPLE HAZE..

YOU KNOW YOU'RE GETTING OLD WHEN…

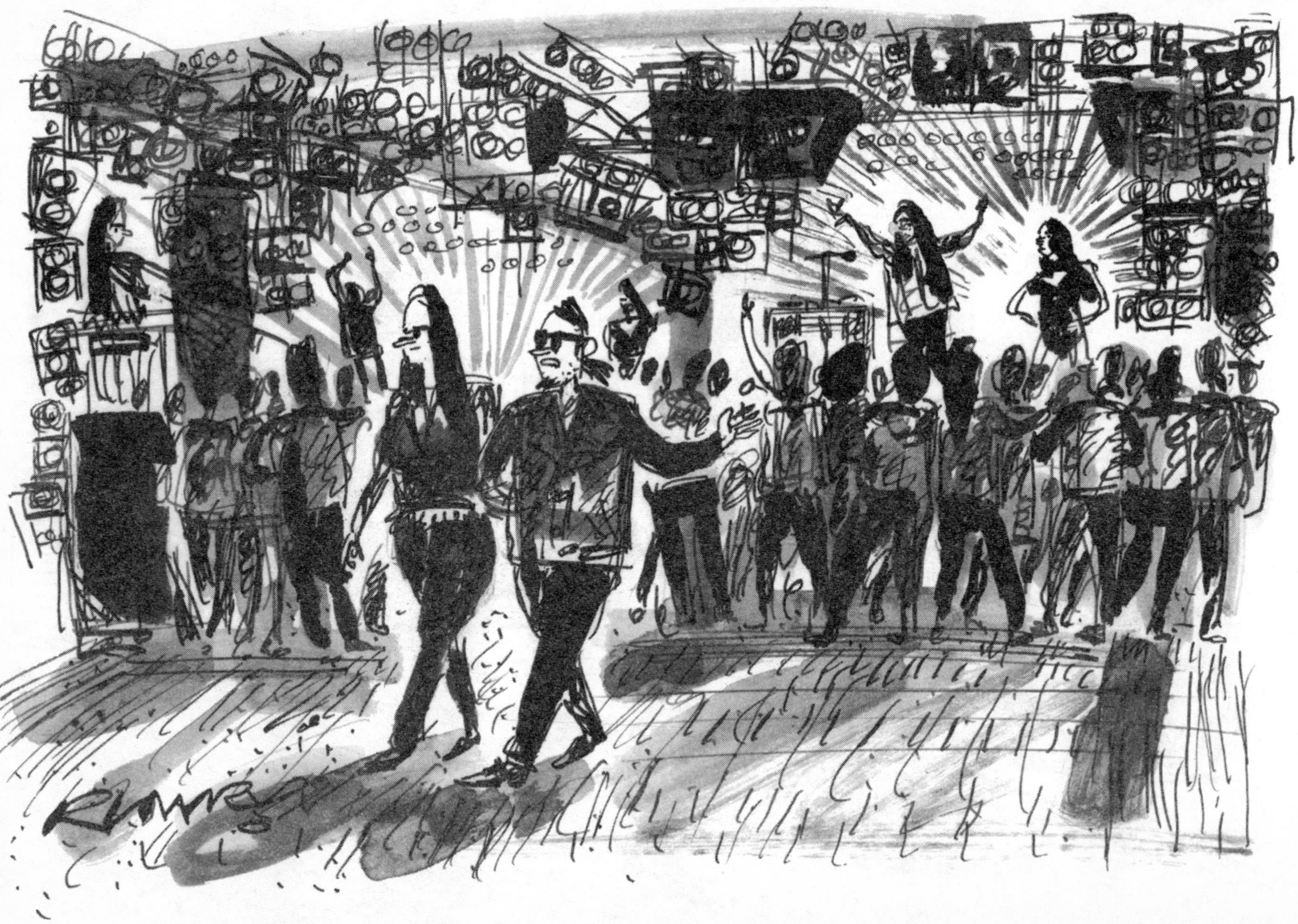

"OK, lets agree to like this in retrospect."

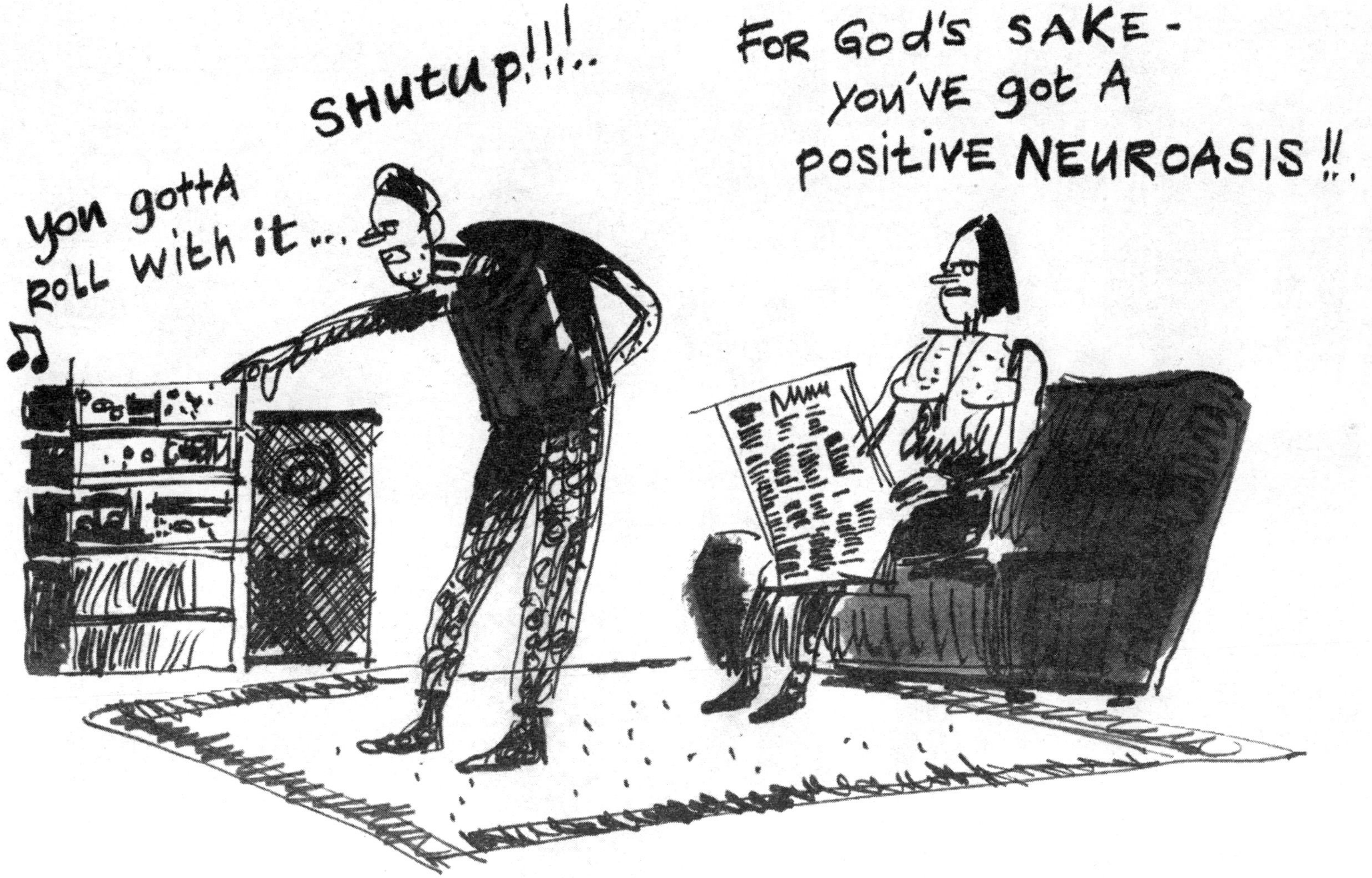
you gottA ROLL with it....
SHUTUP!!!!..
FOR God's SAKE - you've got A positive NEUROASIS !!.

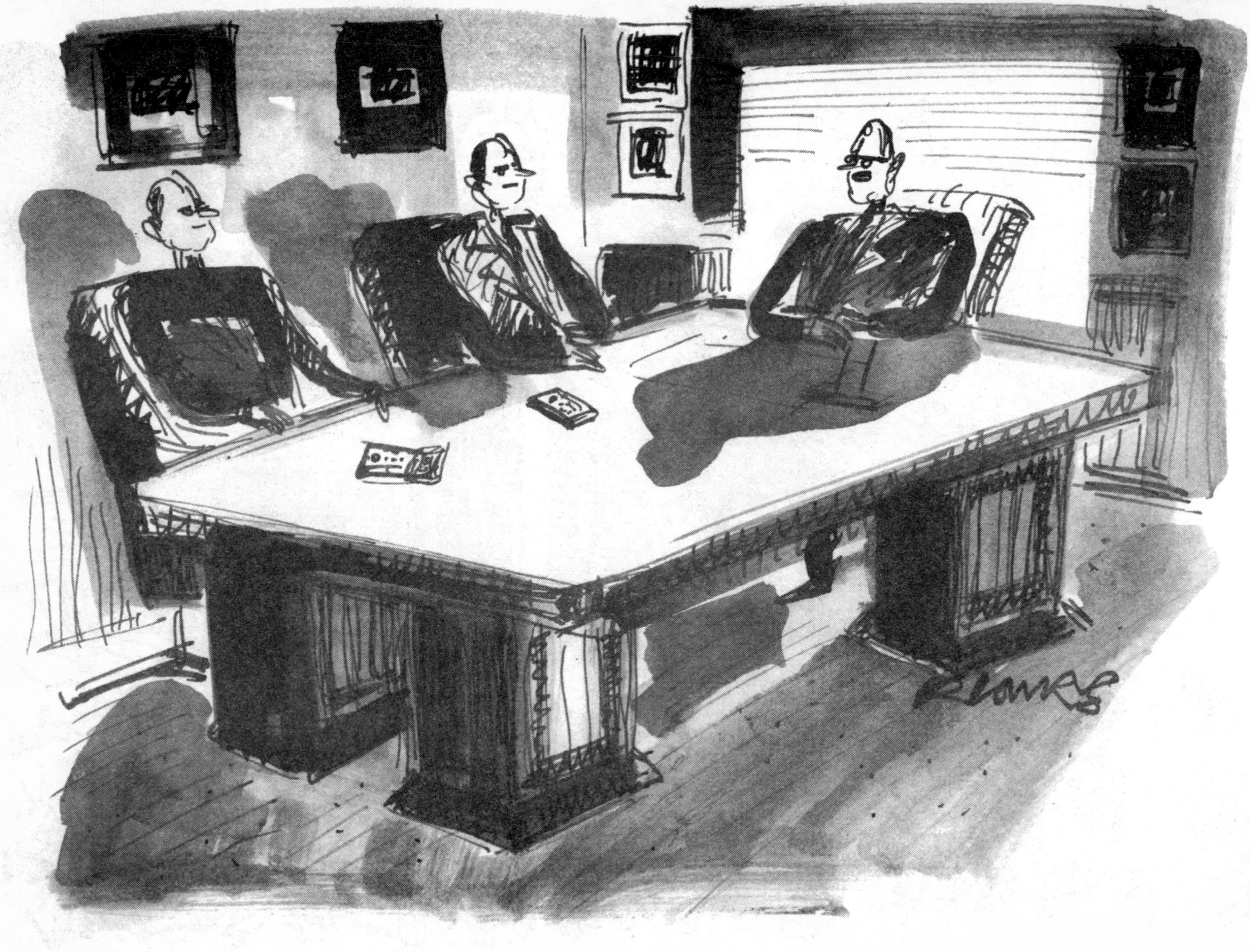

"The electorate have a clear choice before them– either they can get shafted by the opposition or they can get stuffed by us!"

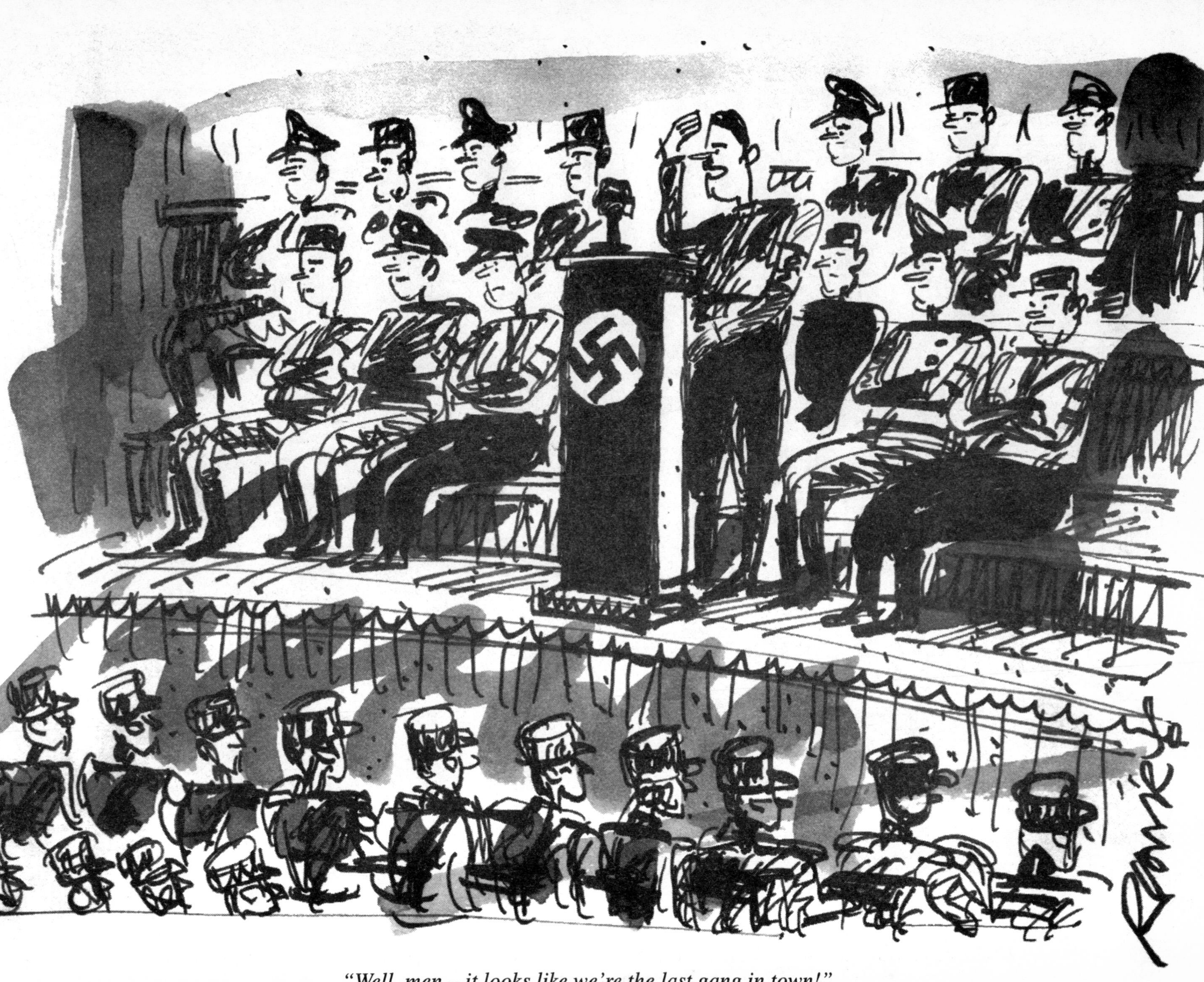

"Well, men – it looks like we're the last gang in town!"

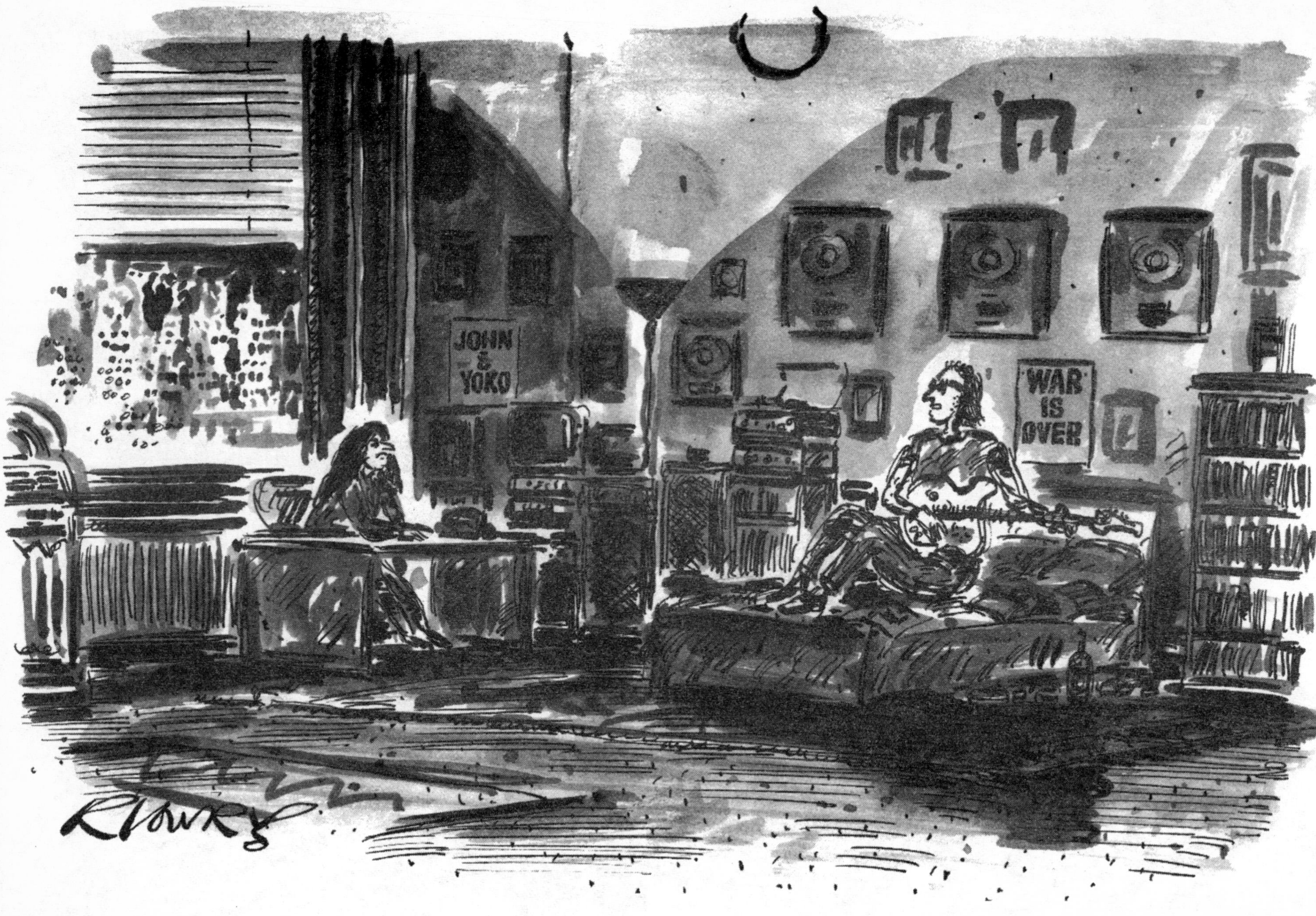
JOHN & YOKO
WAR IS OVER

"I'm so stoned I can't remember – have I been assasinated or not yet?"

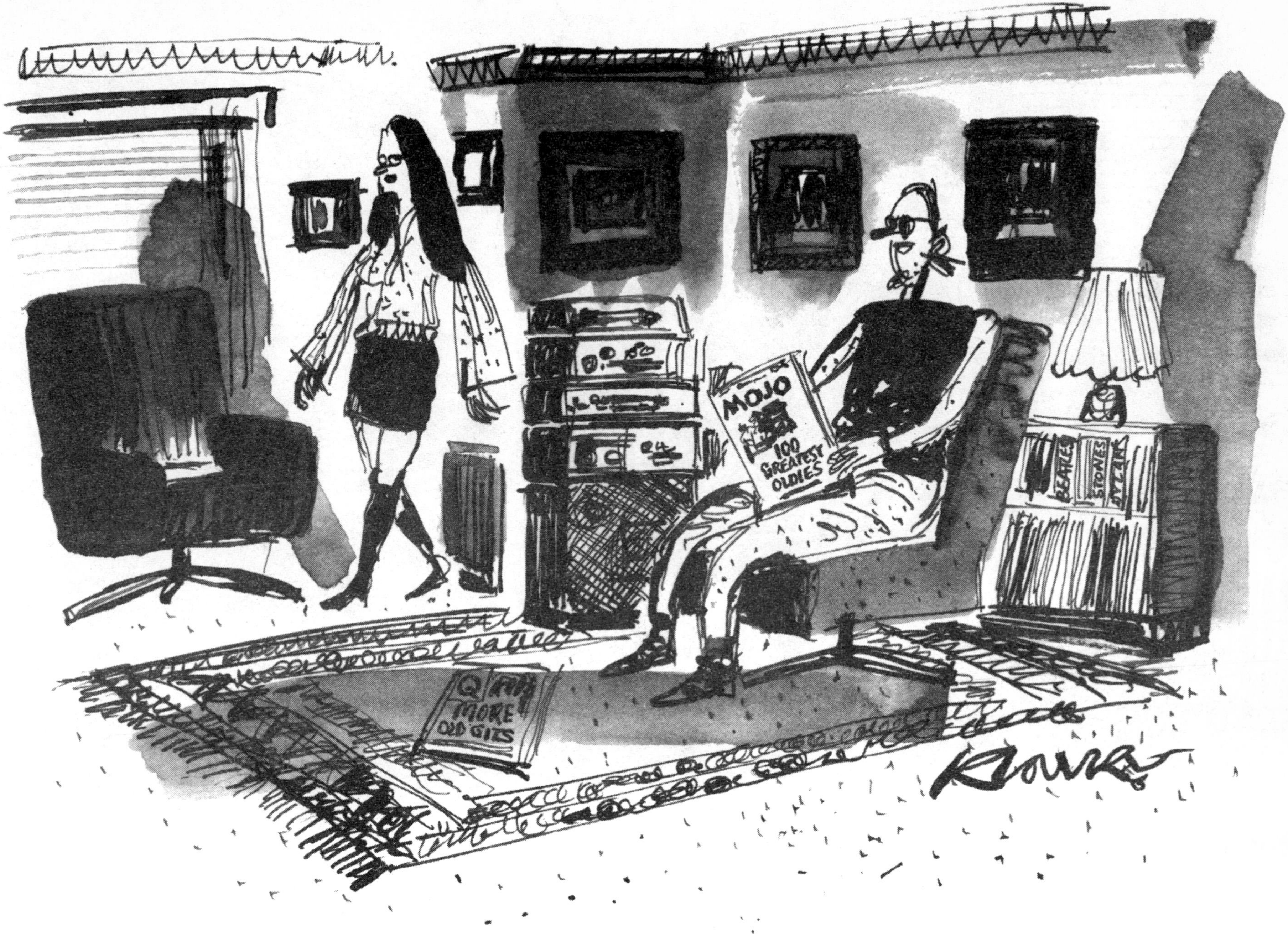
MOJO
100 GREATEST OLDIES
BEATLES
STONES
DYLAN
Q
MORE
OLD GITS

"Looked at another way dear, we're not really a pair of sad old farts. We're actually at the cutting edge of contemporary rock nostalgia."

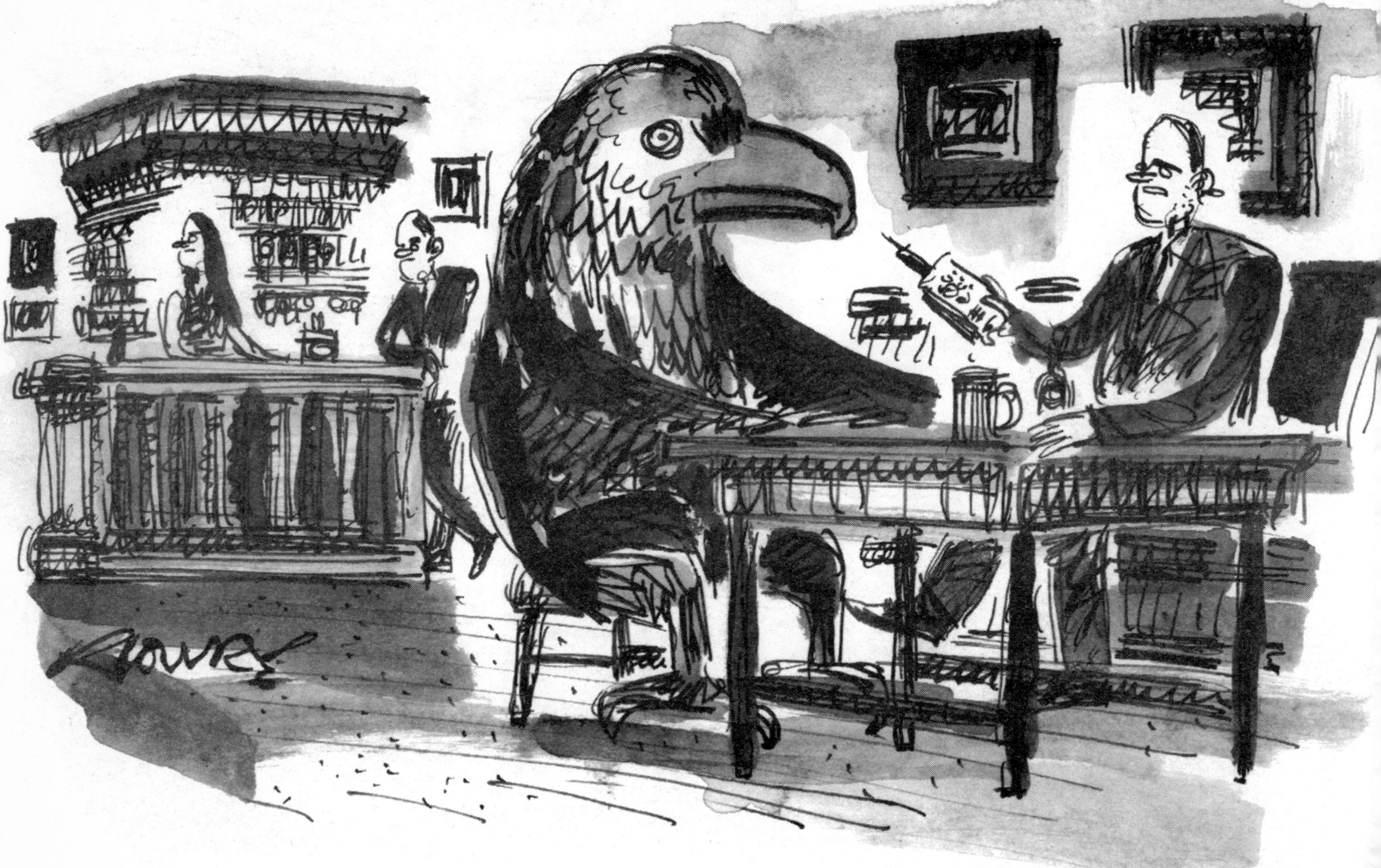

"It's my analyst – are you in?"

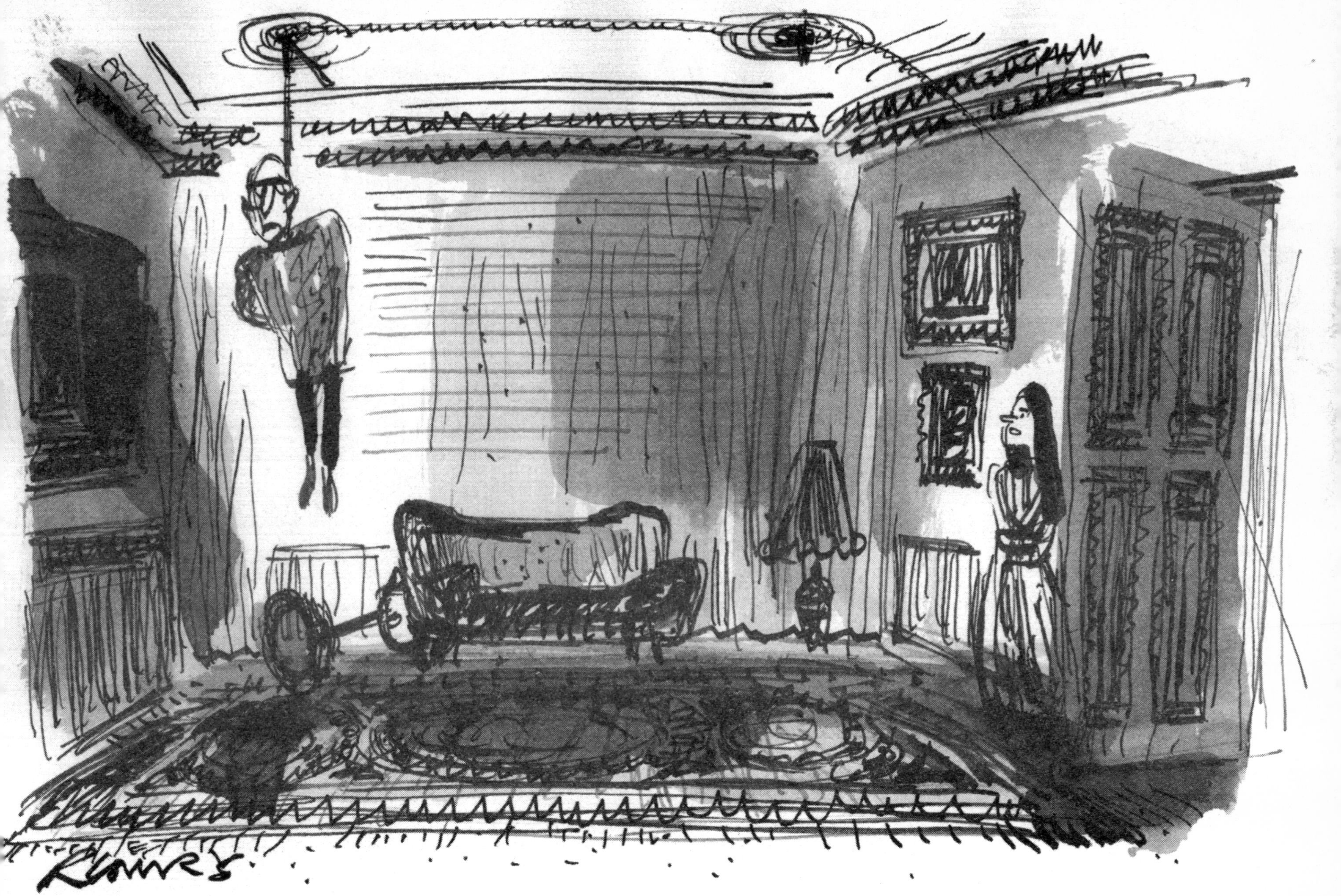

"You're so highly strung, Gerald!"

Nick Logan was unwise enough to ask me to contribute a 'humorous' column to early editions of THE FACE. We lasted about two years before the occasional ranting Spartism and incorrect *paaaarrrttty* line became too much for him. These are a few of the lighter pieces.

December 1980

Ray Lowry

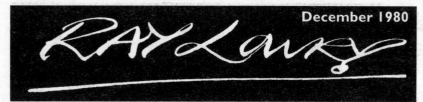

WOULDN'T it have been great if the Sex Pistols (Bernard Rhodes and Malcolm McLaren) had achieved all they set out to do in 1917? No more stinking rock and roll military/industrial complex. No more puffed up turds prancing about in diamond studded jockstraps. No more boring rags like this one. No more wars or famine or poverty!

The only good records were those that were never made! Who wants something when you can have nothing? Send in the first victim!…

MALCOLM McLAREN: Does Anyone Remember Me?

Everybody knows that Malcolm McLaren's mum was the only real Sex Beatle.

SID VICIOUS: The Corpse Speaks (Ranking Records).

Good old Sid! True Punk etc, etc. Everybody knows that Sid was the only true Sex Beatle. The only one who actually lived and DIED the ideals of Punk. Johnny Rotten was only a whining revanchist, middle of the road little sod who accidentally walked into Margaret McLaren's bloody Sex shop one time looking for some Germoloids ointment for his piles, and Ronnie Biggs was only a poovy old John McVicar style sensitive criminal type with two hundred '0' levels and always wanting to play Hamlet and that. I ask you! And Paul Jones and that other little twerp Raymond Glendenning? Naw, Sid was the one who stabbed himself and showed all those dopey, long-haired,faggot Texas cowboys what punk was all about. Stabbing yourself.

THE CLASH: What Are We Gonna Do Now?

Everybody knows that the Sex Pistols were the only real Clash! Joe gorblimey Gormley's so worried about remembering not to sound his aitches with a haitch and using the right knife and fork at all these banquets and not farting in public or wiping his nose on his sleeve and learning to say bellshit instead of bullshit like his heroes, integrated Northerners such as Harold Wilson and Michael Parkinson, so he'll wind up with a peerage to put on his mantelpiece next to the framed reproduction of the "Haywain At Bay" that he's forgotten what he was elected to do in the first place! What was I talking about in the first sodding place?

EDDIE COCHRAN: Come Off It Everybody.

Everybody knows that Eddie Cochran wasn't in the Sex Pistols was he?

BOB DYLAN: I've Saved A Bloody Fortune.

Everybody knows that A. J. Weberman was the real Bob Dylan. Bob Dylan died in 1968 when his Triumph Troubadour motorcycle skidded on a patch of adulation and he lost his ball bearings and drowned in his own vitriol.

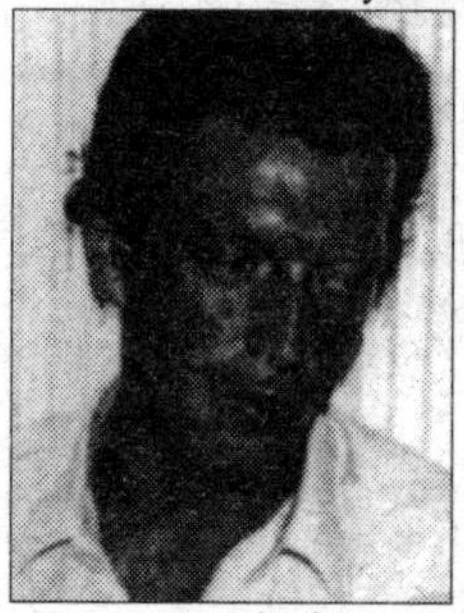

ALBERT COSTELLO: I Can Only See The First Couple Of Rows.

If Bob Dylan's the opium of the masses then this guy must be the dopey one with glasses.

Everyone knows that Malcolm Muggeridge was the only true Sex Pistol.

EDDIE COCHRANE…

Everybody knows that you spell it Eddie Cochran!

DEXY'S FIVE MINUTES ARE UP: Nothing Was Delivered.

Dexy's are so fed up with gormless journalists and stupid fans and positively cretinous audiences and ordinary people in the street and minority groups and children and animals and anyone who isn't actually in the band that they're not going to make any more records, ever, but have paid for this space to let you know what truly fabulous, awe-inspiring, brilliant music you're going to miss because you're so bloody thick! So wake up!! Prostrate yourselves you miserable scum!! Talk about pearls before swine…

THE ABSOLUTELY AND TOTALLY EXCLUSIVES AND NO ONE ELSE PERMITTED, AND THAT MEANS YOU, YOU LITTLE WORM! GET OUT!: Private Sound (Unobtainable Records).

The Abs achieve a similar amount of elder hessian by approaching the business of making records in a similarly ADVANCEDE (so much more modern than moderne) frame of mind. The Abs pack the studio with rich and beautiful people who languish around holding thin stemmed cocktail glasses, puffing languorously on Sobranie Virginias and occasionally approaching one of the microphones with a disdainful glance to deliberately abstain from saying ANYTHING WHATSOEVER, thus demonstrating their absolute and unimpeachable superiority to mere word jugglers and purveyors of opinions, ideas, attitudes and other ephemera. No photographs were allowed during the recording and the fabulous costumes especially created for the Abs were burned along with the studio and the recording equipment. The producer and engineer had their eyes torn out of the living flesh.

STOP PRESS – Rather than compromise their Art the Abs have decided that they won't, after all, allow their record to be circulated to the general public, so that it will remain an enigmatic and unattainable ideal. Bravo, etc.

STEVE SPONGE: A Day In The Life Of Steve Sponge (Sponge-Beat).

Steve is the latest, most magnificent, most tedious and boring example of that awe-inspiring breed – the great tressilated wemick. See Steve painting squiggly lines on his face! Look at Steve taking tea with his demented friends! By night they recreate the decadence of the Plaistow Republic and the great days of Babylon and by day they lack the wit or originality to get out of bed! See Steve brave the cruel stares of Chinese tourists and little old Chelsea pensioners down the Kings Road as he wilts about in an old chimney brush and a Little Lord Fauntleroy suit. Hang on a minute though, OH MY GAWD, he's in trouble! He's run into a gang of skinheads who haven't had the advantage of spending their formative years with gormless types like Steve and his pals. Cries of "Lay orf," "Shame!" etc, etc.

ELVIS PRESLEY: The Legendary Rat Up His Trousers Sessions (Sun).

Rock and roll died when Buddy Holly drowned. Naw, rock and roll died when Eddie Cochran caught a painful hangnail in one of those bloody awful silky-look shirts with the furry surface that attract painful hangnails like iron filings to a magnet! Naw, rock and roll died when Elvis's second cousin thrice removed absent-mindedly sliced through her knuckle while cutting a fruity-bake malt loaf and humming "There's a pawnshop on the corner in Pittsburgh, Pennsylvania!"

CAPTAIN BEEFRAT: Uh, Oh, I'm Rumbled (Vacuum).

This man's a wizard, a charlatan, a true fraud! I once went to interview the Captain and after waiting around nervously for about two or three hours in his agent's office, chewing on my nails, shifting nervously in my chair, scratching my earlobes, taking surreptitious hits on a hipflask of Jack Bibby's Old Jockstrap, coughing, and shuffling through the notes that I'd prepared, I was finally told that he was over two hundred miles away recording an album in Topanga Canyon. What a character! When I finally met the Captain, some years later, he greeted me with an enigmatic "Hi!" Some people can't take these dazzling verbal pyrotechnics, and despair at his wacky wisdoms and wandering imagery. One day the Captain will cease to be a fringe figure and will become completely unknown!

SHREDDED WITS: Leave Me Alone Again Or.

Alienation and icy images are out this week, boys. Decadence is back! Positive, old fashioned values like the Spanish Inquisition and the Last Days of Rome. People are smiling as they stub cigarettes out on bare flesh and grind jackboots into upturned faces. For ever!

CARTER & RAYGUN: Who Won?

Yeah, who won? Are we all still here?

EDDIE COCKROACH: Somethin' Or Other.

Everybody knows that Eddie Cockroach was the only real Beetle and Evils Perversely the only real Sex Pistol. Lucas Mazda will bring back the golden age of the torch song after in-store Muzak rioting sends teenage shoppers crazy over the Christmas period, ripping up loaves of bread and smashing eggs on the floor! Rock's rich rug! Genius is a pain in the art! ▲

January 1982

RAY LOWRY

Friends, I've been having you on! I'm not really an appaling, balding, crapulous old arsepain (FACE No 20) with hate in his heart for everyone under the age of 47, and a headful of pseudo-Marxist, junior Socialist club ranting nonsense about how the world is going to end next Wednesday if young people don't stop watching Top Of The Pops and buying Blue Rondo a la Turbot style zooting suits instead of winter-weight greatcoats and peaked caps with little red stars on them.

Not a bit of it! In fact I'm a perfectly respectable, ageing hippy type who's only ever been in trouble with the law on the odd occasion for trivial drinking misdemeanours and similar rags and I've always been most contrite, not to say positively cringing, the next morning about causing such a lot of unnecessary fuss and bother over a spot of the old tight and emulsionals.

So, reader Jon Paul of Benfleet, Essex, no politicals from me, this time out. Should there have been a major nuclear confrontation/situation/ scenario before the next issue, rest assured that I will have adjusted my perspectives accordingly and we can start a meaningful dialogue about what to do with zed million tons of fried vinyl just as soon as the need arises. For this issue only, it's party time!

"Bring on the narcotics, wipe clean the groaning board and lay out the pale powders," screams reader A. Gaga of Roehampton. "Naw, make it Rumba rhythms and Pina Colandas for me," rants reader A. Darnell of Kilmamock (obviously a pseudonym).

Forget the end of the civilised world as we know it, I'll take a raincheck on the Moscow gold shipment. Cancel this month's roubles, Leonid, and I'll endeavour to string together a handful of coherent sentences about a couple of this year's records ("Records! Bloody hell, cancel my subscription" – Furious, Devizes) that I thought were REALLY GOOD. Of course, if you don't agree with my estimations we may have a difference of opinion leading to an altercation, what you might call a matter of politics, on a small scale. The rock of politics, the politics of rock.

NME watchers may recall that for a brief period this summer I enjoyed the infinite rewards and dazzling career prospects of being a fully-fledged album reviewer for that most stimulating of our pop prints. Alas, pride goeth before a fall, as the Guinness Book of Records has it, and I emerged from the spotlight's blinding glare a sadder but wiser man, with a handful of the worst records ever made and one certified masterwork in the legendary Blue Angel (Polydor-2391 486) album.

This, simply, is the best I heard in '81, performed in the traditional rock and roll style. That is, the instruments held the right way round, no arty videos, and the whole performed with a ton of genuine heart, soul, truth and conviction, mostly cranked Out fast and powerful. What Bruce Springsteen intermittently delivered, but better. The sort of thing, the only sort of thing, that's ever been able to allow me to suspend disbelief for the duration of its playing time and surrender completely to the music.

I even did a phone interview with them – they live in New York, incidentally, how strange! – which never got into the paper, fellas!!

Their singer is a young lady called Cyndi Lauper who is blessed with the most compelling, convincing female voice I've heard in rock and roll. Simply magnificent. She's backed by four brilliant geezers on guitars, keyboards, drums, sax and all the usual stuff. The album did, and still does, knock me out more than anything I've heard since 1977, and nobody seems to give a flying one, for fuck's sake! Incredible, the apathetics who run this business. It's like being Brian Epstein trying to persuade an uncaring world to give a listen to The Beatles. Will someone please care about these people?!

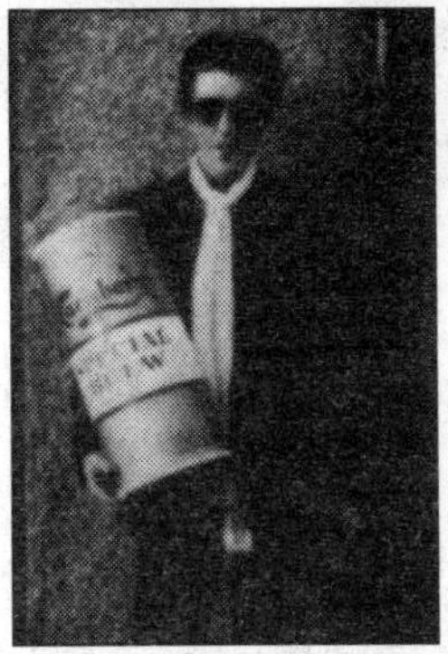

◀ Children, don't do what I have done. Author ponders Ms Burchill's words – "The big thing in life is, don't make yourself a mess in the first place."

To conclude – If you are going to buy yourself one damned thing this Christmas, then do yourself a real favour and make it a copy of "Blue Angel" on the Polydor record label. I have taken no bribes or accepted any offers of similar emoluments for this unsolicited rave, cross my heart and hope to die.

Just do this thing and you will write in to swear your undying gratitude to THE FACE and myself for putting something positive into your life, as soon as the mail starts moving again after the Yuletide festerings. Remember, baggy black trousers tucked into pointy-toed, red boots do not a prison make, nor iron bars a cage. I think Abraham Lincoln said that.

Okay, that's the traditional, deathless, rockunroll sound revitalised, redefined, resurrected and sent toddling around the room all over again by a fine bunch of young American people. It doesn't change the world, cure acne and eczema, defeat right-wing governments or Stalinist style dictatorships, relieve embarrassing itching or feed a family of four, but by God, it makes you feel greater than most leading brands of painkiller.

For those of you who are already fretting and biting your fingernails while tossing your hair imperiously out of your eyes and breathing superciliously down those flared nostrils (the ones that come with the nice cheekbones and the rest) fret no more. I heard another record this year! Honest, government cuts and all.

Oh, by the way, don't come all poverty-struck and moneyless at me after giving me shit for attempting to sort out the capitalist economic system, hear! You can afford a couple of bloody records. Grab some to that gold dust that's been flying around this year! Leave off buying makeup for a week. You'll soon have enough for a album or three.

Finally, this year "Jesus, is there more," wails FACE Major domo, 'Honest' Dick Logan, slugging away at his Remington portable and hip-flask of shaving lotion – from behind the 'Toxteth' brand blazing, riotshield style, Comfiglow incendiary roombeater comes the sound of the massed choirs of Liverpool wailing "What about Pete Wylie you f-----g b------d!!'??". Yes indeed!

A sprig of Taiwanese plastic holly to Pete Wylie for "Nah Poo – The Blart Of Puff"! I love it. Wylie and a few others like him are keeping the flame alive in Liverpool ("Ho ho," guffaws our man on the barricades, Lunchtime O'Shrapnel).

"Will this do?" hisses your columnist sidling into the FACE office trying to butter up FACE supremo 'Jolly' Mick Logan with an opened bottle of 'Blows under the Sheets' and a handful of pounds sterling. "The reincarnation of rock and roll, false bonhomie, sickly good humour and phoney sentiment, and no mention of Vladimir Ilyich Lenin. What do you want, the Queen's Speech?

RAY LOWRY

ALL HUMAN LIFE IS HERE! (This month only) BOOK REVIEW DEPT.:

Fred and Judy Vermorel put it best in the revised edition of "The Sex Pistols – The Inside Story" (Star Books).

"We will never understand the Sex Pistols if we think of them as a rock and roll band. The band was an excuse, the occasion, a blank canvas."

And –

"They count, not as items in the rock and roll reliquary, but as household names: for their universal impact, a rallying point of social bogies, the figment of anxious controversy. And like a dye released on the ocean floor, they show us some of history's deepest currents – upon which the 'events' of royalty or politics or rock and roll 'history' merely float.

"The Sex Pistols was a work of art. The artists: Malcolm, John and Jamie (albeit with many helpers and assistants, scene changers and stand-ins). It was their collective masterpiece, a work of genius."

And finally–

"The Sex Pistols masterpiece stands at the furthermost point where artists have recognised that publicity is as important and, what is more, as malleable a medium as their traditional paints and clay. A point where you may anticipate and plan for the fact that the media does not simply transmit or reproduce your work, but effectively repaints – remakes – it."

HURRAH FOR YOUTH! Youth in the 'twenties had energy and enthusiasm. Youth played the flute, sackbut, psaltery and all kinds of music. But what now?

That's so good, isn't it? The EVENT, the 'swindle', the creation of this notorious Sex Pistols entity was THE work of art. The art created by the Sex Pistols as a rock and roll band – their records – was secondary. The fact that they succeeded in creating some wonderful records confused traditionalists like myself into thinking that their artefacts/records were the whole point, the peg on which to hang one's judgement of them as a 'band', to assess their eventual position in some mythical rock and roll league table. Something to collect and place into the context of a continuing popular music conveyor-belt type history.

Thanks to Fred and Judy Vermorel's book I see what a DUMB attitude this was. Pissing all over the rock and roll process ('killing' rock and roll) or just using the idea of a 'band' to create a new art form or art event or socio/political art event – whatever it was the Sex Pistols did – was a brilliant idea, brilliantly realized.

The disappointment and cause of so much malice from ancient rockists, like me, is that journalists and bands in the wake of the event have accepted half of the idea – the killing off of rock and roll – but have been unwilling or unable to contemplate replacing it with anything but another MUSICAL form, which the Vermorels show is only a part of the story.

The idea of the Sex Pistols wrapping up an era and leaving us all on the edge of hitherto undreamed of possibilities and situations is awesome. The idea of kissing off rock and roll in favour of the MUSIC of post-punk bands is a dismal prospect. As is trading the larger implications of the EVENT for pantomime stage shows and an unexciting, conservative world view from today's 'pop' stars. Adam Ant has achieved the greatest media awareness since the Sex Pistols, and good luck to him, but far from being any kind of catalyst or uncoverer of deep social currents, he's… Marc Bolan with hod-carrier's shoulders.

Whatever else they were, the Sex Pistols were a threat. A firecracker rather than a time-bomb in 30-odd volumes filed under 'Politics', but "God Save The Queen" and the safety pin poster were beautifully direct and untheoretical where theory and perspective can be so uninspiring. After the failure of Bow Wow Wow to spark similar fireworks, maybe Malcolm McLaren or some other visionary can apply the Sex Pistols confrontation tactics to some other field of endeavour, though it's hard to imagine where or how. (And this is too reminiscent of NEXT BIG THING discussions of the pre-Pistols era. Like – "Maybe some giant will appear in another sphere of activity…")

Whatever, I'm grateful to Fred and Judy Vermorel for making the effort to educate slow learners like myself about what was really going down in those far off days of ancient hysteria. Read the book and learn. Then forget PUNK ever happened, throw away "Never Mind The Bollocks", and devise a strategy for combating the new complacency.

OLDIES BUT GOLDIES DEPT.

(Bear with me for this one. The punchline's at the end.) Here's a quote from Leon Trotsky in Where Is Britain Going, written in 1925. He's discussing the concept of "the inevitability of gradualness" in the development of political ideas and political change. The phrase had been coined by a British Labour politician but was being touted by the Conservative prime minister of the day, Stanley Baldwin.

Trotsky writes: "Is it not possible to draw

from all this the conclusion that the greater the success with which Britain applied force to other peoples, the greater the degree of 'gradualness' she managed to realise within her own frontiers? Indeed it is! Britain, over three centuries, conducted an uninterrupted succession of wars directed at extending her arena of exploitation, removing foreign riches, killing foreign commercial competition and annihilating foreign naval forces, all by means of piracy and violence against other nations, and thereby enriching the British governing classes.

"A diligent investigation of the facts and their inner linkages leads to the inescapable conclusion that the British governing classes managed to avoid revolutionary shocks within their own country in so far as they were successful at increasing their own material power by means of wars and shocks of all sorts in other countries.

"In this way did they gain the possibility of restraining the revolutionary indignation of the masses through timely, and always very niggardly, concessions.

"But such a conclusion, which is completely irrefutable in itself, proves the exact opposite of what Baldwin wanted to prove, for the very history of Britain testifies in practice that 'peaceful development' can only be ensured by means of a succession of wars, colonial acts of violence and bloody shocks. This is a strange form of 'gradualness'!"

There are countless more examples given by Trotsky of the wrong-headedness of the idea of 'gradualness'. Now, listen to Michael Foot writing about "My Kind Of Socialism" in the Observer of January 10, 1982. I quote:

"After all, we should have learnt something from half a century of such tumult and terror in human affairs. And part of what we have learnt, or should have learnt, adds up to a direct refutation of apocalyptic Marxism, or, if you wish, a justification, in a quite different sense from the old one, of the inevitability of gradualness."

We here at the edge of the abyss say, "WAKE UP WORZEL! WAKE UP WORZEL! WAKE UP WORZEL! WAKE UP WORZEL! WAKE UP WORZEL!'

ROCK AND ROLL MADNESS DEPT.:

I was glancing through an old *Melody Maker* recently when I was struck by an observation made by Neil Rowland concerning 'Flavour du Temps' Altered Images. He pointed out that their work "doesn't make the slightest protest, but it does remind us of what we are protesting for."

I thought that was a neat point, well made. The Altered Images album is an incredible

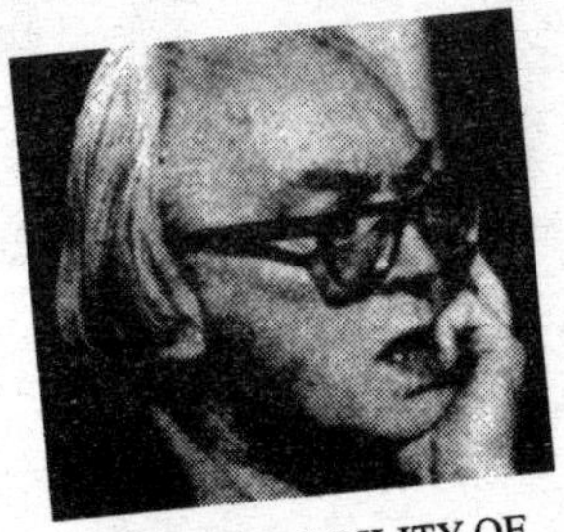

THE INEVITABILITY OF LUDICROUS HAIRSTYLES

triumph of sheer form over any kind of conventional content, any message or story. It's the object of beauty rather than the description of something beautiful. Abstract as opposed to representational. (I reserve the right to 'go off' it of course. Critical consistency not being my strongpoint, as you may have noticed). Artists, musicians, creators, situationists, whatever you call them – how about originals – pop up all over the place under all kinds of historical conditions and circumstances. They've no obligation to 'protest' or bring a specific 'message' or anything else. If they spread a little joy that's more than most of us do.

The reason why 'politics' and art, and 'politics' and everything else are so inextricable is because the economy – the seedbed on which the flowers of art, music and everything else grow – is controlled by the government. Ours is obviously in a great deal of trouble at the moment and the people who say they have the alternative – the Marxists – offer us tantalising glimpses like this one from a Militant pamphlet:

"Under a socialist plan of production, from being seen as a cause of mass unemployment, and a threat to the jobs of working people, the new technology would become the means of freeing the working class from all the monotonous, boring and soul-destroying jobs which are necessary under capitalism."

And, "Within a generation it would mean the abolition of classes, with the possibility opening up, for the first time, of the full flowering and development of the human personality, which is presently stifled under capitalism."

But read the originals. Read Lenin. Trotsky, Marx, Engels. I know how boring and tedious it is seeing Socialists constantly adjusting their "perspectives' in their periodicals. Get the white-heat, the excitement from the people who actually did it. The architects of a revolution that happened, however quickly their work was perverted.

IMPORTANT NEW SERIES STARTS NEXT MONTH: Was McLaren a Marxist/Spencerist? Did Branson wield the ice pick? One lump or two? How does it FEEL?!!

WE'D LOIK TO FINISH NAR WIV A NUMBER FROM OUR NOO ALBUM: Would any American reader be kind enough to send me a pot or two of the sublime Three Flowers hair grease? It's made by Warner-Lambert Co of Morris Plains, N.J., and has the best smell of any brilliantine I've ever encountered. I'll gladly reimburse anyone who obliges.

I don't believe that haircuts can save the world or that ideological purity can only be maintained by soaking your head in engine oil every other day or so. But I do find the disadvantages of grease – filthy shirt collars, disgusting pillow slips etc – outweighed by the fact that it prevents dandruff, one of the great bains of my life.

With grease applied I wander through life like a man wearing a severely mauled pontefract cake on his head but, since everybody looks weird nowadays, who's looking? English grease is, of course, generally rubbish; hence this crie de barnet.

Who's got the world's most absurd hairstyle? Is It Andre Previn… Dave Lee Travesty… Bruce Forsyth… Mike Reid… Kevin Keegan… Bobby Charlton? Only history will provide the answer, I fear.

Finally tonight, I'd like to thank the millions who've written from all corners of the room, particularly Greg Graham of Canada, Terri Sinai (it looks like. Thanks a lot anyway) of Hampstead and Wild Billy Childish of The Milkshakes. Thanks to The Quads and Johnny Green for cards. I will reply, shamelessly plug your records etc., if I haven't done so already. Don't forget what Karl Marx had to say on the subject: "The problem with the philosophers is that they have only interpreted the world, the point is to change it." CAN YOU DIG IT!!!!????

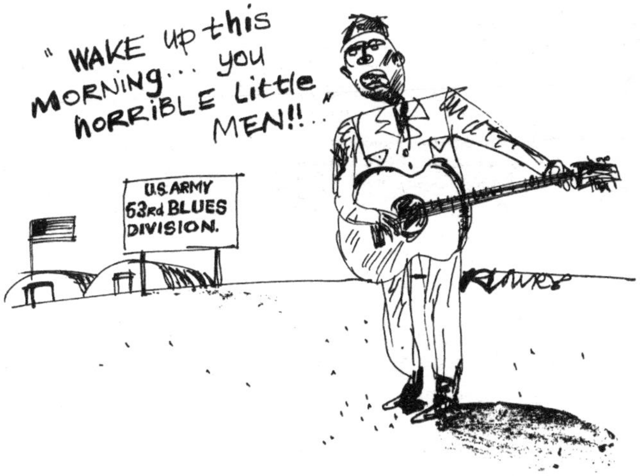
"WAKE up this MORNING… you horrible Little MEN!!…"
U.S. ARMY 53rd BLUES DIVISION.

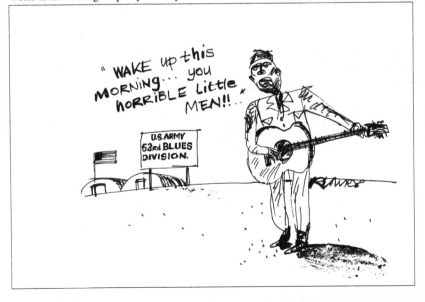

RAY LOWRY

May, July 1982

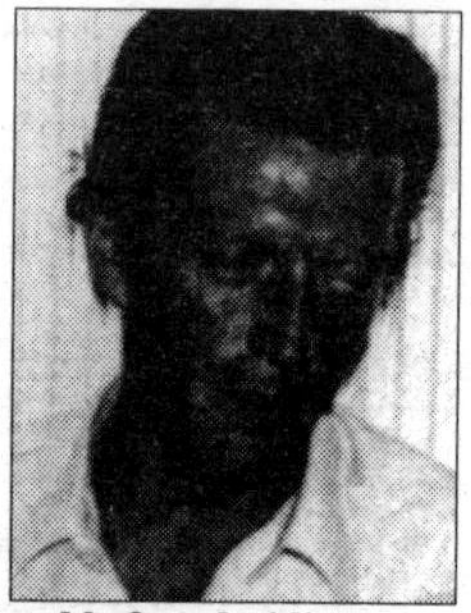

SNAATCHI SPEAKS: In a specially pre-recorded, 1984 Christmas message from the Fuehrerbunker, Mrs Snaatchi spoke movingly of the light at the end of the tunnel, the corner of our great struggle being finally turned by a new streamlined-style, British mini-industryette freed from the constraints of unnecessary burdens like factories, shipyards, machinery and a workforce.

Likening our new, compact industry to a finely tuned, Hitaatchi, battery-operated pocket calculator, Mrs Snaatchi (3,000,000) announced:

"I have a dream! Now that we have totally eradicated the scourge of full employment and created in its place vast, new armies of highly trained and ferociously bloodthirsty Special Assault Groups, Tactical Aid Penetration Squads, Inter-county Parachute Attack Teams, Anti-tank Civil Disorder Defence Patrols, Neighbourhood Cossack Patrol Groups, Ski-teams, Anti-Mugging Groups, Community Bren-gun Carrier Patrols and Germ Warfare Liaison Committees, we can all pull up our drawbridges at night, set the Securalarm, throw the switch on the Deteraburglar electrified fence and settle down with a good book.

"If discontented foreigners, of whatever colour or stripe, choose not to integrate into our million year island tapestry, our peaceful social fabric, then we can only offer them the boot and the lash," sighed Mrs Thaatchel (Military Tendency).

"No one can be more disappointed than Mr Whipmore (Hom. Sec.) and myself that we've found it necessary to establish special internment camps on the New Falklands (formerly Isle of Wight) to house the growing number of political militants, subversives and anti-social elements in our midst," added a tired and emotional McHatchet.

"Mr Wafflemore and I agonized long and hard before deciding that we had no recourse but to return to the rope and the cat," said a visibly shaken Mrs Thatchedhouse (V.C. and Fiery Cross).

In a final, emotional outburst Mrs A. Hitlaach (V.C.R.) screamed, "As I speak to you tonight, crack divisions of our highly-trained shock troops, supported by tanks, heavy artillery and air strikes, are speeding through Glamorgan to repel the brutish Welsh aggressor! We will not tolerate this violation of our borders! Lebensraum! There is no alternative! No alternative... snap!... bzzzz... click. Malfunction. Malfunction."
(Mrs Hitlaach is a dead loss.)

Cheering millions thronged Fleet Street recently after hearing of the appointment of Simone De Frithe to the 'rock' chair of the *Sundry Tribes* 'newspaper'. Outgoing pop scribe, Sir Derek Jewellery (247) said at a stormy press conference, "I'm a drunken man. Er, I mean a broken man. They've appointed this young punk over my dead body against all the dictates of common sense and musical good taste.

"For 500 years now I have bored to tears succeeding generations of rock fans with my tireless championing of Cleo Laine, er, Tommy Bennet, Genesnores, Pink Fluke etc, etc. I was good for at least another 77 years, but they drag in this mewling, be-safety-pinned brat over my head! There'll be rioting in the streets when my fans (Mrs D. Jewellery, deceased) hear about this," warned Sir Derek, envisaging a 1981 style summer of discontent.

A spokesthug for Violence of Victims, the new pre-emptive anti-mugging strike force established by Welifed Wafflemore (Hom. Sec.) and 'Sony' Jim Jardine (Scot. Nit.), speaking on the World At One to Sir Rubic Cubeday, outlined their plans to:

"Rid our great society of the creeping cancer of disaffected Commonwealth immigrants waiting on our street corners to pounce on the passing flower of our British womanhood (believed to refer to Eunice Thugee, Bart.) and rob them of their purses full of life savings. I'm not suggesting that we should set up vigilante groups and Tactical Assault Forces to ride the streets and motorways armed with flame-throwers and Ousi submachine guns, but it's come to a pretty pass when an Englishman can't call a spade a spade, or a wop or a spic for that matter, in the privacy of his own neighbourhood with a loudhailer, don't you think Sir Robin?" added the spokesperson.

"I think that we should look for the root causes of the Shame of our City Streets and grasp the nettle firmly to remove it root and branch in one fell swoop, so to speak, Sir Roddy," editorialised the spokesperson.

"To this end, Sir Rabbie, we've canvassed Parliamentary support for the idea of filling the old Ark Royal up with the little buggers and dumping them off the coast of Argentina,in a manner of speaking. Unhappily I must report that we were only able to obtain assurances of a sympathetic view being taken should we be driven beyond endurance to the point of entering the homes of sleeping subversives and pouring quantities of boiling lead in their ears, in view of the appaling rise in the crime rate.

"I mean, Sir Rupert, where's the sense in putting half the nation's youth into the uniform of blue if they're so bloody incompetent that all they can do is snort up huge quantities of confiscated drugs and accept bribes while the muggers have a field day in our inner-city conurbations?

"What the hell do we pay our rates and electricity bills for, Sir Robbish, if we can't..." (cont. p94 of Mein Kampf.)

I was lying, close to death, in my scuzz pit recently, locked into black neurosis and HEAVY PARANOIA. I'd surfaced into the same old stinking, steamy a.m. horrors from

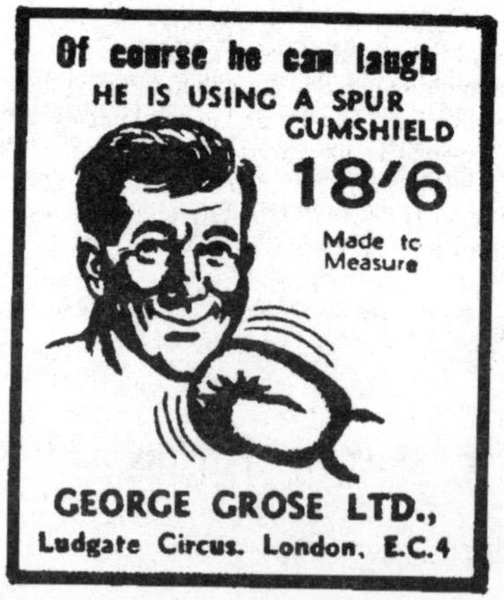
Of course he can laugh
HE IS USING A SPUR
GUMSHIELD
18/6
Made to
Measure
GEORGE GROSE LTD.,
Ludgate Circus. London. E.C.4

a dream of approaching corpses; collapsed into a heap of empty beer cans, eyeballs stabbing into decaying eye whites, mouth full of chewed aspirin and cigarette ash, damped down and quivering with hate for the world and his wife, as usual.

The video machine was full to overflowing with beer and cigarette butts and it looked very much as if some inventive soul had attempted to cram a maggot and tomato style pizza into the feed slot. The cassettes looked to have been comprehensively stomped and ripped open and the tapes eaten or shredded and thrown around the environs like a celluloid version of party streamers.

The TV had been turned on its glass belly, its insides torn out and the shell used as a receptacle for more empty beer cans, bottles and strange glutinous lumps that were probably foodstuffs or the detritus from intimate surgical operations, a touching attempt by some strung-out dingbat to make things a little neater, a tad more presentable. Like trying to sweep up after the battle of the Somme. Futile, but nice that someone had made an attempt.

I was lying in the wreckage of a sofa that had been righteously stomped by a party of visigoths in spiked boots, a window was smashed, and a Polar Bear was weeping softly to itself behind the remains of a Swiss Cheese plant that had been tortured to extract information about a drug deal by a biker on a satanist trip. I decided it was wisest to ignore the bear for the time being. Perhaps it was just an hallucination; with any luck it might turn out to be only a Hell's Angel on an evil downer from a horse tranquilliser.

If it was going to be another of THOSE days I obviously needed to listen to something positive enough to blowout the black disease horror and general negative, uh, vibes that seemed to be fluttering in like clouds of rabid bats. I needed to GET THE WORLD OFF OF MY BACK. I needed some KILLER LICKS!!!!

I crawled to a heap of albums that had miraculously survived the sacking and filleting of my neighbourhood and copped all the old favourites. "Knife In Your Eyes" by the Nazi Baby Stompers. Naw, protest music was dead "Your Best Party Hits From The Pornosnuff Movies". I didn't need SEASONAL music, dammit! The Haemorrhages Of Doom. The Skin

Complaint From Hell. Adam Ant and Diana Dors – Together. Hmmmmmm... no, I was after something REALLY HEAVY…

Ah, yes, it's easy to be a gonzoid journalist after the event, isn't it? I never followed *CREEM* **magazine under the late Lester Bangs' editorial hand but I did follow his and others contributions to** *Rolling Stone* **through the late Sixties/early Seventies with a mixture of awe and delighted admiration. When Lester Bangs and those other early Stone contributors were good they were BAAAAD!** *Rolling Stone* **was the first paper I saw that regularly carried the new, enlightened style of writing that was later picked up on over here and used to transform our own** *NME.*

How about a record review that starts out with this kind of brio: "It's about goddamn fucking time these Groundhogs started to get some recognition! And this may be just the album to turn the trick. These guys have been hanging in there, albeit under a different name or two, through the whole gauntlet of Sixties stylistic changes from student-blues to Beefheart, and even though they're generally thought of as the transcendence of hasty pudding in their crosspond homeland they still haven't managed to crack the walls of the U.S. of A."

The transcendence of hasty pudding?! Does anybody know what that meant? The same review finishes up like this: "Who needs bagpipes when you've got the Groundhogs? Who needs to say thanks for the memories by dropping another good four bucks on another sorry Hendrix stewpot for that matter, when you've got the Groundhogs? Who needs to ever have to say you're sorry, when the Groundhogs are ranting and romping free, cutting a swath as wide as the outer spaces of a Mohawk haircut across these lands of ours?"

That was Lester Bangs in *Rolling Stone* **1972, reviewing an album that probably didn't deserve that delicious, infectious enthusiasm. No icy poses for those guys; when they liked something they raved in a manner that had me running round to record shops shelling out for a hundred and one horrible stiffers. I even bought early Blue Oyster Cult albums, but I**

always forgave the guilty reviewers and was ready to indulge their next flight of oversell. Because they often got it right.

They didn't just write about records, of course. The next time that I or anyone else is trying to urge you to take seriously the words and works of our professional politicians it would be as well to mark the words of the legendary Hunter S. Thompson on the subject: "This may explain why McGovern blew his gig with Kennedy. It was a perfectly rational notion – and that was the flaw, because a man on the scent of the White House is rarely rational. He is more like a beast in heat, crashing blindly through the

A member of Wally Witless' Special Assault Group on patrol in Glasgow

timber in a fever for something to fuck. Anything! A cow, a calf, a mare – any flesh and blood beast with a hole in it…

"A career politician finally smelling the White House is not much different from a bull elk in the rut. He will stop at nothing, trashing anything that gets in his way; and anything he can't handle personally he will hire out – or, failing that, make a deal. It is a difficult syndrome for most people to understand, because few of us ever come close to the kind of Ultimate Power and achievement that the White House represents

to a career politician.

"The Presidency is as far as he can go. There is no more. The currency of politics is power, and once you've been the Most Powerful Man in the World for four years, everything else is downhill – except four more years on the same trip."

That about says it all really, doesn't it? Terrific insights salted with that cynical, savage wit. An added bonus with most of Thompson's wonderful pieces was some of the VERY BEST EVER of Ralph Steadman's nightmare illustrations. If you haven't seen them you've no idea of how perfectly words and illustrations can complement each other.

If you want to see where most of the good, modern rock/politricks/ human condition journalism was demonstrated to best, most stylish effect, ask your Grandad to show you his old copies of early **Rolling Stone** magazine.

Still on the subject of journalism, albeit of an, er, different order, I'm becoming more and more convinced of the presence of some kind of demented genius at work behind those *Sun* headlines. Whoever was responsible for those Super-Patriot, Argy-bashing classics has to be some kind of twisted, terminal cynic, n'est ce pas? "GOTCHA", "HUNDREDS OF ARGYS DROWNED" etc spring to mind. Journalism of that lofty order can only come from a conviction that your readership comprises a bunch of intellectual flea-weights and a righteous determination to rub their noses in their own stupid, animal prejudices.

I have a mental picture of the three cackling witches out of Macbeth dancing around a huge cauldron of neat malt whisky in the middle of the *Sun* editorial offices. They're laughing hysterically as they scoop out a tumbler full from time to time and quaff it with great relish; all the while chanting the ingredients for the next day's issue:

Liver of blaspheming Jew;
Gall of goat; and slips of yew;
Silver'd in the moon's eclipse;
Nose of Turk; and Tarter's lip,
Finger of birth-strangled babe,
Ditch-delivered by a drab,
Make the gruel thick and slab.

I salute the unsung *Sun* headline writers. Demented genius of this kind should be recognised and appreciated. ■

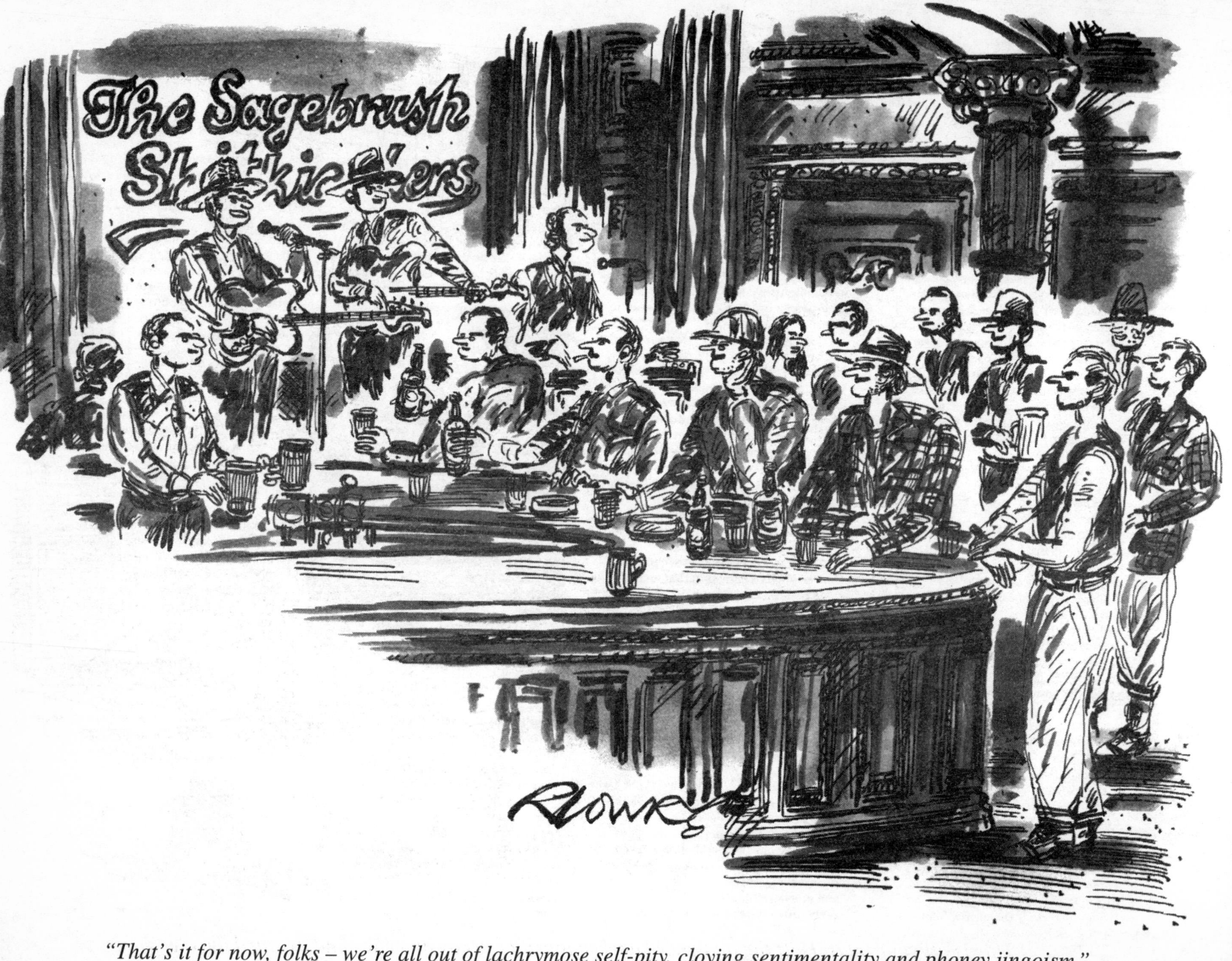
The Sagebrush

"That's it for now, folks – we're all out of lachrymose self-pity, cloying sentimentality and phoney jingoism."

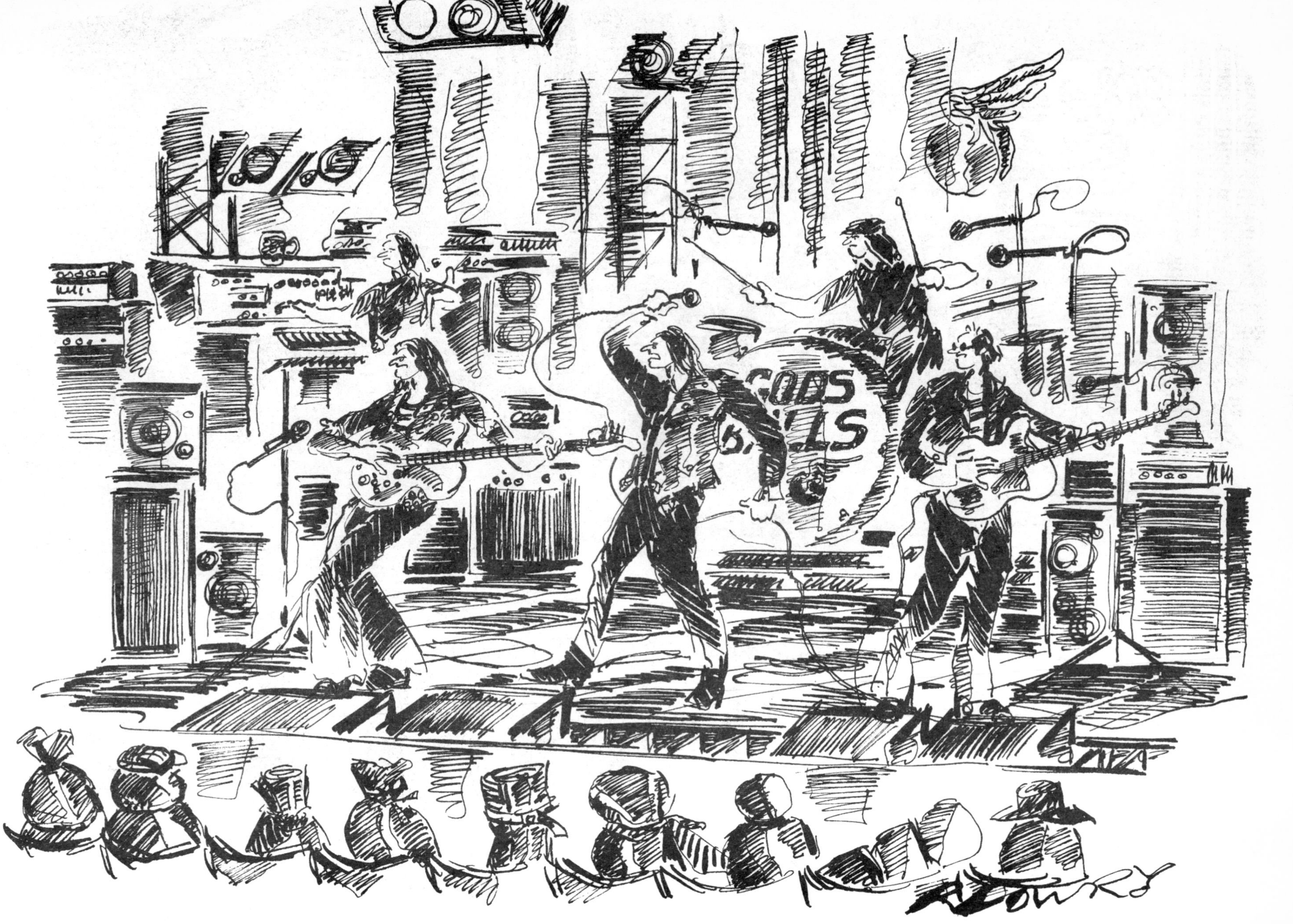

"This is all your fault. Half the audience knocked together decoy dummies and escaped during your interminably boring guitar soloing!"

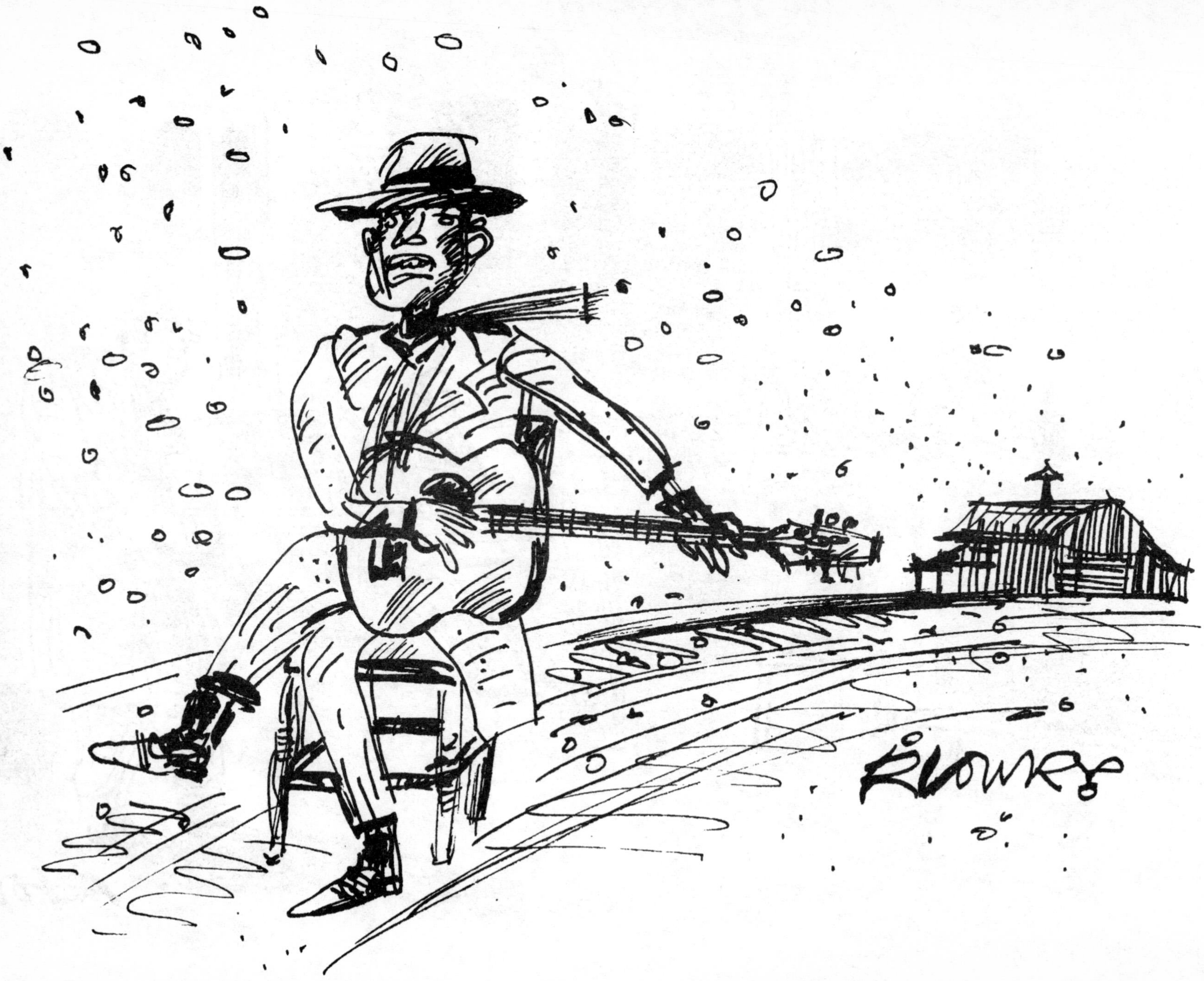

"Woke up this morning and, stupidly enough, I had the summertime blues!"

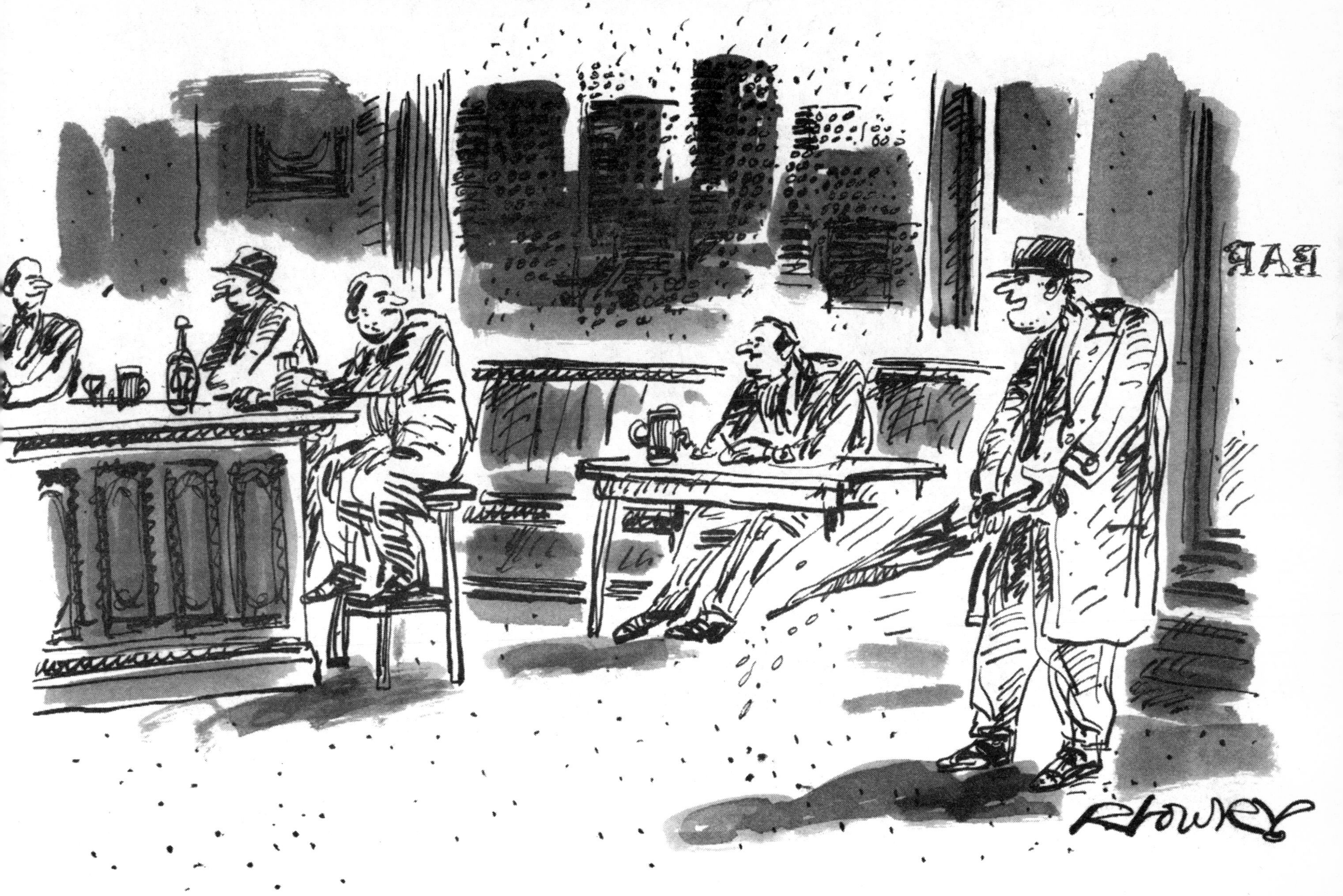

"Hi, fellows. I just ducked in here to get out of the human race."

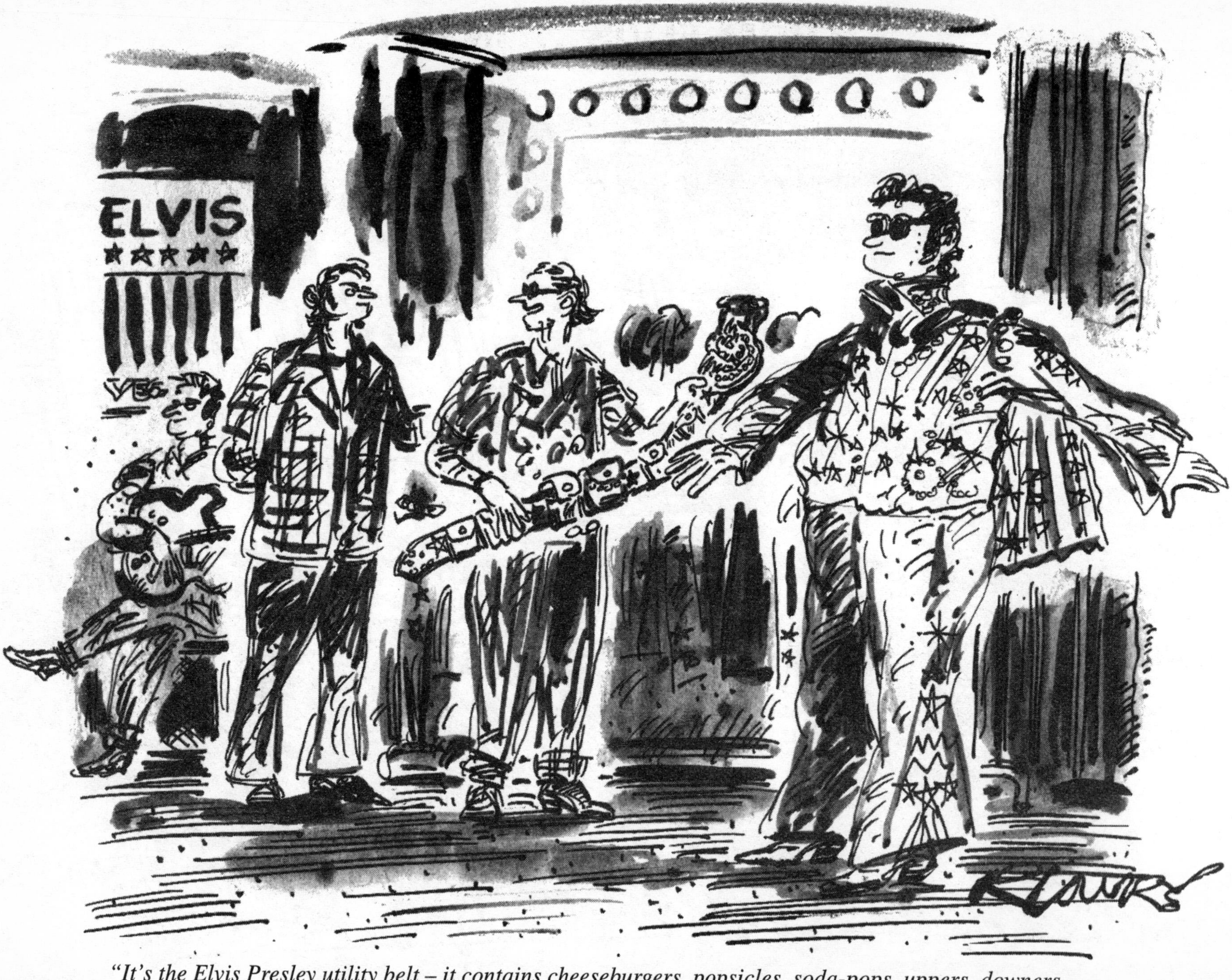
ELVIS

"It's the Elvis Presley utility belt – it contains cheeseburgers, popsicles, soda-pops, uppers, downers a couple of lines of coke and a supply of candy bars."

FROM ELVIS... IN HELL

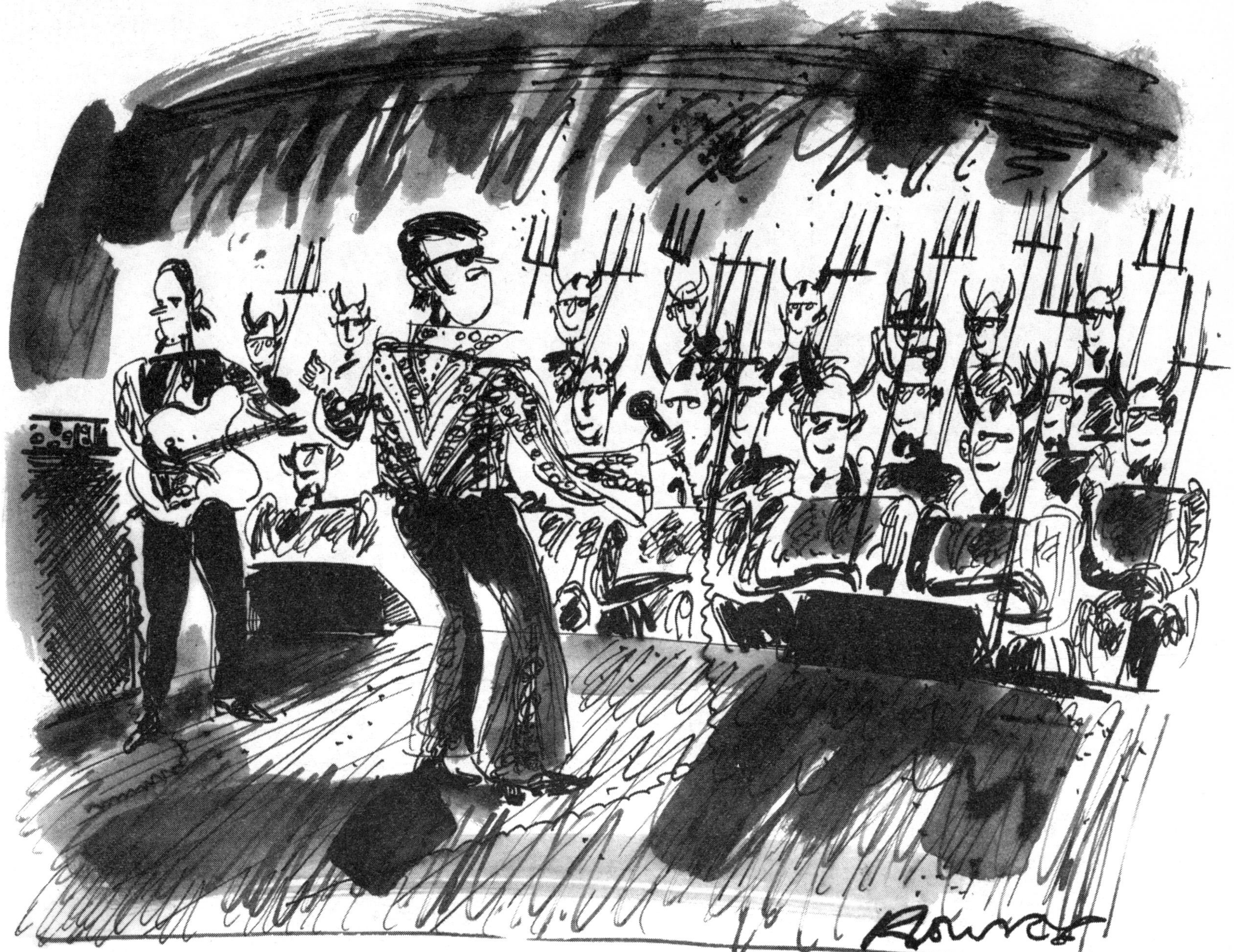

"It looks like the knockers were right after all... it WAS the devil's music!"

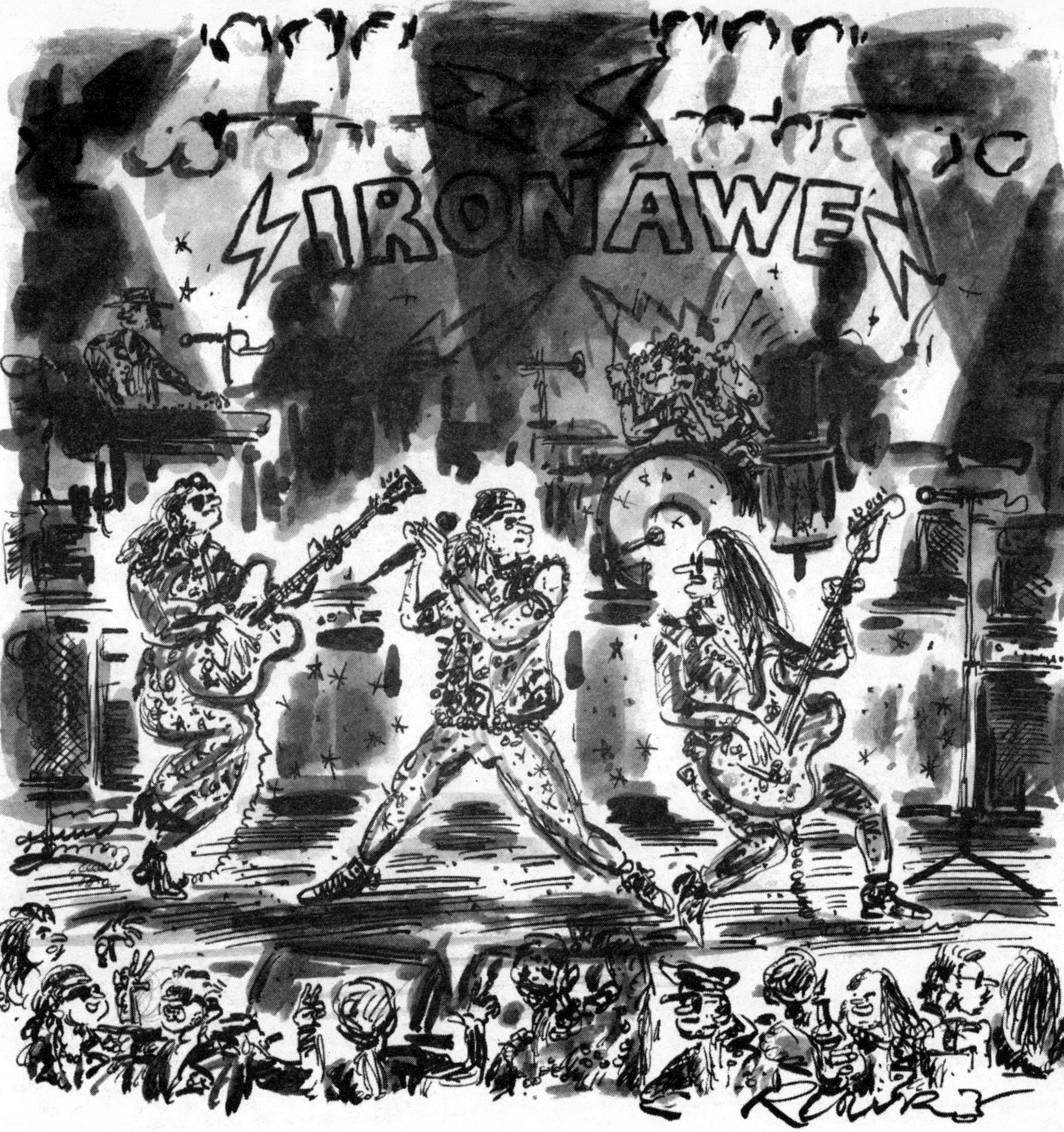
IRON AWE

"Do you ever long to escape from mundane hyper-reality and get back to something challenging like hideous normality?"

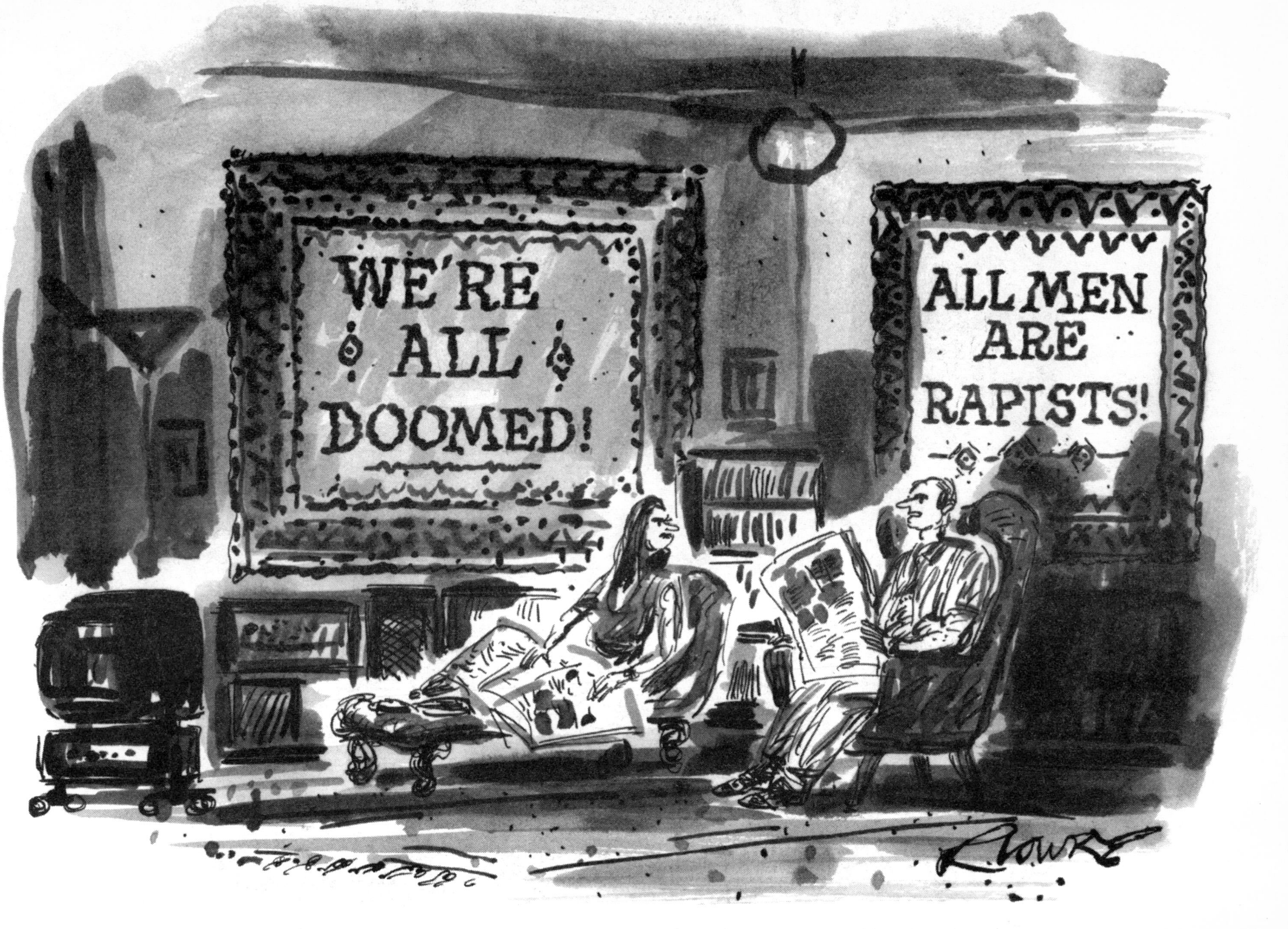

WE'RE
ALL
DOOMED!
ALL MEN
ARE
RAPISTS!

"You and your homespun philosophies…"

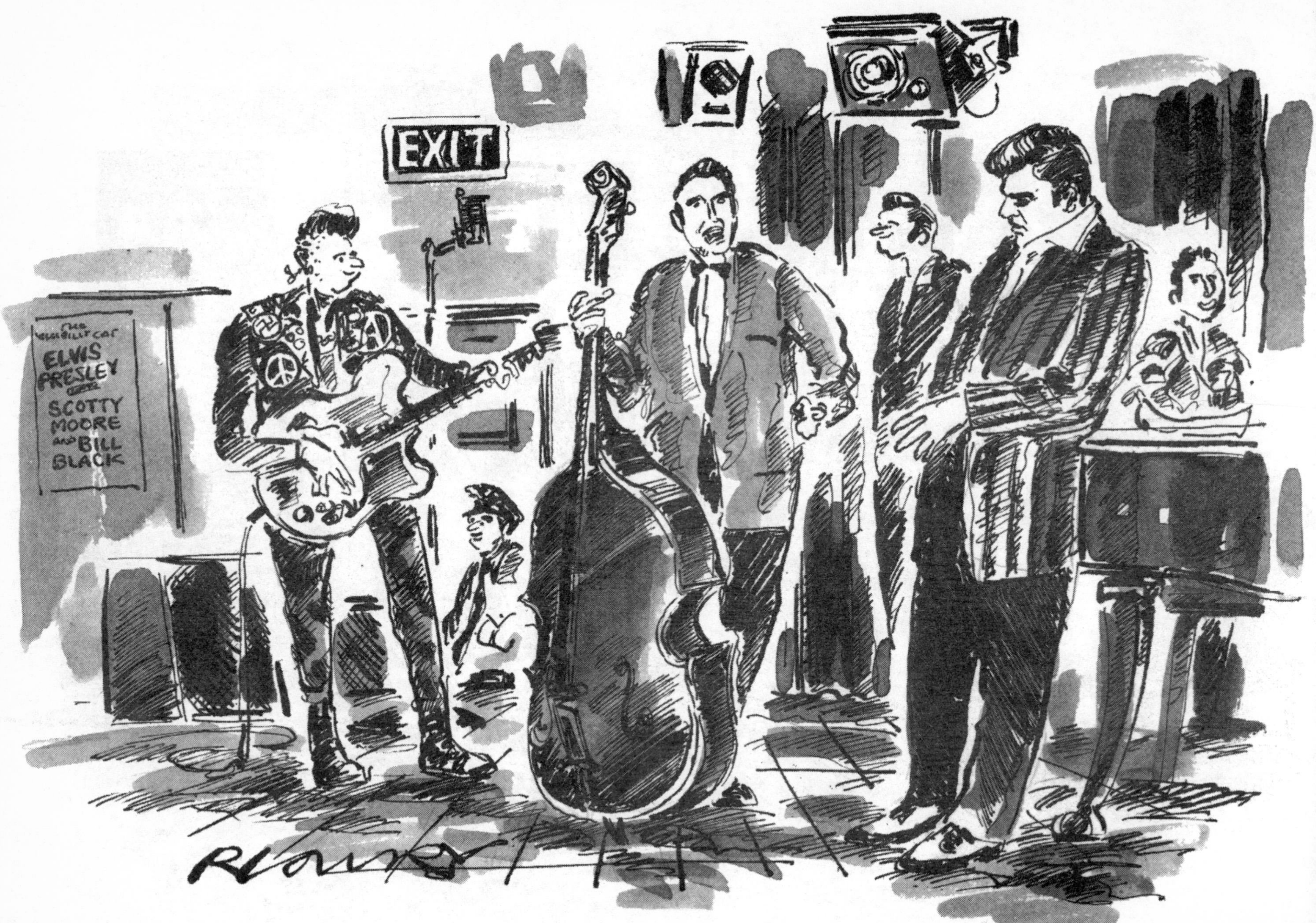
EXIT
ELVIS
PRESLEY
SCOTTY
MOORE
BILL
BLACK

"Just think about it for a minute and you'll see he's years ahead of his time with this idea – a punk band called Elvis, Snotty and Bill!"

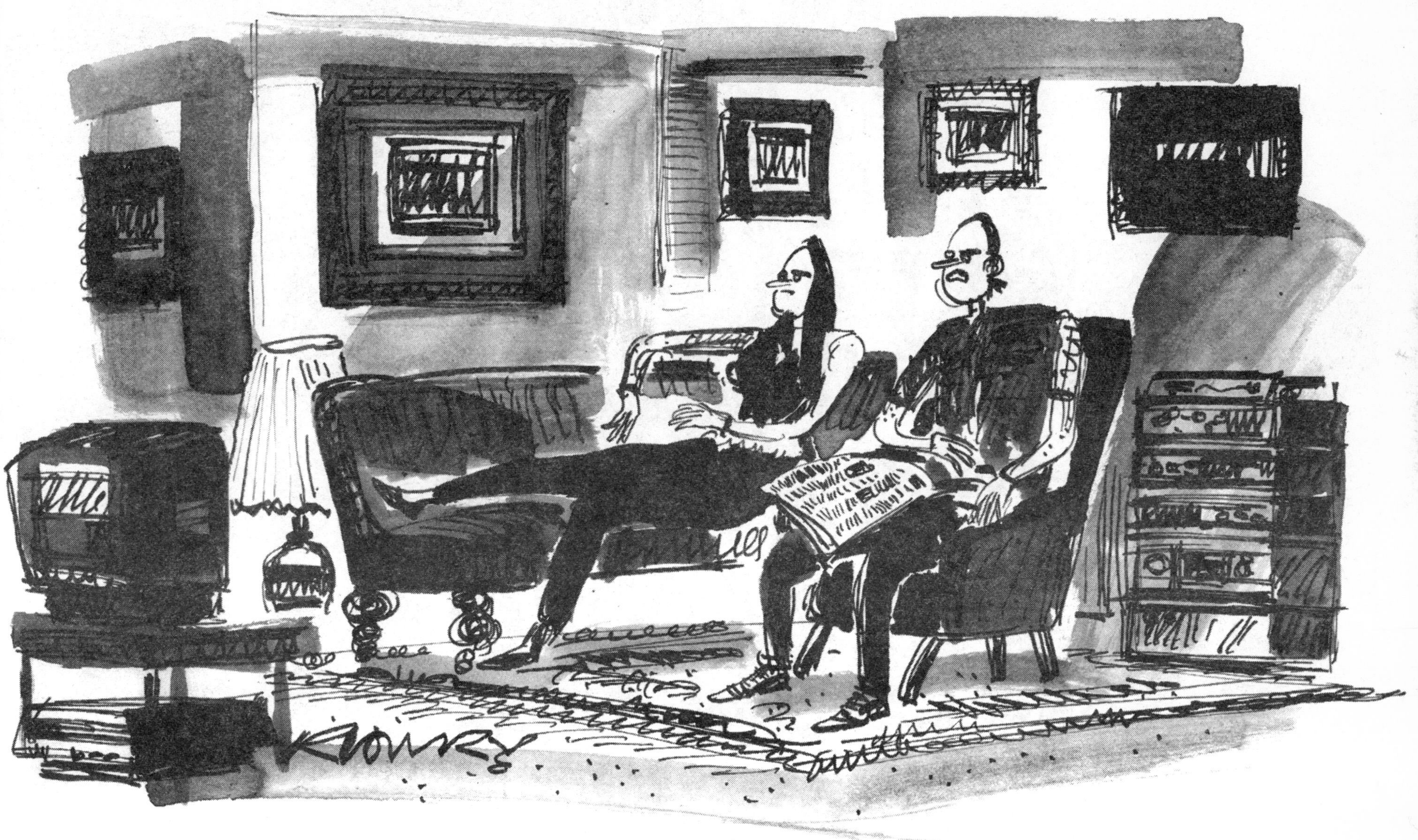

"It says here it's a wacky, structuralist sit-com set in a typical post-modern family, written by Michael Ignatieff..."

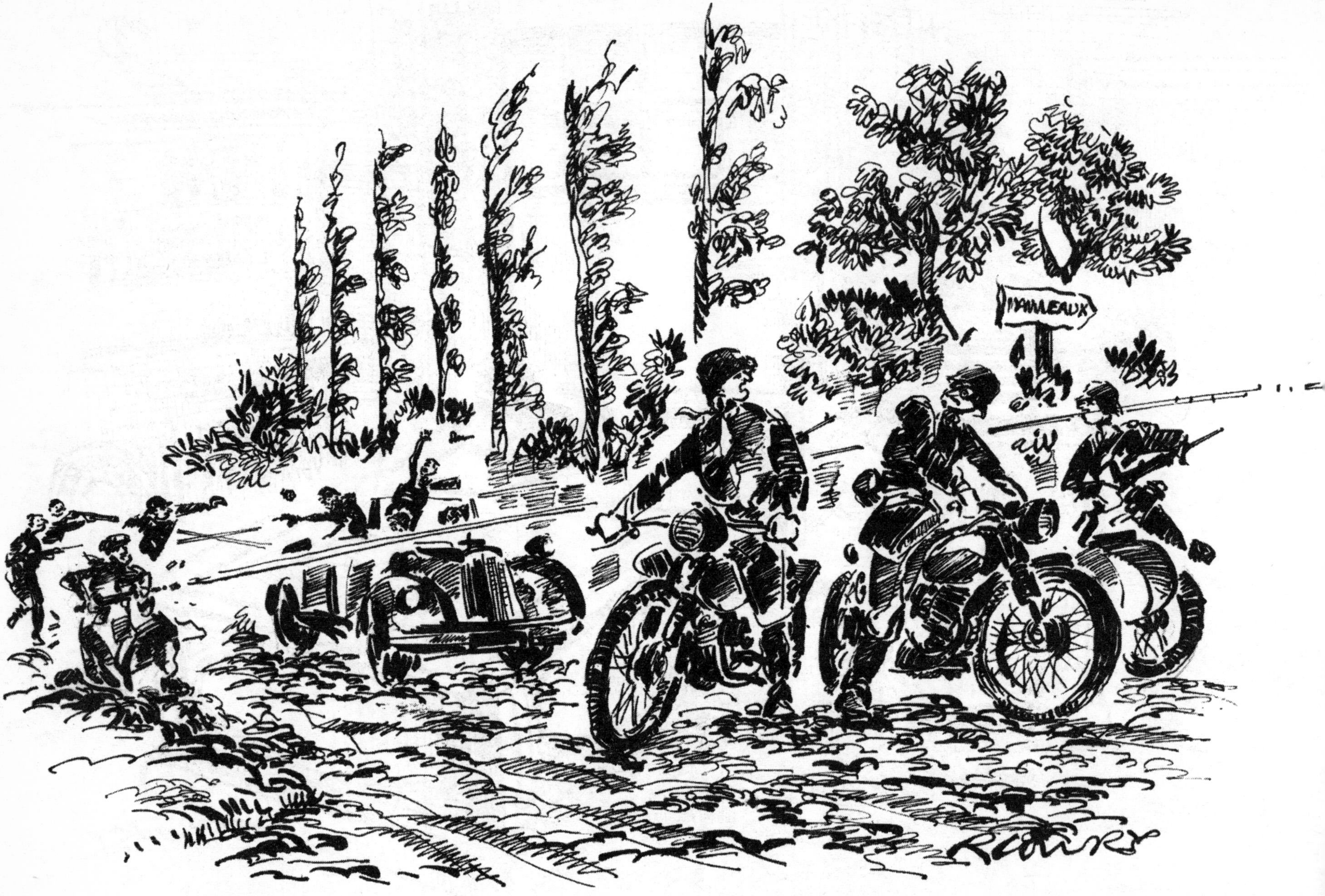

"I don't know what the world's coming to. There was a time when you could occupy half of Europe without all this unnecessary violence in the streets!"

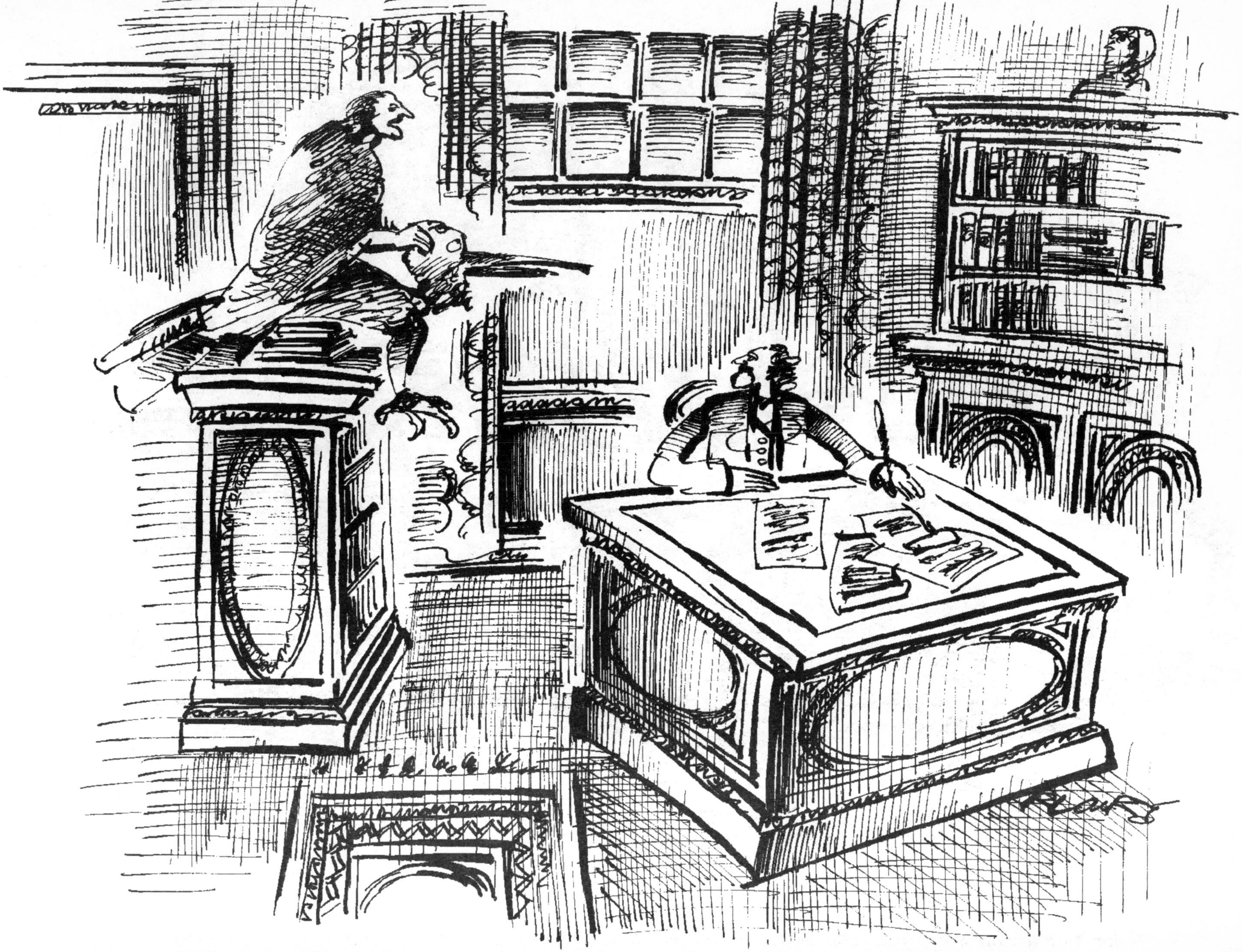

"Take my word for it, guv, you won't see any genuine talking ravens about at this time of the year."

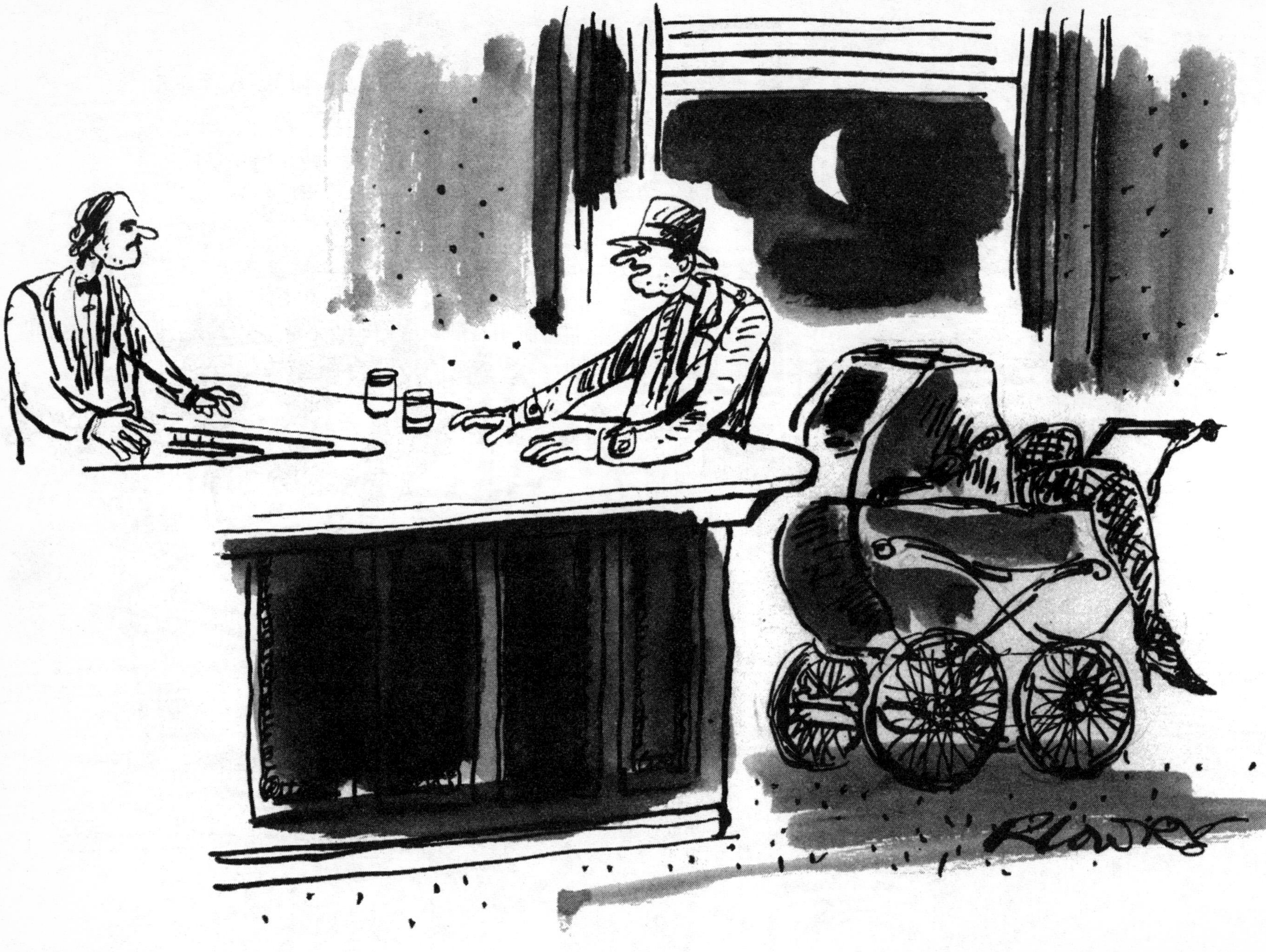

"Make it one for my baby and one more for the road."

CAT STEVENS SINGS THE BLUES…

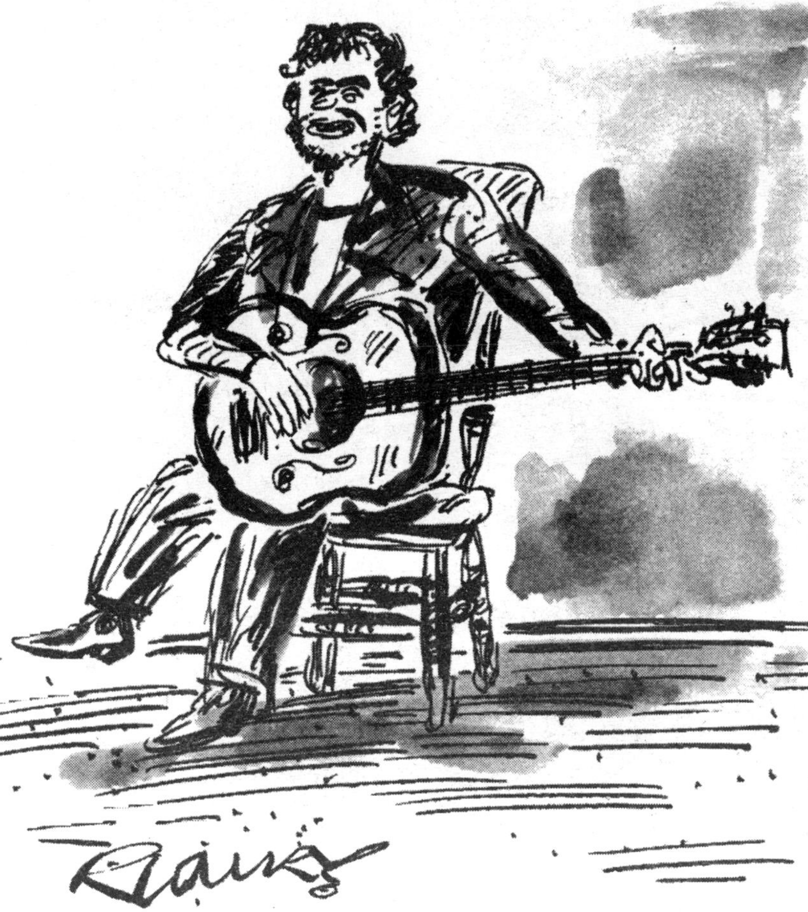

"Woke up this mornin'…."

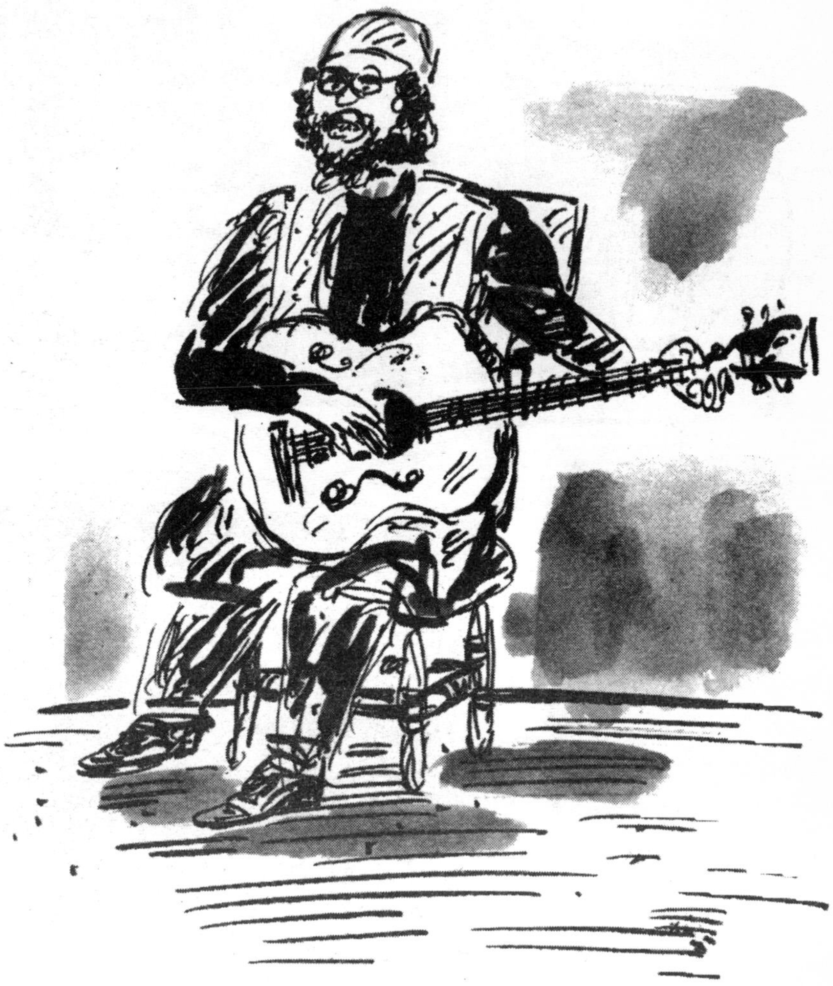

"Islam-bam-boom!"

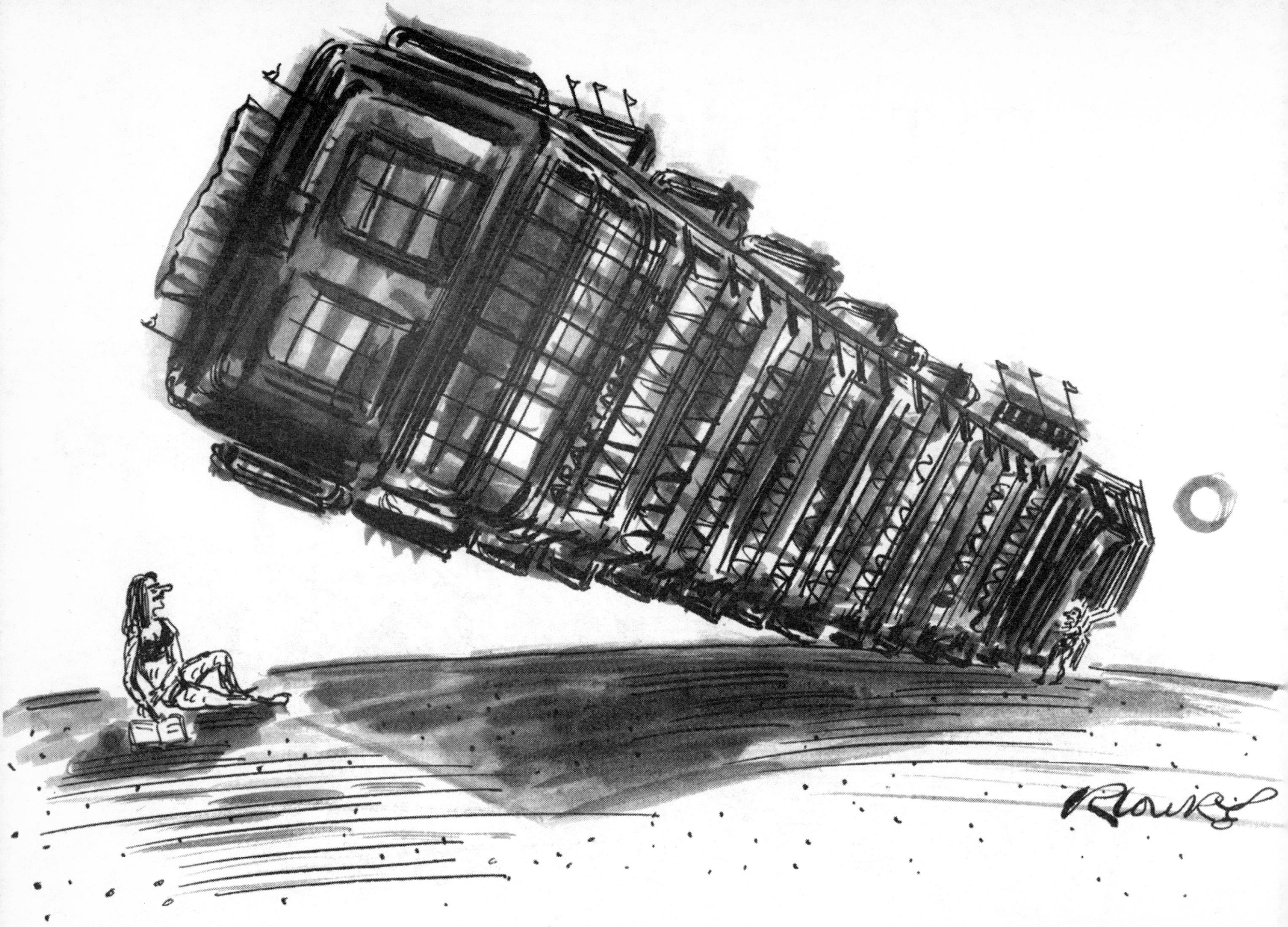

"It's quite safe – I'm wearing a condominium."

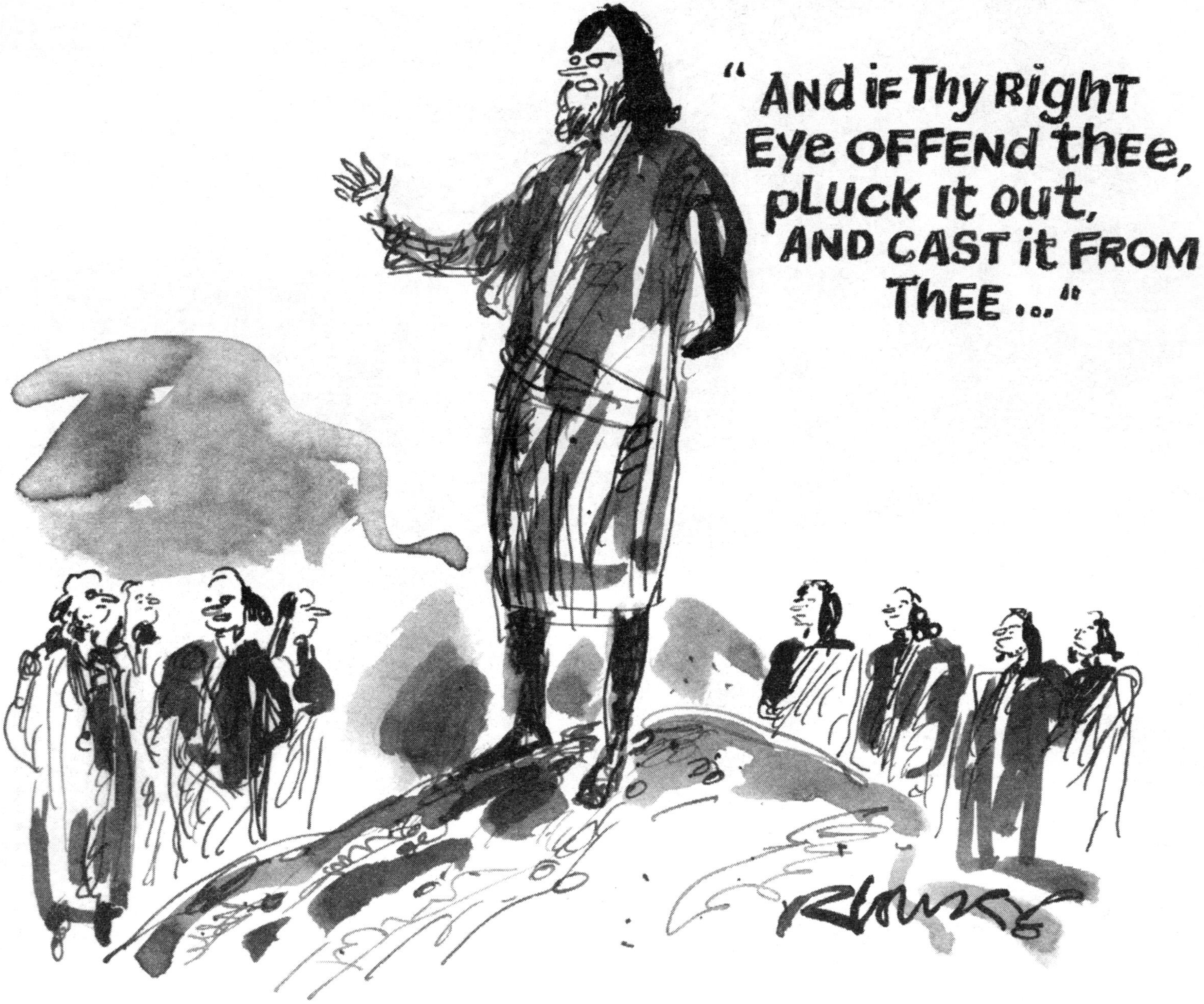
"And if Thy Right Eye OFFEND thee, pluck it out, AND CAST it FROM ThEE ..."

"He's like a cross between Steven Wright and Woody Allen – only not as funny as either of them."

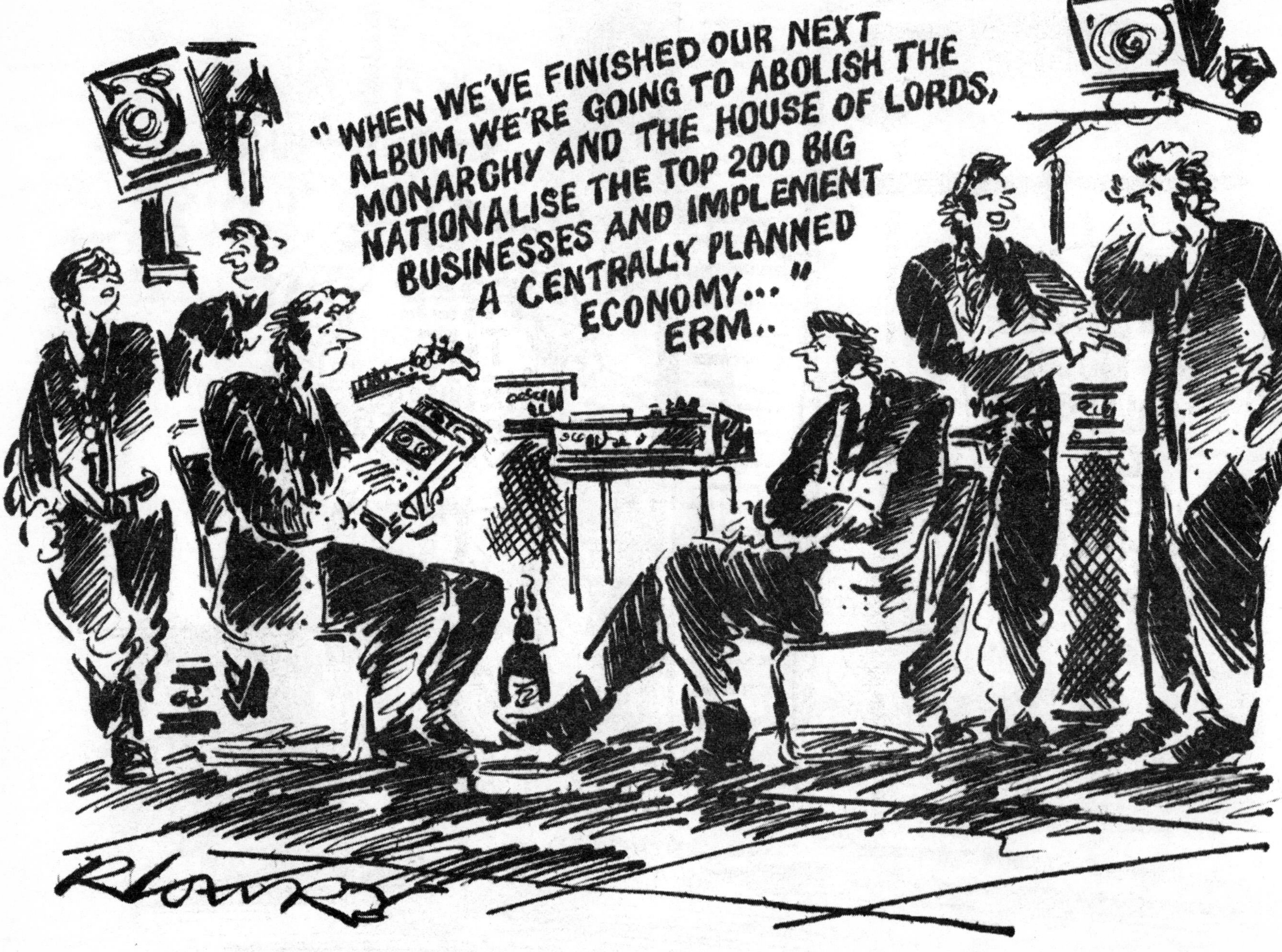
"WHEN WE'VE FINISHED OUR NEXT ALBUM, WE'RE GOING TO ABOLISH THE MONARCHY AND THE HOUSE OF LORDS, NATIONALISE THE TOP 200 BIG BUSINESSES AND IMPLEMENT A CENTRALLY PLANNED ECONOMY..." ERM..

"Search me – it's something to do with the New Positivism that's sweeping the nation's youth."

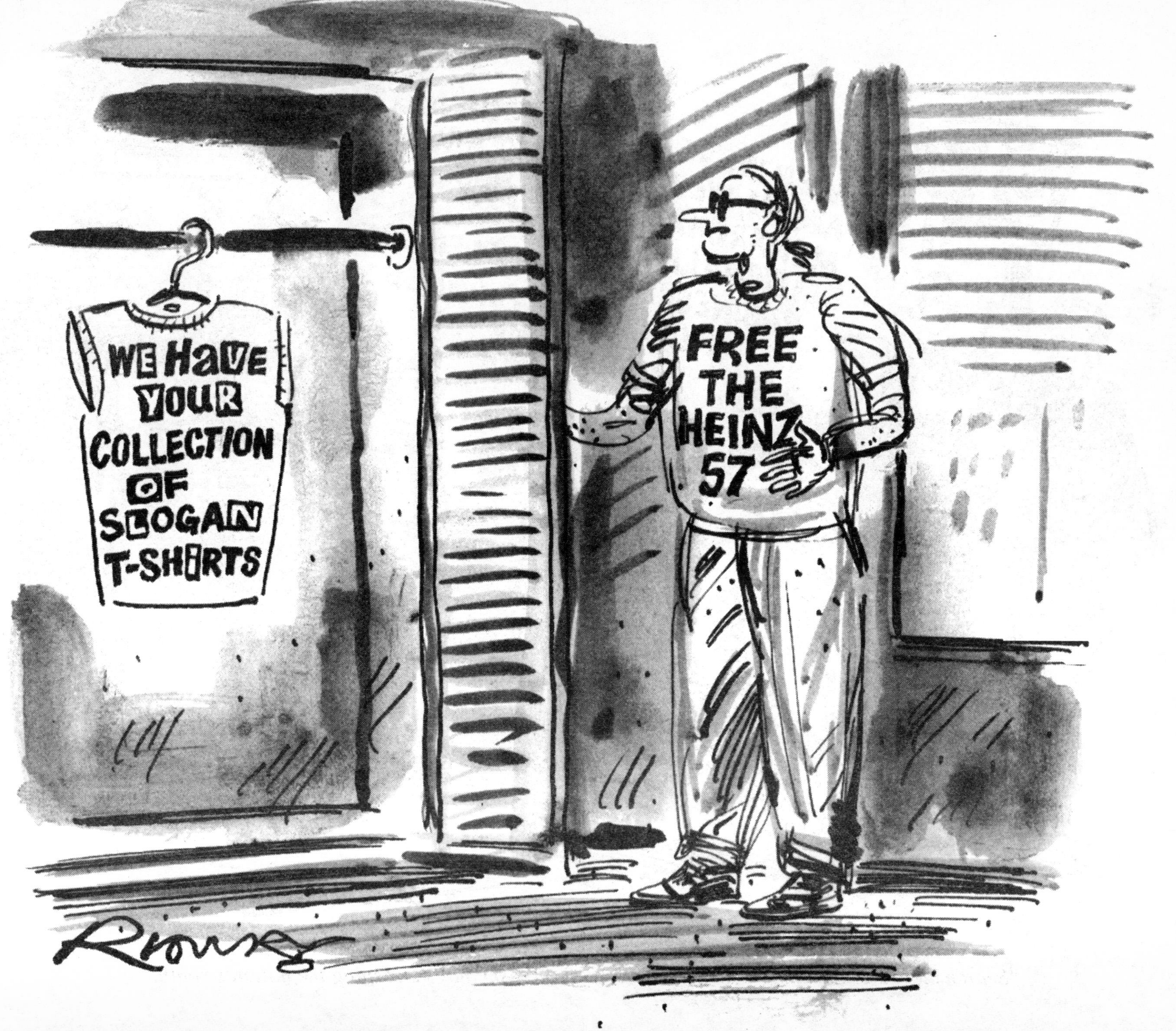
WE HAVE YOUR COLLECTION OF SLOGAN T-SHIRTS
FREE THE HEINZ 57

I drew a number of differing styles of strips for the NME in the late nineteen seventies through to the middle of the 'eighties and some of these were published in a small collection called Only Rock 'n' Roll in 1980. The conventional style strip eventually mutated into the Biff inspired collage style insanity originally titled Note Oilskin Base and later retitled 78 RPM. This was cobbled together from other strips, adverts and text illustrations from a pile of mid to late nineteen-fifties Tit Bits magazines that my old man had shoved in an attic at home and forgotten about. This purported to show the weekly travails of a would-be rock star and socialist revolutionary, one Monty Montgomery. A fair number of them have been lost or mislaid but I think the ones that are left are worth reproducing here – despite the lack of continuity and general confusion of story line (or lack of same).

I went back to a conventional hand drawn style of strip once I'd reduced the pile of Tit Bits to a shredded heap.

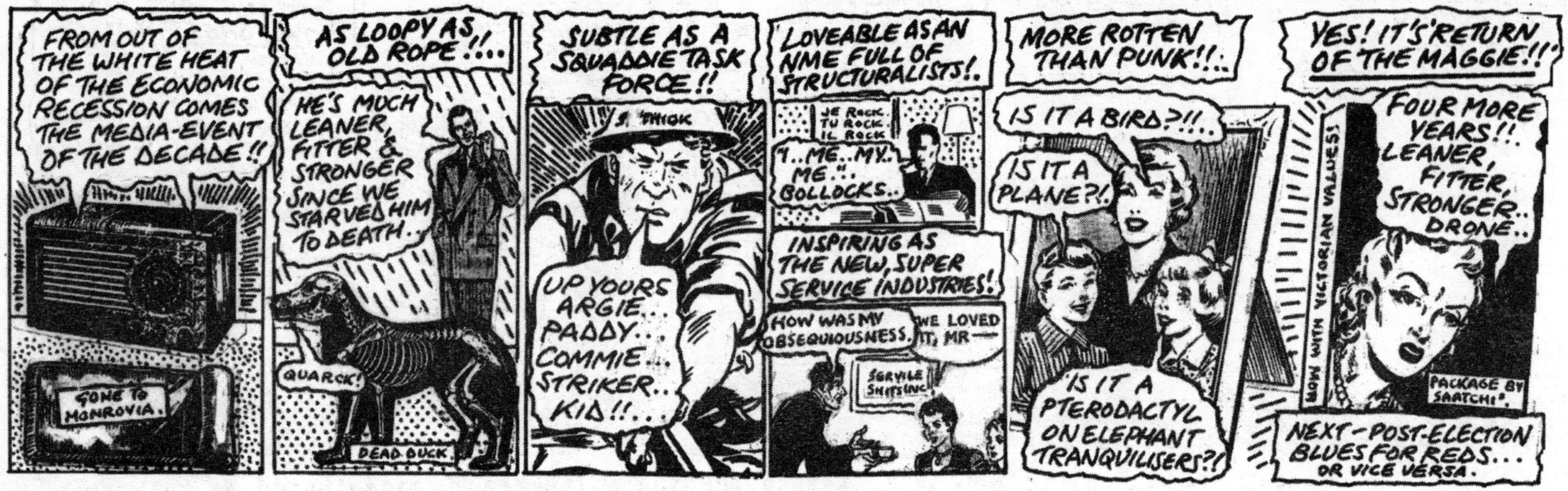
FROM OUT OF THE WHITE HEAT OF THE ECONOMIC RECESSION COMES THE MEDIA-EVENT OF THE DECADE!!
GONE TO MONROVIA.
AS LOOPY AS OLD ROPE!!...
HE'S MUCH LEANER, FITTER & STRONGER SINCE WE STARVED HIM TO DEATH..
QUARCK!
DEAD DUCK
SUBTLE AS A SQUADDIE TASK FORCE!!
UP YOURS ARGIE.. PADDY.. COMMIE.. STRIKER.. KID!!...
LOVEABLE AS AN NME FULL OF STRUCTURALISTS!.
"I..ME..MY.. ME".. BOLLOCKS..
INSPIRING AS THE NEW, SUPER SERVICE INDUSTRIES!
HOW WAS MY OBSEQUIOUSNESS.
WE LOVED IT, MR—
SERVILE SHITS INC.
MORE ROTTEN THAN PUNK!!...
IS IT A BIRD?!!..
IS IT A PLANE?!.
IS IT A PTERODACTYL ON ELEPHANT TRANQUILISERS?!
YES! IT'S RETURN OF THE MAGGIE!!
FOUR MORE YEARS!! LEANER, FITTER, STRONGER.. DRONE..
NOW WITH VICTORIAN VALUES!
PACKAGE BY SAATCHI
NEXT - POST-ELECTION BLUES FOR REDS... OR VICE VERSA.

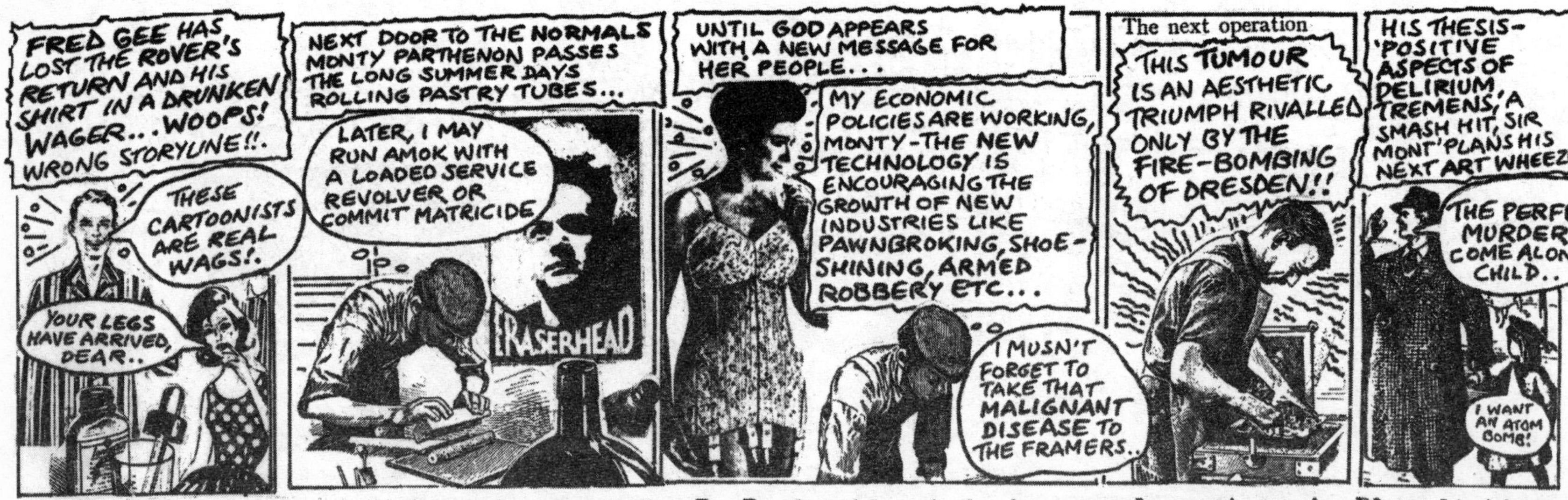
FRED GEE HAS LOST THE ROVER'S RETURN AND HIS SHIRT IN A DRUNKEN WAGER... WOOPS! WRONG STORYLINE!!.
THESE CARTOONISTS ARE REAL WAGS!.
YOUR LEGS HAVE ARRIVED, DEAR..
NEXT DOOR TO THE NORMALS MONTY PARTHENON PASSES THE LONG SUMMER DAYS ROLLING PASTRY TUBES...
LATER, I MAY RUN AMOK WITH A LOADED SERVICE REVOLVER OR COMMIT MATRICIDE
ERASERHEAD
UNTIL GOD APPEARS WITH A NEW MESSAGE FOR HER PEOPLE...
MY ECONOMIC POLICIES ARE WORKING, MONTY - THE NEW TECHNOLOGY IS ENCOURAGING THE GROWTH OF NEW INDUSTRIES LIKE PAWNBROKING, SHOE-SHINING, ARMED ROBBERY ETC...
I MUSN'T FORGET TO TAKE THAT MALIGNANT DISEASE TO THE FRAMERS..
The next operation
THIS TUMOUR IS AN AESTHETIC TRIUMPH RIVALLED ONLY BY THE FIRE-BOMBING OF DRESDEN!!
HIS THESIS- 'POSITIVE ASPECTS OF DELIRIUM TREMENS,' A SMASH HIT, SIR MONT' PLANS HIS NEXT ART WHEEZE..
THE PERFECT MURDER!!.. COME ALONG CHILD..
I WANT AN ATOM BOMB!

Next Week: Sir Monty De Parthenon and the Ra Ra Skirt, a study in sexual psychomania. Plus: Lighting a fire with two old-aged pensioners.

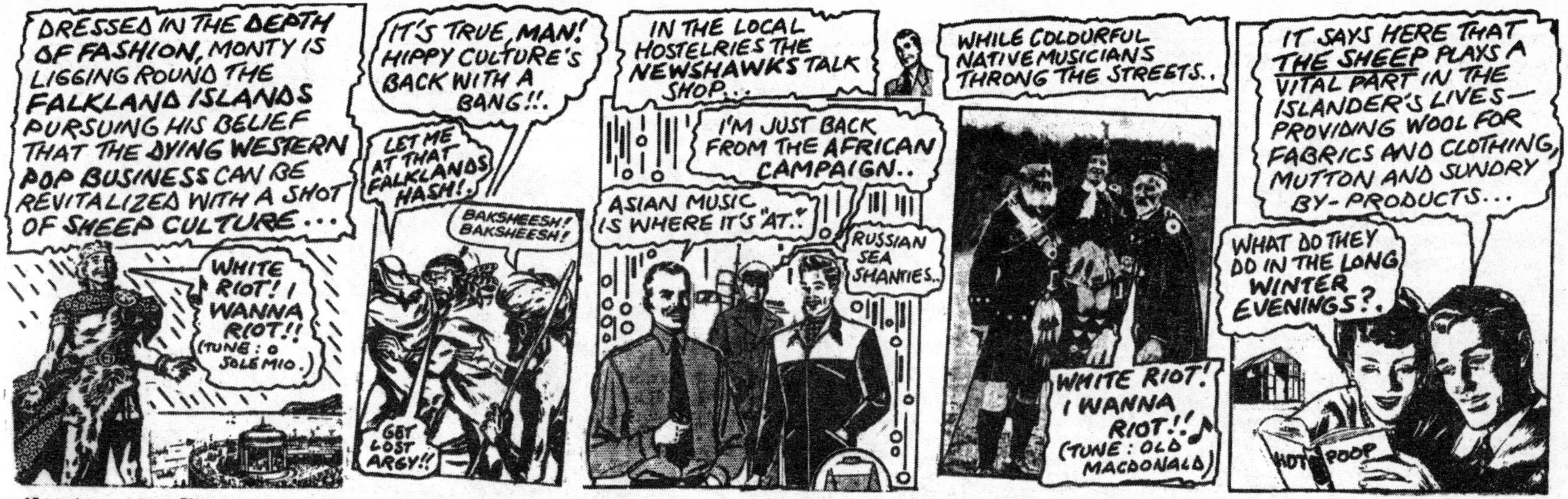
DRESSED IN THE DEPTH OF FASHION, MONTY IS LIGGING ROUND THE FALKLAND ISLANDS PURSUING HIS BELIEF THAT THE DYING WESTERN POP BUSINESS CAN BE REVITALIZED WITH A SHOT OF SHEEP CULTURE...
WHITE RIOT! I WANNA RIOT!! (TUNE: O SOLE MIO.)
IT'S TRUE, MAN! HIPPY CULTURE'S BACK WITH A BANG!!.
LET ME AT THAT FALKLANDS HASH!.
BAKSHEESH! BAKSHEESH!
GET LOST ARGY!!
IN THE LOCAL HOSTELRIES THE NEWSHAWKS TALK SHOP...
I'M JUST BACK FROM THE AFRICAN CAMPAIGN..
ASIAN MUSIC IS WHERE IT'S "AT."
RUSSIAN SEA SHANTIES..
WHILE COLOURFUL NATIVE MUSICIANS THRONG THE STREETS..
WHITE RIOT! I WANNA RIOT!! (TUNE: OLD MACDONALD)
IT SAYS HERE THAT THE SHEEP PLAYS A VITAL PART IN THE ISLANDER'S LIVES— PROVIDING WOOL FOR FABRICS AND CLOTHING, MUTTON AND SUNDRY BY-PRODUCTS...
WHAT DO THEY DO IN THE LONG WINTER EVENINGS?.
HOT POOP

Next week: The economy collapses, riots in the streets, leading politicians assassinated. We talk to a Falkland islander about passing the long winter evenings with a sheep and wellington boots.

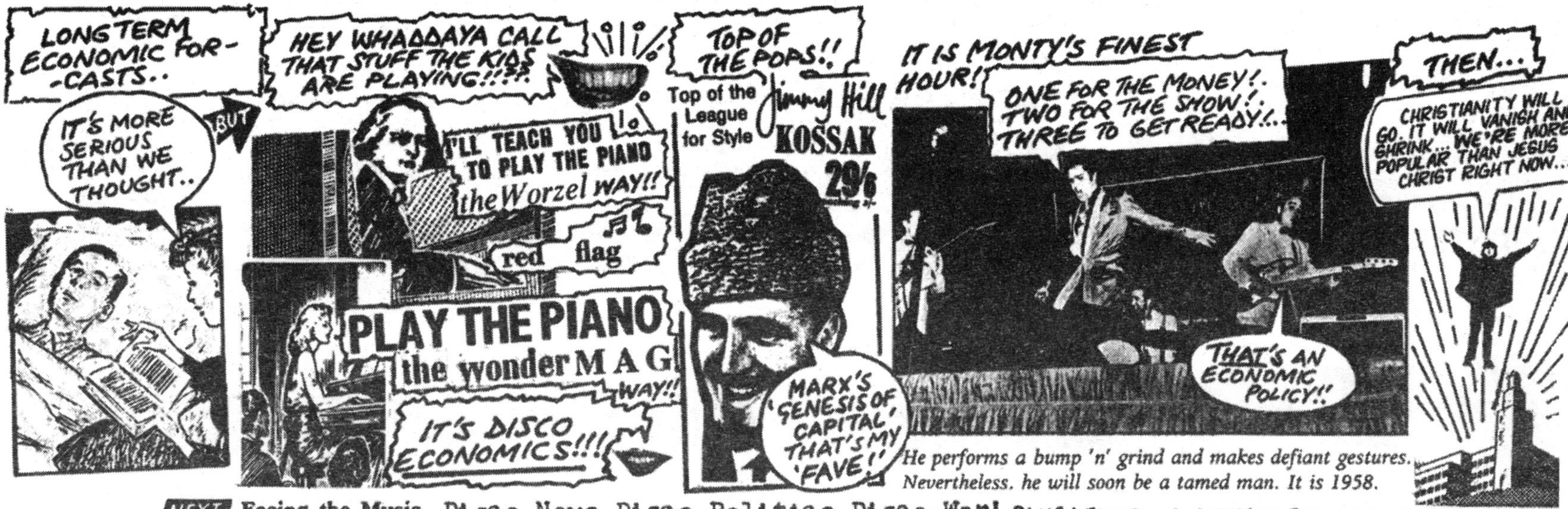
LONG TERM ECONOMIC FOR-CASTS..
IT'S MORE SERIOUS THAN WE THOUGHT..
BUT
HEY WHADDAYA CALL THAT STUFF THE KIDS ARE PLAYING!!??
I'LL TEACH YOU TO PLAY THE PIANO the Worzel WAY!!
red flag
PLAY THE PIANO the wonder MAG WAY!!
IT'S DISCO ECONOMICS!!!
TOP OF THE POPS!!
Top of the League for Style
Jimmy Hill
KOSSAK
29/6
MARX'S GENESIS OF CAPITAL, THAT'S MY 'FAVE'!!
IT IS MONTY'S FINEST HOUR!
ONE FOR THE MONEY!. TWO FOR THE SHOW!. THREE TO GET READY!..
THAT'S AN ECONOMIC POLICY!!
He performs a bump 'n' grind and makes defiant gestures. Nevertheless, he will soon be a tamed man. It is 1958.
THEN...
CHRISTIANITY WILL GO. IT WILL VANISH AND SHRINK... WE'RE MORE POPULAR THAN JESUS CHRIST RIGHT NOW...

NEXT Facing the Music Disco-News, Disco-Politics, Disco-War! PLUS: CHARLES ALWAYS SEEMS ALRIGHT TO GAV

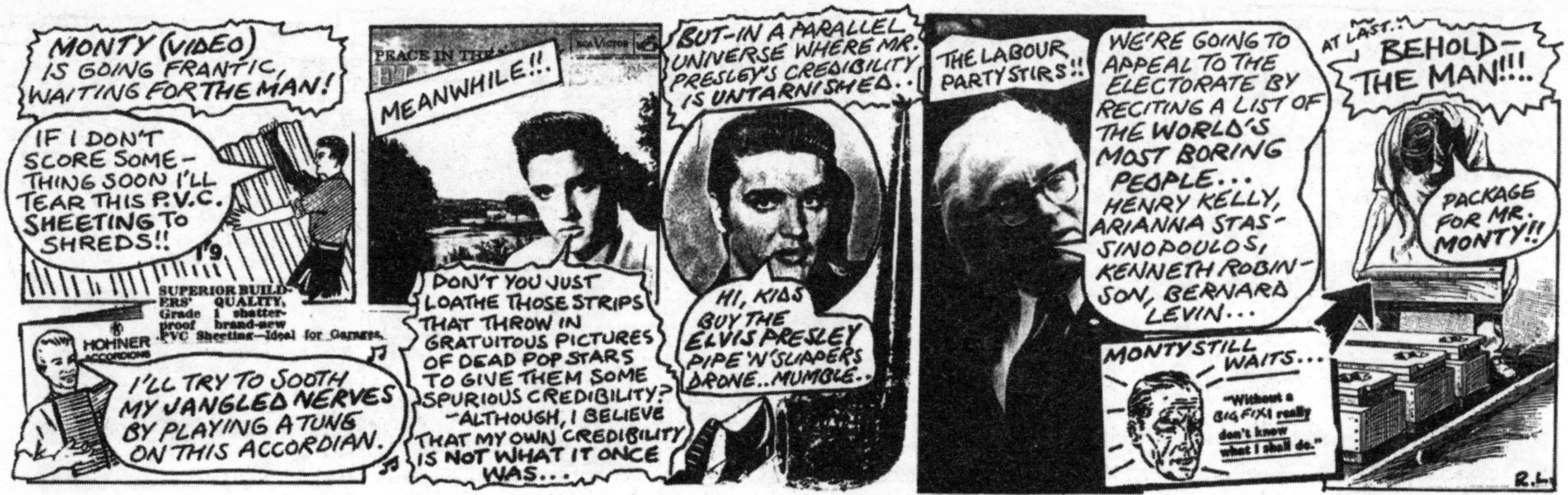
MONTY (VIDEO) IS GOING FRANTIC, WAITING FOR THE MAN!
IF I DON'T SCORE SOME-THING SOON I'LL TEAR THIS P.V.C. SHEETING TO SHREDS!!
1'9
SUPERIOR BUILDERS' QUALITY, Grade 1 shatter-proof brand-new PVC Sheeting—Ideal for Garages.
HOHNER ACCORDIONS
I'LL TRY TO SOOTH MY JANGLED NERVES BY PLAYING A TUNE ON THIS ACCORDIAN.
MEANWHILE!!
DON'T YOU JUST LOATHE THOSE STRIPS THAT THROW IN GRATUITOUS PICTURES OF DEAD POP STARS TO GIVE THEM SOME SPURIOUS CREDIBILITY? —ALTHOUGH, I BELIEVE THAT MY OWN CREDIBILITY IS NOT WHAT IT ONCE WAS...
BUT—IN A PARALLEL UNIVERSE WHERE MR. PRESLEY'S CREDIBILITY IS UNTARNISHED..
HI, KIDS BUY THE ELVIS PRESLEY PIPE 'N' SLIPPERS DRONE...MUMBLE..
THE LABOUR PARTY STIRS!!
WE'RE GOING TO APPEAL TO THE ELECTORATE BY RECITING A LIST OF THE WORLD'S MOST BORING PEOPLE... HENRY KELLY, ARIANNA STASSINOPOULOS, KENNETH ROBINSON, BERNARD LEVIN...
MONTY STILL WAITS...
"Without a BIG FIX I really don't know what I shall do."
AT LAST..
BEHOLD—THE MAN!!!..
PACKAGE FOR MR. MONTY!!
R.L.

Owing to reports of imminent rail strike/nuclear strike/Second Coming etc,etc,etc,thisstrip drawn AGES ago.23/6/82.Next issue:Monty scores for England!!

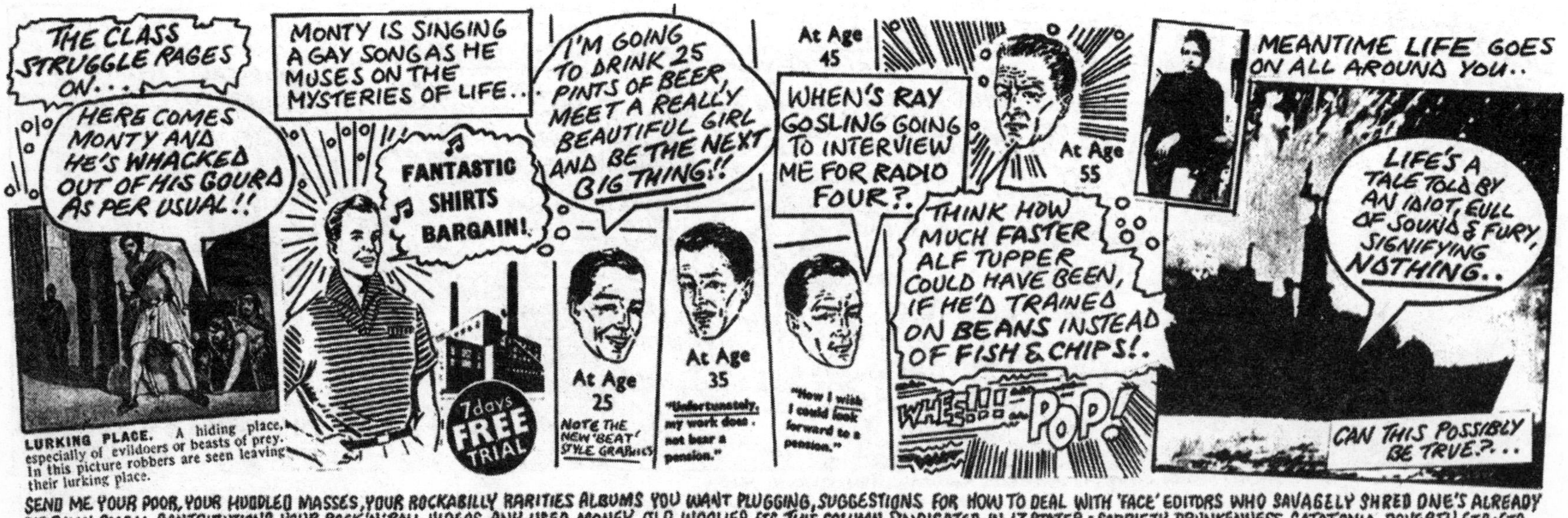
THE CLASS STRUGGLE RAGES ON...
HERE COMES MONTY AND HE'S WHACKED OUT OF HIS GOURD AS PER USUAL!!
LURKING PLACE. A hiding place, especially of evildoers or beasts of prey. In this picture robbers are seen leaving their lurking place.
MONTY IS SINGING A GAY SONG AS HE MUSES ON THE MYSTERIES OF LIFE..
FANTASTIC SHIRTS BARGAIN!
7days FREE TRIAL
I'M GOING TO DRINK 25 PINTS OF BEER, MEET A REALLY BEAUTIFUL GIRL AND BE THE NEXT BIG THING!!
At Age 25
NOTE THE NEW 'BEAT' STYLE GRAPHICS
At Age 35
"Unfortunately, my work does not bear a pension."
At Age 45
WHEN'S RAY GOSLING GOING TO INTERVIEW ME FOR RADIO FOUR?.
"How I wish I could look forward to a pension."
At Age 55
THINK HOW MUCH FASTER ALF TUPPER COULD HAVE BEEN, IF HE'D TRAINED ON BEANS INSTEAD OF FISH & CHIPS!.
WHEE!!!... POP!
MEANTIME LIFE GOES ON ALL AROUND YOU..
LIFE'S A TALE TOLD BY AN IDIOT, FULL OF SOUND & FURY, SIGNIFYING NOTHING..
CAN THIS POSSIBLY BE TRUE?...

SEND ME YOUR POOR, YOUR HUDDLED MASSES, YOUR ROCKABILLY RARITIES ALBUMS YOU WANT PLUGGING, SUGGESTIONS FOR HOW TO DEAL WITH 'FACE' EDITORS WHO SAVAGELY SHRED ONE'S ALREADY PITIFULLY SMALL CONTRIBUTIONS, YOUR ROCK'N'ROLL VIDEOS, ANY USED MONEY, OLD WOOLIES ETC. THIS COLUMN SINDICATED IN 17 STATES : SOBRIETY, DRUNKENNESS, CATATONIA, POVERTY ETC·ETC·

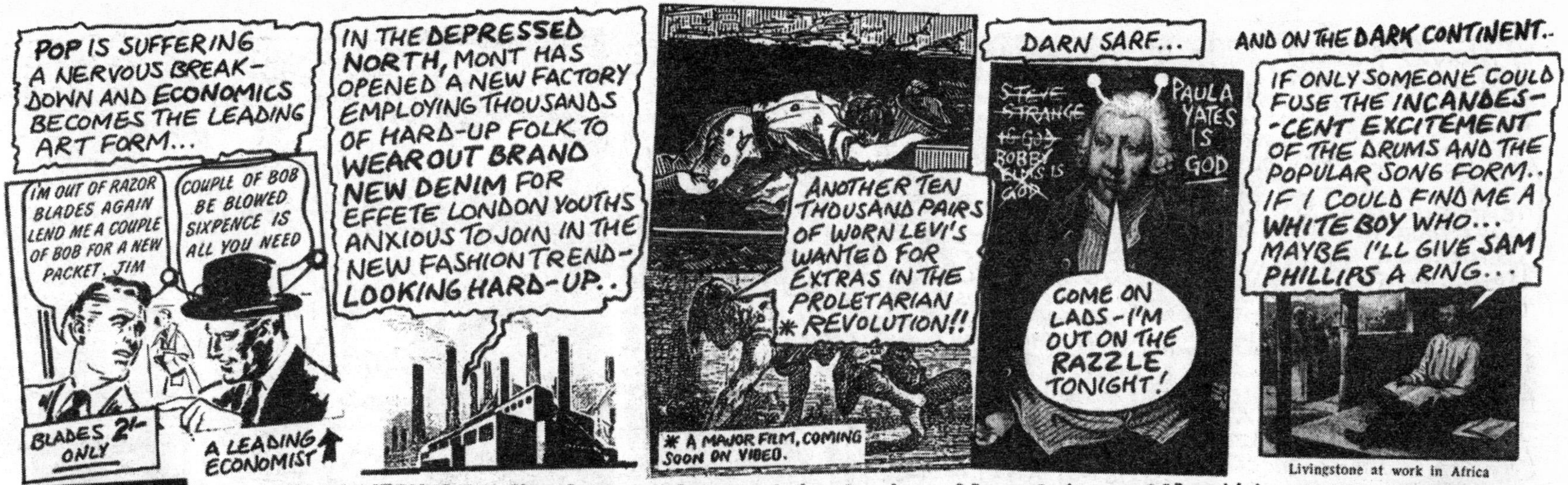
POP IS SUFFERING A NERVOUS BREAK-DOWN AND ECONOMICS BECOMES THE LEADING ART FORM...
I'M OUT OF RAZOR BLADES AGAIN LEND ME A COUPLE OF BOB FOR A NEW PACKET, JIM
COUPLE OF BOB BE BLOWED SIXPENCE IS ALL YOU NEED
BLADES 2/- ONLY
A LEADING ECONOMIST
IN THE DEPRESSED NORTH, MONT HAS OPENED A NEW FACTORY EMPLOYING THOUSANDS OF HARD-UP FOLK TO WEAR OUT BRAND NEW DENIM FOR EFFETE LONDON YOUTHS ANXIOUS TO JOIN IN THE NEW FASHION TREND-LOOKING HARD-UP..
ANOTHER TEN THOUSAND PAIRS OF WORN LEVI'S WANTED FOR EXTRAS IN THE PROLETARIAN * REVOLUTION!!
* A MAJOR FILM, COMING SOON ON VIDEO.
DARN SARF...
STEVE STRANGE IS GOD
PAULA YATES IS GOD
COME ON LADS - I'M OUT ON THE RAZZLE TONIGHT!
AND ON THE DARK CONTINENT..
IF ONLY SOMEONE COULD FUSE THE INCANDES--CENT EXCITEMENT OF THE DRUMS AND THE POPULAR SONG FORM.. IF I COULD FIND ME A WHITE BOY WHO... MAYBE I'LL GIVE SAM PHILLIPS A RING...
Livingstone at work in Africa

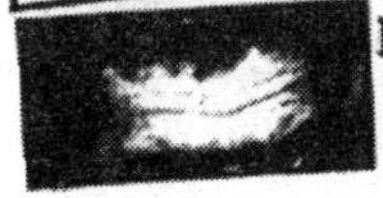

Next: THOSE WRINKLES! Should middle-aged hacks be allowed to peddle this filth to today's pop kids? Should all deejays and Stephen Pile be hit repeatedly with flat stones? Errol revival, anyone?

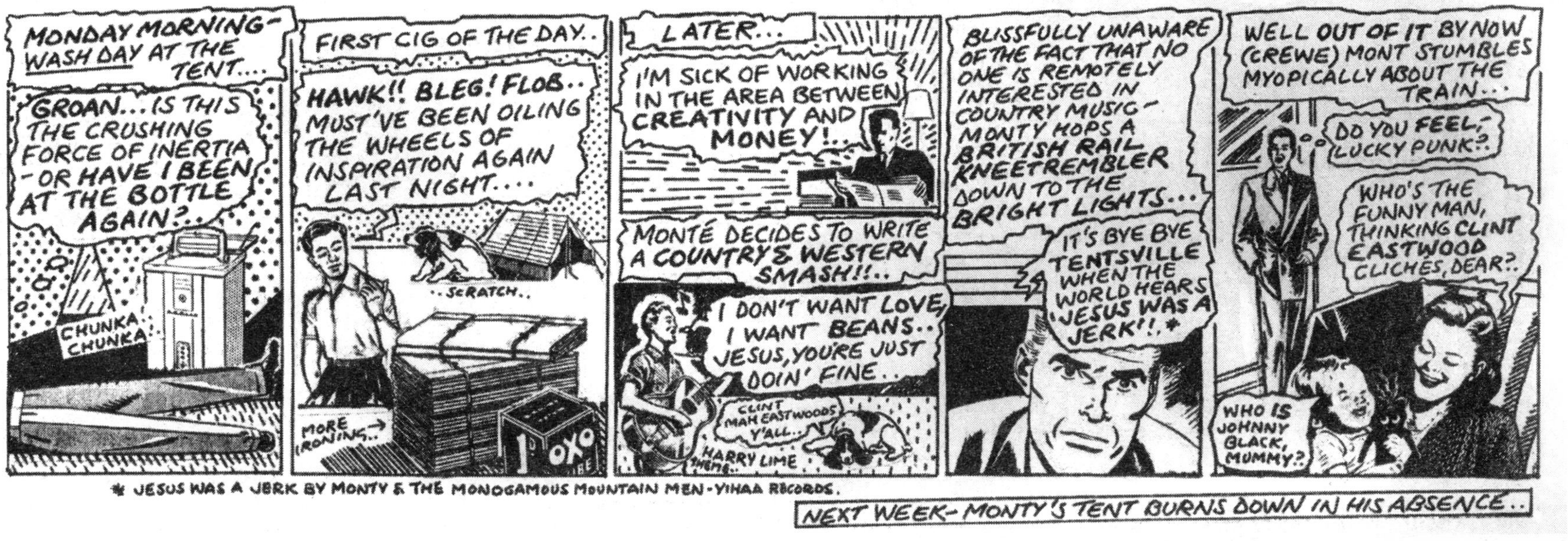
MONDAY MORNING-WASH DAY AT THE TENT...
GROAN... IS THIS THE CRUSHING FORCE OF INERTIA - OR HAVE I BEEN AT THE BOTTLE AGAIN?..
CHUNKA CHUNKA
FIRST CIG OF THE DAY..
HAWK!! BLEG! FLOB.. MUST'VE BEEN OILING THE WHEELS OF INSPIRATION AGAIN LAST NIGHT....
..SCRATCH..
MORE IRONING..
OXO
LATER...
I'M SICK OF WORKING IN THE AREA BETWEEN CREATIVITY AND MONEY!..
MONTÉ DECIDES TO WRITE A COUNTRY & WESTERN SMASH!!..
I DON'T WANT LOVE, I WANT BEANS.. JESUS, YOU'RE JUST DOIN' FINE..
CLINT MAH EASTWOODS Y'ALL..
HARRY LIME THEME..
BLISSFULLY UNAWARE OF THE FACT THAT NO ONE IS REMOTELY INTERESTED IN COUNTRY MUSIC-MONTY HOPS A BRITISH RAIL KNEETREMBLER DOWN TO THE BRIGHT LIGHTS...
IT'S BYE BYE TENTSVILLE WHEN THE WORLD HEARS JESUS WAS A JERK'!.*
WELL OUT OF IT BY NOW (CREWE) MONT STUMBLES MYOPICALLY ABOUT THE TRAIN...
DO YOU FEEL, LUCKY PUNK?
WHO'S THE FUNNY MAN, THINKING CLINT EASTWOOD CLICHES, DEAR?..
WHO IS JOHNNY BLACK, MUMMY?
* JESUS WAS A JERK BY MONTY & THE MONOGAMOUS MOUNTAIN MEN-YIHAA RECORDS.
NEXT WEEK- MONTY'S TENT BURNS DOWN IN HIS ABSENCE..

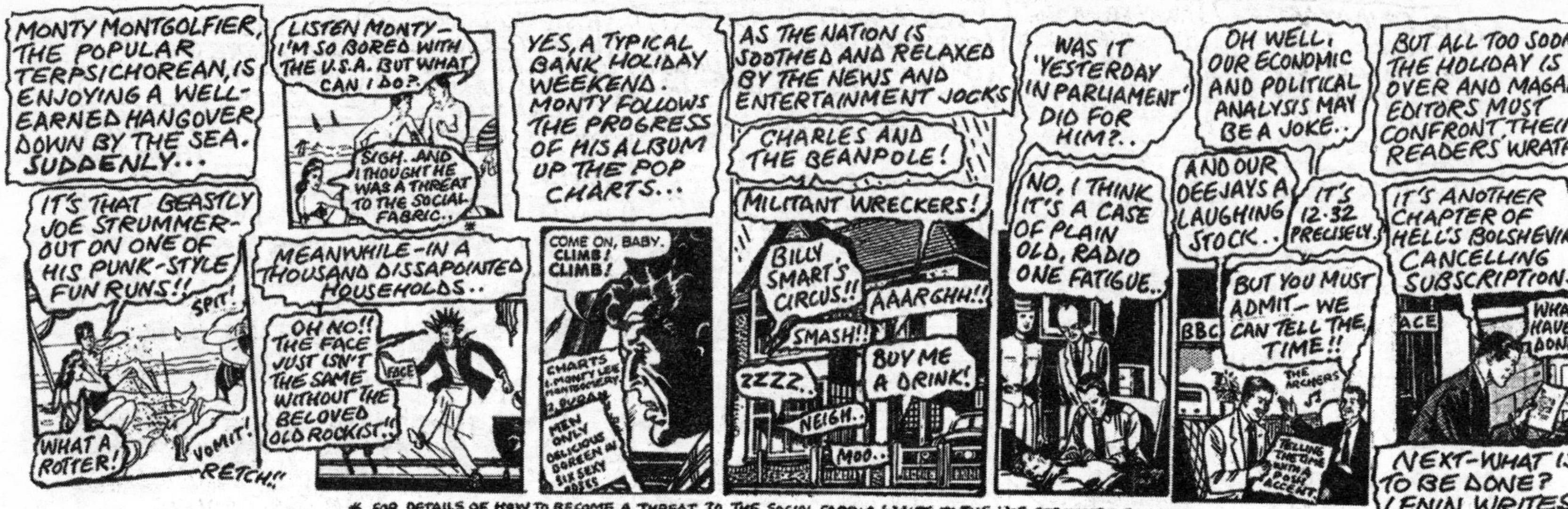
MONTY MONTGOLFIER, THE POPULAR TERPSICHOREAN, IS ENJOYING A WELL-EARNED HANGOVER DOWN BY THE SEA. SUDDENLY...
IT'S THAT BEASTLY JOE STRUMMER- OUT ON ONE OF HIS PUNK-STYLE FUN RUNS!!
SPIT!
WHAT A ROTTER!
VOMIT!
RETCH!!
LISTEN MONTY- I'M SO BORED WITH THE U.S.A. BUT WHAT CAN I DO?
SIGH.. AND I THOUGHT HE WAS A THREAT TO THE SOCIAL FABRIC..*
MEANWHILE- IN A THOUSAND DISSAPOINTED HOUSEHOLDS..
OH NO!! THE FACE JUST ISN'T THE SAME WITHOUT THE BELOVED OLD ROCKIST!
FACE
YES, A TYPICAL BANK HOLIDAY WEEKEND. MONTY FOLLOWS THE PROGRESS OF HIS ALBUM UP THE POP CHARTS...
COME ON, BABY. CLIMB! CLIMB!
AS THE NATION IS SOOTHED AND RELAXED BY THE NEWS AND ENTERTAINMENT JOCKS
CHARLES AND THE BEANPOLE!
MILITANT WRECKERS!
BILLY SMART'S CIRCUS!!
AAARGHH!!
SMASH!!
BUY ME A DRINK!
ZZZZ..
NEIGH..
MOO..
WAS IT 'YESTERDAY IN PARLIAMENT' DID FOR HIM?..
NO, I THINK IT'S A CASE OF PLAIN OLD, RADIO ONE FATIGUE..
OH WELL, OUR ECONOMIC AND POLITICAL ANALYSIS MAY BE A JOKE..
AND OUR DEEJAYS A LAUGHING STOCK..
IT'S 12·32 PRECISELY.
BUT YOU MUST ADMIT- WE CAN TELL THE TIME!!
BBC
BUT ALL TOO SOON THE HOLIDAY IS OVER AND MAGAZINE EDITORS MUST CONFRONT THEIR READERS WRATH..
IT'S ANOTHER CHAPTER OF HELL'S BOLSHEVIKS CANCELLING SUBSCRIPTIONS!!
WHAT HAVE I DONE?
ACE
NEXT- WHAT IS TO BE DONE? LENIN WRITES..

* FOR DETAILS OF HOW TO BECOME A THREAT TO THE SOCIAL FABRIC WRITE TO THE 'JOE STRUMMER FUN RUN'.

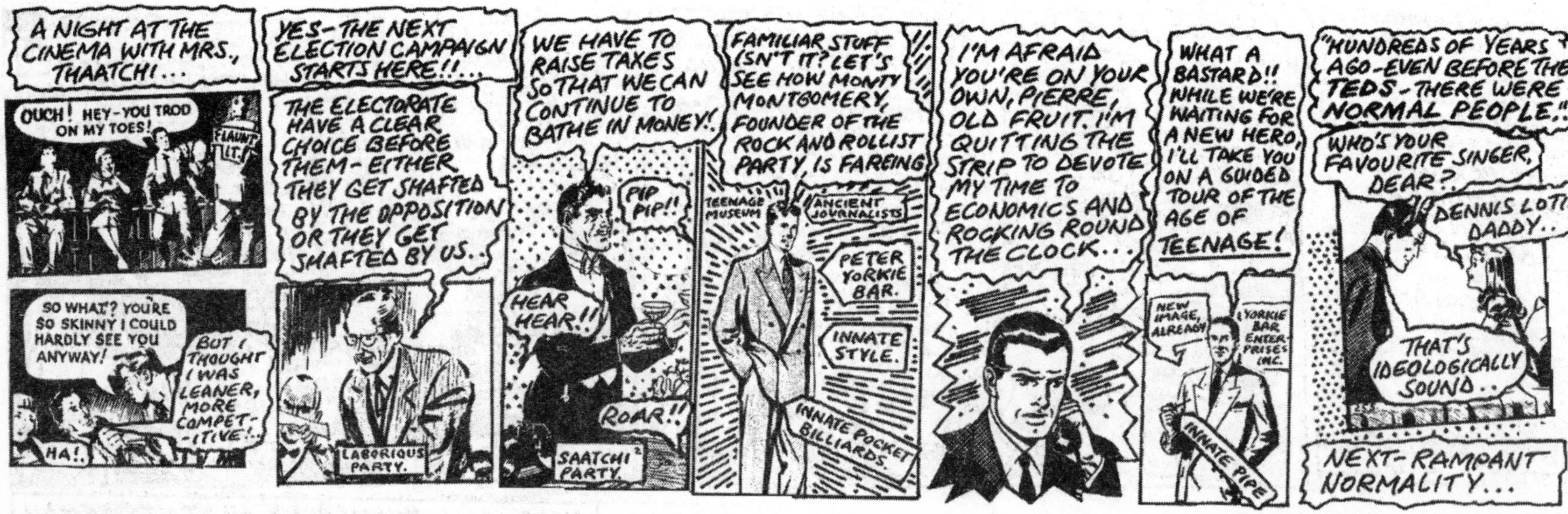
A NIGHT AT THE CINEMA WITH MRS., THAATCH!...
OUCH! HEY- YOU TROD ON MY TOES!
FLAUNT IT.
SO WHAT? YOU'RE SO SKINNY I COULD HARDLY SEE YOU ANYWAY!
BUT I THOUGHT I WAS LEANER, MORE COMPET- -ITIVE!
HA!
YES- THE NEXT ELECTION CAMPAIGN STARTS HERE!!...
THE ELECTORATE HAVE A CLEAR CHOICE BEFORE THEM- EITHER THEY GET SHAFTED BY THE OPPOSITION OR THEY GET SHAFTED BY US..
LABORIOUS PARTY.
WE HAVE TO RAISE TAXES SO THAT WE CAN CONTINUE TO BATHE IN MONEY!
PIP PIP!!
HEAR HEAR!!
ROAR!!
SAATCHI² PARTY.
FAMILIAR STUFF ISN'T IT? LET'S SEE HOW MONTY MONTGOMERY, FOUNDER OF THE ROCK AND ROLLIST PARTY, IS FAREING
TEENAGE MUSEUM
ANCIENT JOURNALISTS
PETER YORKIE BAR.
INNATE STYLE.
INNATE POCKET BILLIARDS.
I'M AFRAID YOU'RE ON YOUR OWN, PIERRE, OLD FRUIT. I'M QUITTING THE STRIP TO DEVOTE MY TIME TO ECONOMICS AND ROCKING ROUND THE CLOCK...
WHAT A BASTARD!! WHILE WE'RE WAITING FOR A NEW HERO, I'LL TAKE YOU ON A GUIDED TOUR OF THE AGE OF TEENAGE!
NEW IMAGE, ALREADY
YORKIE BAR ENTER- PRISES INC.
INNATE PIPE
"HUNDREDS OF YEARS AGO- EVEN BEFORE THE TEDS- THERE WERE NORMAL PEOPLE."
WHO'S YOUR FAVOURITE SINGER, DEAR?
DENNIS LOTIS, DADDY..
THAT'S IDEOLOGICALLY SOUND..
NEXT- RAMPANT NORMALITY...

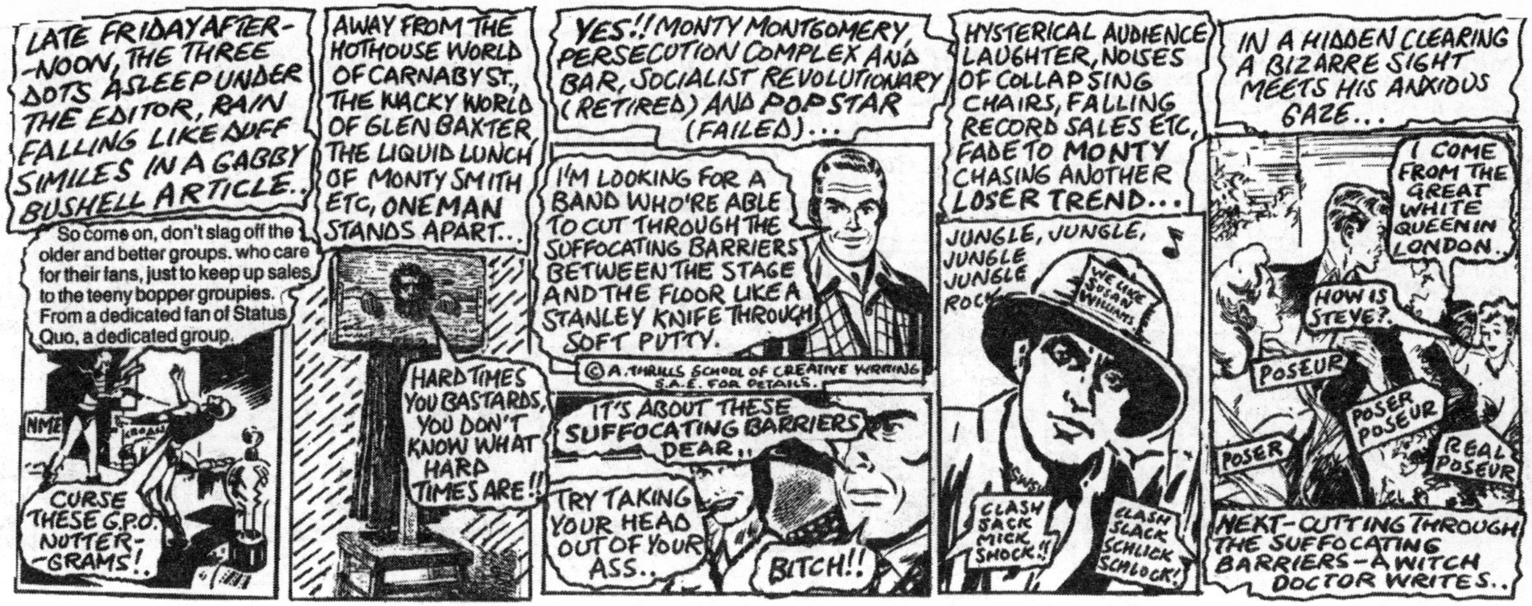
LATE FRIDAY AFTER-NOON, THE THREE DOTS ASLEEP UNDER THE EDITOR, RAIN FALLING LIKE DUFF SIMILES IN A GABBY BUSHELL ARTICLE..
So come on, don't slag off the older and better groups. who care for their fans, just to keep up sales to the teeny bopper groupies. From a dedicated fan of Status Quo, a dedicated group.
NME
CURSE THESE G.P.O. NUTTER-GRAMS!.
AWAY FROM THE HOTHOUSE WORLD OF CARNABY ST., THE WACKY WORLD OF GLEN BAXTER THE LIQUID LUNCH OF MONTY SMITH ETC, ONE MAN STANDS APART..
HARD TIMES YOU BASTARDS, YOU DON'T KNOW WHAT HARD TIMES ARE!!
YES!! MONTY MONTGOMERY, PERSECUTION COMPLEX AND BAR, SOCIALIST REVOLUTIONARY (RETIRED) AND POP STAR (FAILED)...
I'M LOOKING FOR A BAND WHO'RE ABLE TO CUT THROUGH THE SUFFOCATING BARRIERS BETWEEN THE STAGE AND THE FLOOR LIKE A STANLEY KNIFE THROUGH SOFT PUTTY.
© A. THRILLS SCHOOL OF CREATIVE WRITING S.A.E. FOR DETAILS.
IT'S ABOUT THESE SUFFOCATING BARRIERS DEAR..
TRY TAKING YOUR HEAD OUT OF YOUR ASS..
BITCH!!
HYSTERICAL AUDIENCE LAUGHTER, NOISES OF COLLAPSING CHAIRS, FALLING RECORD SALES ETC, FADE TO MONTY CHASING ANOTHER LOSER TREND...
JUNGLE, JUNGLE, JUNGLE JUNGLE ROCK
CLASH SACK MICK SHOCK!!
CLASH SLACK SCHLICK SCHLOCK!
IN A HIDDEN CLEARING A BIZARRE SIGHT MEETS HIS ANXIOUS GAZE...
I COME FROM THE GREAT WHITE QUEEN IN LONDON.
HOW IS STEVE?
POSEUR
POSER POSEUR
POSER
REAL POSEUR
NEXT—CUTTING THROUGH THE SUFFOCATING BARRIERS—A WITCH DOCTOR WRITES..

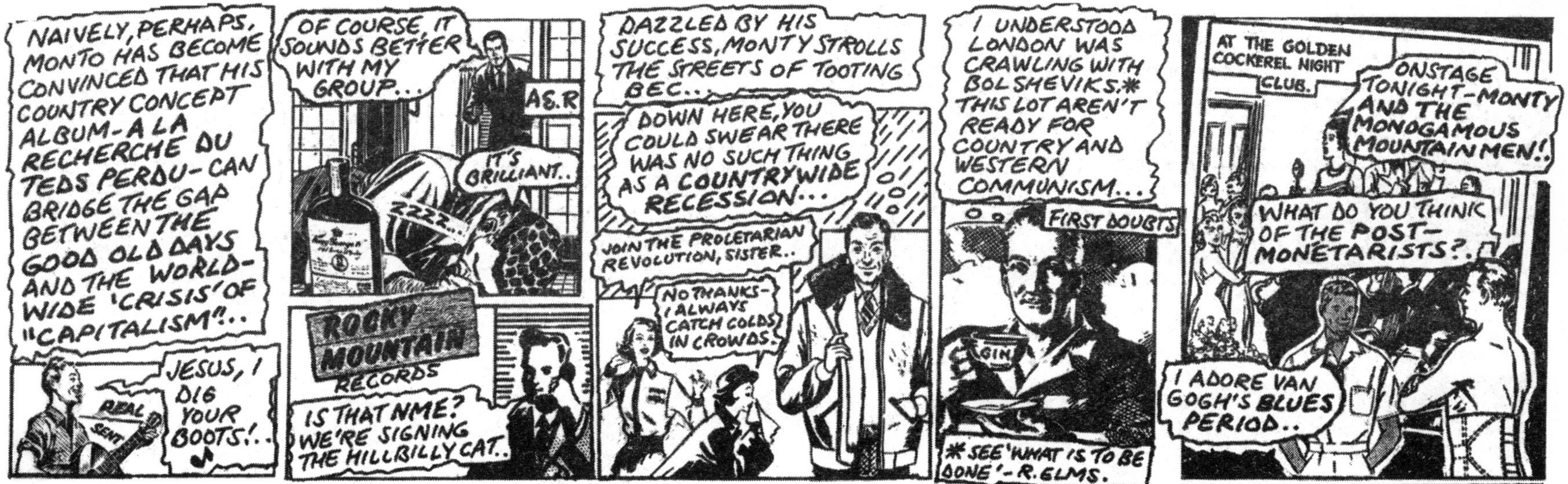
NAIVELY, PERHAPS, MONTO HAS BECOME CONVINCED THAT HIS COUNTRY CONCEPT ALBUM—A LA RECHERCHE DU TEDS PERDU—CAN BRIDGE THE GAP BETWEEN THE GOOD OLD DAYS AND THE WORLD-WIDE 'CRISIS' OF "CAPITALISM"!..
REAL SENT
JESUS, I DIG YOUR BOOTS!..
OF COURSE, IT SOUNDS BETTER WITH MY GROUP...
A&R
IT'S BRILLIANT..
ZZZZ...
ROCKY MOUNTAIN RECORDS
IS THAT NME? WE'RE SIGNING THE HILLBILLY CAT.
DAZZLED BY HIS SUCCESS, MONTY STROLLS THE STREETS OF TOOTING BEC..
DOWN HERE, YOU COULD SWEAR THERE WAS NO SUCH THING AS A COUNTRYWIDE RECESSION...
JOIN THE PROLETARIAN REVOLUTION, SISTER..
NO THANKS—I ALWAYS CATCH COLDS IN CROWDS.
I UNDERSTOOD LONDON WAS CRAWLING WITH BOLSHEVIKS.* THIS LOT AREN'T READY FOR COUNTRY AND WESTERN COMMUNISM...
FIRST DOUBTS
GIN
* SEE 'WHAT IS TO BE DONE' - R. ELMS.
AT THE GOLDEN COCKEREL NIGHT CLUB.
ONSTAGE TONIGHT—MONTY AND THE MONOGAMOUS MOUNTAIN MEN!.
WHAT DO YOU THINK OF THE POST-MONETARISTS?.
I ADORE VAN GOGH'S BLUES PERIOD..

NEXT—A LA RECHERCHE DU TENTS PERDU.

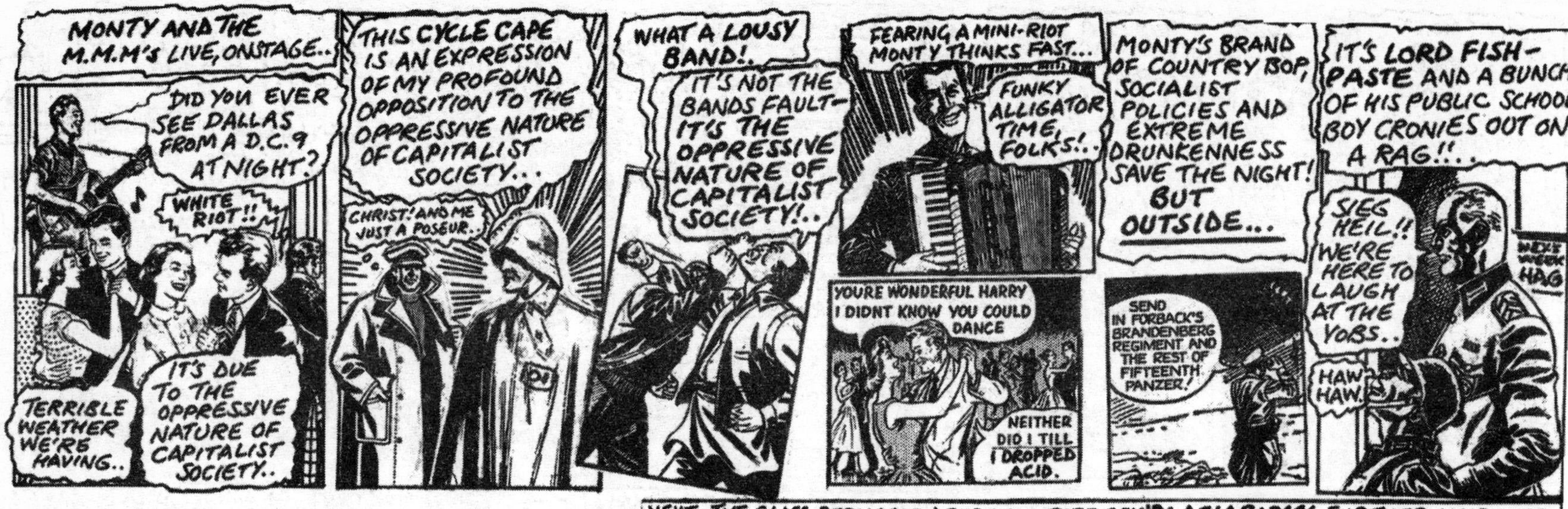
MONTY AND THE M.M.M's LIVE, ONSTAGE..
DID YOU EVER SEE DALLAS FROM A D.C.9 AT NIGHT?
WHITE RIOT!!
IT'S DUE TO THE OPPRESSIVE NATURE OF CAPITALIST SOCIETY..
TERRIBLE WEATHER WE'RE HAVING..
THIS CYCLE CAPE IS AN EXPRESSION OF MY PROFOUND OPPOSITION TO THE OPPRESSIVE NATURE OF CAPITALIST SOCIETY...
CHRIST! AND ME JUST A POSEUR..
WHAT A LOUSY BAND!.
IT'S NOT THE BANDS FAULT- IT'S THE OPPRESSIVE NATURE OF CAPITALIST SOCIETY!..
FEARING A MINI-RIOT MONTY THINKS FAST...
FUNKY ALLIGATOR TIME, FOLKS!..
YOU'RE WONDERFUL HARRY I DIDNT KNOW YOU COULD DANCE
NEITHER DID I TILL I DROPPED ACID.
MONTY'S BRAND OF COUNTRY BOP, SOCIALIST POLICIES AND EXTREME DRUNKENNESS SAVE THE NIGHT! BUT OUTSIDE...
SEND IN FORBACK'S BRANDENBERG REGIMENT AND THE REST OF FIFTEENTH PANZER!
IT'S LORD FISH-PASTE AND A BUNCH OF HIS PUBLIC SCHOOL-BOY CRONIES OUT ON A RAG!!...
SIEG HEIL!! WE'RE HERE TO LAUGH AT THE YOBS..
HAW HAW.

NEXT - THE CLASS STRUGGLE DEEPENS - BIFF CRY 'PLAGIARISM' - FURTHER HAIR LOSS.

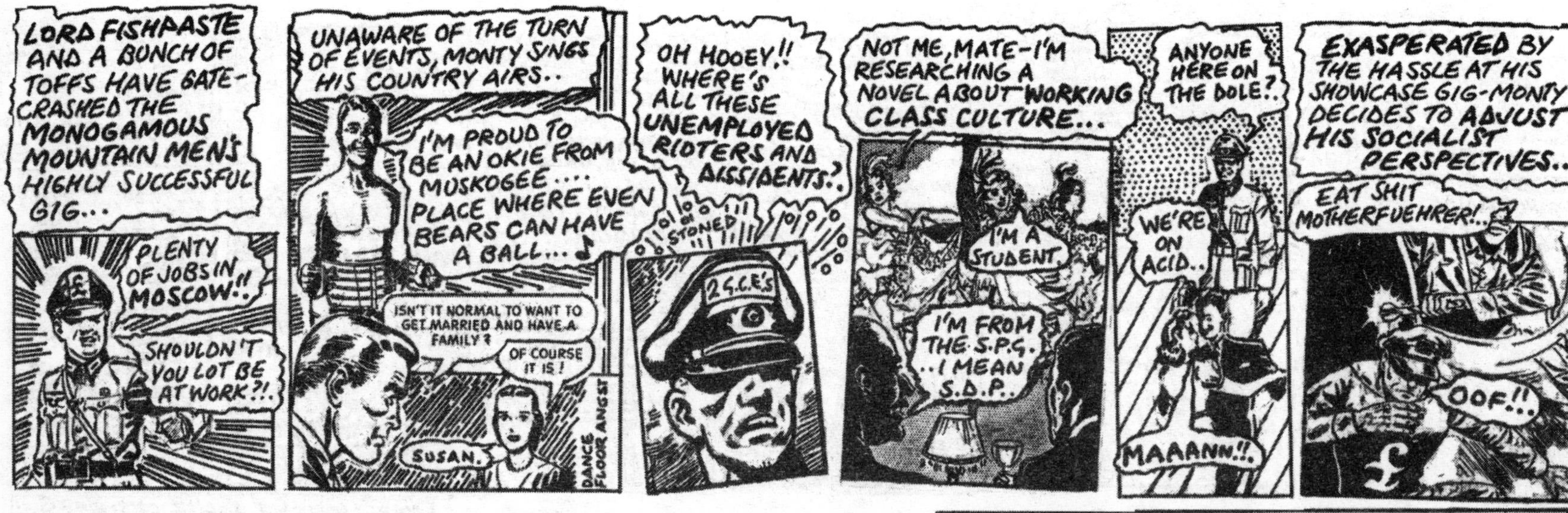
LORD FISHPASTE AND A BUNCH OF TOFFS HAVE GATE-CRASHED THE MONOGAMOUS MOUNTAIN MEN'S HIGHLY SUCCESSFUL GIG...
PLENTY OF JOBS IN MOSCOW!!
SHOULDN'T YOU LOT BE AT WORK?!.
UNAWARE OF THE TURN OF EVENTS, MONTY SINGS HIS COUNTRY AIRS..
I'M PROUD TO BE AN OKIE FROM MUSKOGEE.... PLACE WHERE EVEN BEARS CAN HAVE A BALL...
ISN'T IT NORMAL TO WANT TO GET MARRIED AND HAVE A FAMILY?
OF COURSE IT IS!
SUSAN.
DANCE FLOOR ANGST
OH HOOEY!! WHERE'S ALL THESE UNEMPLOYED RIOTERS AND DISSIDENTS?.
STONED
2 G.C.E's
NOT ME, MATE - I'M RESEARCHING A NOVEL ABOUT WORKING CLASS CULTURE...
I'M A STUDENT.
I'M FROM THE S.P.G. ..I MEAN S.D.P..
ANYONE HERE ON THE DOLE?.
WE'RE ON ACID..
MAAANN!!.
EXASPERATED BY THE HASSLE AT HIS SHOWCASE GIG - MONTY DECIDES TO ADJUST HIS SOCIALIST PERSPECTIVES..
EAT SHIT MOTHERFUEHRER!..
OOF!!..

NEXT WEEK - RIDING AROUND LOOKING FOR WORK

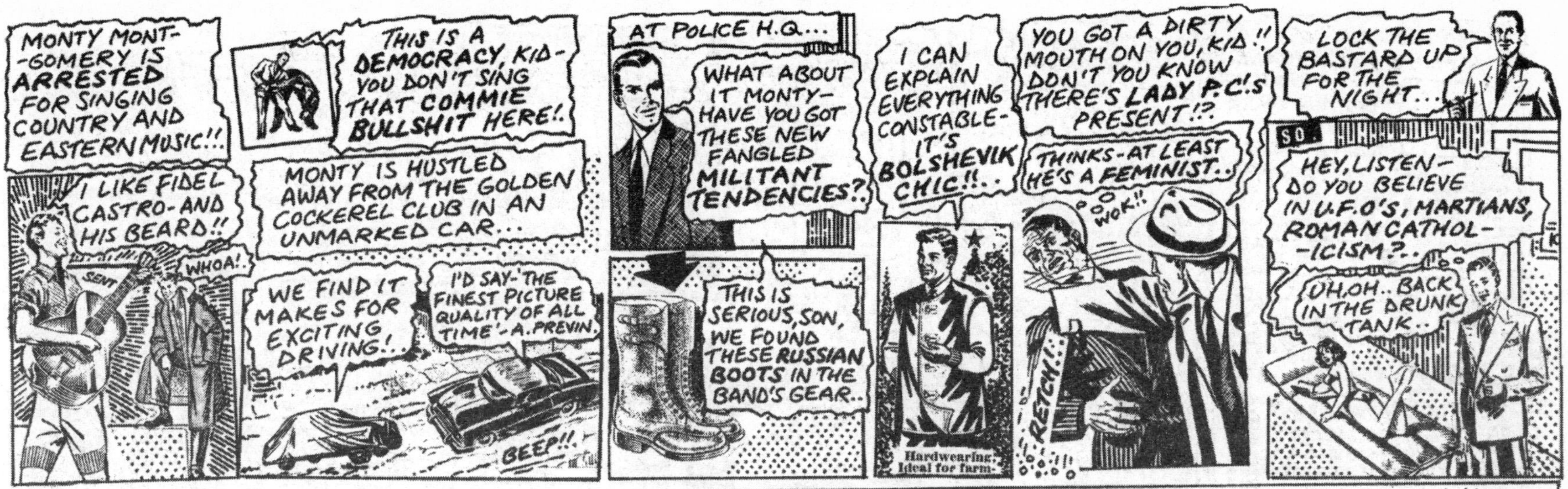
MONTY MONT--GOMERY IS ARRESTED FOR SINGING COUNTRY AND EASTERN MUSIC!!
I LIKE FIDEL CASTRO- AND HIS BEARD!!
SENT
WHOA!
THIS IS A DEMOCRACY, KID- YOU DON'T SING THAT COMMIE BULLSHIT HERE!.
MONTY IS HUSTLED AWAY FROM THE GOLDEN COCKEREL CLUB IN AN UNMARKED CAR...
WE FIND IT MAKES FOR EXCITING DRIVING!...
I'D SAY- 'THE FINEST PICTURE QUALITY OF ALL TIME' - A. PREVIN.
BEEP!!
AT POLICE H.Q...
WHAT ABOUT IT MONTY- HAVE YOU GOT THESE NEW FANGLED MILITANT TENDENCIES?.
THIS IS SERIOUS, SON, WE FOUND THESE RUSSIAN BOOTS IN THE BAND'S GEAR..
I CAN EXPLAIN EVERYTHING CONSTABLE- IT'S BOLSHEVIK CHIC!!..
Hardwearing. Ideal for farm.
RETCH!
YOU GOT A DIRTY MOUTH ON YOU, KID!! DON'T YOU KNOW THERE'S LADY P.C.'s PRESENT!?
THINKS- AT LEAST HE'S A FEMINIST..
WOK!!
LOCK THE BASTARD UP FOR THE NIGHT...
SO.
HEY, LISTEN- DO YOU BELIEVE IN U.F.O'S, MARTIANS, ROMAN CATHOL--ICISM?..
UH,OH.. BACK IN THE DRUNK TANK...

NEXT- THE MASSES FINALLY RISE!! — BUT ONLY AGAINST PAULA YATES..

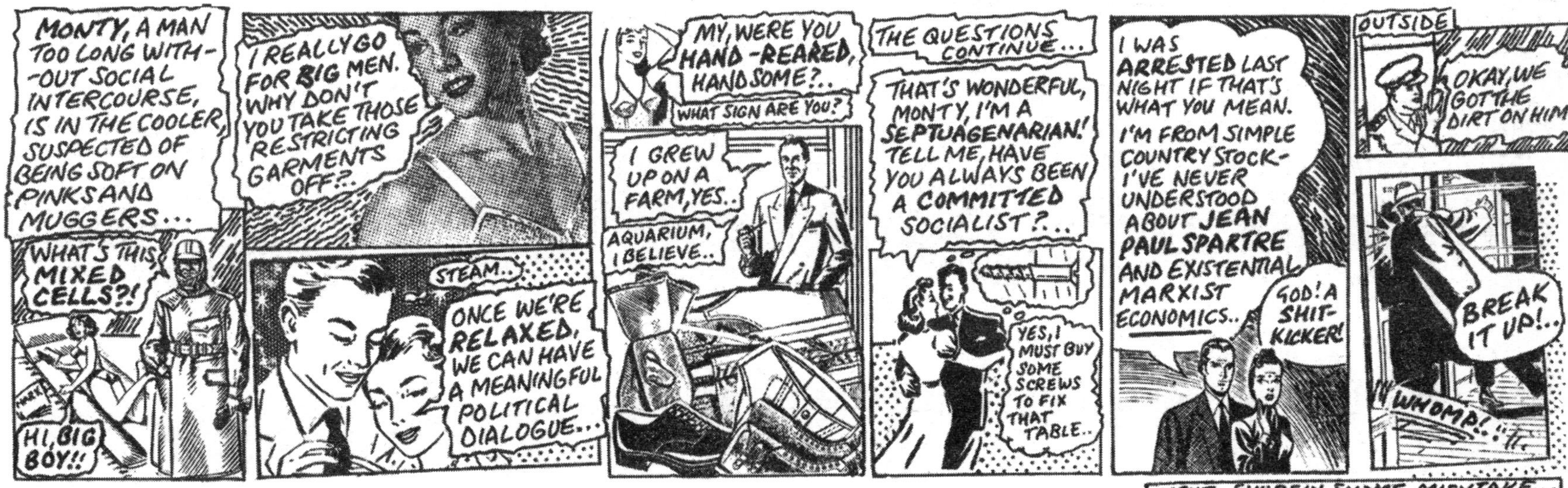
MONTY, A MAN TOO LONG WITH--OUT SOCIAL INTERCOURSE, IS IN THE COOLER, SUSPECTED OF BEING SOFT ON PINKS AND MUGGERS...
WHAT'S THIS MIXED CELLS?!
HI, BIG BOY!!
I REALLY GO FOR BIG MEN. WHY DON'T YOU TAKE THOSE RESTRICTING GARMENTS OFF?..
STEAM..
ONCE WE'RE RELAXED, WE CAN HAVE A MEANINGFUL POLITICAL DIALOGUE...
MY, WERE YOU HAND-REARED, HANDSOME?..
WHAT SIGN ARE YOU?
I GREW UP ON A FARM, YES..
AQUARIUM, I BELIEVE..
THE QUESTIONS CONTINUE...
THAT'S WONDERFUL, MONTY, I'M A SEPTUAGENARIAN! TELL ME, HAVE YOU ALWAYS BEEN A COMMITTED SOCIALIST?...
YES, I MUST BUY SOME SCREWS TO FIX THAT TABLE..
I WAS ARRESTED LAST NIGHT IF THAT'S WHAT YOU MEAN.
I'M FROM SIMPLE COUNTRY STOCK- I'VE NEVER UNDERSTOOD ABOUT JEAN PAUL SPARTRE AND EXISTENTIAL MARXIST ECONOMICS..
GOD! A SHIT-KICKER!
OUTSIDE
OKAY, WE GOT THE DIRT ON HIM!
BREAK IT UP!..
WHOMP!

NEXT- SHURELY SHOME MISHTAKE..

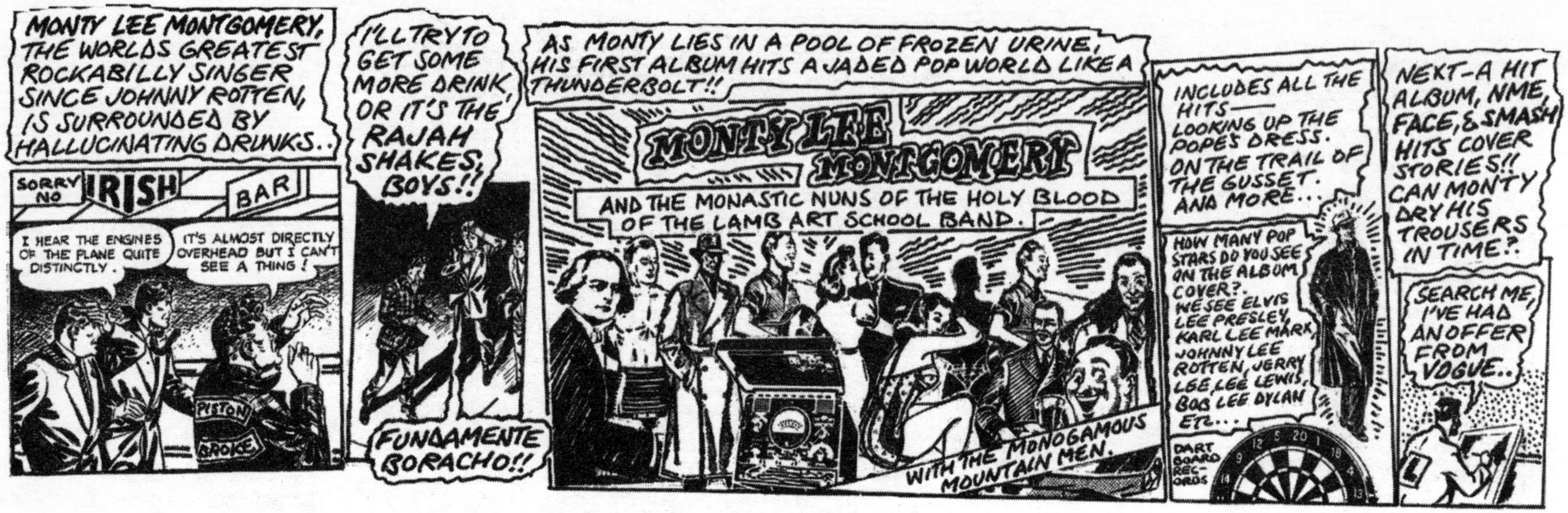

MONTY LEE MONTGOMERY, THE WORLDS GREATEST ROCKABILLY SINGER SINCE JOHNNY ROTTEN, IS SURROUNDED BY HALLUCINATING DRUNKS..
SORRY NO IRISH
BAR
I HEAR THE ENGINES OF THE PLANE QUITE DISTINCTLY.
IT'S ALMOST DIRECTLY OVERHEAD BUT I CAN'T SEE A THING!
PISTON BROKE
I'LL TRY TO GET SOME MORE DRINK, OR IT'S THE RAJAH SHAKES, BOYS!!
FUNDAMENTE BORACHO!!
AS MONTY LIES IN A POOL OF FROZEN URINE, HIS FIRST ALBUM HITS A JADED POP WORLD LIKE A THUNDERBOLT!!
MONTY LEE MONTGOMERY
AND THE MONASTIC NUNS OF THE HOLY BLOOD OF THE LAMB ART SCHOOL BAND.
WITH THE MONOGAMOUS MOUNTAIN MEN.
INCLUDES ALL THE HITS— LOOKING UP THE POPE'S DRESS. ON THE TRAIL OF THE GUSSET. AND MORE...
HOW MANY POP STARS DO YOU SEE ON THE ALBUM COVER?. WE SEE ELVIS LEE PRESLEY, KARL LEE MARX, JOHNNY LEE ROTTEN, JERRY LEE, LEE LEWIS, BOB LEE DYLAN ETC...
DART BOARD REC-ORDS
NEXT—A HIT ALBUM, NME, FACE, & SMASH HITS COVER STORIES!! CAN MONTY DRY HIS TROUSERS IN TIME?.
SEARCH ME, I'VE HAD AN OFFER FROM VOGUE..

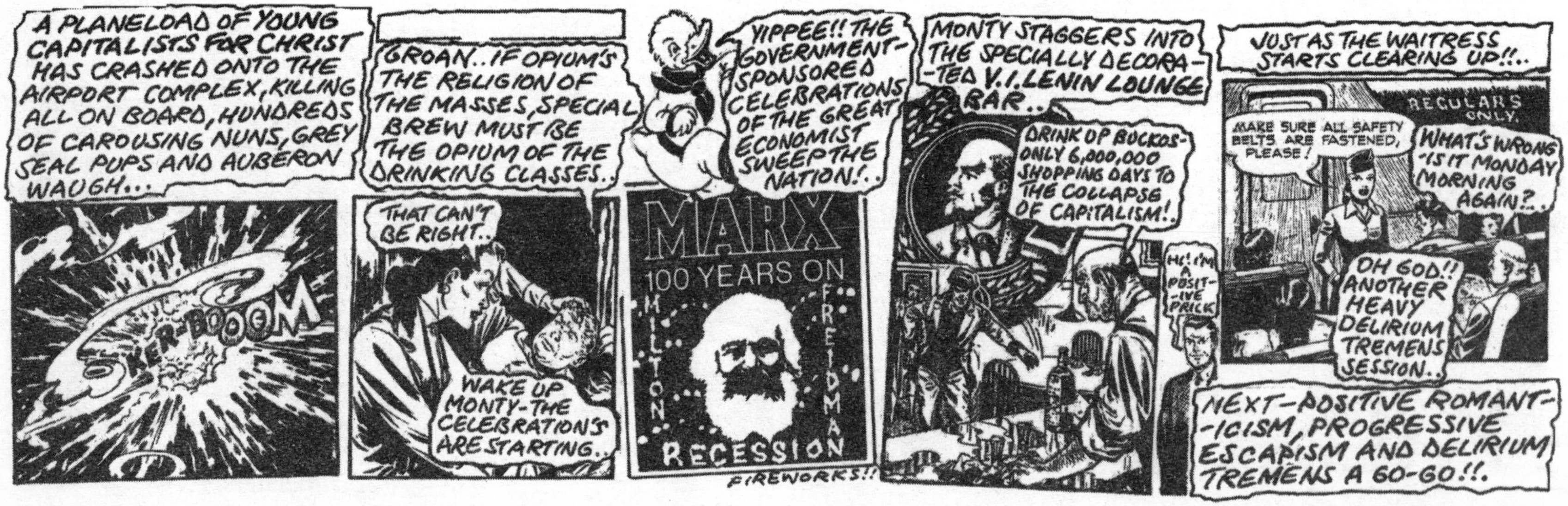

A PLANELOAD OF YOUNG CAPITALISTS FOR CHRIST HAS CRASHED ONTO THE AIRPORT COMPLEX, KILLING ALL ON BOARD, HUNDREDS OF CAROUSING NUNS, GREY SEAL PUPS AND AUBERON WAUGH...
SKER-BOOOM
GROAN.. IF OPIUM'S THE RELIGION OF THE MASSES, SPECIAL BREW MUST BE THE OPIUM OF THE DRINKING CLASSES..
THAT CAN'T BE RIGHT..
WAKE UP MONTY—THE CELEBRATION'S ARE STARTING..
YIPPEE!! THE GOVERNMENT-SPONSORED CELEBRATIONS OF THE GREAT ECONOMIST SWEEP THE NATION!..
MARX
100 YEARS ON
MILTON FREIDMAN
RECESSION
FIREWORKS!!
MONTY STAGGERS INTO THE SPECIALLY DECORA--TED V.I. LENIN LOUNGE BAR..
DRINK UP BUCKOS-ONLY 6,000,000 SHOPPING DAYS TO THE COLLAPSE OF CAPITALISM!.
HI! I'M A POSIT--IVE PRICK
JUST AS THE WAITRESS STARTS CLEARING UP!!..
REGULARS ONLY.
MAKE SURE ALL SAFETY BELTS ARE FASTENED, PLEASE!
WHAT'S WRONG-IS IT MONDAY MORNING AGAIN?..
OH GOD!! ANOTHER HEAVY DELIRIUM TREMENS SESSION..
NEXT—POSITIVE ROMANT--ICISM, PROGRESSIVE ESCAPISM AND DELIRIUM TREMENS A GO-GO!!.

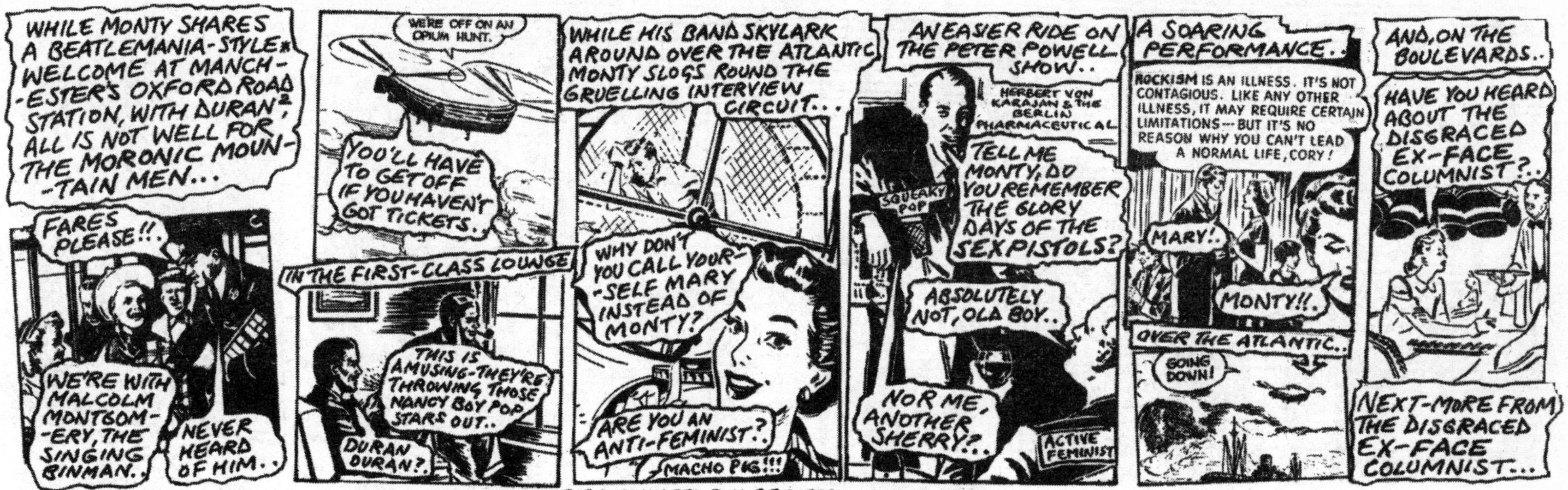
WHILE MONTY SHARES A BEATLEMANIA-STYLE* WELCOME AT MANCH-ESTER'S OXFORD ROAD STATION, WITH DURAN², ALL IS NOT WELL FOR THE MORONIC MOUN-TAIN MEN...
FARES PLEASE!!..
WE'RE WITH MALCOLM MONTGOM-ERY, THE SINGING BINMAN..
NEVER HEARD OF HIM...
WE'RE OFF ON AN OPIUM HUNT.
YOU'LL HAVE TO GET OFF IF YOU HAVEN'T GOT TICKETS..
IN THE FIRST-CLASS LOUNGE
THIS IS AMUSING-THEY'RE THROWING THOSE NANCY BOY POP STARS OUT..
DURAN DURAN?..
WHILE HIS BAND SKYLARK AROUND OVER THE ATLANTIC MONTY SLOGS ROUND THE GRUELLING INTERVIEW CIRCUIT...
WHY DON'T YOU CALL YOUR-SELF MARY INSTEAD OF MONTY?
ARE YOU AN ANTI-FEMINIST?..
MACHO PIG!!!
AN EASIER RIDE ON THE PETER POWELL SHOW..
HERBERT VON KARAJAN & THE BERLIN PHARMACEUTICAL
TELL ME MONTY, DO YOU REMEMBER THE GLORY DAYS OF THE SEX PISTOLS?
SQUEAKY POP
ABSOLUTELY NOT, OLD BOY..
NOR ME, ANOTHER SHERRY?..
ACTIVE FEMINIST
A SOARING PERFORMANCE..
ROCKISM IS AN ILLNESS. IT'S NOT CONTAGIOUS. LIKE ANY OTHER ILLNESS, IT MAY REQUIRE CERTAIN LIMITATIONS--- BUT IT'S NO REASON WHY YOU CAN'T LEAD A NORMAL LIFE, CORY!
MARY!..
MONTY!!..
OVER THE ATLANTIC..
GOING DOWN!
AND, ON THE BOULEVARDS..
HAVE YOU HEARD ABOUT THE DISGRACED EX-FACE COLUMNIST?..
NEXT-MORE FROM THE DISGRACED EX-FACE COLUMNIST...

* FOR YOUR NEXT BEATLE STYLE MINI-RECEPTIONETTE, BAR MITZVAH ETC. RING B.B.C., SPECIAL EFFECTS DEPT

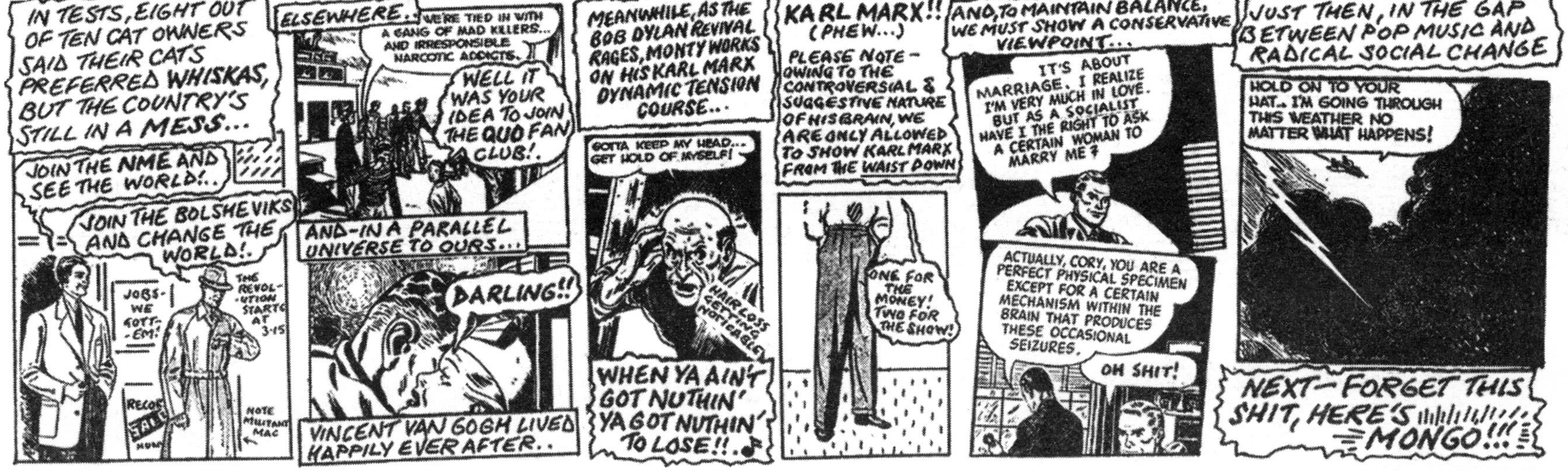
IN TESTS, EIGHT OUT OF TEN CAT OWNERS SAID THEIR CATS PREFERRED WHISKAS, BUT THE COUNTRY'S STILL IN A MESS...
JOIN THE NME AND SEE THE WORLD!..
JOIN THE BOLSHEVIKS AND CHANGE THE WORLD!.
JOBS-WE GOTT-EM!
THE REVOL-UTION STARTS AT 3:15
NOTE MILITANT MAC
ELSEWHERE..
WE'RE TIED IN WITH A GANG OF MAD KILLERS... AND IRRESPONSIBLE NARCOTIC ADDICTS.
WELL IT WAS YOUR IDEA TO JOIN THE QUO FAN CLUB!.
AND-IN A PARALLEL UNIVERSE TO OURS...
DARLING!!
VINCENT VAN GOGH LIVED HAPPILY EVER AFTER..
MEANWHILE, AS THE BOB DYLAN REVIVAL RAGES, MONTY WORKS ON HIS KARL MARX DYNAMIC TENSION COURSE..
GOTTA KEEP MY HEAD... GET HOLD OF MYSELF!
WHEN YA AIN'T GOT NUTHIN' YA GOT NUTHIN' TO LOSE!!
KARL MARX!! (PHEW...)
PLEASE NOTE - OWING TO THE CONTROVERSIAL & SUGGESTIVE NATURE OF HIS BRAIN, WE ARE ONLY ALLOWED TO SHOW KARL MARX FROM THE WAIST DOWN
ONE FOR THE MONEY! TWO FOR THE SHOW!
AND, TO MAINTAIN BALANCE, WE MUST SHOW A CONSERVATIVE VIEWPOINT...
IT'S ABOUT MARRIAGE. I REALIZE I'M VERY MUCH IN LOVE. BUT AS A SOCIALIST HAVE I THE RIGHT TO ASK A CERTAIN WOMAN TO MARRY ME?
ACTUALLY, CORY, YOU ARE A PERFECT PHYSICAL SPECIMEN EXCEPT FOR A CERTAIN MECHANISM WITHIN THE BRAIN THAT PRODUCES THESE OCCASIONAL SEIZURES.
OH SHIT!
JUST THEN, IN THE GAP BETWEEN POP MUSIC AND RADICAL SOCIAL CHANGE
HOLD ON TO YOUR HAT.. I'M GOING THROUGH THIS WEATHER NO MATTER WHAT HAPPENS!
NEXT-FORGET THIS SHIT, HERE'S MONGO!!!

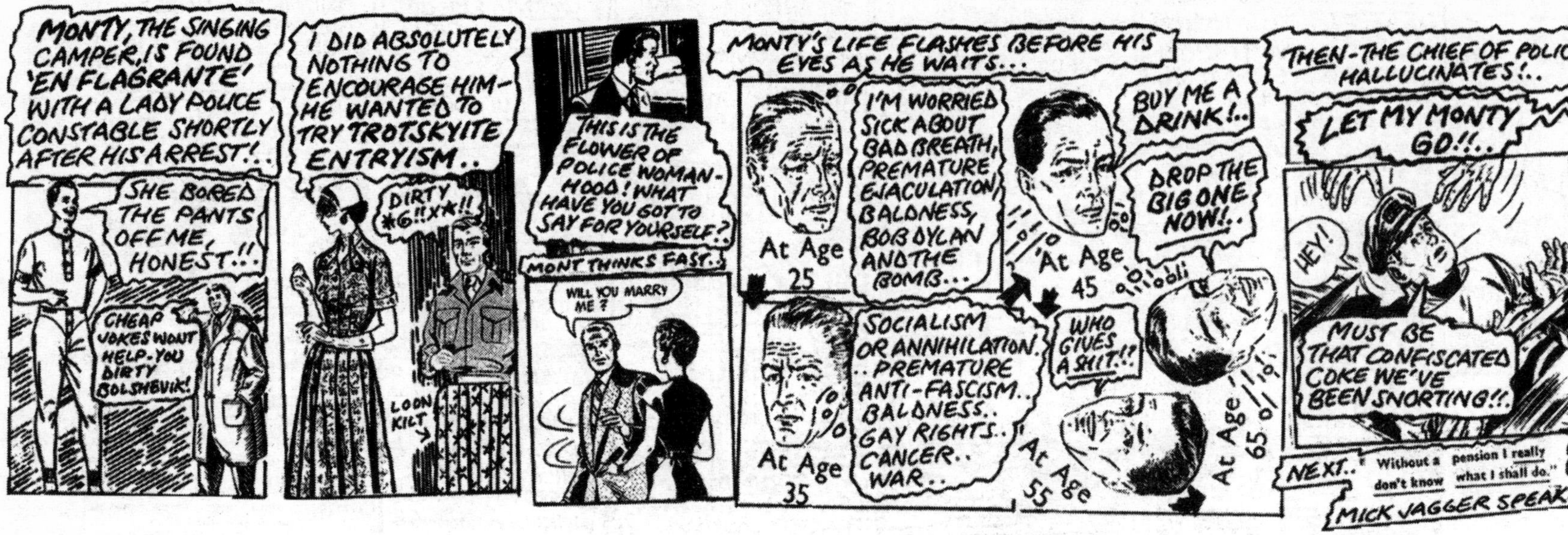

MONTY, THE SINGING CAMPER, IS FOUND 'EN FLAGRANTE' WITH A LADY POLICE CONSTABLE SHORTLY AFTER HIS ARREST!..
SHE BORED THE PANTS OFF ME, HONEST!!..
CHEAP JOKES WONT HELP-YOU DIRTY BOLSHEVIK!
I DID ABSOLUTELY NOTHING TO ENCOURAGE HIM-HE WANTED TO TRY TROTSKYITE ENTRYISM..
DIRTY *6!!X*!!
LOON KILT
THIS IS THE FLOWER OF POLICE WOMAN-HOOD! WHAT HAVE YOU GOT TO SAY FOR YOURSELF?
MONT THINKS FAST..
WILL YOU MARRY ME ?
MONTY'S LIFE FLASHES BEFORE HIS EYES AS HE WAITS...
At Age 25
I'M WORRIED SICK ABOUT BAD BREATH, PREMATURE EJACULATION, BALDNESS, BOB DYLAN AND THE BOMB...
At Age 35
SOCIALISM OR ANNIHILATION.. PREMATURE ANTI-FASCISM.. BALDNESS.. GAY RIGHTS.. CANCER.. WAR..
At Age 45
BUY ME A DRINK!..
DROP THE BIG ONE NOW!..
At Age 55
WHO GIVES A SHIT!!
At Age 65
THEN-THE CHIEF OF POLICE HALLUCINATES!..
LET MY MONTY GO!!..
HEY!
MUST BE THAT CONFISCATED COKE WE'VE BEEN SNORTING!!.
NEXT.. "Without a pension I really don't know what I shall do."
MICK JAGGER SPEAKS..

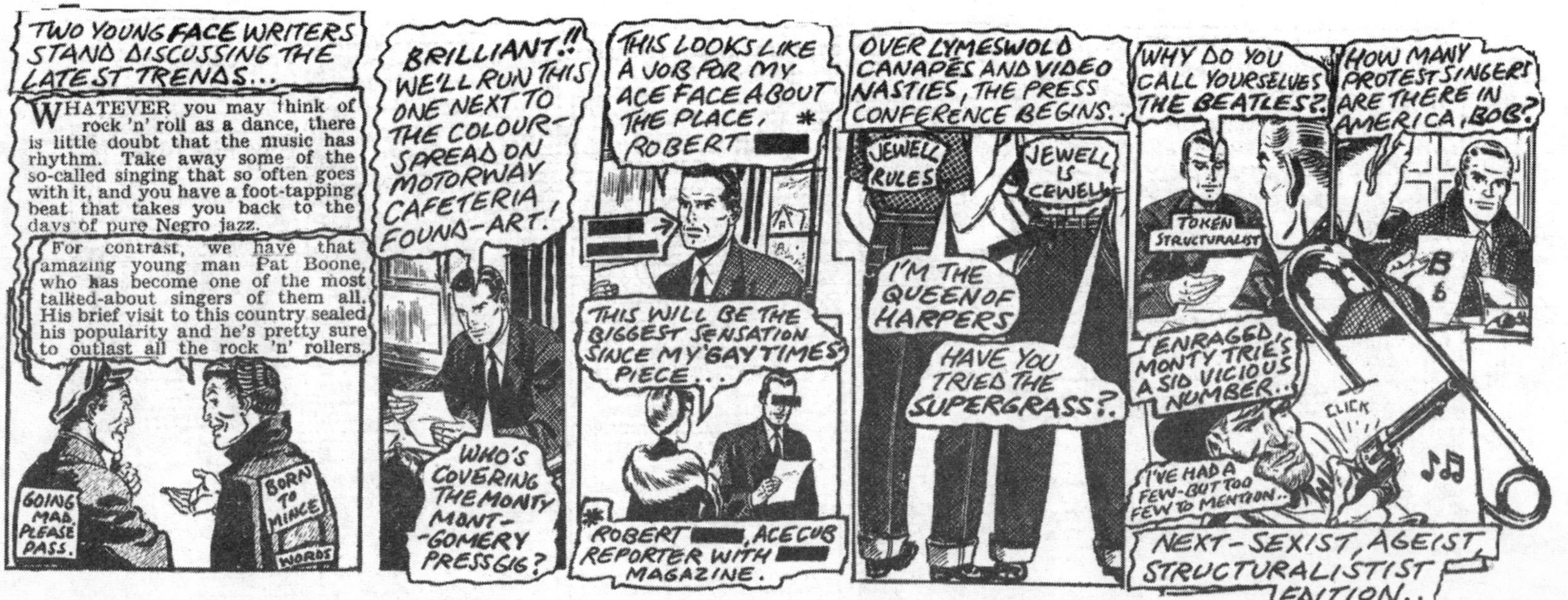

TWO YOUNG FACE WRITERS STAND DISCUSSING THE LATEST TRENDS...
WHATEVER you may think of rock 'n' roll as a dance, there is little doubt that the music has rhythm. Take away some of the so-called singing that so often goes with it, and you have a foot-tapping beat that takes you back to the days of pure Negro jazz.
For contrast, we have that amazing young man Pat Boone, who has become one of the most talked-about singers of them all. His brief visit to this country sealed his popularity and he's pretty sure to outlast all the rock 'n' rollers.
GOING MAD PLEASE PASS.
BORN TO MINCE
WORDS
BRILLIANT!! WE'LL RUN THIS ONE NEXT TO THE COLOUR-SPREAD ON MOTORWAY CAFETERIA FOUND-ART!
WHO'S COVERING THE MONTY MONT-GOMERY PRESS GIG?
THIS LOOKS LIKE A JOB FOR MY ACE FACE ABOUT THE PLACE, ROBERT [redacted] *
THIS WILL BE THE BIGGEST SENSATION SINCE MY 'GAY TIMES' PIECE...
*ROBERT [redacted], ACE CUB REPORTER WITH [redacted] MAGAZINE.
OVER LYMESWOLD CANAPÉS AND VIDEO NASTIES, THE PRESS CONFERENCE BEGINS..
JEWELL RULES
JEWELL IS CEWELL
I'M THE QUEEN OF HARPERS
HAVE YOU TRIED THE SUPERGRASS?.
WHY DO YOU CALL YOURSELVES THE BEATLES?
HOW MANY PROTEST SINGERS ARE THERE IN AMERICA, BOB?
TOKEN STRUCTURALIST
ENRAGED, MONTY TRIES A SID VICIOUS NUMBER..
CLICK
I'VE HAD A FEW-BUT TOO FEW TO MENTION..
NEXT-SEXIST, AGEIST, STRUCTURALISTIST EDITION..

DEATH IN THE NIGHT ONLY THE OVERTHROW OF THE GOVERNMENT, THE DISBANDING OF THE POLICE AND THE ARMED FORCES, THE BREAKDOWN OF THE POSTAL AND TELECOMMUNICATION SERVICES, THE HEALTH SERVICE AND ORGANISED RELIGION, A GENERAL STRIKE AND A SUBSEQUENT INCREASE IN POLITICAL UNREST STANDS BETWEEN THE COUNTRY AND **ANARCHY**!!!...

TIME FOR A STRONG MAN!!

ALL DAY, PEACEFUL CITIZENS PURSUE THEIR LAWFUL ACTIVITIES — COLLECTING GIROS, BUYING GLUE, WATCHING POSTMAN PAT, BUT, AT NIGHT, SINISTER FIGURES EMERGE...

C.D. OR D.A.T? V.A.T. AND N.I.C., B.T. AND T.S.B., HIGH N.R.G.!!
V.I.P.?.
CLUB
OUI!..
AIDS.
B.O.F.

THE ARROGANT **YUPPIES** (THOUGHT POLICE) STROLL UNMOLESTED WHILE THE LEADERS OF THE GREAT P.U.N.K. REVOLT LANGUISH IN EXILE...

PUT THE HANDS UP, AND YOU DON'T GET NO TROUBLE!
P.O.U.M!!!
STRAIGHT TO HELL!!

JOE STRUMMER - EX-LEADER OF THE ONCE FEARED CLASHIST TENDENCY!!!

FORCED TO EKE OUT A LIVING ON THE FRINGES OF SOCIETY, THE DEPOSED P.U.N.K. KINGS CUT SORRY FIGURES...

I DID IT MY WAY!!

ROTTEN FORCED TO GO STRAIGHT AND DEAL IN REAL ESTATE IN THE FAR OFF U.S.A. WHILE STRUMMER SLEEPS IN OLD CARS WITHOUT A CHANGE OF CLOTHING!!

ONLY IN THE UNDERGROUND MAQUIS CLUB, DOES THE TRUE SPIRIT OF P.U.N.K. LIVE...

HERE'S AN OLD SIOUXSIE NUMBER!..
LONG LIVE LOVE!
OUT DEMONS OUT!!

NEXT- Hilda Schratzendorf is suddenly recognized by the half-mad Polish girl, Janka, as an ex-Nazi. Furiously, her room-mates fall on the German woman and force poison down her throat.
PLUS-EDGAR BROUGHTON REVIVAL.

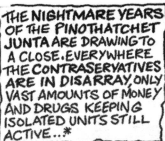

THE NIGHTMARE YEARS OF THE **PINOTHATCHET** JUNTA ARE DRAWING TO A CLOSE. EVERYWHERE THE **CONTRASERVATIVES** ARE IN DISARRAY, ONLY VAST AMOUNTS OF MONEY AND DRUGS KEEPING ISOLATED UNITS STILL ACTIVE...*

THE SOCIALISTS AREN'T IN SIGHT YET, BUT I CAN HEAR THEIR DOGS..
JOHNNY, I CAN'T SWIM!
STONED
CREEK
CRACKED
YOU'D BETTER GET ON YOUR BIKE, THEN!!

* THE GOVERNMENT, FEDERATION OF CONSERVATIVE STUDENTS ETC,

WHILE HARD-LINE OLD TORIES CURSE THEIR CHANGING FORTUNES..

IT'S THAT GREY SOCIALIST UNIFORMITY I CAN'T STAND!!
I CAN'T STAND IT, EITHER
NOR ME!!

YOUNG DESIGNER SOCIALISTS PLAN THE COMING SOCIETY..
WE'RE GOING TO BEAT OUR GUITARS INTO PLOUGHSHARES
AND RECORD IT ON EIGHTEEN TRACK!.

THE NATIONAL HEALTH SERVICE...

MR. PHARMACIST!! I WANT EVERYTHING! I WANT IT NOW!!!
CRUNGE!
YES MA'AM
BLART!

NOTE THE NEAT COMBINING OF THE SNOT ROCK ANTHEMS OF THE DAY-FALL, GODFATHERS-IN ONE TYPICAL DOMESTIC SCENE.

Up in the air—and no mistake about it—are Nick Adams and Andy Griffith in a hilarious shot from "No Time For Sergeants," to be released on August 18th (ELVIS PRESLEY IS ON HOLIDAY.)

MORE TEEN-POWER !!

IF WE THINK ABOUT IT HARD ENOUGH – I'M SURE WE CAN ABOLISH POVERTY!!
THERE..
I'VE ABOLISHED POVERTY!!
SOCIALISM IN ONE BRAIN!!

NOW WE WANT NEIL KINNOCK AT NUMBER 10
IN THE HIP HOP CHARTS!!

BUT-OLDER HEADS PREVAIL AT THE POLITBUREAU ANNUAL CONGRESS..

WE HAVE TO GET RID OF THE ENEMY WITHIN!
THE CONTRASERVATIVES ?!?
NO! THE TROTSKYITES!! THE REVOLUTIONARY SOCIALISTS!.

NEXT-ALL THAT'S NEW IN ELECTRO BEAT AND HIP HOP! ROY HATTERSLEY & GERALD KAUFMAN WRITE...

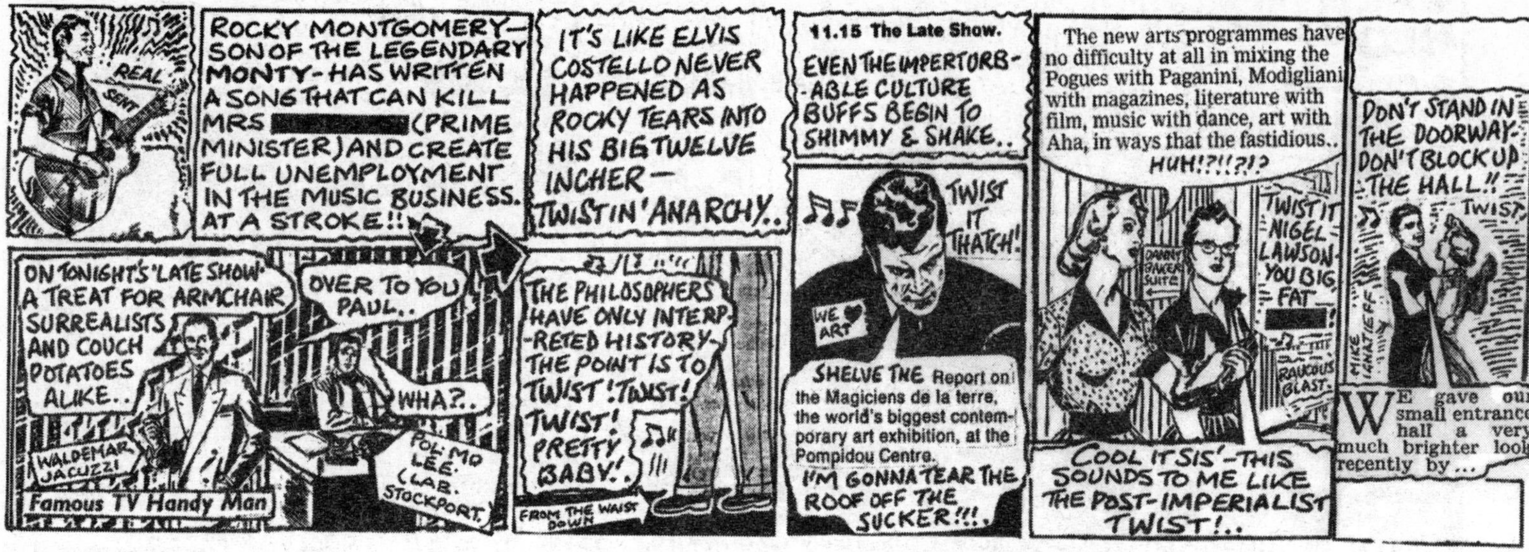

REAL SENT
ROCKY MONTGOMERY- SON OF THE LEGENDARY MONTY- HAS WRITTEN A SONG THAT CAN KILL MRS [redacted] (PRIME MINISTER) AND CREATE FULL UNEMPLOYMENT IN THE MUSIC BUSINESS. AT A STROKE!!
IT'S LIKE ELVIS COSTELLO NEVER HAPPENED AS ROCKY TEARS INTO HIS BIG TWELVE INCHER — TWISTIN' ANARCHY..
11.15 The Late Show.
EVEN THE IMPERTURB- -ABLE CULTURE BUFFS BEGIN TO SHIMMY & SHAKE..
The new arts programmes have no difficulty at all in mixing the Pogues with Paganini, Modigliani with magazines, literature with film, music with dance, art with Aha, in ways that the fastidious..
HUH!?!!?!?
DON'T STAND IN THE DOORWAY- DON'T BLOCK UP THE HALL!!
TWIST
ON TONIGHT'S 'LATE SHOW' A TREAT FOR ARMCHAIR SURREALISTS AND COUCH POTATOES ALIKE..
OVER TO YOU PAUL..
WHA?..
WALDEMAR JACUZZI
POL: MO LEE. (LAB. STOCKPORT.
Famous TV Handy Man
THE PHILOSOPHERS HAVE ONLY INTERP- -RETED HISTORY- THE POINT IS TO TWIST! TWIST! TWIST! PRETTY BABY!
FROM THE WAIST DOWN
TWIST IT THATCH!
WE ♥ ART
SHELVE THE Report on the Magiciens de la terre, the world's biggest contemporary art exhibition, at the Pompidou Centre.
I'M GONNA TEAR THE ROOF OFF THE SUCKER!!!
TWIST IT NIGEL LAWSON YOU BIG FAT [redacted]
DANNY BAKER SUITE
RAUCOUS BLAST
COOL IT SIS'- THIS SOUNDS TO ME LIKE THE POST-IMPERIALIST TWIST!..
MIKE GATTING
WE gave our small entrance hall a very much brighter look recently by...

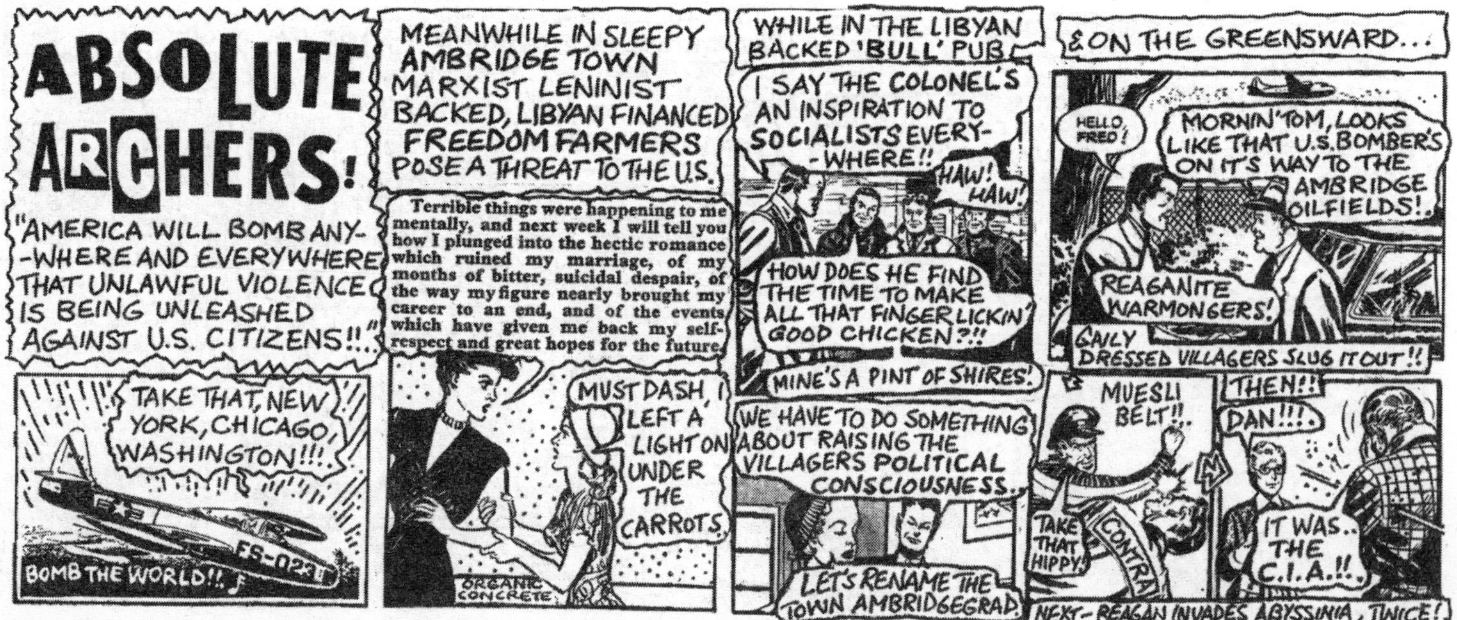

ABSOLUTE ARCHERS!
"AMERICA WILL BOMB ANY- -WHERE AND EVERYWHERE THAT UNLAWFUL VIOLENCE IS BEING UNLEASHED AGAINST U.S. CITIZENS!!"
TAKE THAT, NEW YORK, CHICAGO, WASHINGTON!!!
FS-023
BOMB THE WORLD!!
MEANWHILE IN SLEEPY AMBRIDGE TOWN MARXIST LENINIST BACKED, LIBYAN FINANCED FREEDOM FARMERS POSE A THREAT TO THE U.S.
Terrible things were happening to me mentally, and next week I will tell you how I plunged into the hectic romance which ruined my marriage, of my months of bitter, suicidal despair, of the way my figure nearly brought my career to an end, and of the events which have given me back my self-respect and great hopes for the future.
MUST DASH, I LEFT A LIGHT ON UNDER THE CARROTS.
ORGANIC CONCRETE
WHILE IN THE LIBYAN BACKED 'BULL' PUB
I SAY THE COLONEL'S AN INSPIRATION TO SOCIALISTS EVERY- -WHERE!!
HAW! HAW!
HOW DOES HE FIND THE TIME TO MAKE ALL THAT FINGER LICKIN' GOOD CHICKEN?!!
MINE'S A PINT OF SHIRES!
WE HAVE TO DO SOMETHING ABOUT RAISING THE VILLAGERS POLITICAL CONSCIOUSNESS.
LET'S RENAME THE TOWN AMBRIDGEGRAD.
& ON THE GREENSWARD...
HELLO, FRED!
MORNIN' TOM, LOOKS LIKE THAT U.S. BOMBER'S ON IT'S WAY TO THE AMBRIDGE OILFIELDS!
REAGANITE WARMONGERS!
GAILY DRESSED VILLAGERS SLUG IT OUT!!
MUESLI BELT!!
TAKE THAT HIPPY!
CONTRA
THEN!! DAN!!!
IT WAS.. THE C.I.A.!!
NEXT- REAGAN INVADES ABYSSINIA, TWICE!

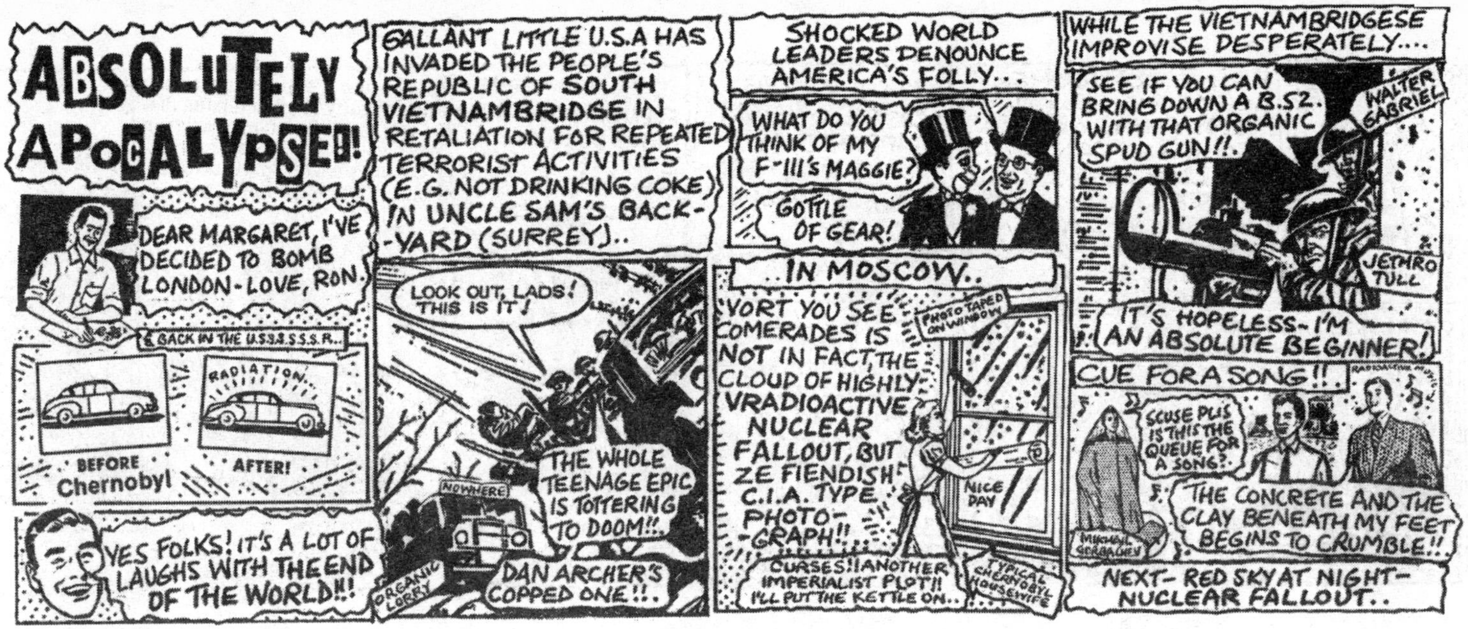
ABSOLUTELY APOCALYPSED!
DEAR MARGARET, I'VE DECIDED TO BOMB LONDON - LOVE, RON.
& BACK IN THE U.S.S.S.S.S.S.R..
RADIATION..
BEFORE Chernobyl
AFTER!
YES FOLKS! IT'S A LOT OF LAUGHS WITH THE END OF THE WORLD!!
GALLANT LITTLE U.S.A HAS INVADED THE PEOPLE'S REPUBLIC OF SOUTH VIETNAMBRIDGE IN RETALIATION FOR REPEATED TERRORIST ACTIVITIES (E.G. NOT DRINKING COKE) IN UNCLE SAM'S BACK-YARD (SURREY)..
LOOK OUT, LADS! THIS IS IT!
THE WHOLE TEENAGE EPIC IS TOTTERING TO DOOM!!
NOWHERE
ORGANIC LORRY
DAN ARCHER'S COPPED ONE!!
SHOCKED WORLD LEADERS DENOUNCE AMERICA'S FOLLY..
WHAT DO YOU THINK OF MY F-111'S MAGGIE?
GOTTLE OF GEAR!
..IN MOSCOW..
"VORT YOU SEE COMERADES IS NOT IN FACT, THE CLOUD OF HIGHLY VRADIOACTIVE NUCLEAR FALLOUT, BUT ZE FIENDISH C.I.A. TYPE PHOTO--GRAPH!!
PHOTO TAPED ON WINDOW
NICE DAY
CURSES!! ANOTHER IMPERIALIST PLOT!! I'LL PUT THE KETTLE ON..
TYPICAL CHERNOBYL HOUSEWIFE
WHILE THE VIETNAMBRIDGESE IMPROVISE DESPERATELY....
SEE IF YOU CAN BRING DOWN A B.52. WITH THAT ORGANIC SPUD GUN!!
WALTER GABRIEL
JETHRO TULL
IT'S HOPELESS - I'M AN ABSOLUTE BEGINNER!
CUE FOR A SONG!!
SCUSE PLIS IS THIS THE QUEUE FOR A SONG?
MICHAIL GORBACHEV
THE CONCRETE AND THE CLAY BENEATH MY FEET BEGINS TO CRUMBLE!!
NEXT - RED SKY AT NIGHT - NUCLEAR FALLOUT..

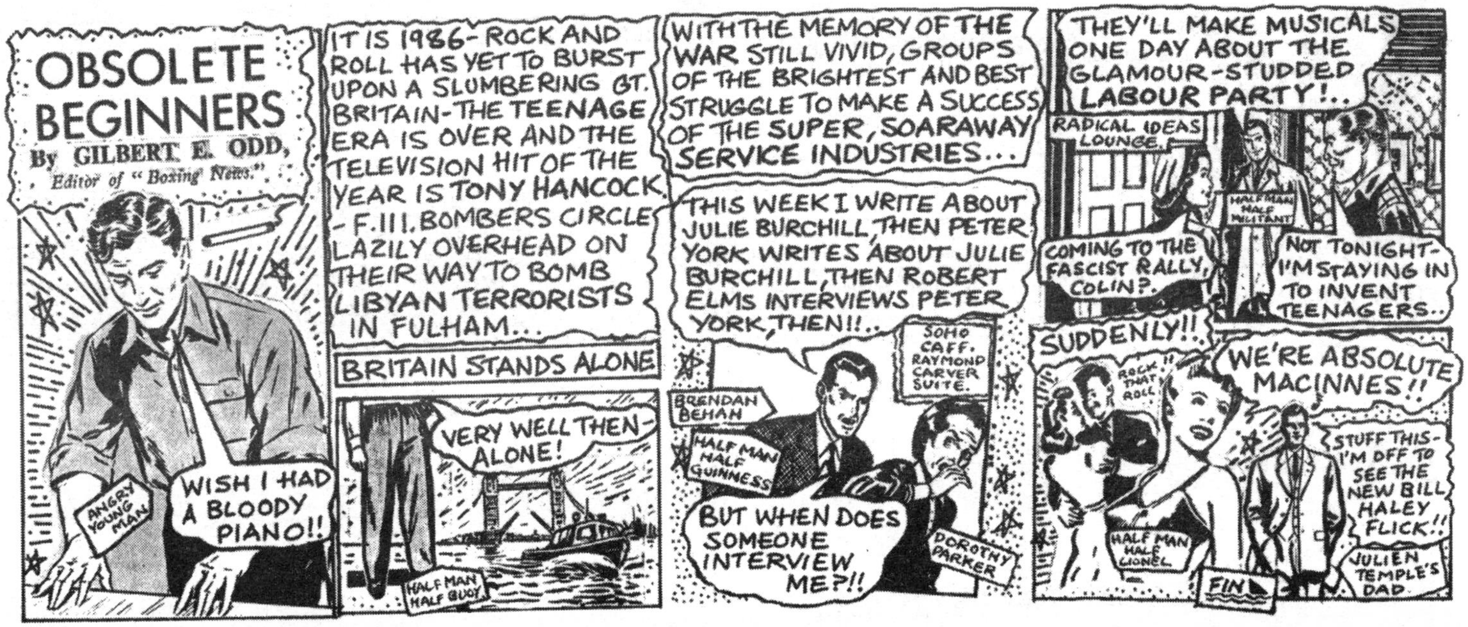
OBSOLETE BEGINNERS
By GILBERT E. ODD,
Editor of "Boxing News."
ANGRY YOUNG MAN
WISH I HAD A BLOODY PIANO!!
IT IS 1986 - ROCK AND ROLL HAS YET TO BURST UPON A SLUMBERING GT. BRITAIN - THE TEENAGE ERA IS OVER AND THE TELEVISION HIT OF THE YEAR IS TONY HANCOCK. - F.111. BOMBERS CIRCLE LAZILY OVERHEAD ON THEIR WAY TO BOMB LIBYAN TERRORISTS IN FULHAM...
BRITAIN STANDS ALONE
VERY WELL THEN - ALONE!
HALF MAN HALF BUOY
WITH THE MEMORY OF THE WAR STILL VIVID, GROUPS OF THE BRIGHTEST AND BEST STRUGGLE TO MAKE A SUCCESS OF THE SUPER, SOARAWAY SERVICE INDUSTRIES...
THIS WEEK I WRITE ABOUT JULIE BURCHILL, THEN PETER YORK WRITES ABOUT JULIE BURCHILL, THEN ROBERT ELMS INTERVIEWS PETER YORK, THEN!!..
SOHO CAFF. RAYMOND CARVER SUITE.
BRENDAN BEHAN
HALF MAN HALF GUINNESS
BUT WHEN DOES SOMEONE INTERVIEW ME?!!
DOROTHY PARKER
THEY'LL MAKE MUSICALS ONE DAY ABOUT THE GLAMOUR-STUDDED LABOUR PARTY!..
RADICAL IDEAS LOUNGE
HALF MAN HALF MILITANT
COMING TO THE FASCIST RALLY, COLIN?
NOT TONIGHT - I'M STAYING IN TO INVENT TEENAGERS..
SUDDENLY!!
WE'RE ABSOLUTE MACINNES!!
HALF MAN HALF LIONEL
STUFF THIS - I'M OFF TO SEE THE NEW BILL HALEY FLICK!!
JULIEN TEMPLE'S DAD
FIN

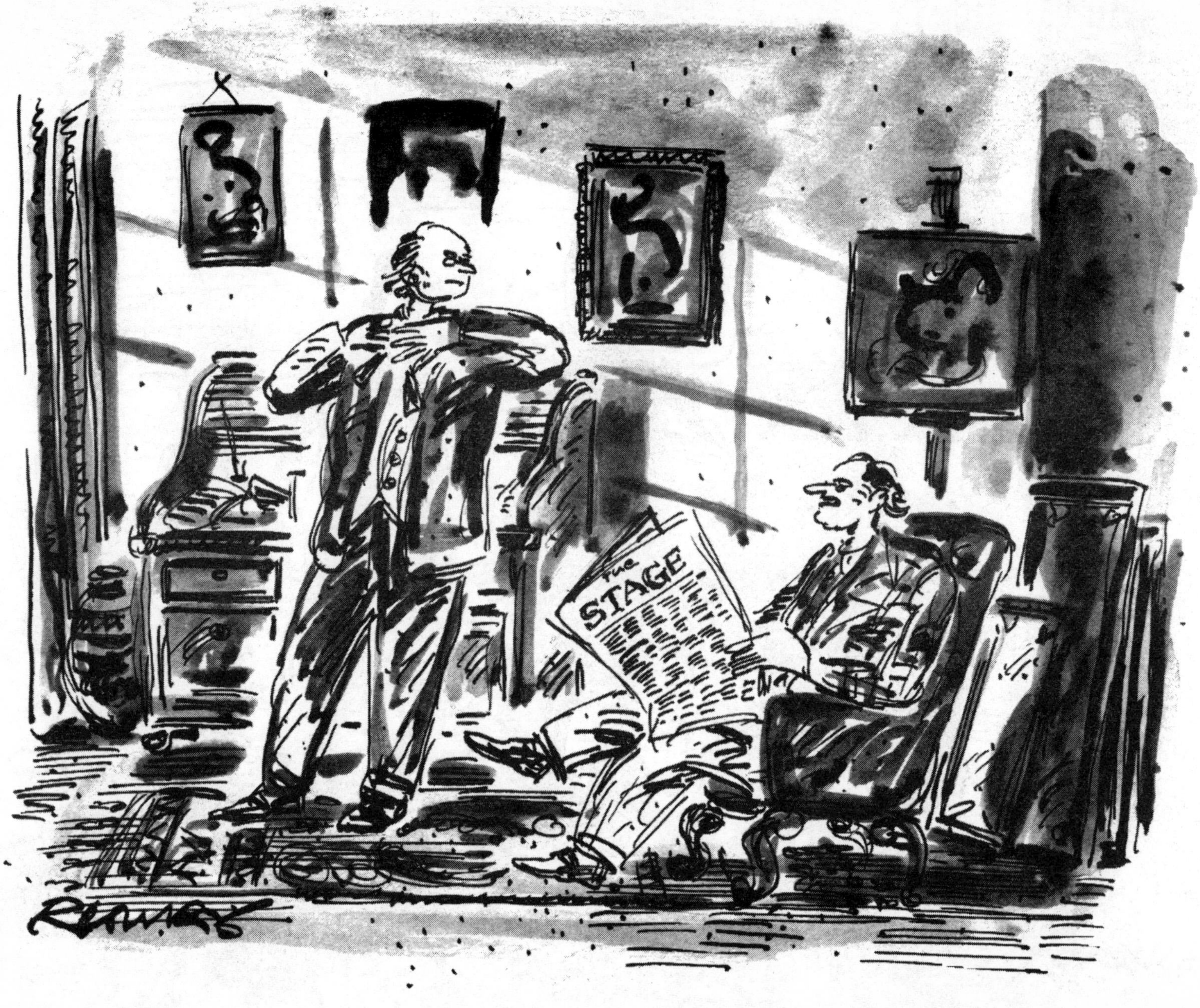
THE STAGE

"This looks promising – they're looking for a stand-up comic for the light entertainment wing of the Bloomsbury group."

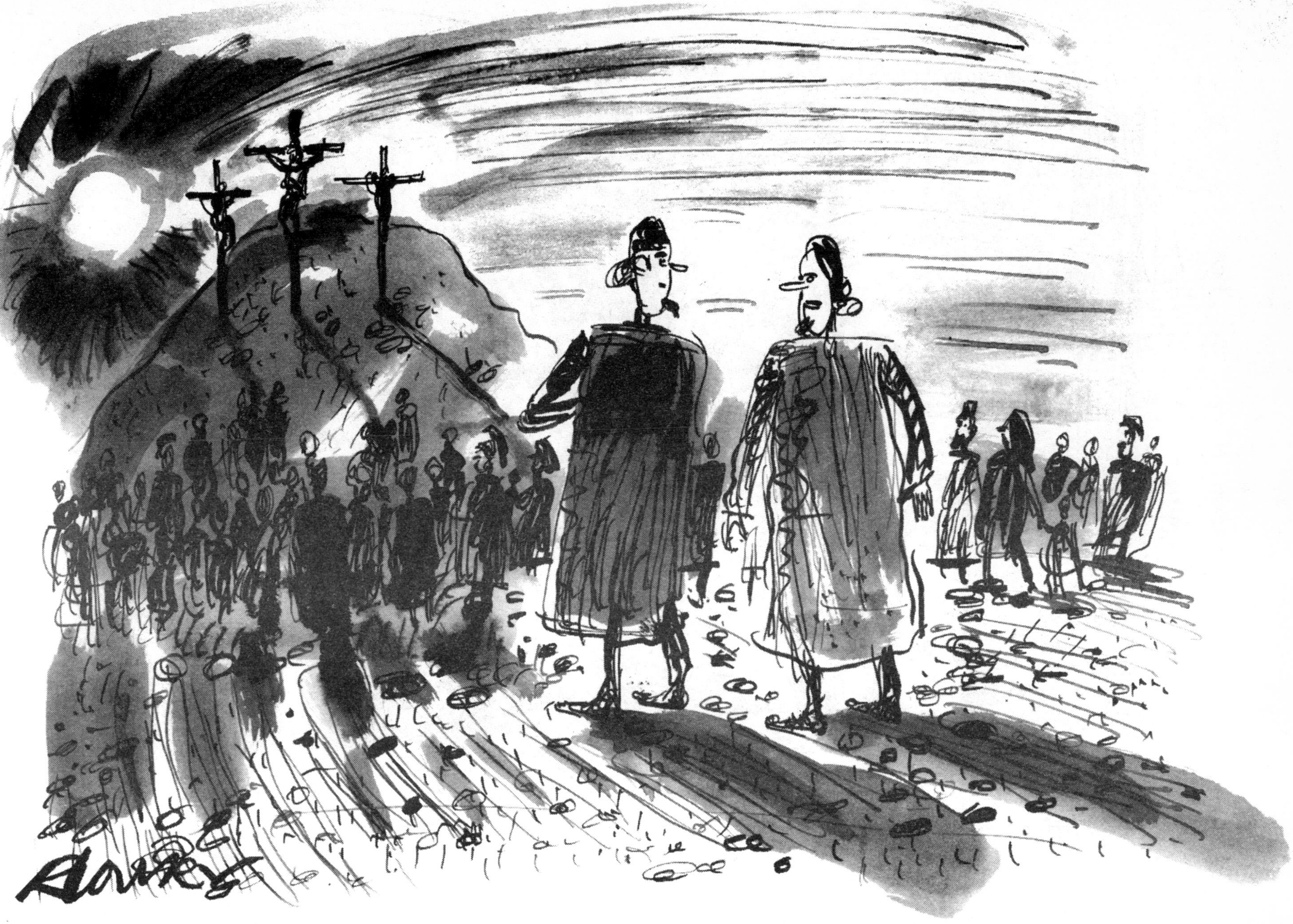

"Brilliant isn't it? And he does all his own stunts..."

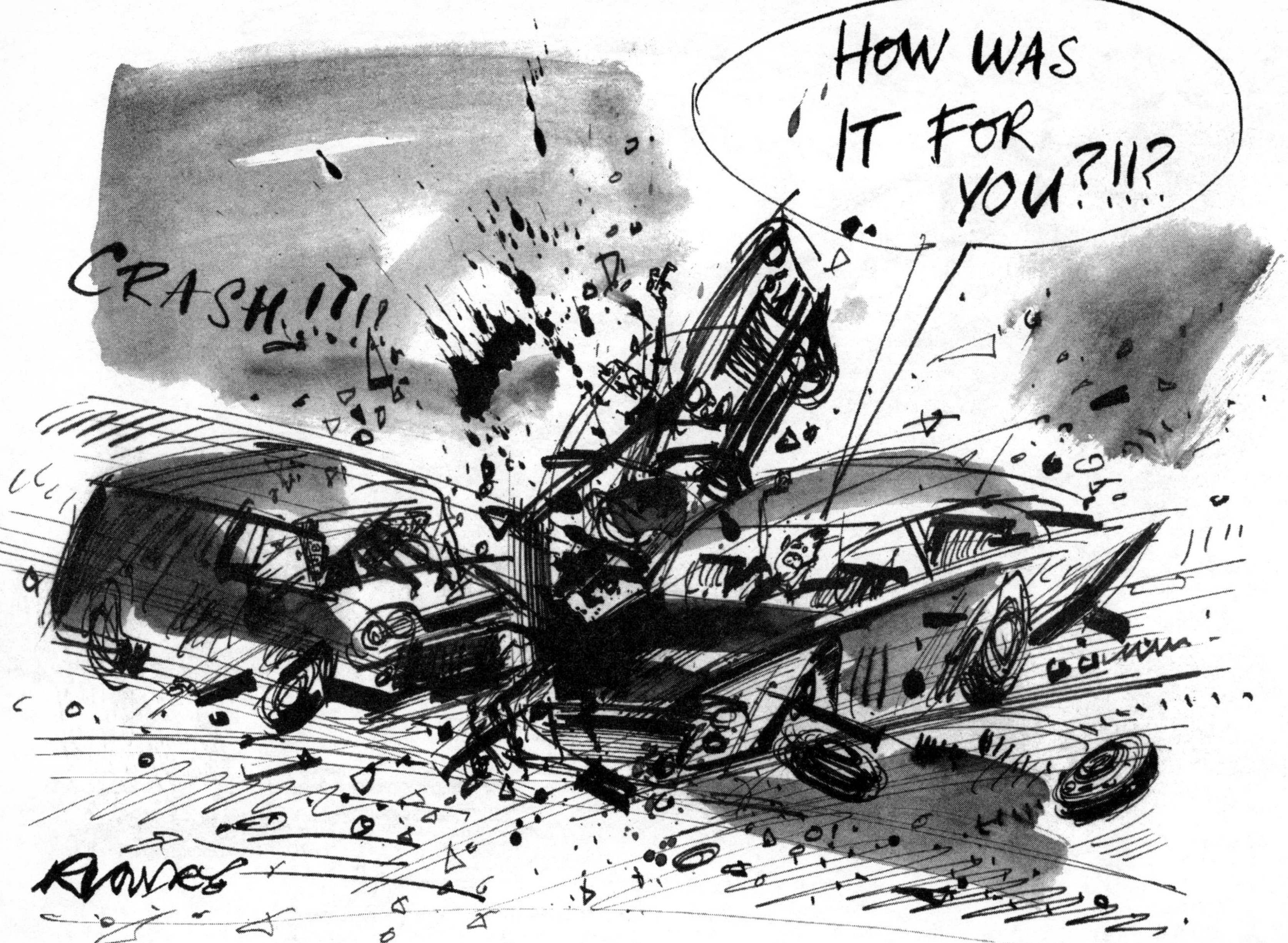

CRASH!!!!!
HOW WAS IT FOR YOU?!!?

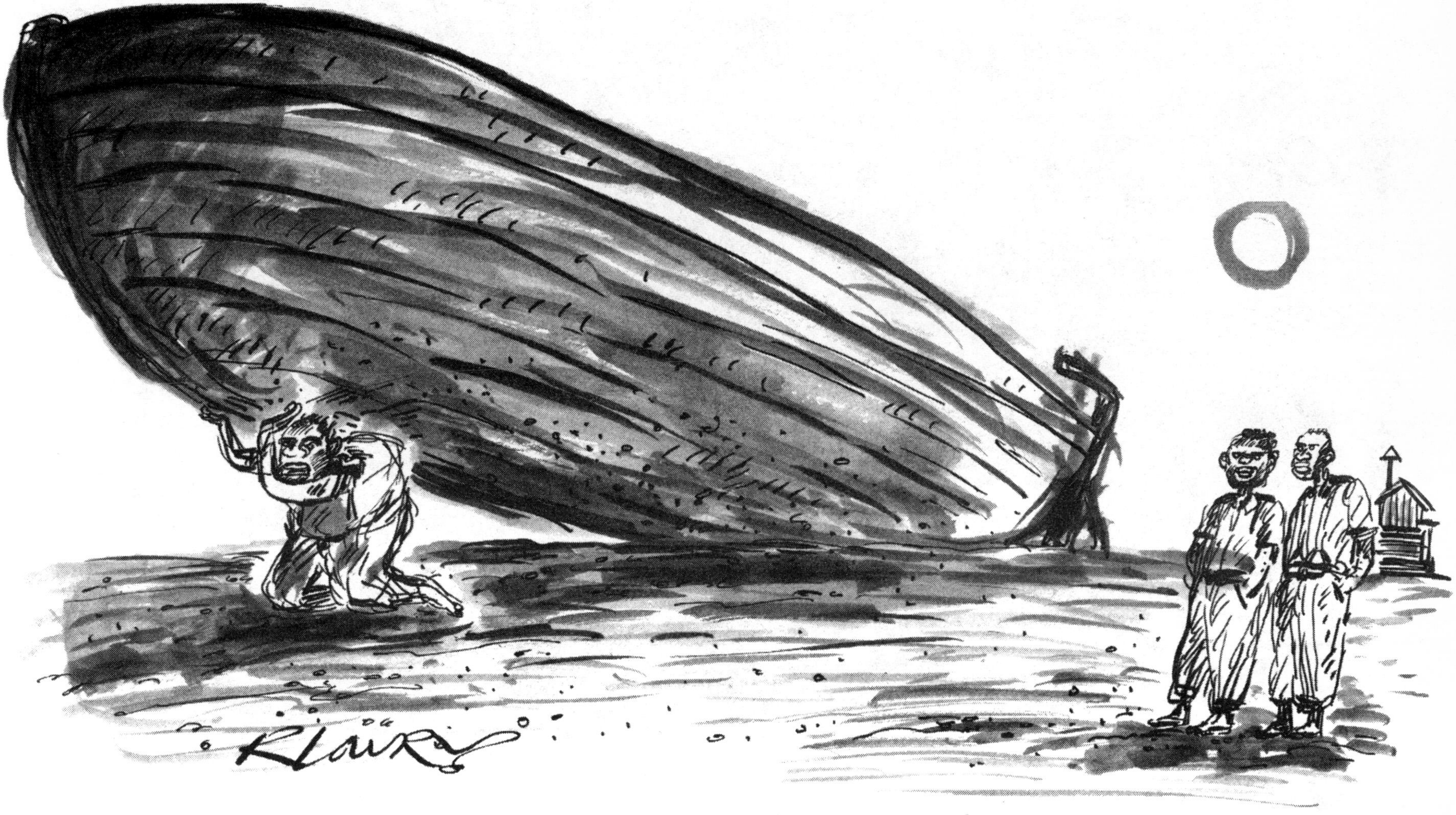

"Don't you think we ought to tell him he's supposed to tote the barges and lift the bales?"

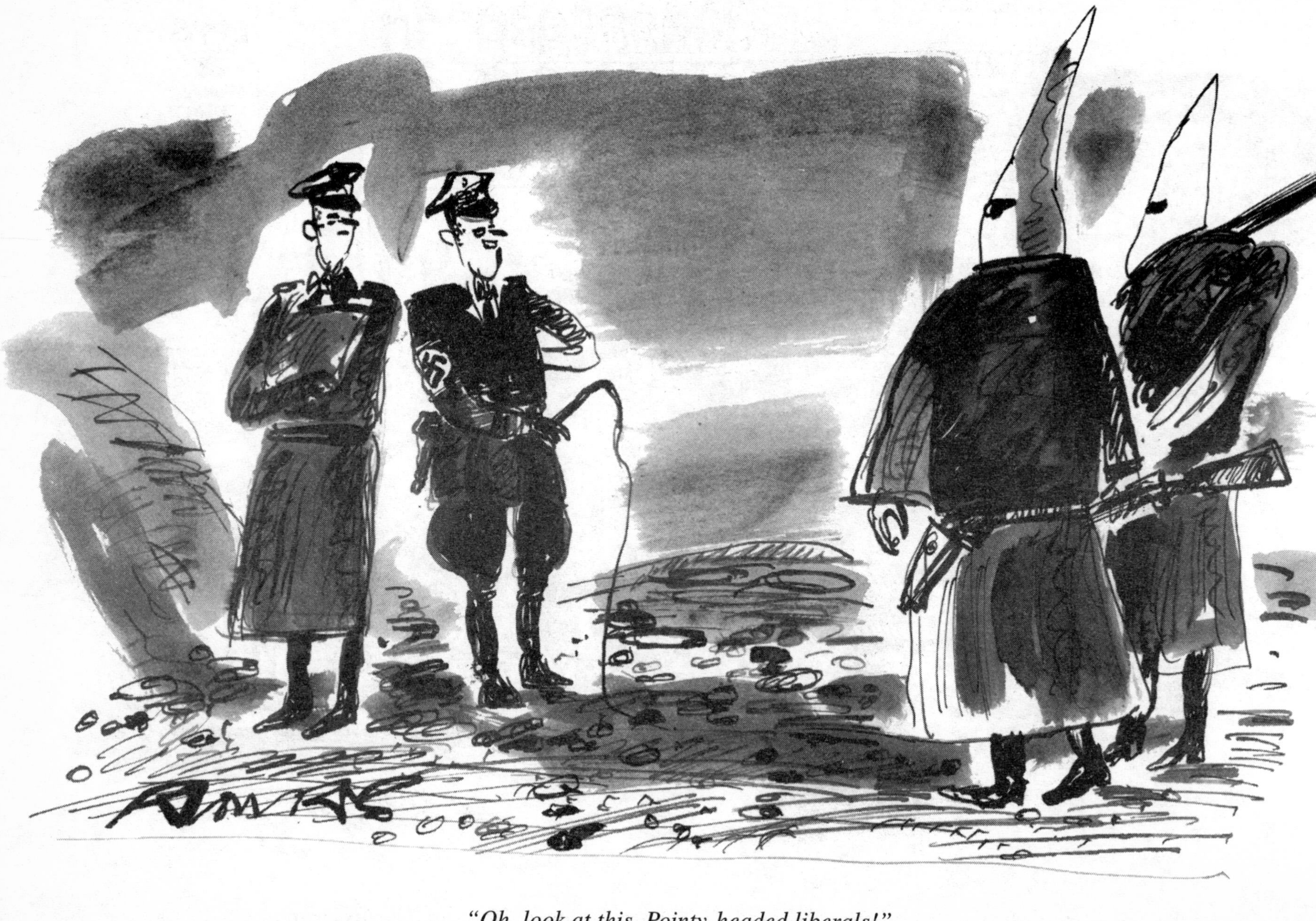

"Oh, look at this. Pointy-headed liberals!"

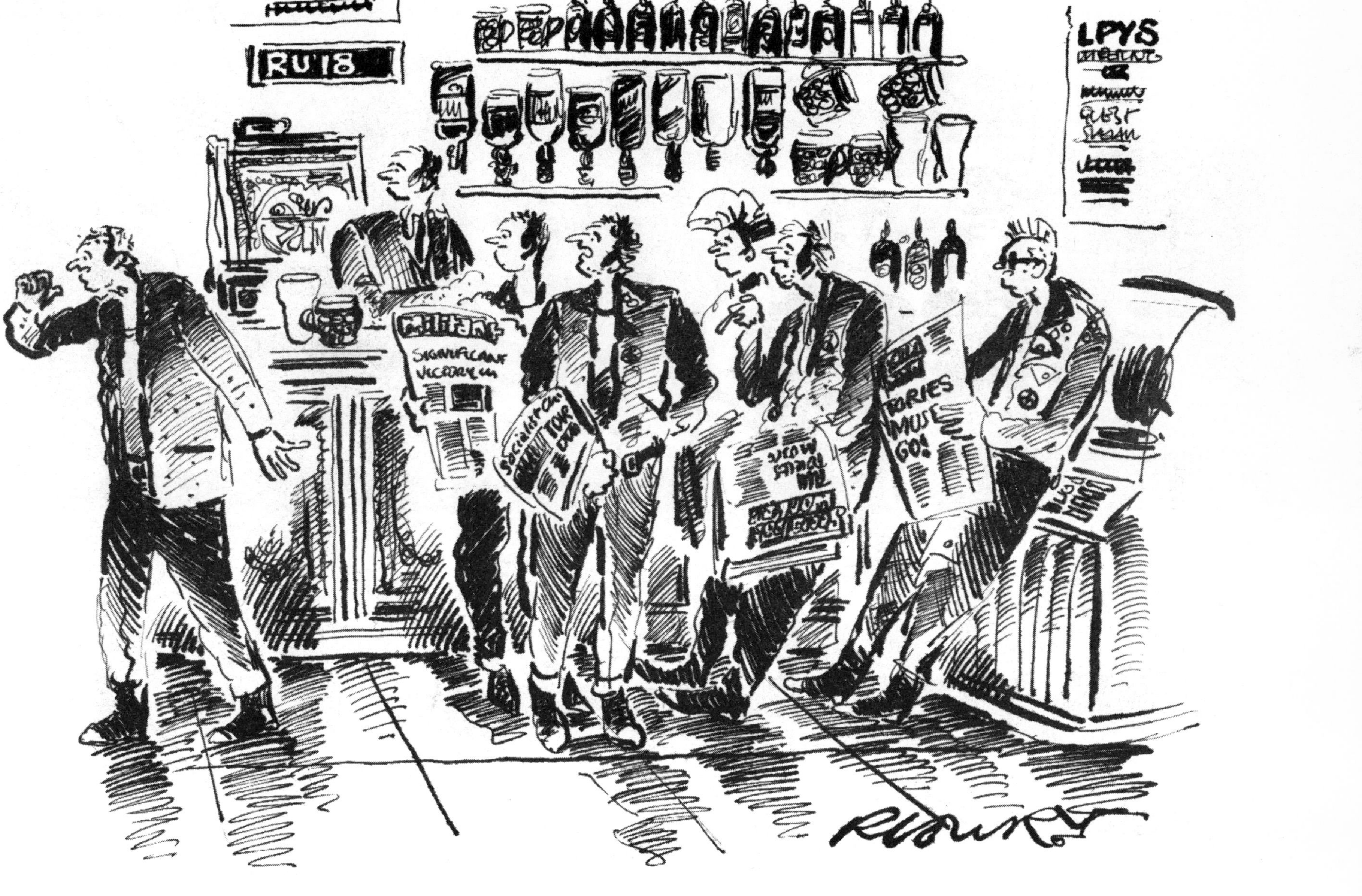
LPYS
TORIES MUST GO!

"He's absolutely pathetic. He says he's a conscientious objector to the class war!"

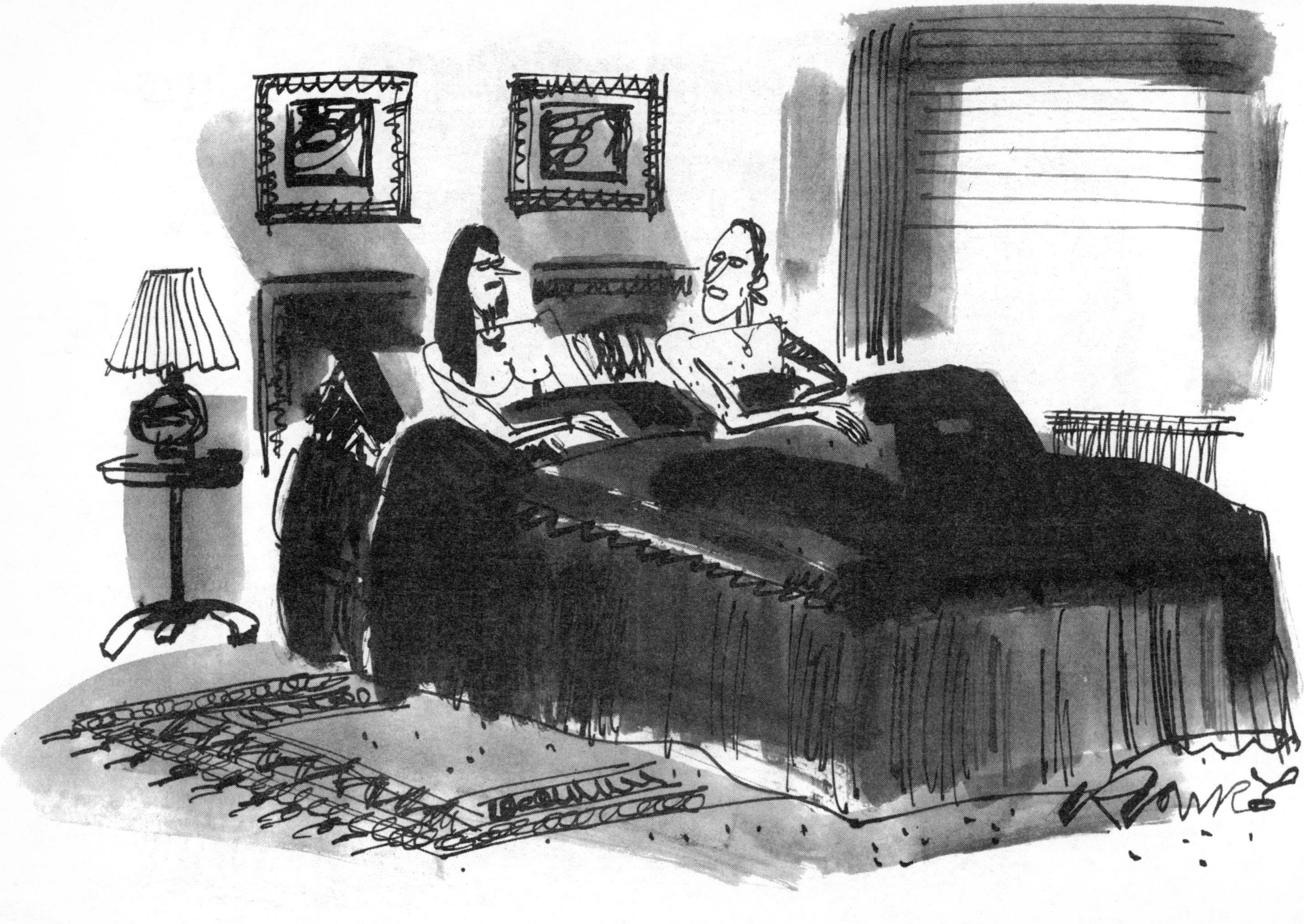

"Of course you're my TYPE dear. You're a naked woman!"

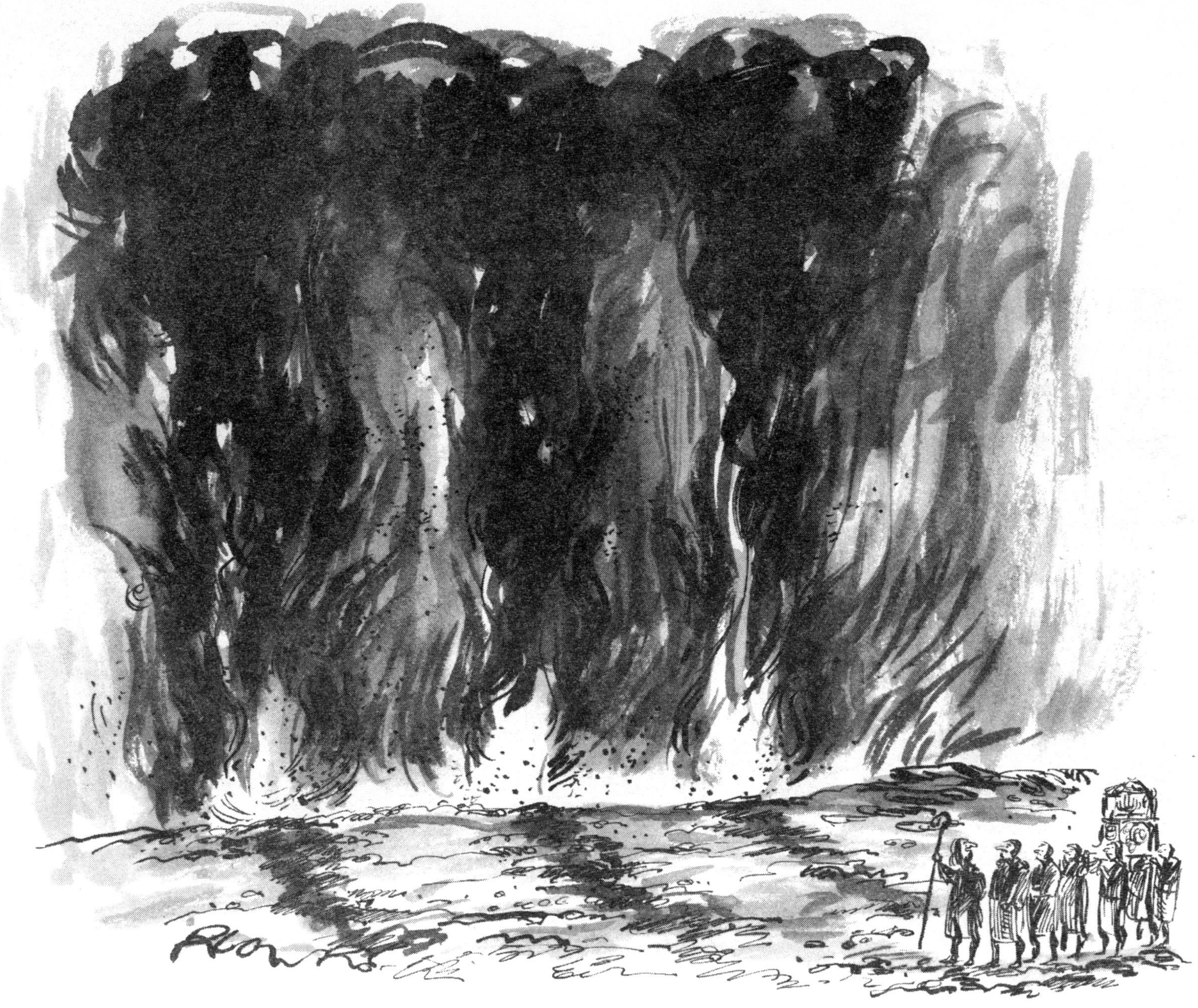

"Isn't that typical – you wait all day for one pillar of fire to come, then three or four show up at once!"

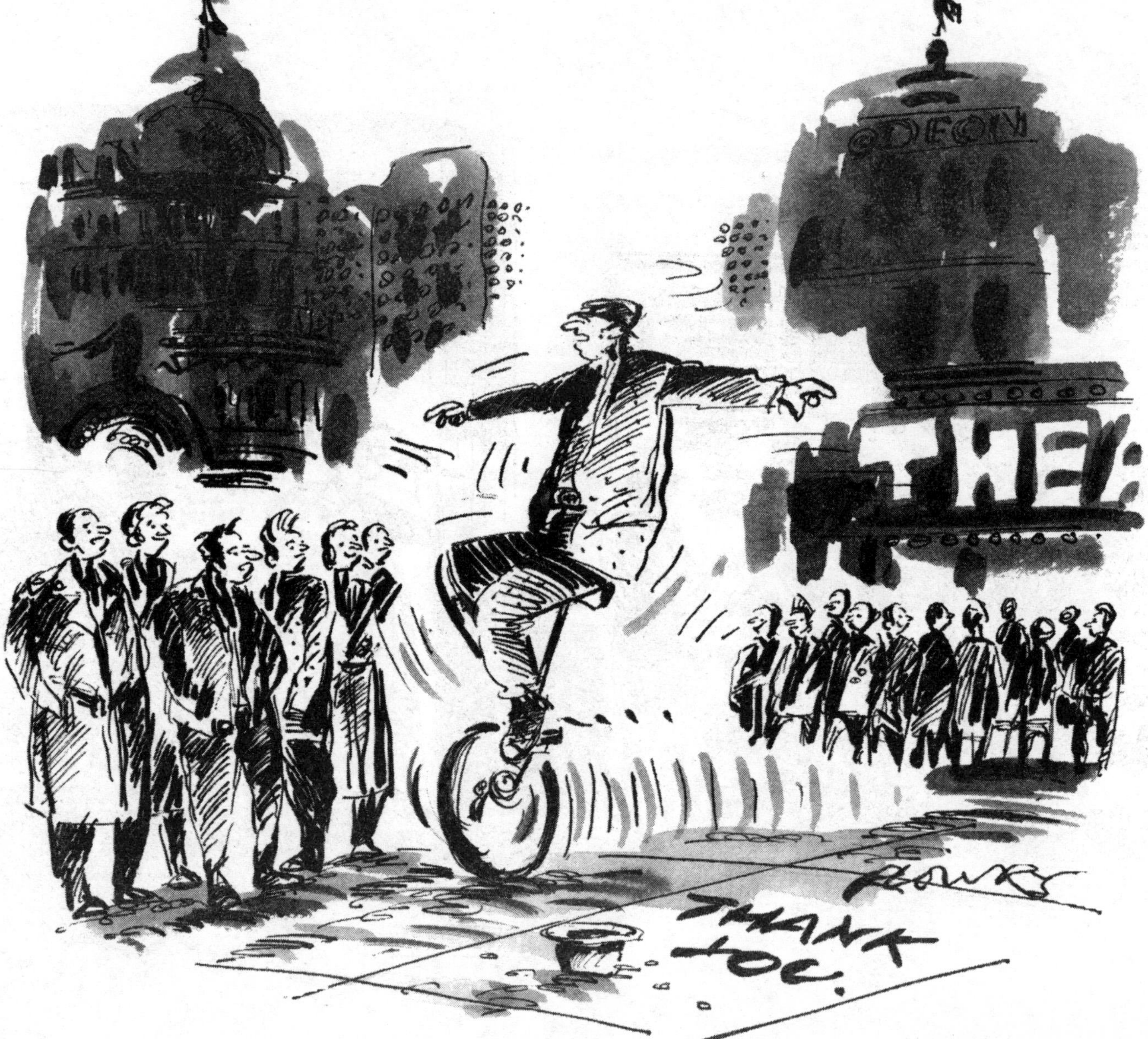
THE
THANK YOU.

"It's the only skill I learned while I was riding around the country looking for work!"

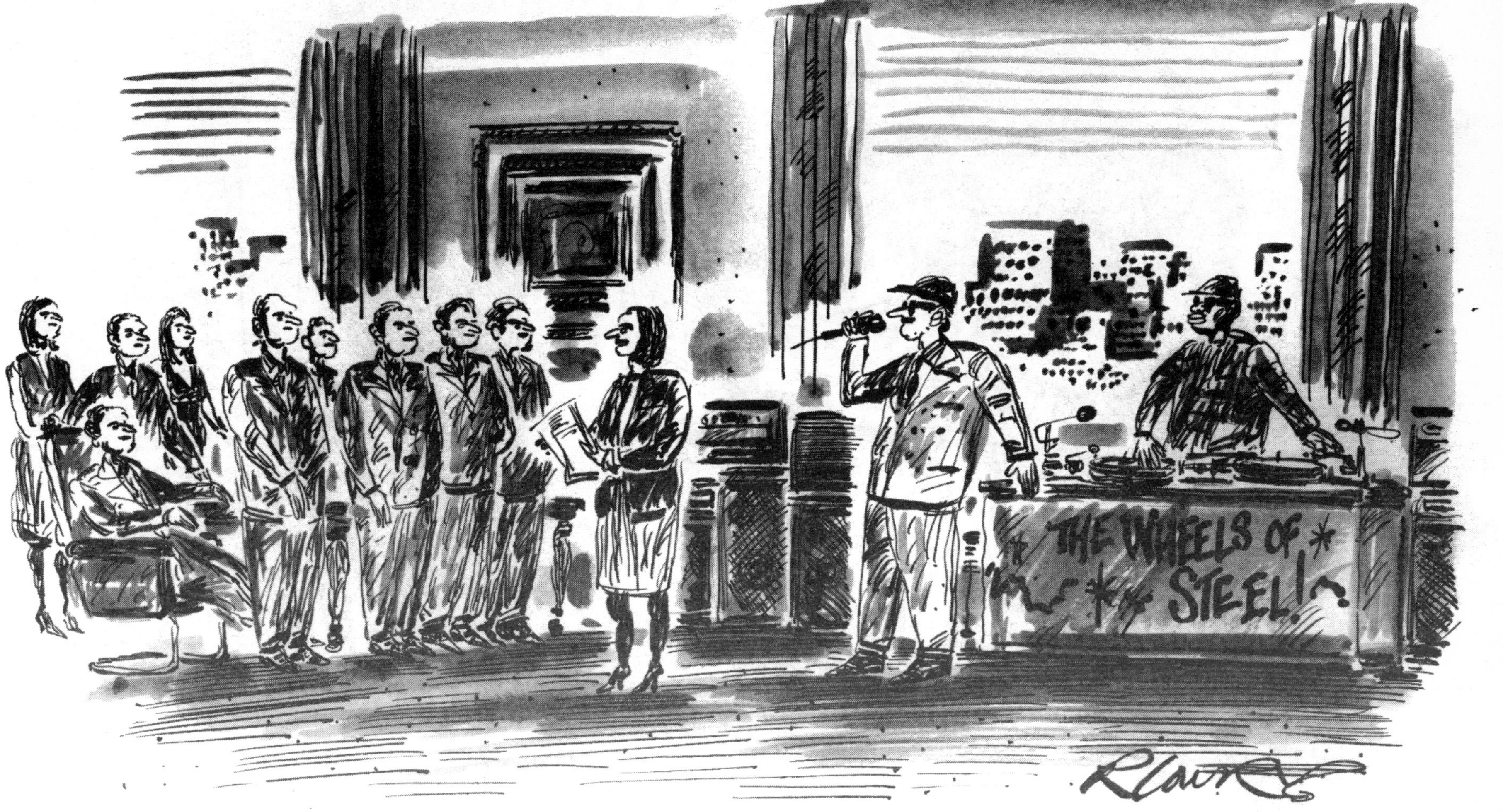
THE WHEELS OF STEEL!

"The Chairman has decided to make a complete break with tradition this year. Instead of reading the annual report and statement of accounts, he's going to hit you all with the company rap."

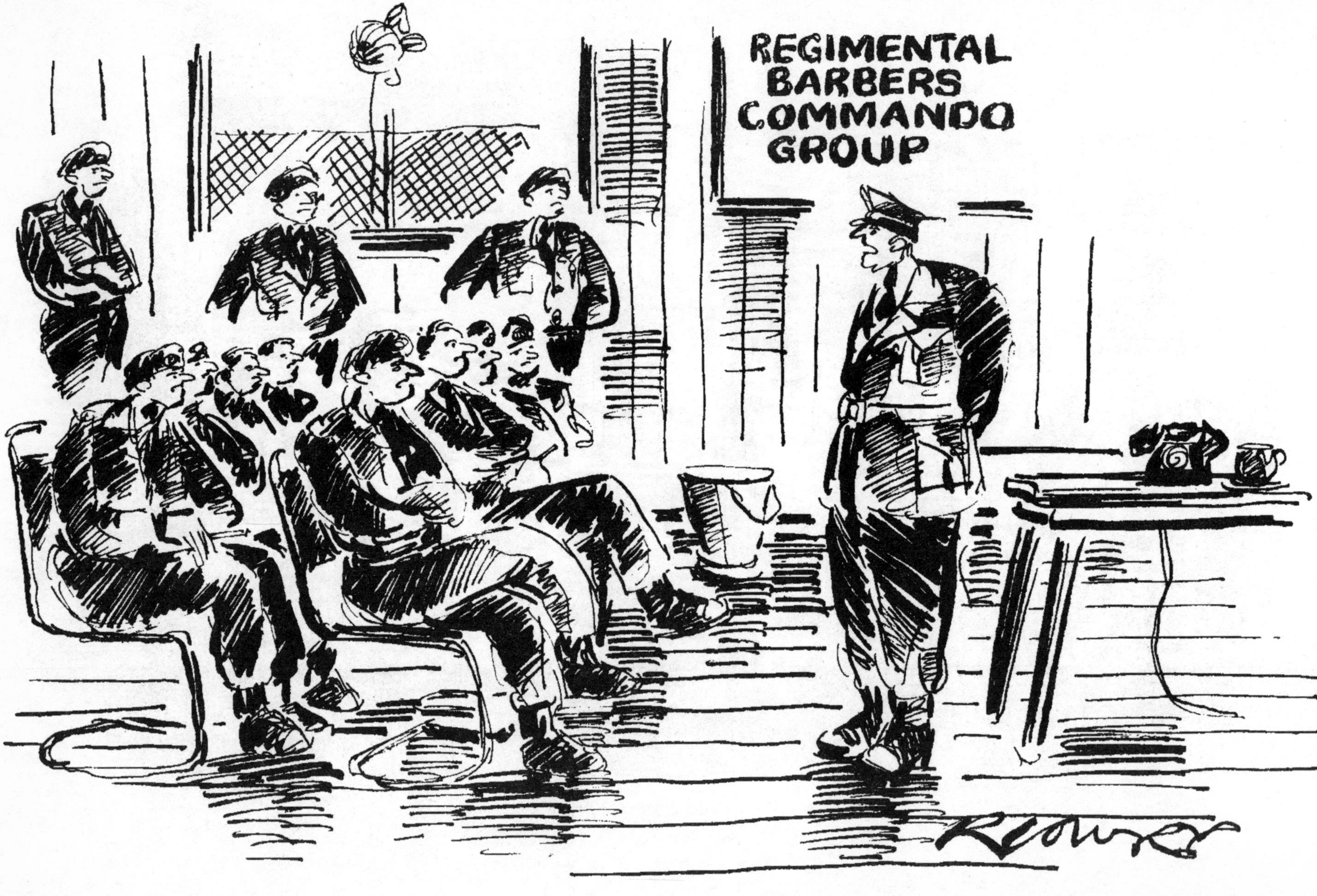

REGIMENTAL BARBERS COMMANDO GROUP

"It's a suicide mission, men. I want two volunteers to parachute into Berlin and give the Führer a compulsory Afro.."

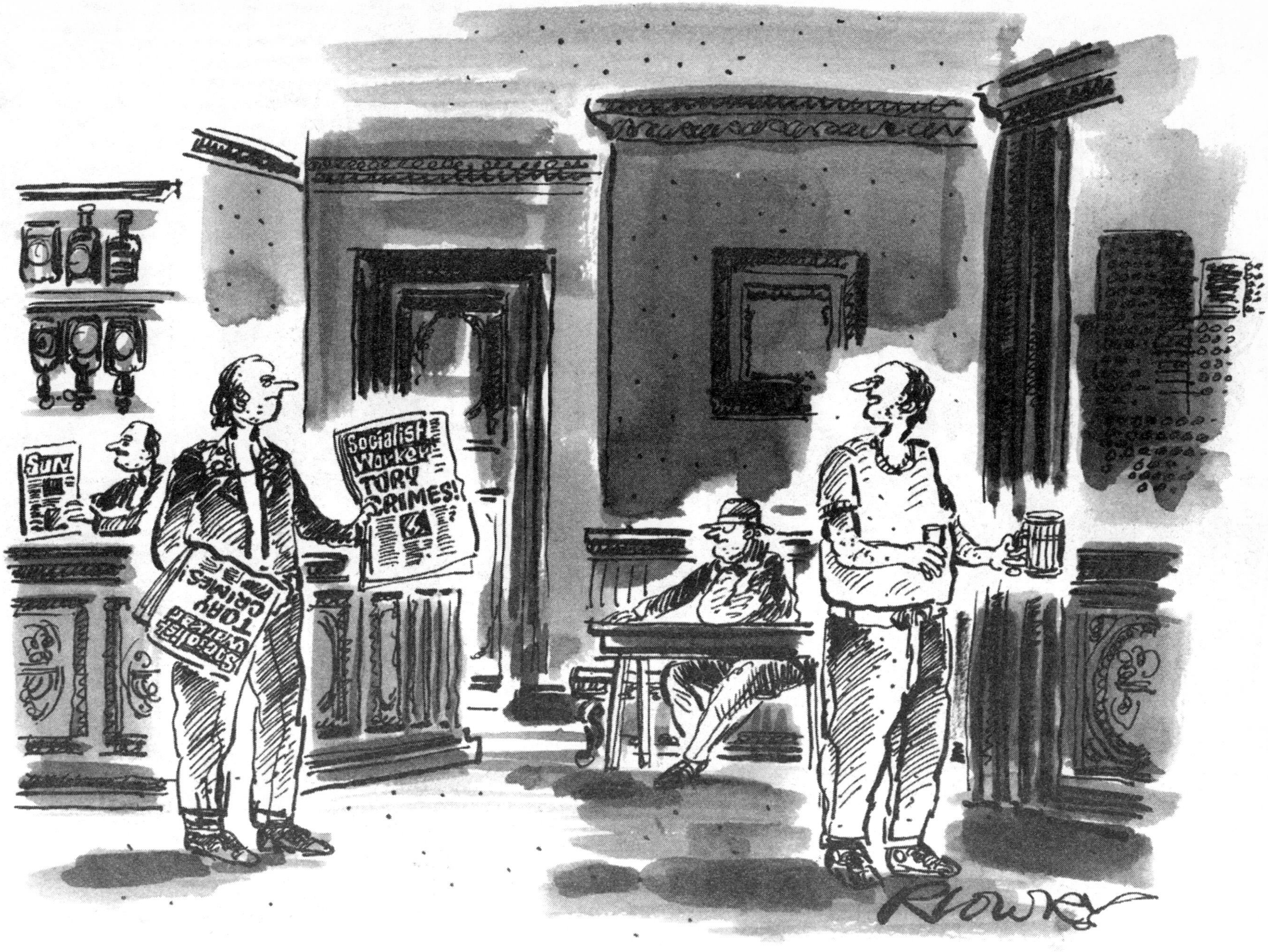
SUN
Socialist Worker
TORY CRIMES!

"Not for me. I've opted out of the struggle between Capitalism and Socialism in order to concentrate more fully on the struggle against alcoholism."

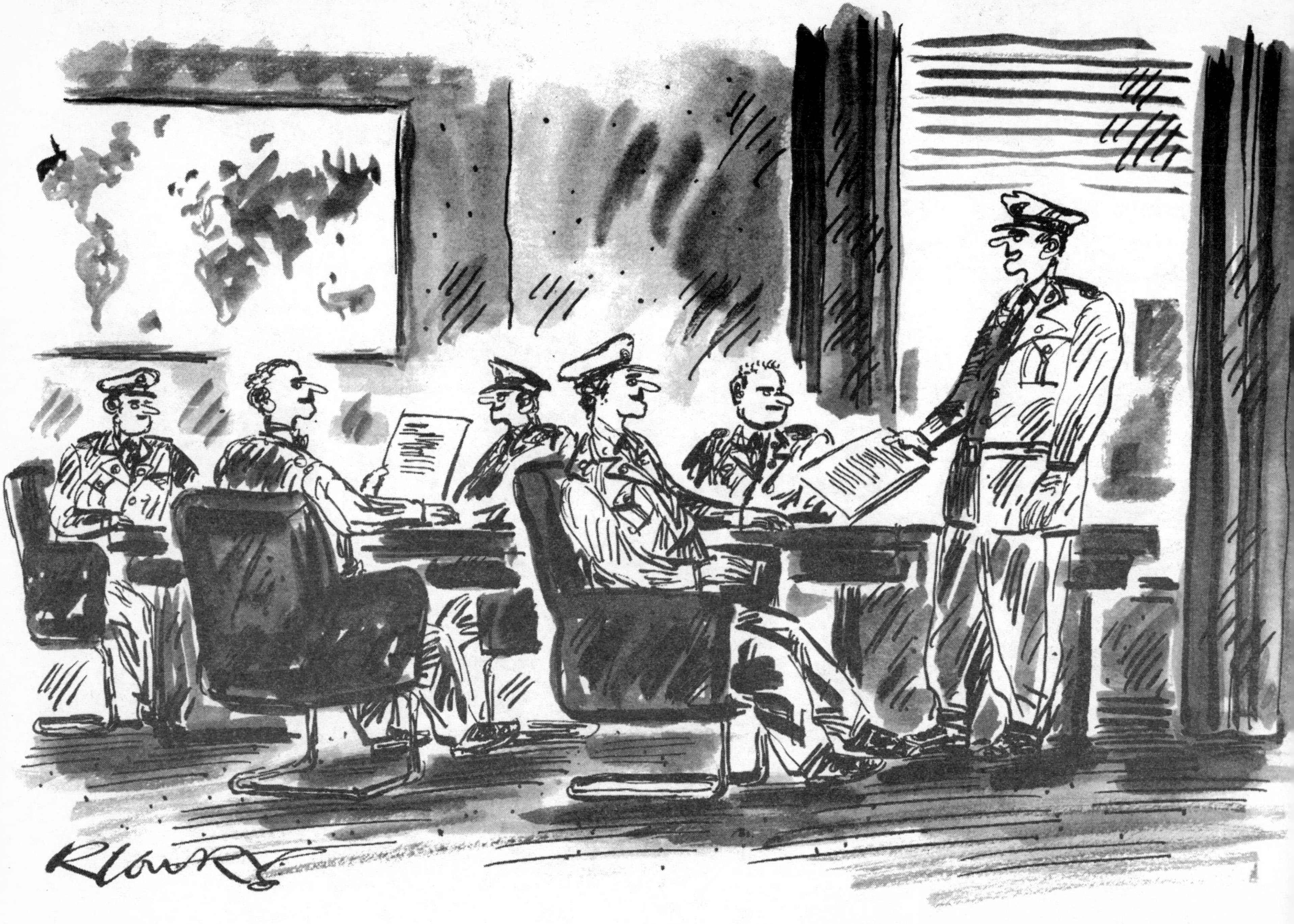

"Right gentlemen – that's enough of that mamby-pamby talk about the defence budget. Let's discuss the ATTACK budget..."

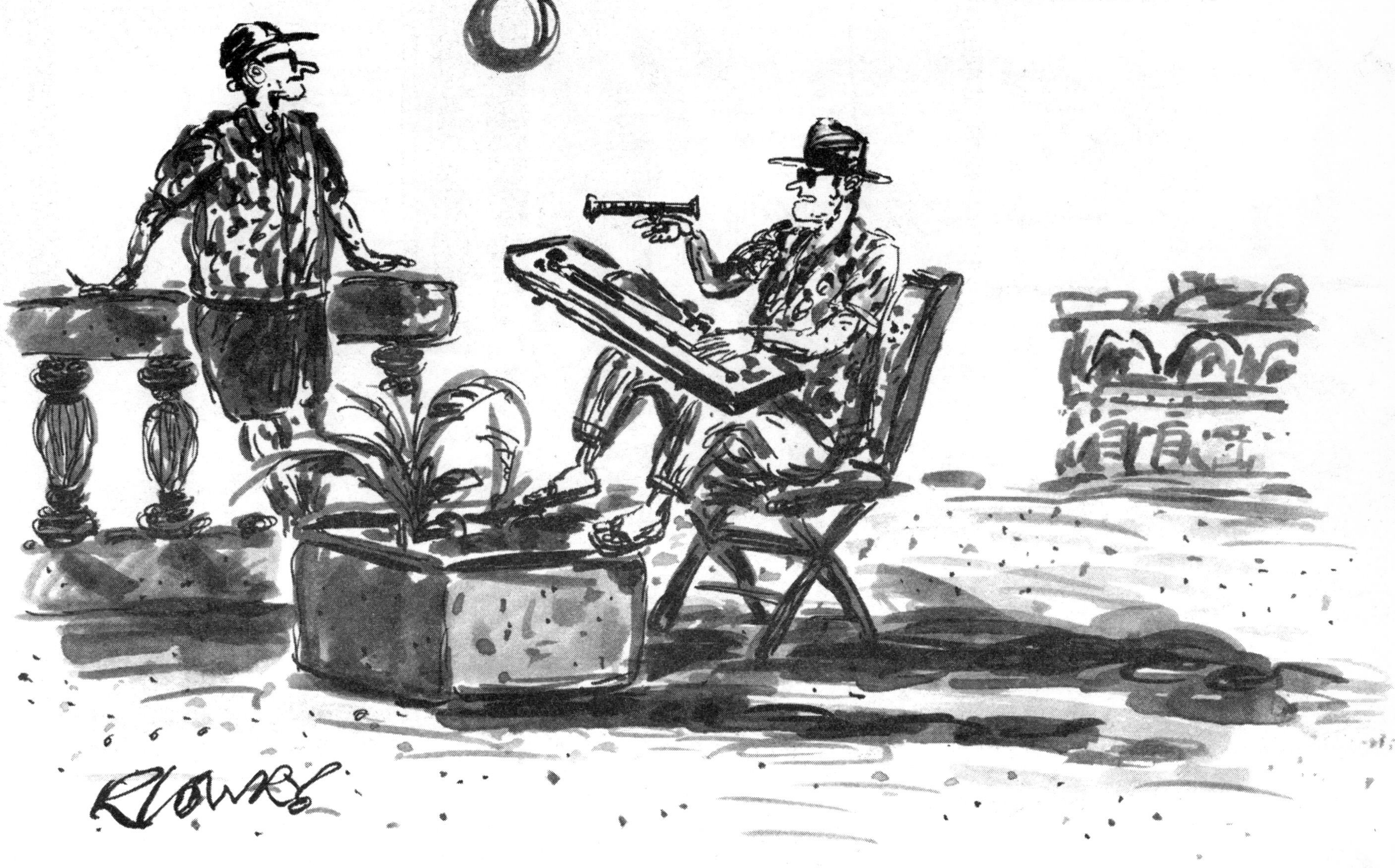

"I can remember exactly what I was doing when President Kennedy was shot."

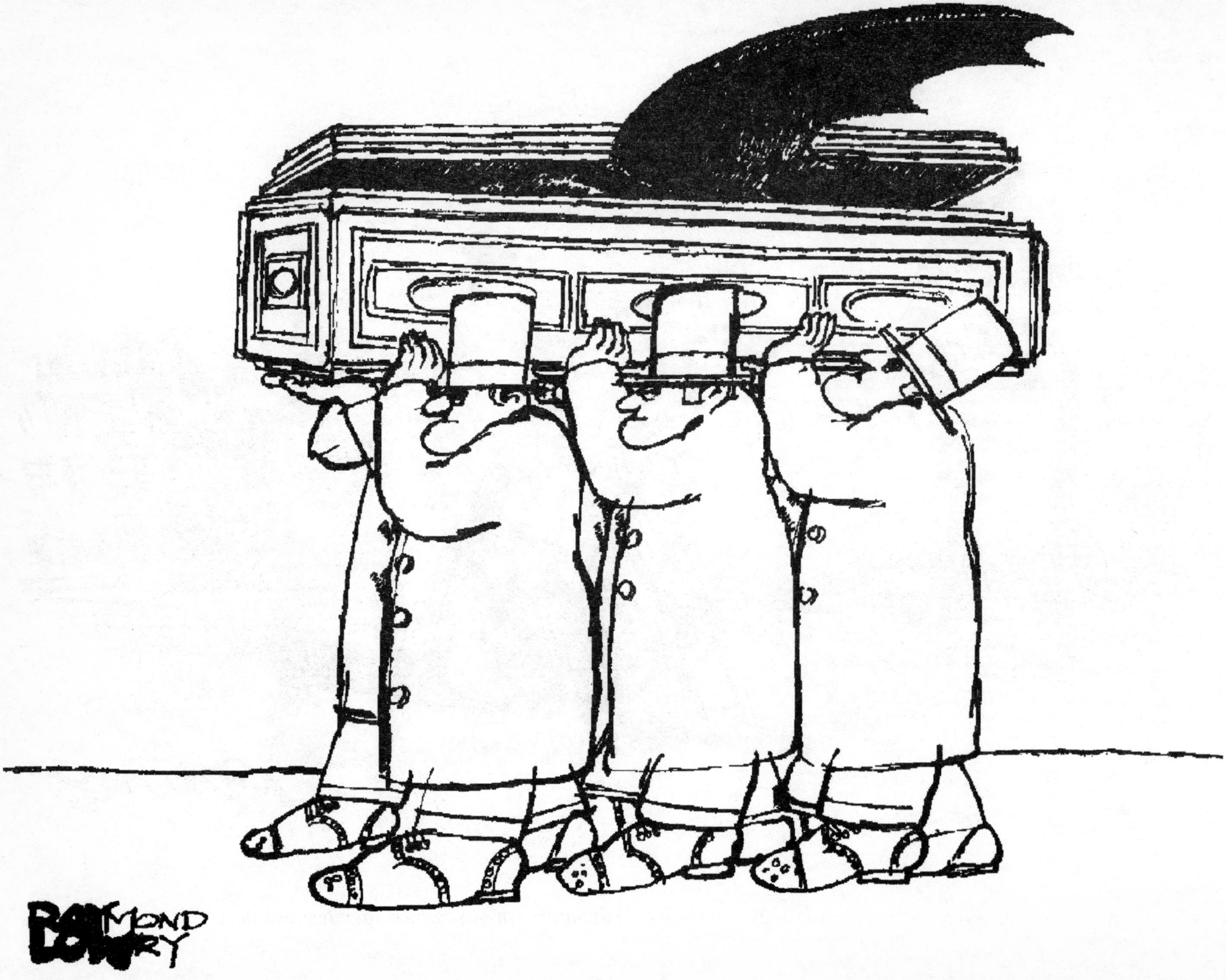

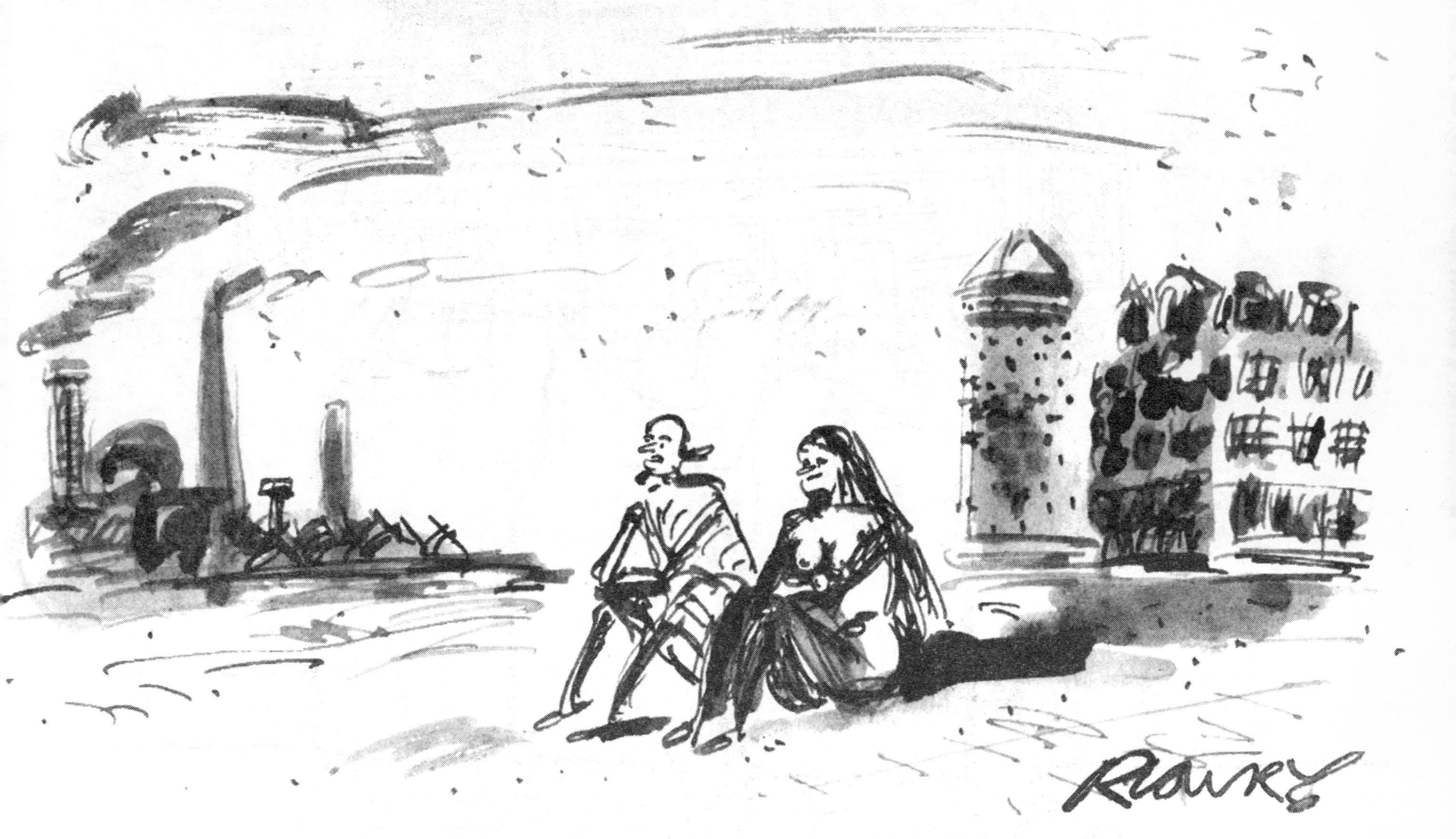
RLOWRY

"OK dear, we're naked as nature intended – but nature isn't as nature intended any more!"

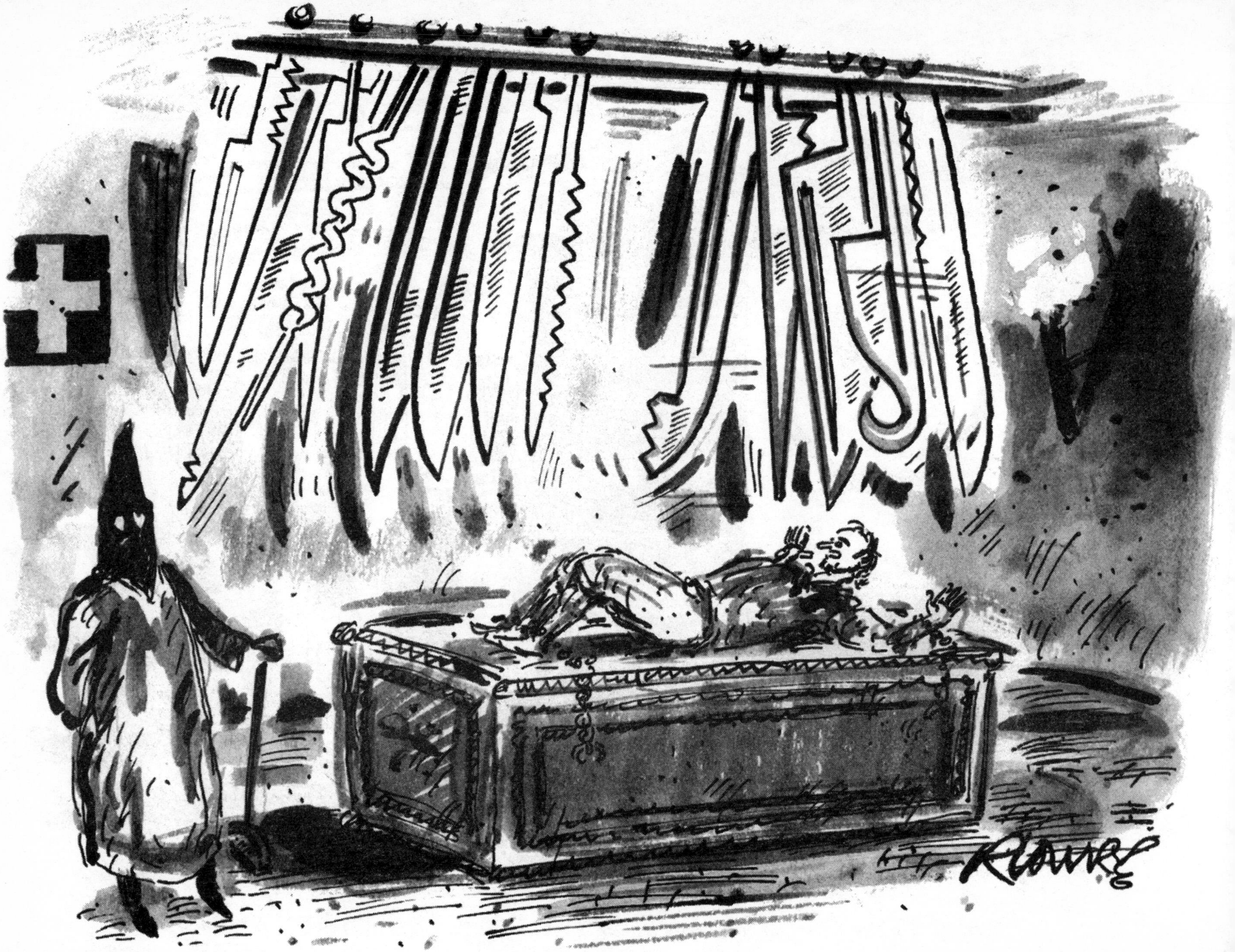

"Oh no! The Swiss Army Inquisition."

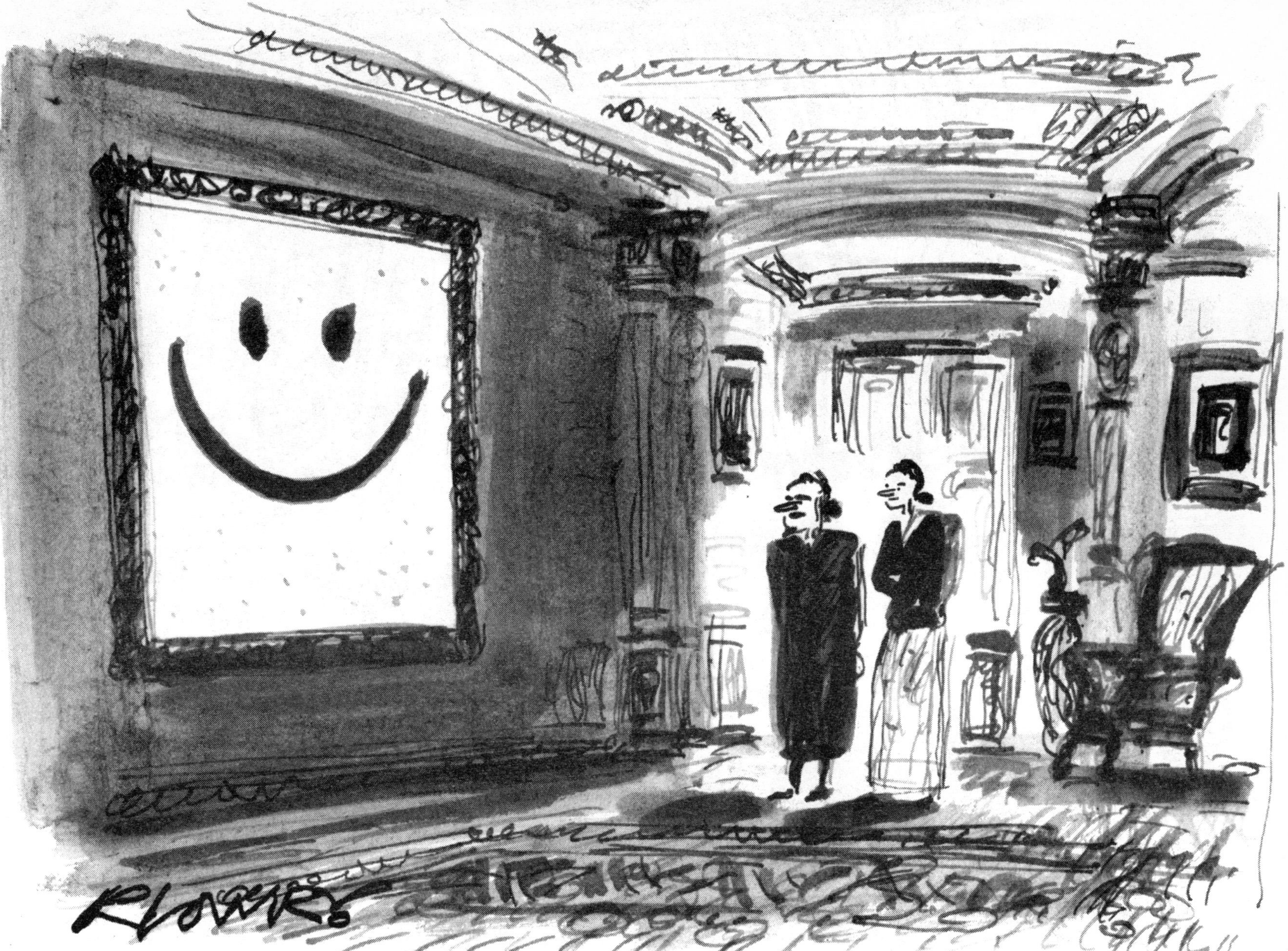

"We keep the funny money behind that one."

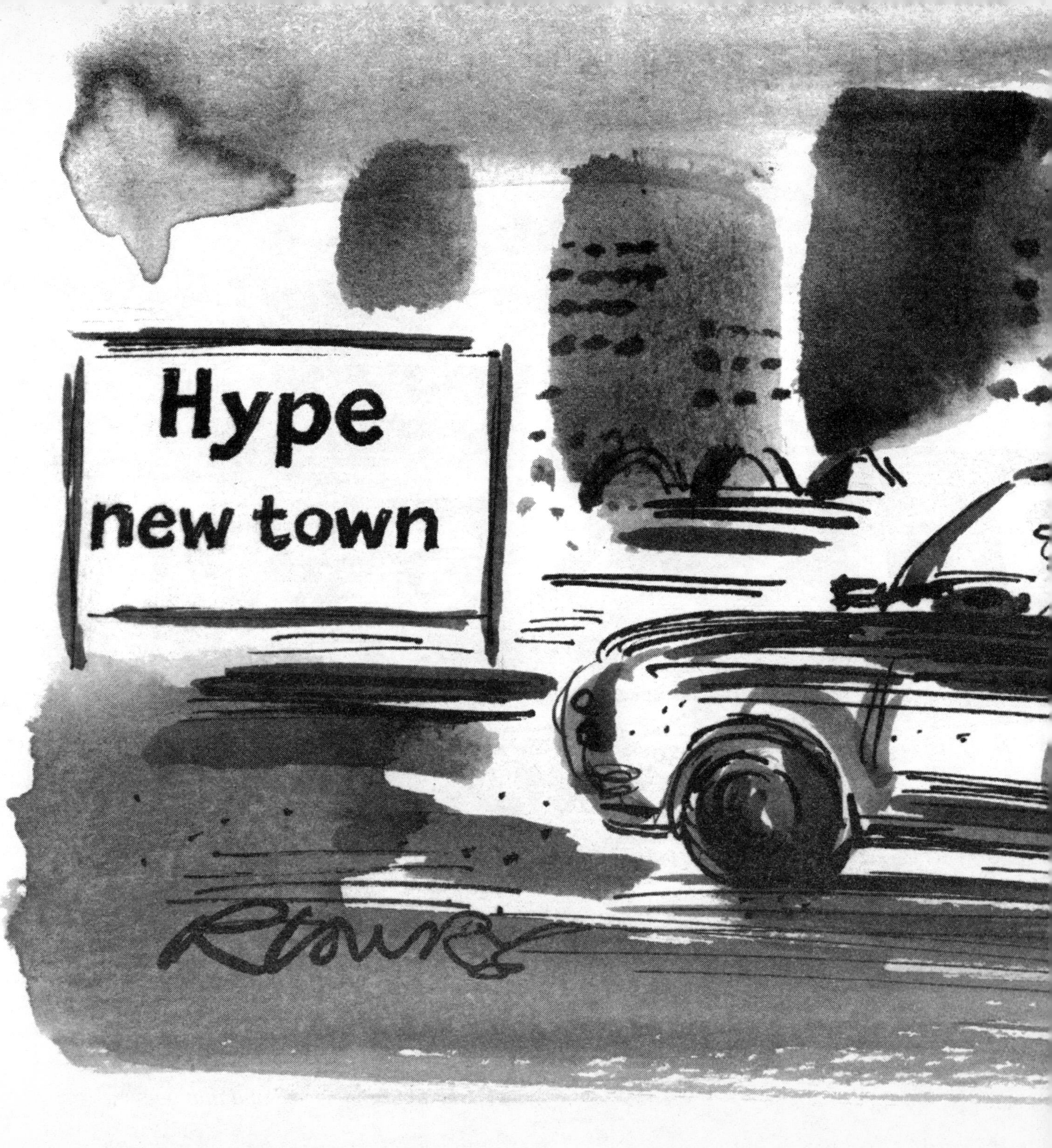
Hype
new town

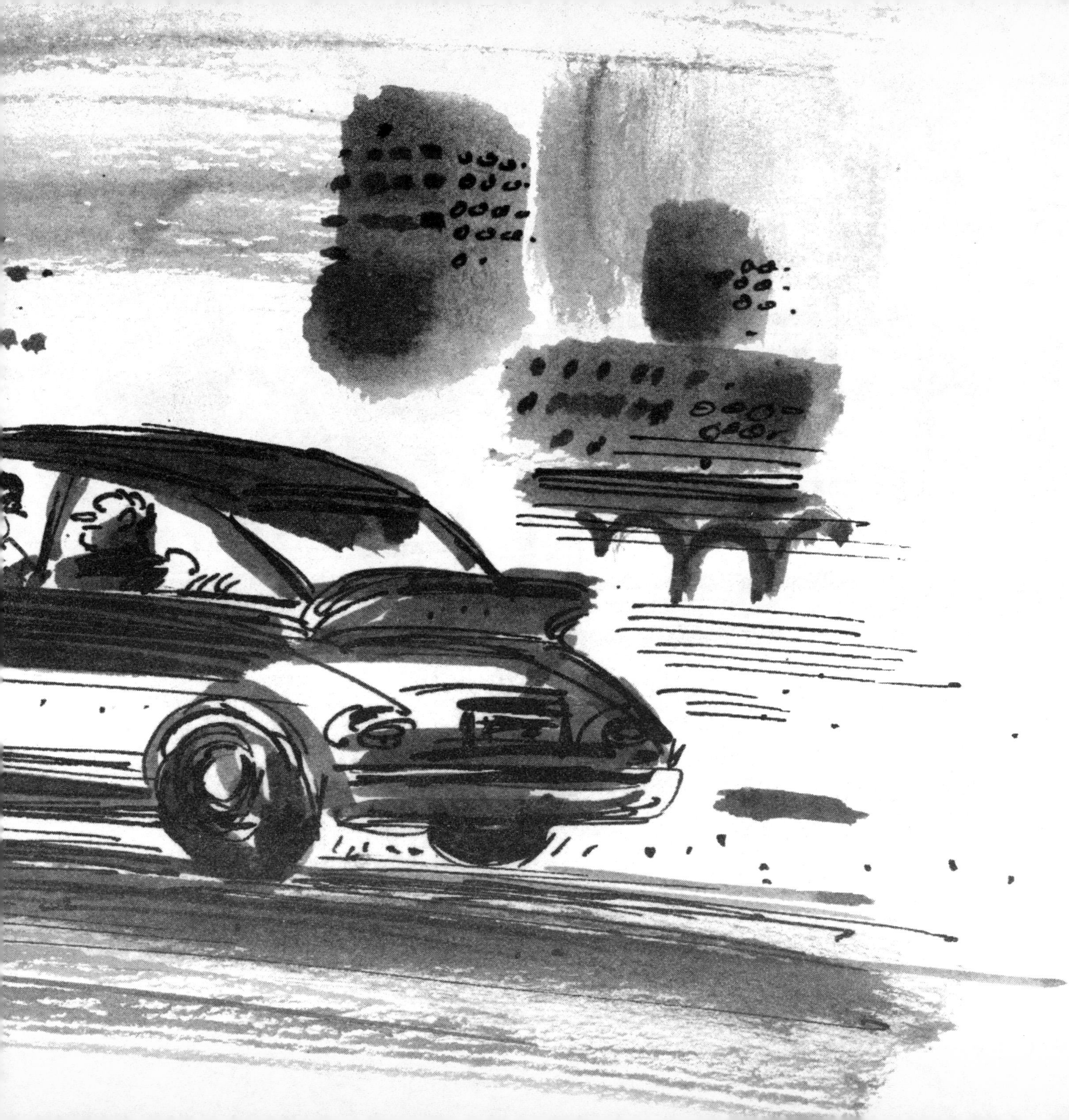

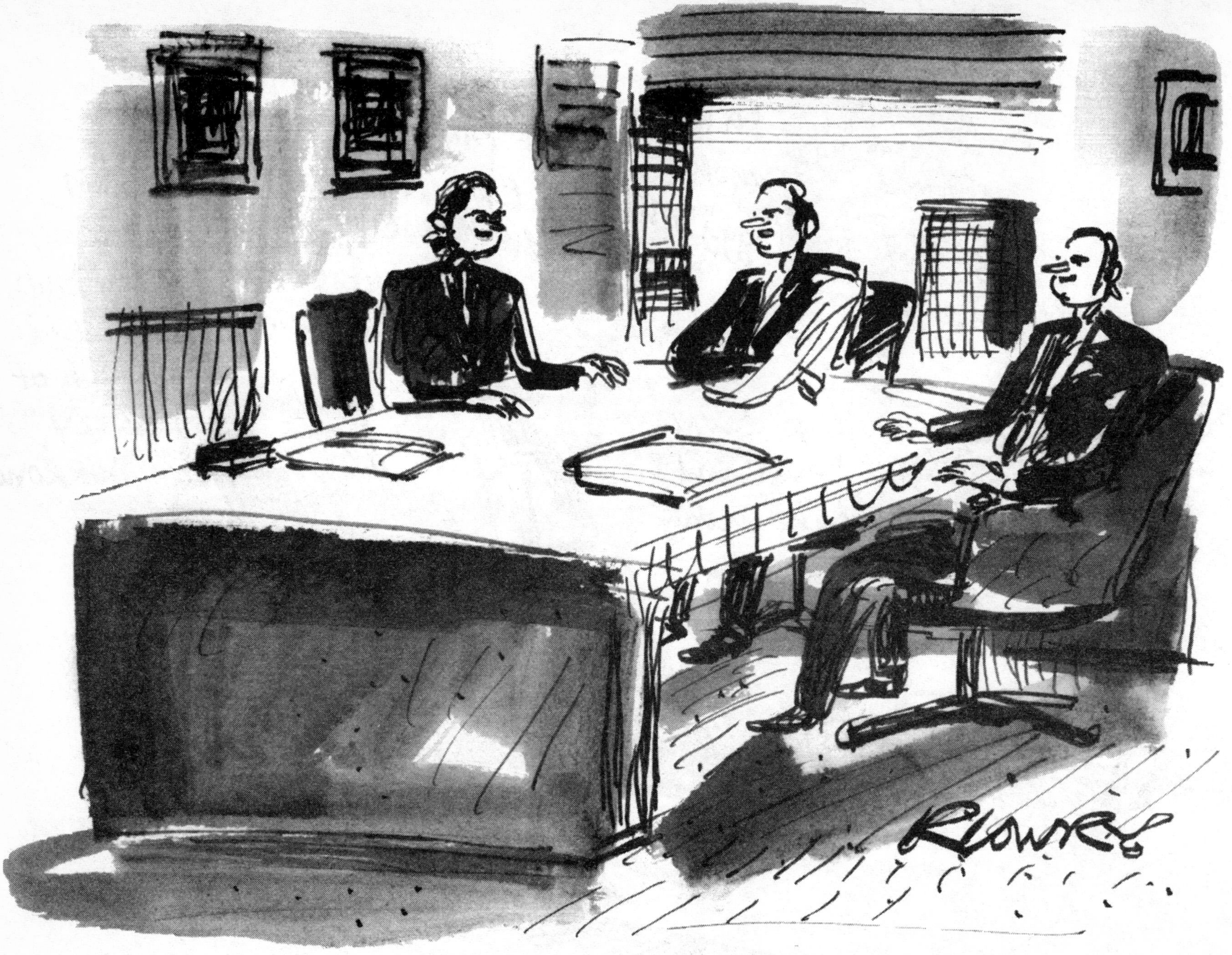
RLOWRS

"This calls for a celebration, gentlemen. Let's open a can of worms."

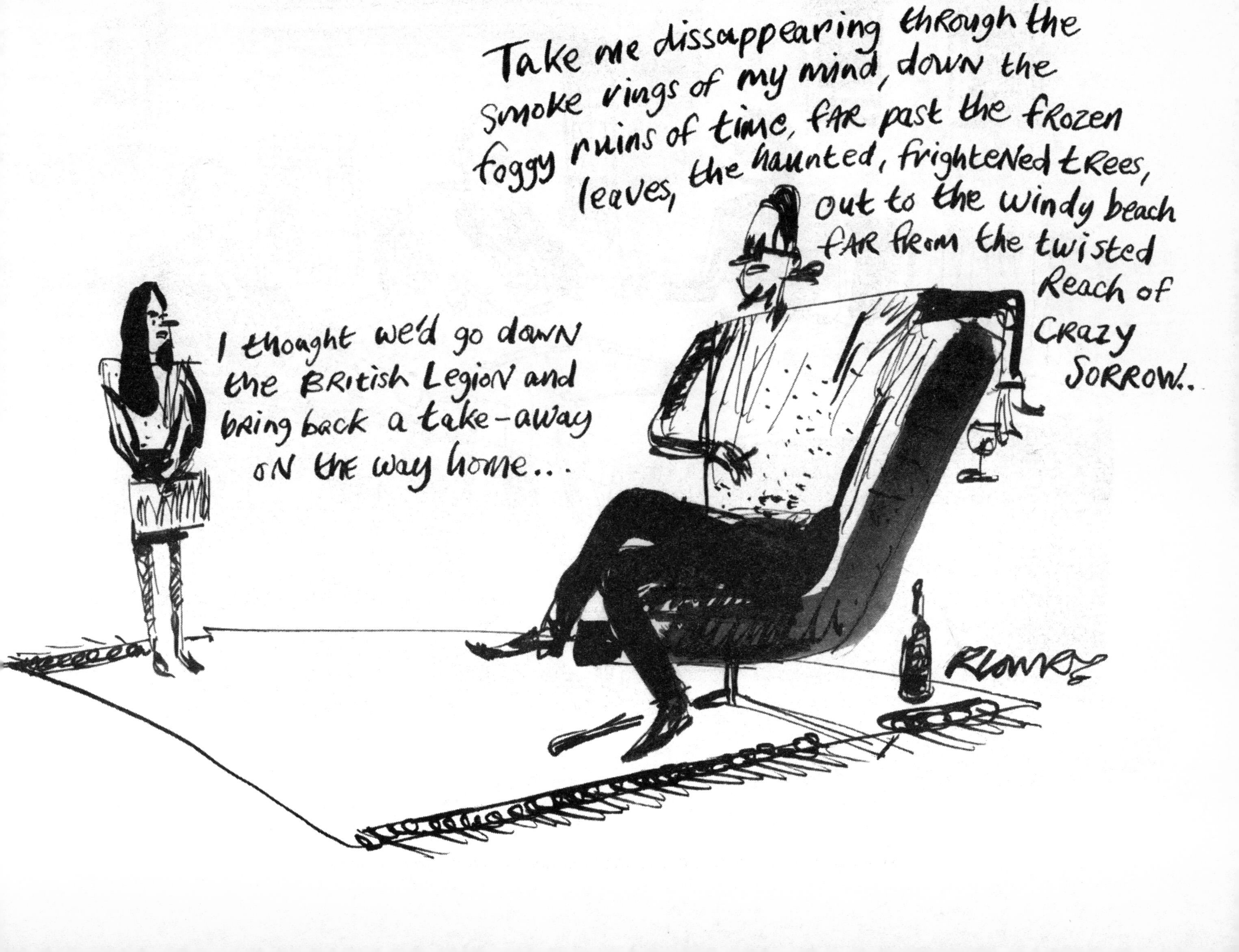

Take me dissappearing through the smoke rings of my mind, down the foggy ruins of time, FAR past the frozen leaves, the haunted, frightened trees, out to the windy beach FAR from the twisted Reach of crazy SORROW..
I thought we'd go down the BRitish Legion and bring back a take-away on the way home...
RLOWRY

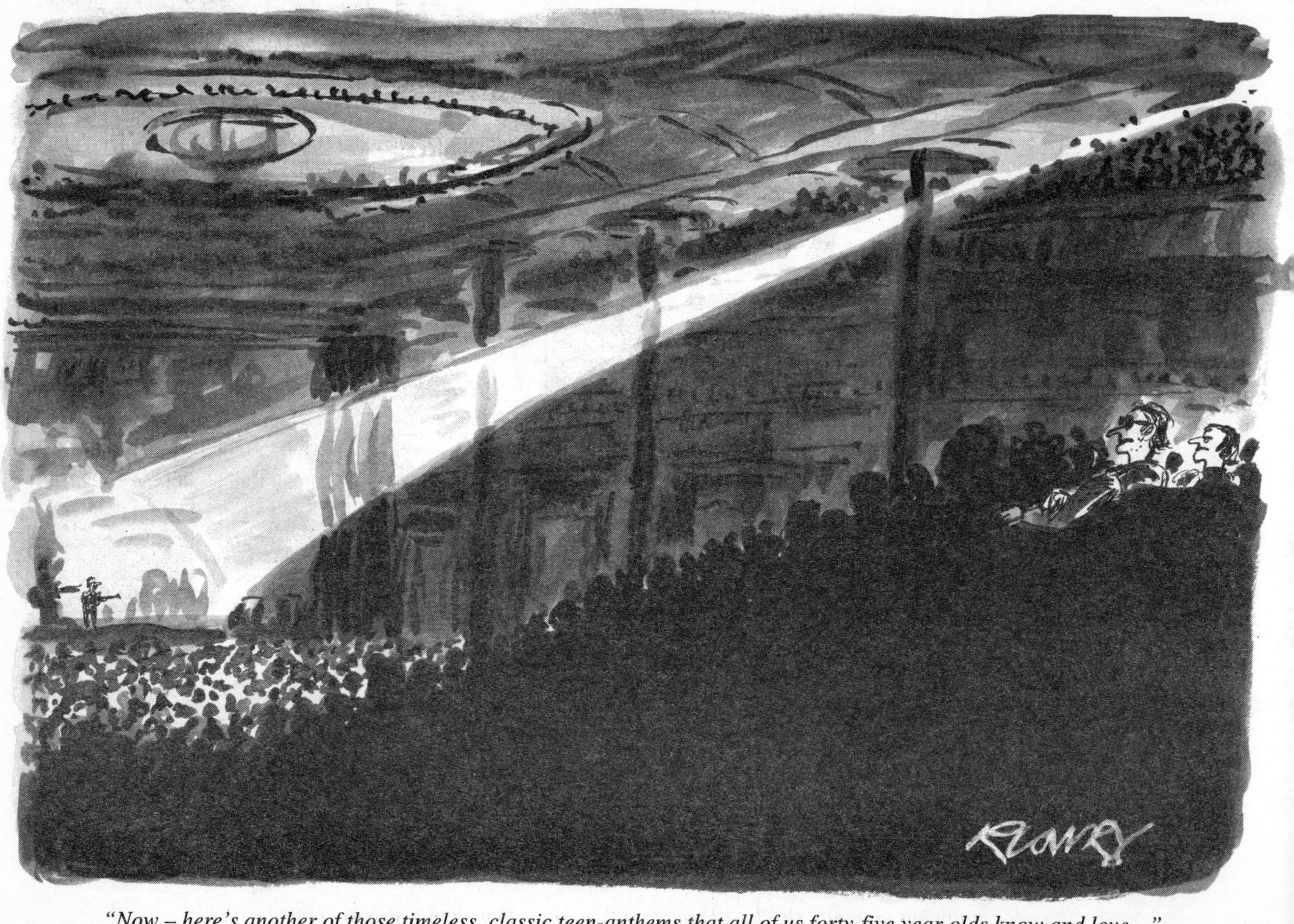
KEANEY

"Now – here's another of those timeless, classic teen-anthems that all of us forty-five year olds know and love…"

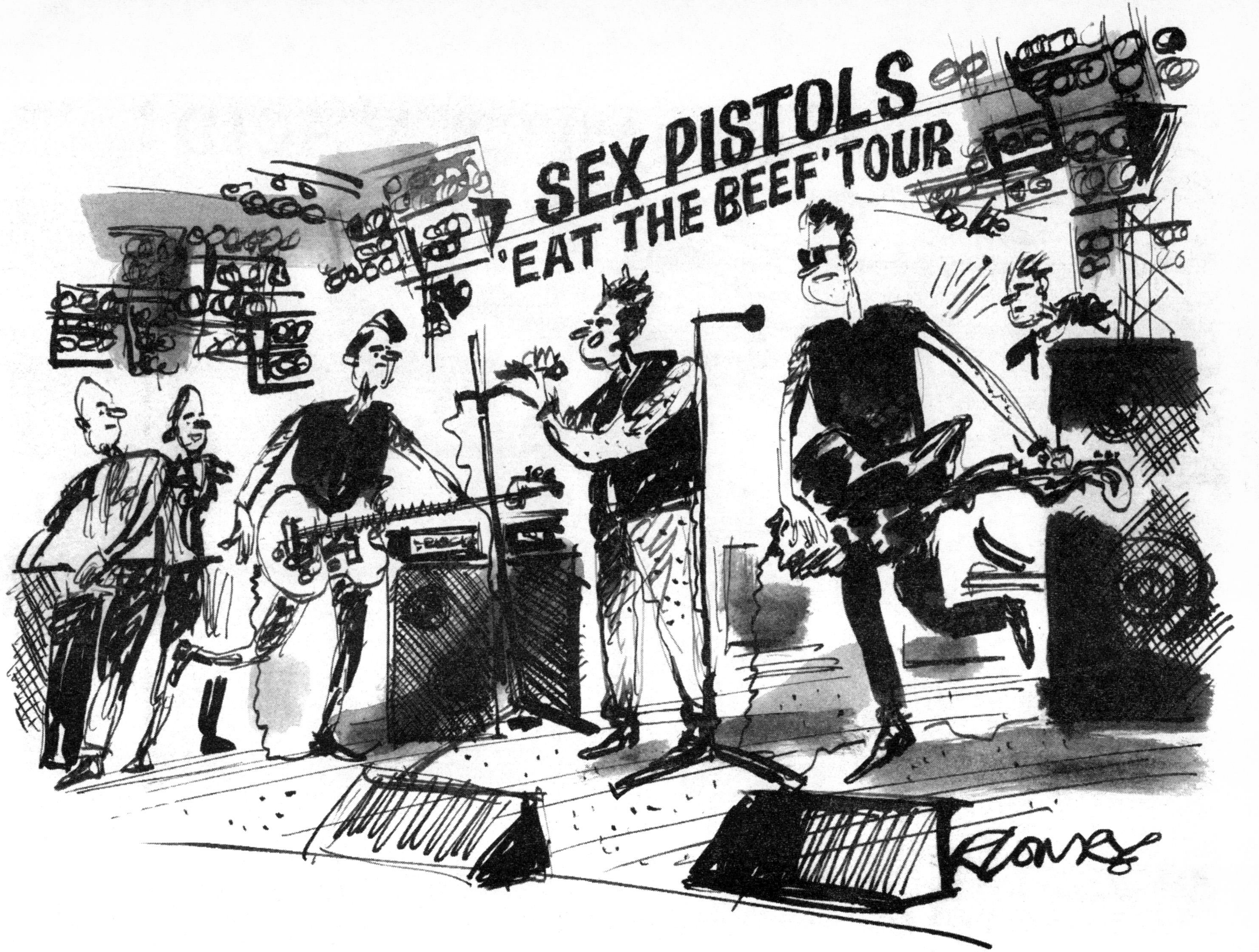
SEX PISTOLS
'EAT THE BEEF' TOUR

"They're really out to totally shock and nauseate this time – look at that sirloin-shaped guitar!"

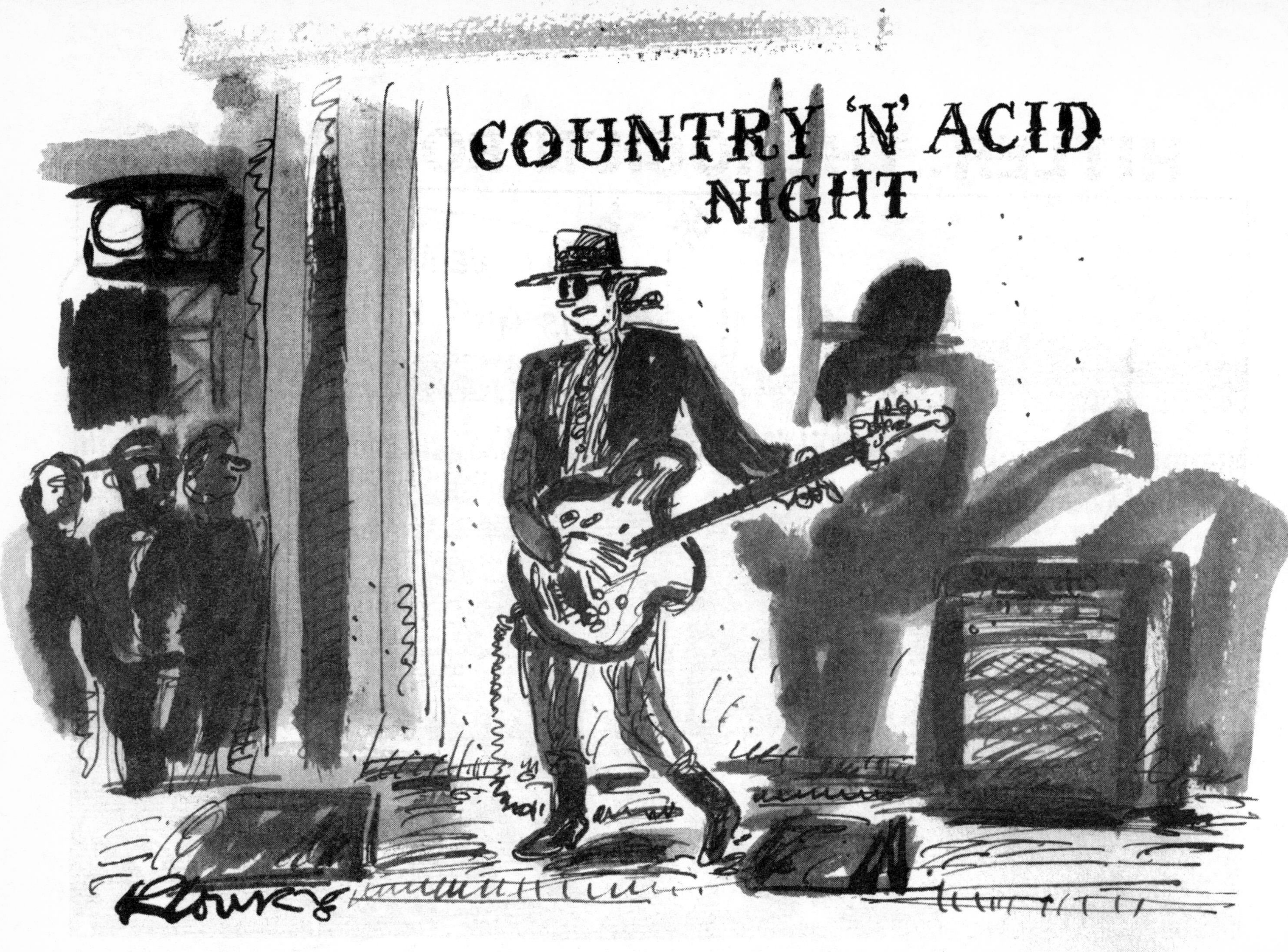
COUNTRY 'N' ACID
NIGHT

"My wife's been cheatin' on me, I lost my job at the factory, and I'm a throbbing fluorescent lobster floating high above the electric, neon night."

HITLER..THE ROCK'N' ROLL YEARS

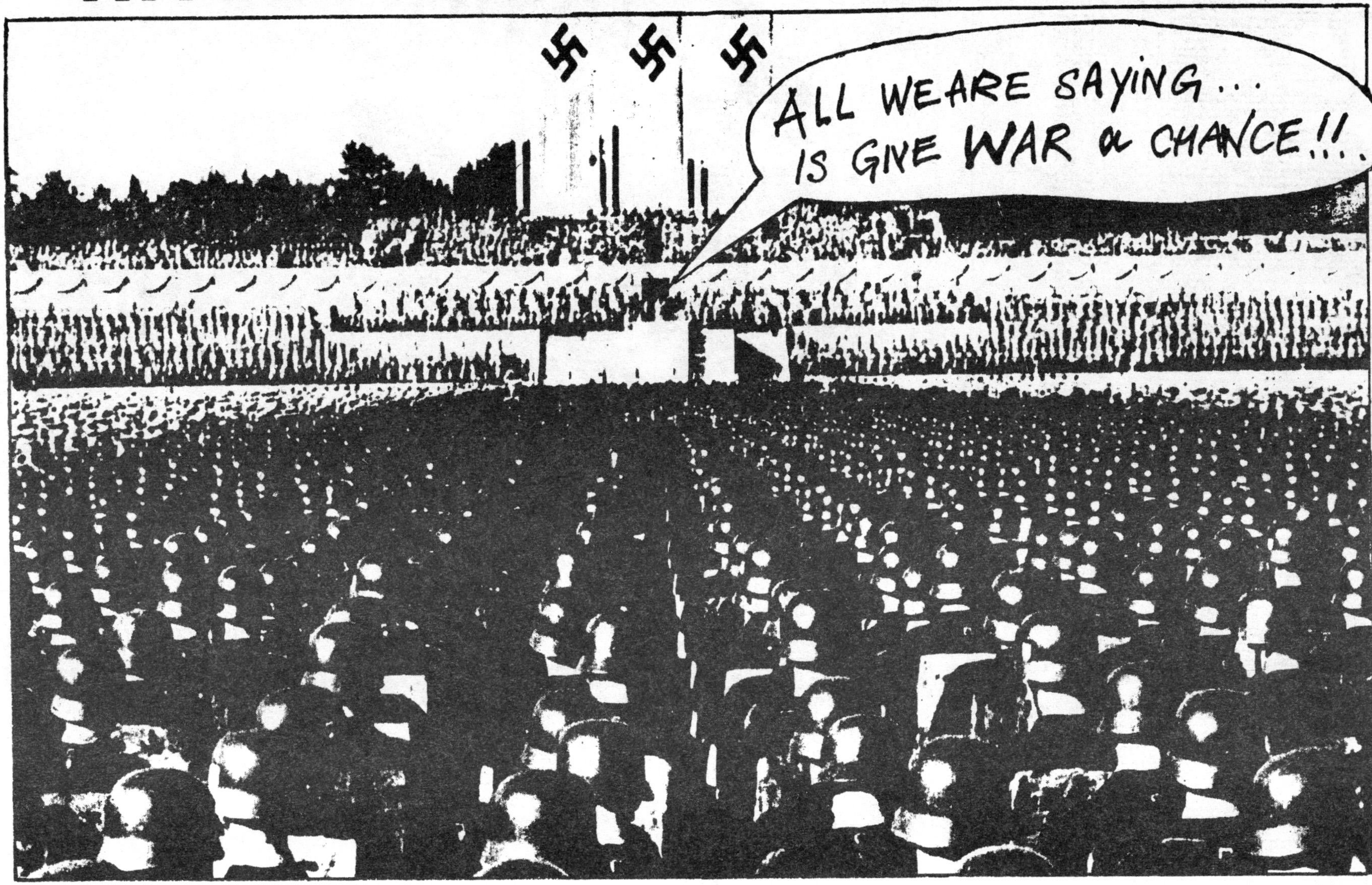
ALL WEARE SAYING...
IS GIVE WAR a CHANCE!!

I deputised for Posy Simmonds in The Guardian for a few heady months in the early '90s.
These are some of the results of that brief dalliance.

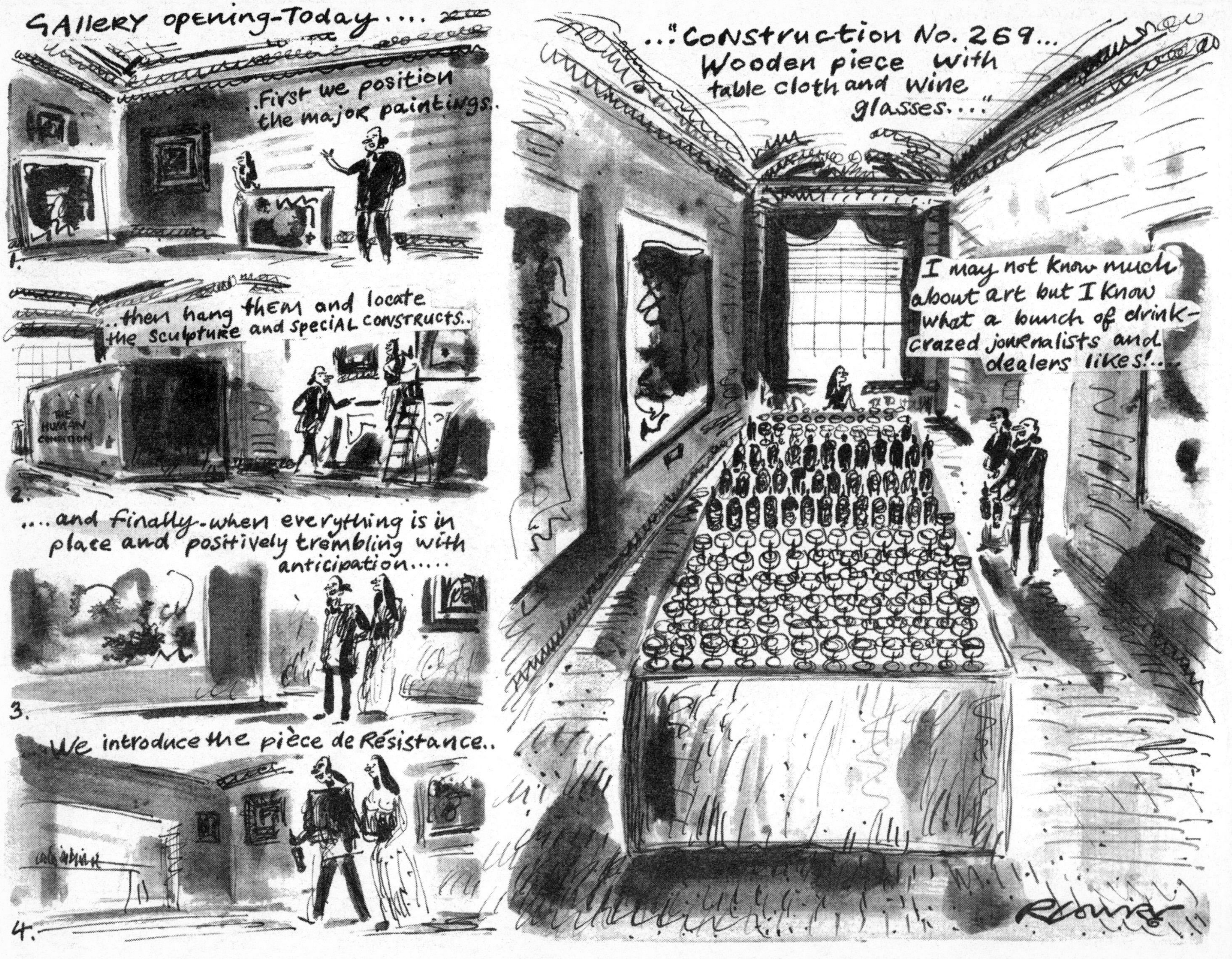
GALLERY opening-Today....
..First we position the major paintings..
1.
..then hang THEM and locate the sculpture and SPECIAL CONSTRUCTS..
THE HUMAN CONDITION
2.
....and finally-when everything is in place and positively trembling with anticipation.....
3.
We introduce the pièce de Résistance..
4.
..."CONSTRUCTION No. 269... Wooden piece with table cloth and wine glasses...."
I may not know much about art but I know what a bunch of drink-crazed journalists and dealers likes!...

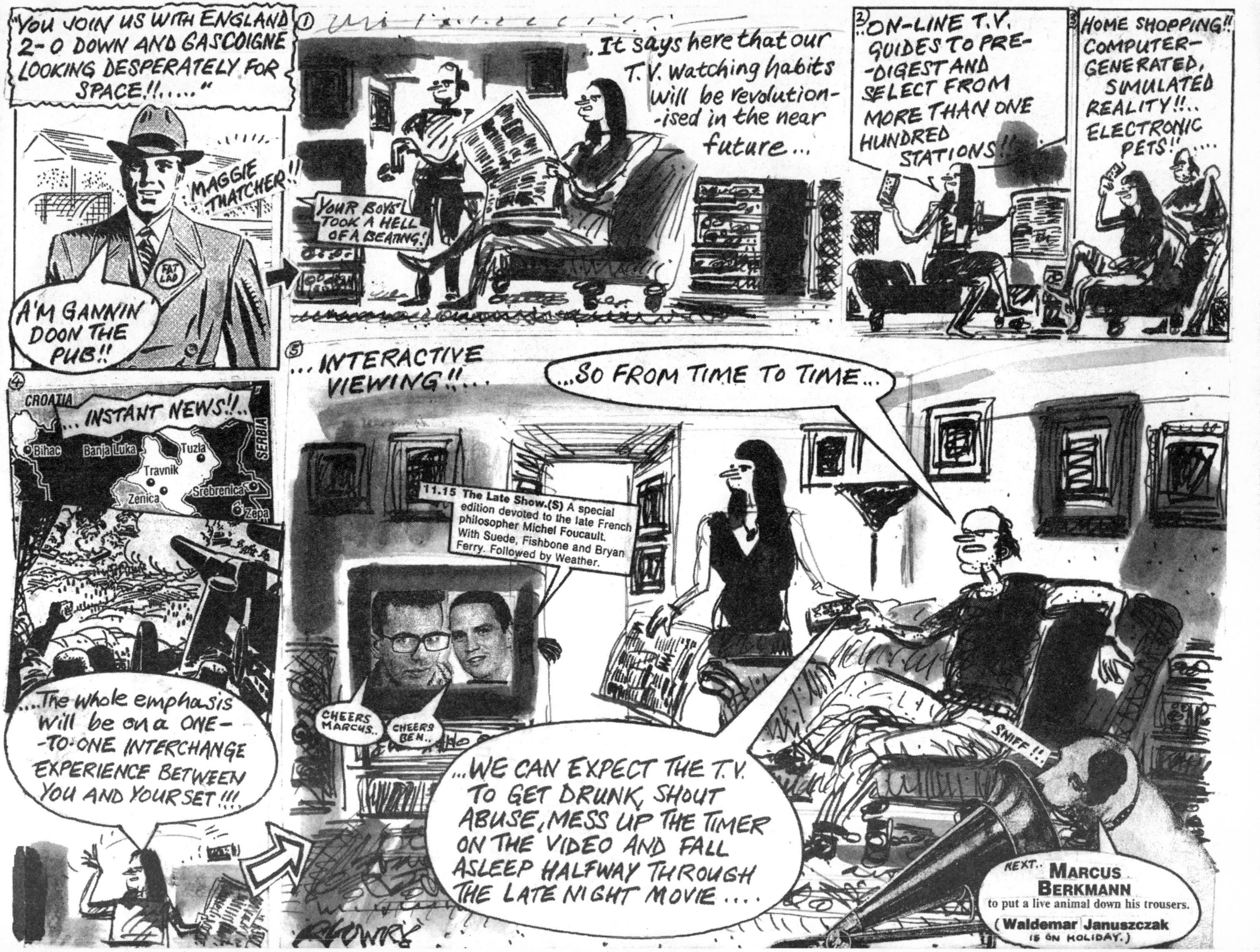
"YOU JOIN US WITH ENGLAND 2-0 DOWN AND GASCOIGNE LOOKING DESPERATELY FOR SPACE!!....."
MAGGIE THATCHER!!
FAT LAD
A'M GANNIN' DOON THE PUB!!
1
...It says here that our T.V. watching habits will be revolution--ised in the near future...
YOUR BOYS TOOK A HELL OF A BEATING!
2
...ON-LINE T.V. GUIDES TO PRE--DIGEST AND SELECT FROM MORE THAN ONE HUNDRED STATIONS!!
3
HOME SHOPPING!! COMPUTER-GENERATED, SIMULATED REALITY!!.. ELECTRONIC PETS!!....
4
CROATIA
...INSTANT NEWS!!..
SERBIA
Bihac
Banja Luka
Tuzla
Travnik
Zenica
Srebrenica
Zepa
...The whole emphasis will be on a ONE--TO-ONE INTERCHANGE EXPERIENCE BETWEEN YOU AND YOUR SET!!!
5
...INTERACTIVE VIEWING!!...
...SO FROM TIME TO TIME...
11.15 The Late Show.(S) A special edition devoted to the late French philosopher Michel Foucault. With Suede, Fishbone and Bryan Ferry. Followed by Weather.
CHEERS MARCUS..
CHEERS BEN..
...WE CAN EXPECT THE T.V. TO GET DRUNK, SHOUT ABUSE, MESS UP THE TIMER ON THE VIDEO AND FALL ASLEEP HALFWAY THROUGH THE LATE NIGHT MOVIE...
SNIFF!!
NEXT.. MARCUS BERKMANN to put a live animal down his trousers.
(Waldemar Januszczak IS ON HOLIDAY.)

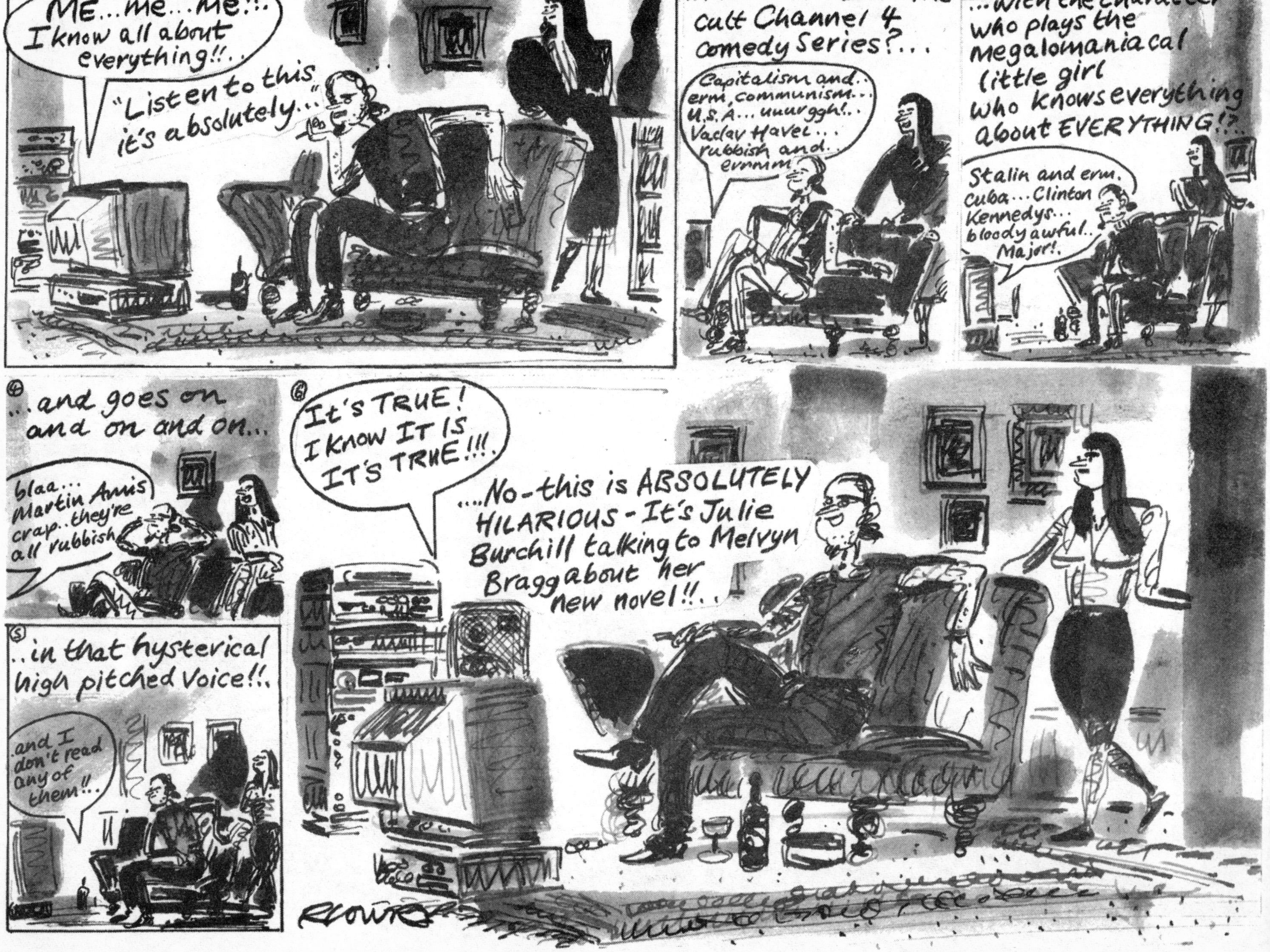
ME...me...me!!. I know all about everything!!..
"Listen to this it's absolutely..."
.."ABSOLUTELY"-The cult Channel 4 comedy Series?...
Capitalism and.. erm, communism.. U.S.A... uuurggh!.. Vaclav Havel... rubbish and.. ermmm
...with the character who plays the Megalomaniacal little girl who knows everything about EVERYTHING!?..
Stalin and erm. Cuba... Clinton Kennedys... bloody awful.. Major!.
...and goes on and on and on...
blaa... Martin Amis crap.. they're all rubbish
..in that hysterical high pitched Voice!!.
.and I don't read any of them!!..
It's TRUE! I Know It Is IT'S TRUE!!!
...No-this is ABSOLUTELY HILARIOUS - It's Julie Burchill talking to Melvyn Bragg about her new novel!!..

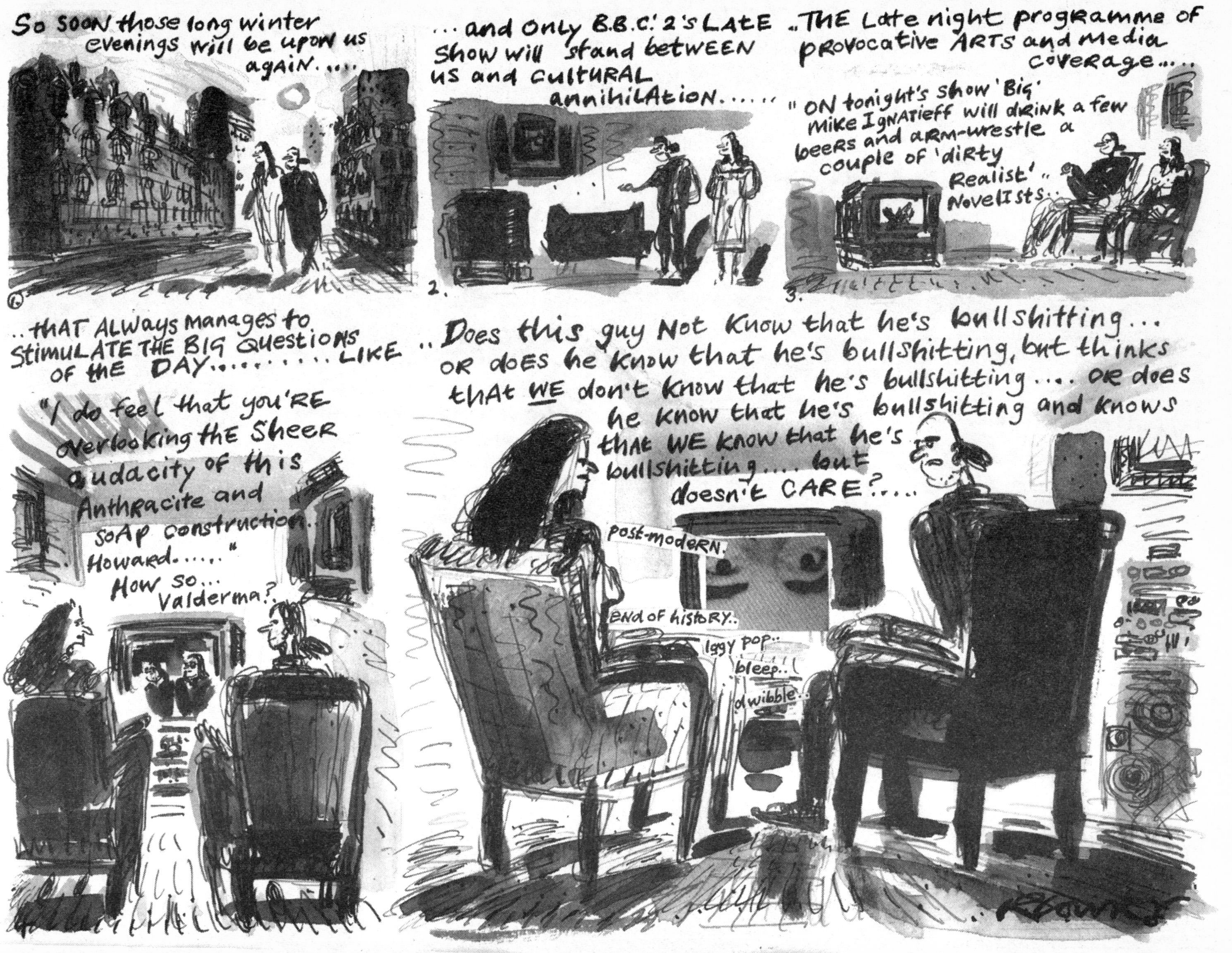

So soon those long winter evenings will be upon us again.....
...and only B.B.C. 2's Late Show will stand between us and cultural annihilation......
...The late night programme of provocative arts and media coverage.....
"On tonight's show 'Big' Mike Ignatieff will drink a few beers and arm-wrestle a couple of 'dirty Realist'.. Novelists..
...that always manages to stimulate the big questions of the day..........like
"I do feel that you're overlooking the sheer audacity of this anthracite and soap construction.. Howard....."
How so... Valderma?
...Does this guy not know that he's bullshitting... or does he know that he's bullshitting, but thinks that WE don't know that he's bullshitting.... or does he know that he's bullshitting and knows that WE know that he's bullshitting.... but doesn't CARE?....
post-modern.
End of history..
iggy pop..
bleep..
dwibble..

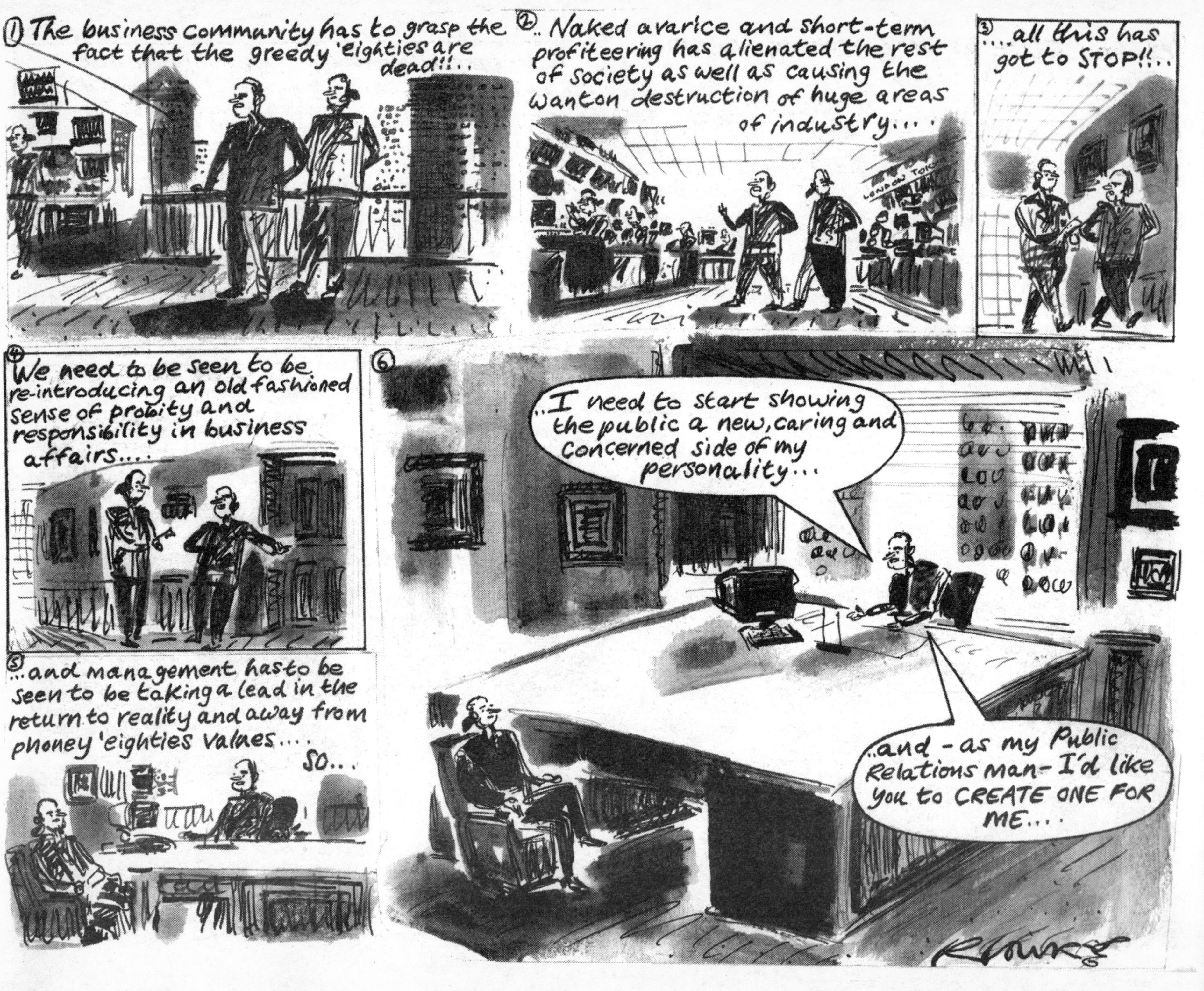
1
The business community has to grasp the fact that the greedy 'eighties are dead!!...
2
.. Naked avarice and short-term profiteering has alienated the rest of society as well as causing the wanton destruction of huge areas of industry...
3
....all this has got to STOP!!...
4
We need to be seen to be re-introducing an old fashioned sense of probity and responsibility in business affairs....
5
...and management has to be seen to be taking a lead in the return to reality and away from phoney 'eighties values....
SO...
6
...I need to start showing the public a new, caring and concerned side of my personality...
...and - as my Public Relations man - I'd like you to CREATE ONE FOR ME...
LONDON TOKYO
RFOWKES

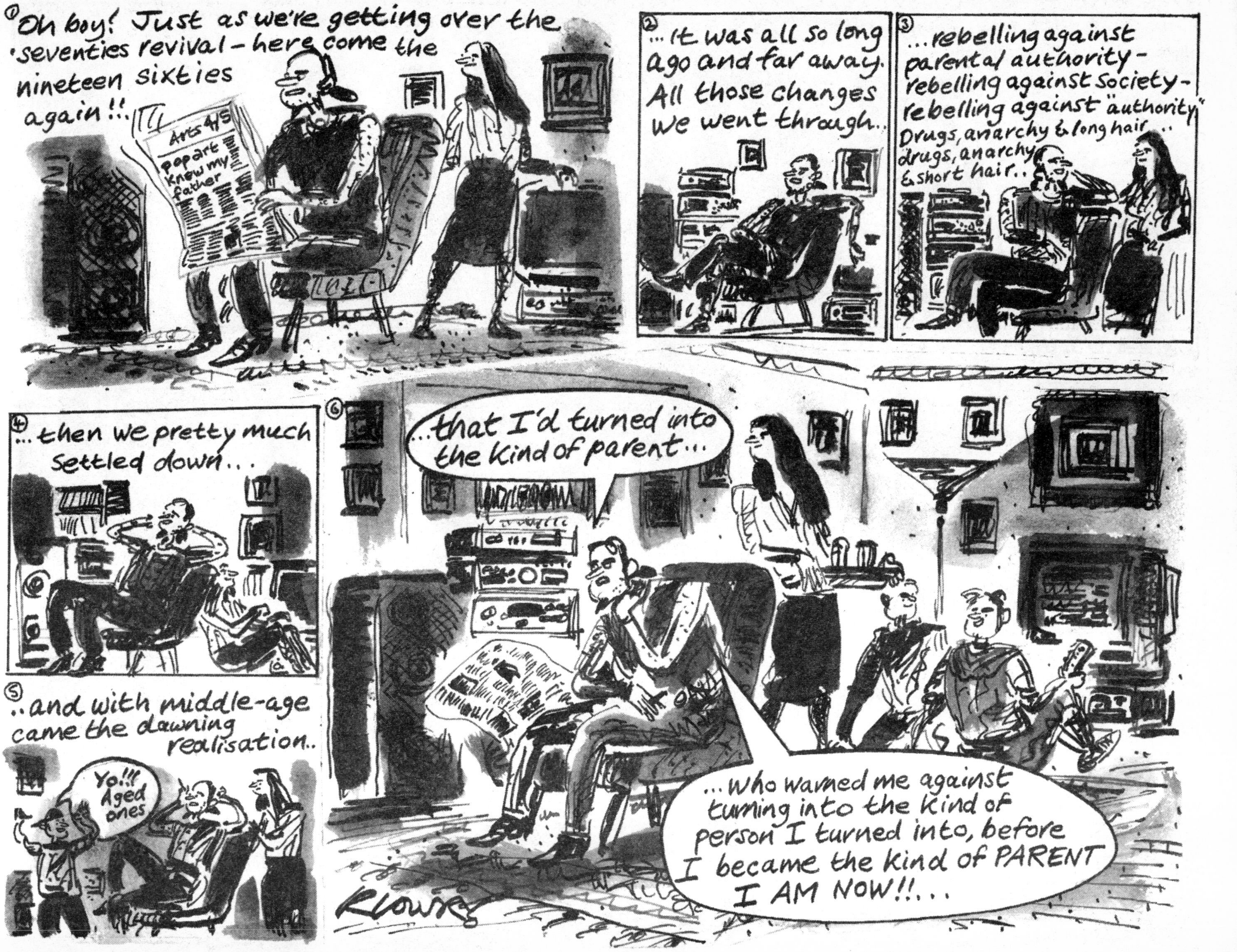
1 "Oh boy! Just as we're getting over the 'seventies revival – here come the nineteen sixties again!!
Arts 4/5
Pop art knew my father
2 ... it was all so long ago and far away. All those changes we went through...
3 ...rebelling against parental authority – rebelling against society – rebelling against "authority"
Drugs, anarchy & long hair... drugs, anarchy & short hair...
4 ... then we pretty much settled down...
5 ..and with middle-age came the dawning realisation..
Yo!!! Aged ones
6 ...that I'd turned into the kind of parent...
...who warned me against turning into the kind of person I turned into, before I became the kind of PARENT I AM NOW!!...
RLOWRY

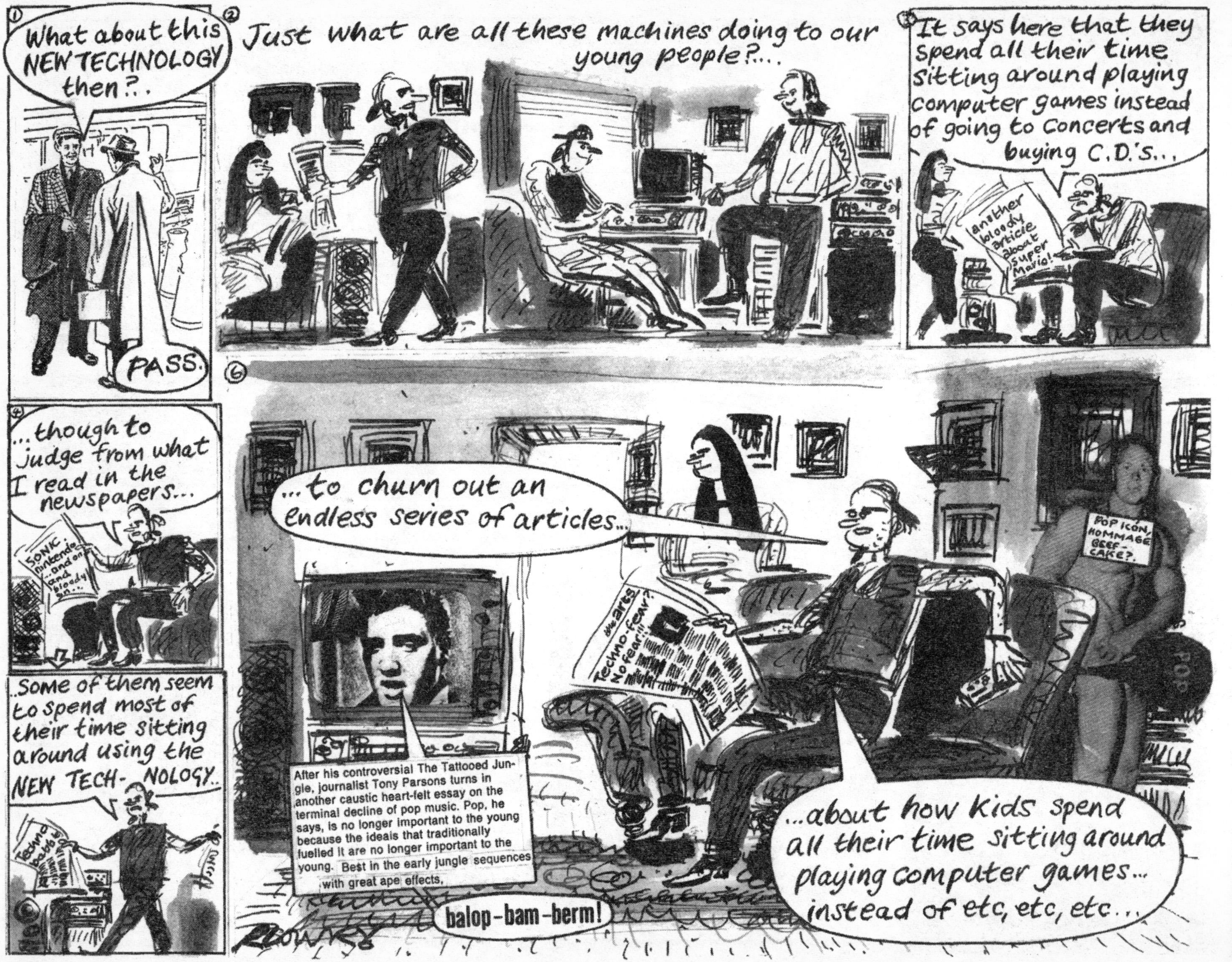

1
What about this NEW TECHNOLOGY then?..
PASS.
2
Just what are all these machines doing to our young people?...
3
It says here that they spend all their time sitting around playing computer games instead of going to Concerts and buying C.D.'s...
another bloody article about Super Mario!
4
...though to judge from what I read in the newspapers...
SONIC. nintendo ...and on and bloody on...
..Some of them seem to spend most of their time sitting around using the NEW TECH- NOLOGY..
Techno babble
6
...to churn out an endless series of articles...
the arts
Techno-fear? No fear!!!
POP ICON, HOMMAGE BEEF-CAKE?.
POP
After his controversial The Tattooed Jungle, journalist Tony Parsons turns in another caustic heart-felt essay on the terminal decline of pop music. Pop, he says, is no longer important to the young because the ideals that traditionally fuelled it are no longer important to the young. Best in the early jungle sequences with great ape effects,
...about how kids spend all their time sitting around playing computer games... instead of etc, etc, etc...
balop-bam-berm!

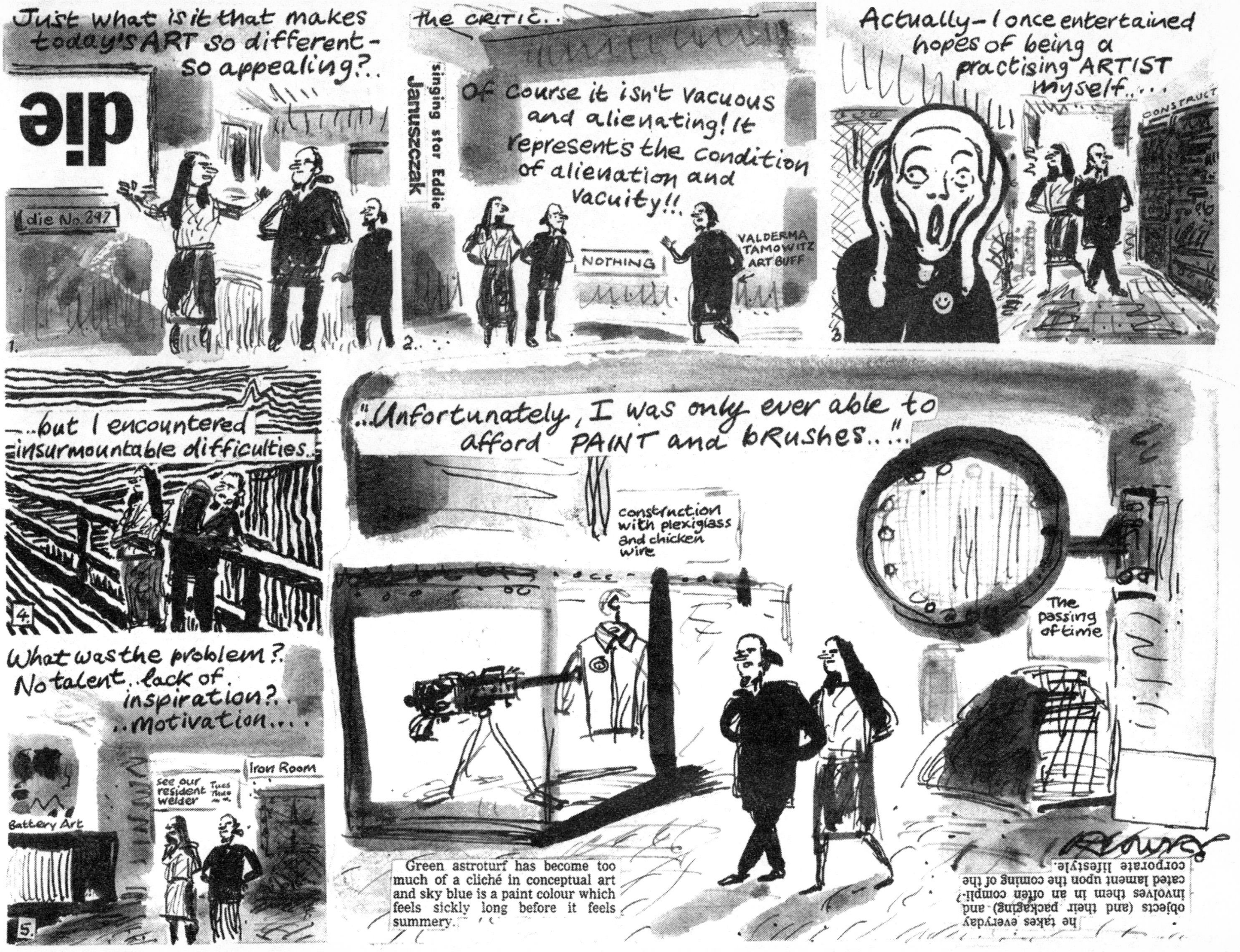
Just what is it that makes today's ART so different - so appealing?..
Edie No. 247
1.
the CRITIC..
singing star Eddie Januszczak
Of course it isn't vacuous and alienating! It represents the condition of alienation and vacuity!!
NOTHING
VALDERMA TAMOWITZ ART BUFF
2.
Actually - I once entertained hopes of being a practising ARTIST myself....
CONSTRUCT
3
..but I encountered insurmountable difficulties..
4.
What was the problem?.. No talent.. lack of.. inspiration?.. ..Motivation....
Battery Art
see our resident welder
Tues Thurs
Iron Room
5.
"..Unfortunately, I was only ever able to afford PAINT and BRUSHES..!"
construction with plexiglass and chicken wire
The passing of time
Green astroturf has become too much of a cliché in conceptual art and sky blue is a paint colour which feels sickly long before it feels summery.
he takes everyday objects (and their packaging) and involves them in an often complicated lament upon the coming of the corporate lifestyle.

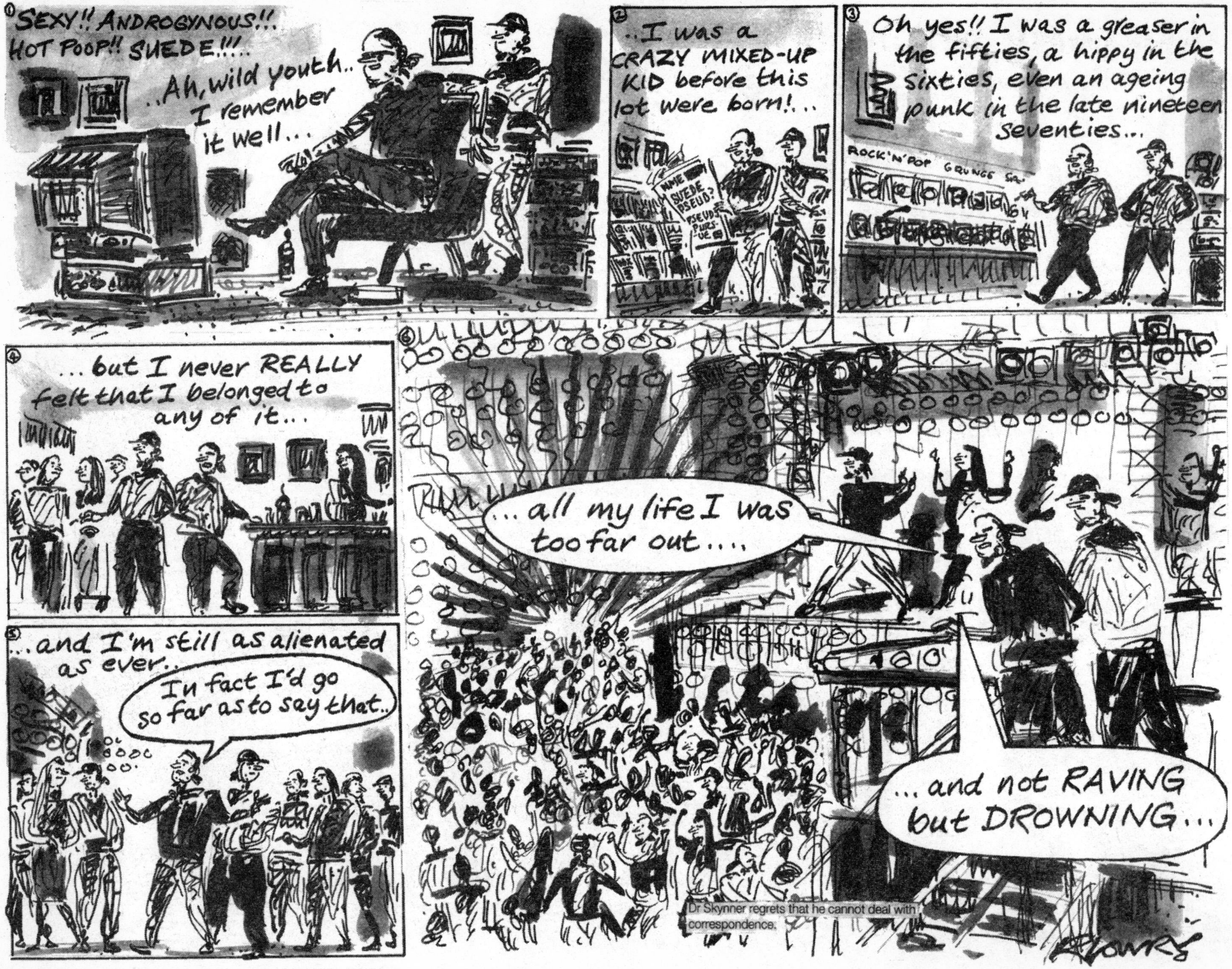
SEXY!! ANDROGYNOUS!! HOT POOP!! SUEDE!!!..
..Ah, wild youth.. I remember it well...
..I was a CRAZY MIXED-UP KID before this lot were born!..
Oh yes!! I was a greaser in the fifties, a hippy in the sixties, even an ageing punk in the late nineteen seventies...
ROCK'N'POP GRUNGE
...but I never REALLY felt that I belonged to any of it...
...and I'm still as alienated as ever..
In fact I'd go so far as to say that..
...all my life I was too far out....
...and not RAVING but DROWNING...

Dr Skynner regrets that he cannot deal with correspondence.

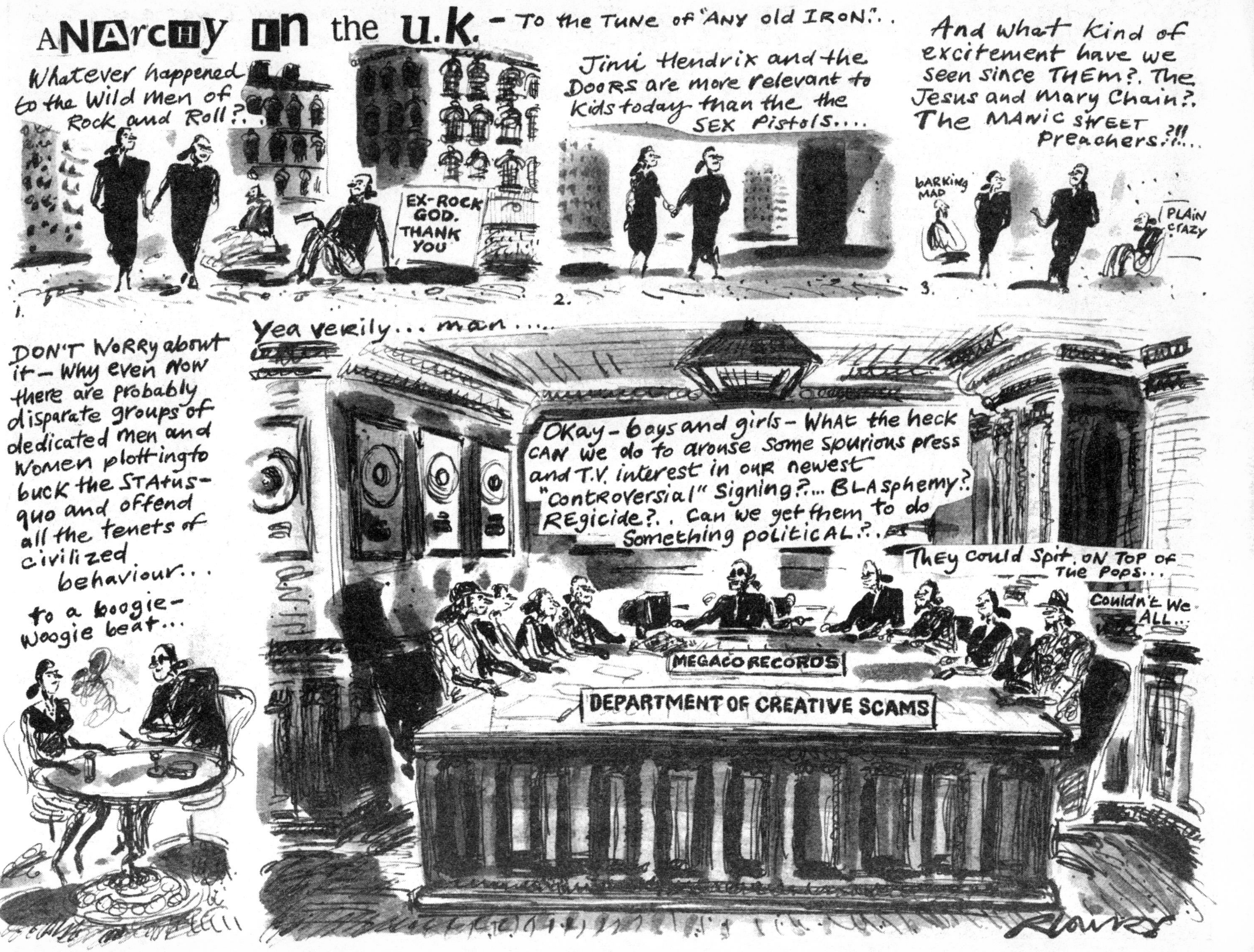

ANARCHY IN the U.K. - TO the TUNE of "ANY old IRON"..
Whatever happened to the Wild Men of Rock and Roll?..
EX-ROCK GOD. THANK YOU
1.
Jimi Hendrix and the Doors are more relevant to kids today than the the SEX Pistols....
2.
And what kind of excitement have we seen since THEM?. The Jesus and Mary Chain?. The MANIC STREET Preachers?!!...
barking mad
PLAIN crazy
3.
Yea verily... man.....
DON'T WORRY about it - Why even NOW there are probably disparate groups of dedicated men and women plotting to buck the STATUS-quo and offend all the tenets of civilized behaviour...
to a boogie-woogie beat...
4.
Okay - boys and girls - WHAT the heck CAN we do to arouse some spurious press and T.V. interest in our newest "controversial" signing?... BLASphemy?. Regicide?.. Can we get them to do something political?..
They could spit ON TOP OF THE POPS...
Couldn't we ALL...
MEGACO RECORDS
DEPARTMENT OF CREATIVE SCAMS

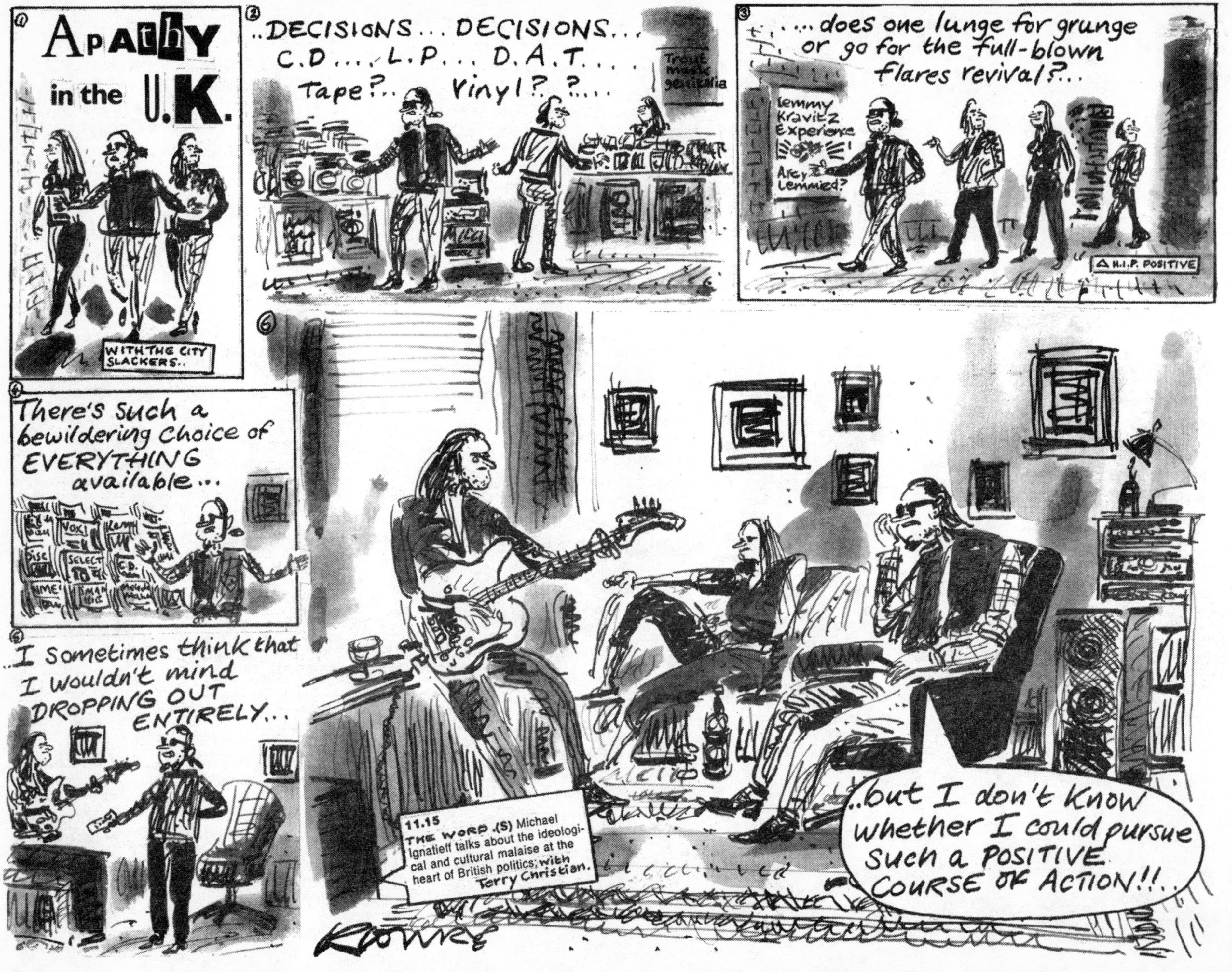
Apathy in the U.K.
WITH THE CITY SLACKERS..
..DECISIONS... DECISIONS... C.D...., L.P... D.A.T..... Tape?.. Vinyl? ?...
Trout mask genitalia
.....does one lunge for grunge or go for the full-blown flares revival?..
Lemmy Kravitz Experience
Are y Lemmied?
H.I.P. POSITIVE
There's such a bewildering choice of EVERYTHING available...
VOX
SELECT
NME
..I sometimes think that I wouldn't mind DROPPING OUT ENTIRELY...
11.15
THE WORD .(S) Michael Ignatieff talks about the ideological and cultural malaise at the heart of British politics; with Terry Christian.
..but I don't know whether I could pursue such a POSITIVE COURSE OF ACTION!!..
RIOWRE

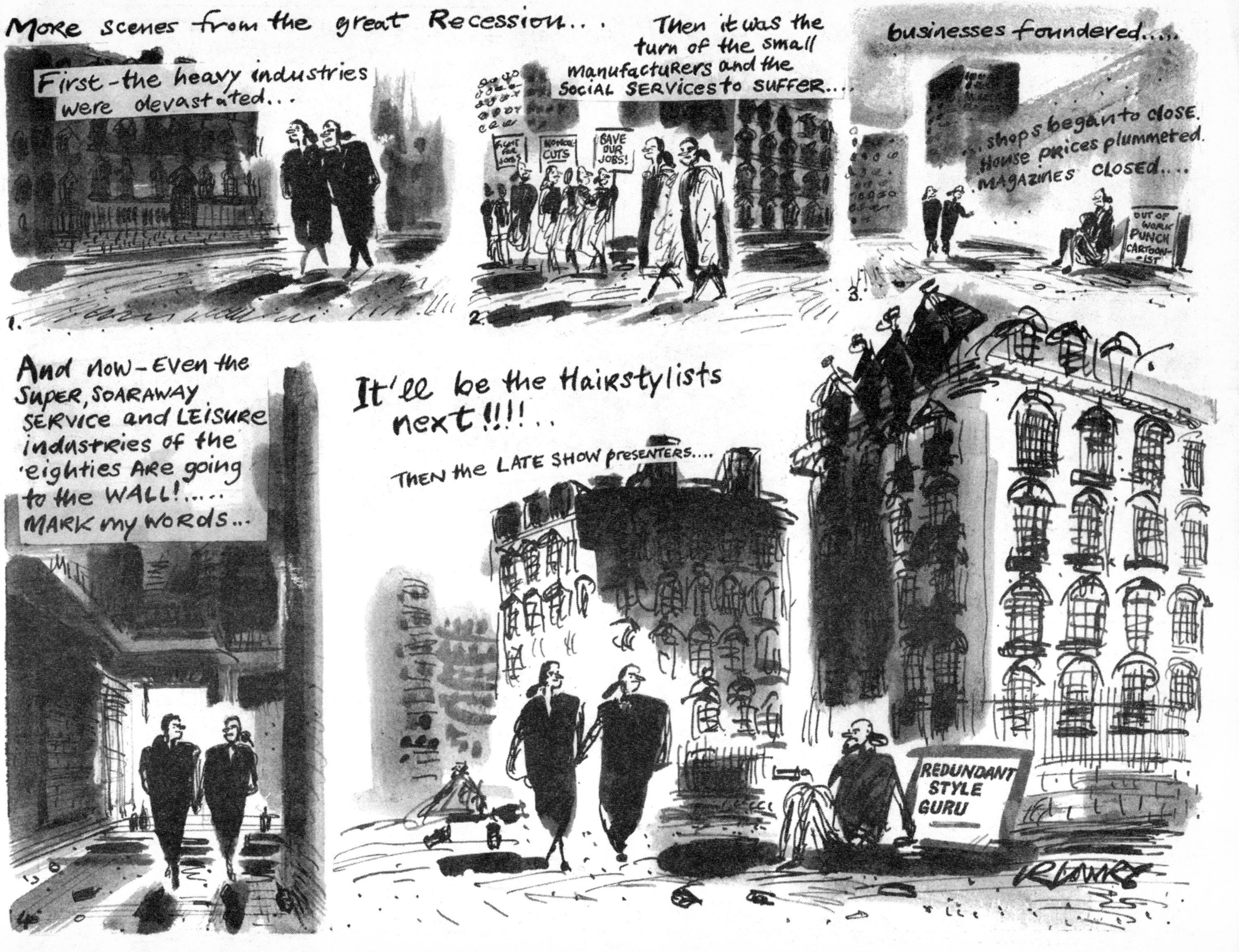
More scenes from the great Recession...
First - the heavy industries were devastated...
1.
Then it was the turn of the small manufacturers and the SOCIAL SERVICES to SUFFER...
CUTS
SAVE OUR JOBS!
2.
businesses foundered.....
...shops began to close. House prices plummeted. MAGAZINES CLOSED....
OUT OF WORK PUNCH CARTOON-IST
3.
And now - Even the SUPER, SOARAWAY SERVICE and LEISURE industries of the 'eighties ARE going to the WALL!..... MARK my words...
4.
It'll be the Hairstylists next!!!!..
THEN the LATE SHOW presenters....
REDUNDANT STYLE GURU

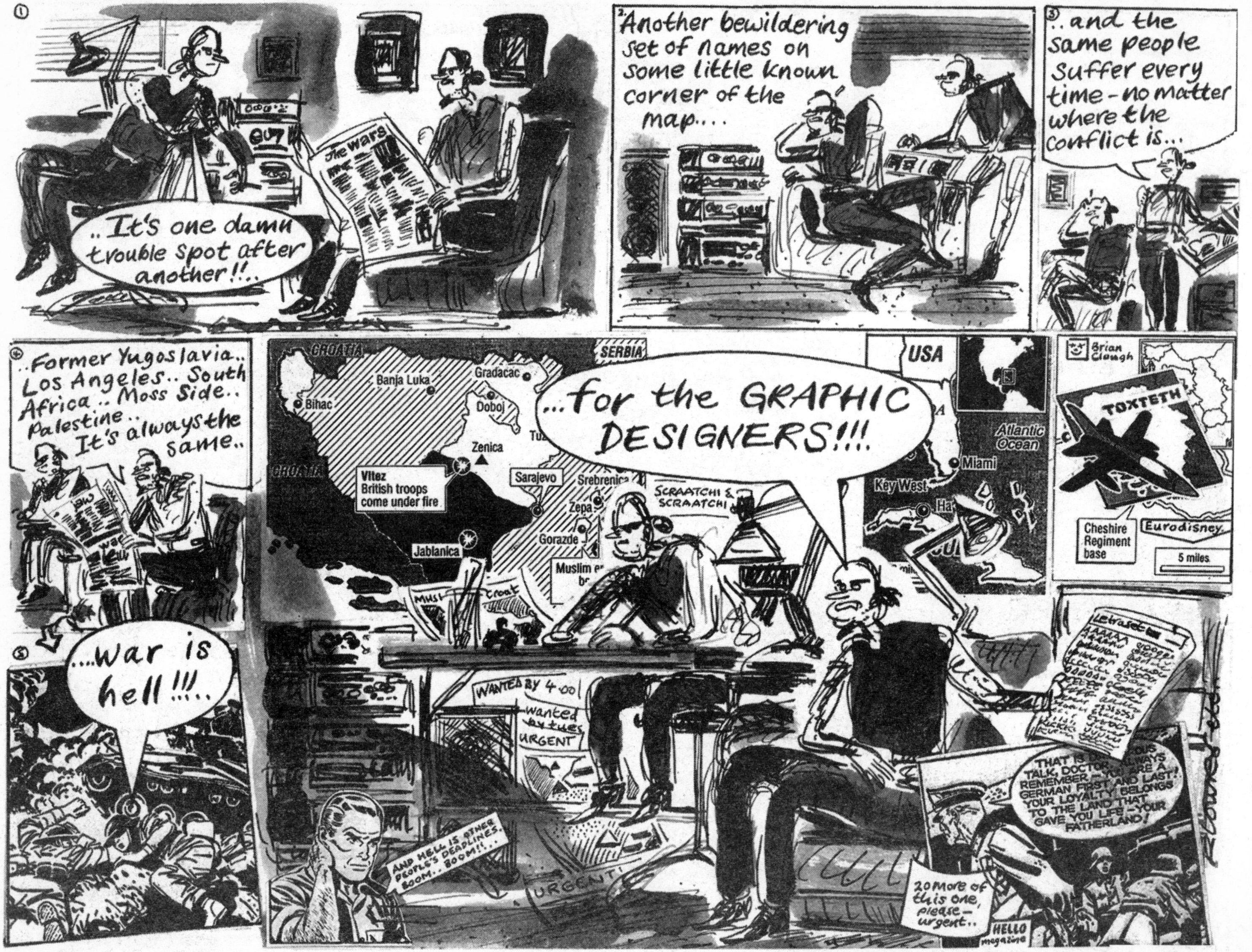

1
The wars
..It's one damn trouble spot after another!!..
2. Another bewildering set of names on some little known corner of the map....
3. ..and the same people suffer every time - no matter where the conflict is...
4. ..Former Yugoslavia.. Los Angeles.. South Africa.. Moss Side.. Palestine.. It's always the same..
CROATIA
SERBIA
Banja Luka
Gradacac
Bihac
Doboj
Zenica
Vitez British troops come under fire
Sarajevo
Srebrenica
Zepa
Gorazde
Jablanica
USA
Atlantic Ocean
Miami
Key West
Brian Clough
TOXTETH
Cheshire Regiment base
Eurodisney
5 miles
...for the GRAPHIC DESIGNERS!!!
SCRAATCHI & SCRAATCHI
5
...War is hell!!!..
WANTED BY 4.00
wanted by tues
URGENT
Letraset
AND HELL IS OTHER PEOPLE'S DEADLINES. BOOM.. BOOM!!..
URGENT!
20 more of this one, please - urgent..
HELLO magazine

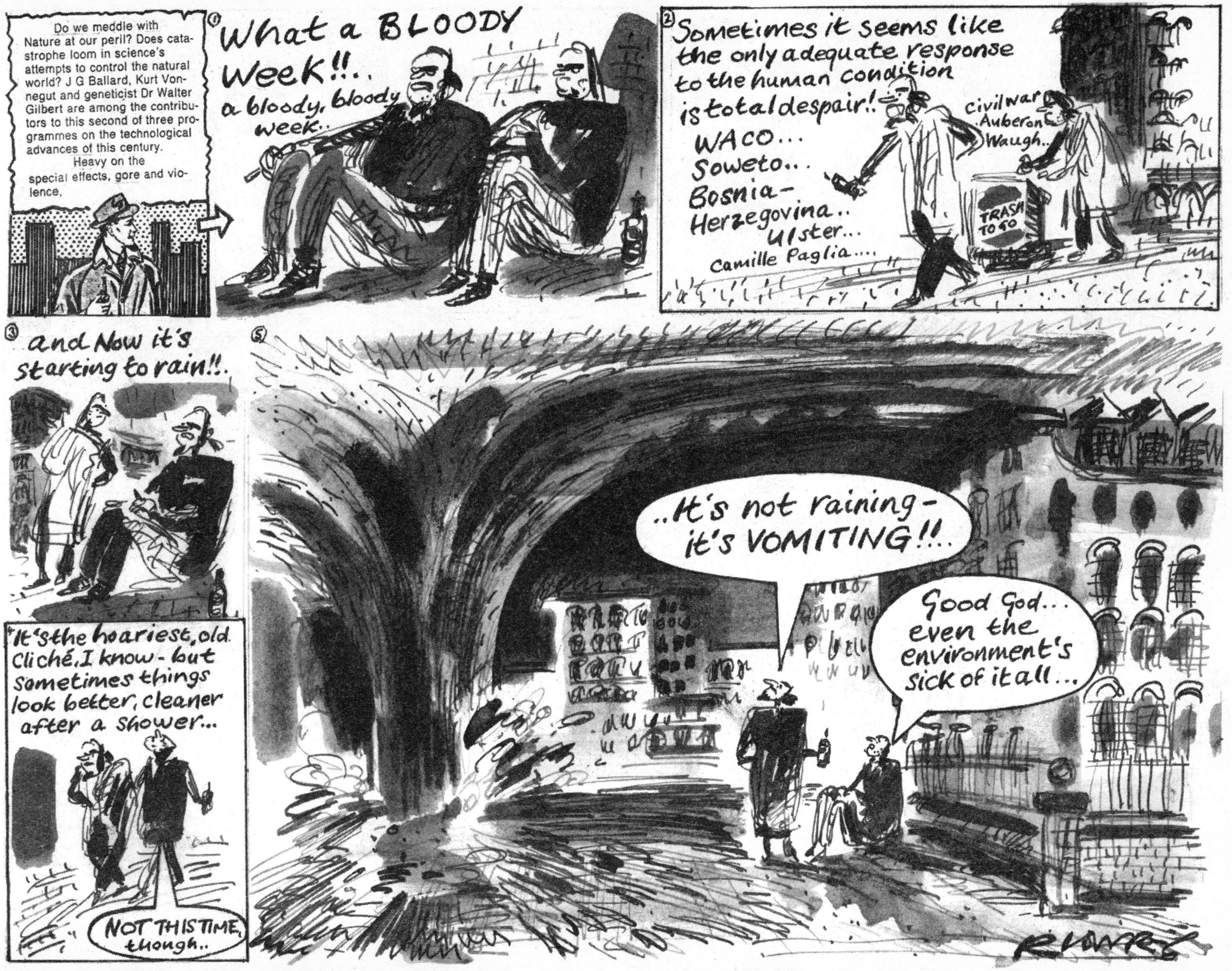

Do we meddle with Nature at our peril? Does catastrophe loom in science's attempts to control the natural world? J G Ballard, Kurt Vonnegut and geneticist Dr Walter Gilbert are among the contributors to this second of three programmes on the technological advances of this century.
Heavy on the special effects, gore and violence.
What a BLOODY Week!!..
a bloody, bloody week..
Sometimes it seems like the only adequate response to the human condition is total despair!..
WACO...
Soweto..
Bosnia-Herzegovina..
Ulster...
Camille Paglia....
Civil war
Auberon Waugh...
TRASH TO GO
and Now it's starting to rain!!..
"It's the hoariest, old Cliché, I know - but sometimes things look better, cleaner after a shower...
NOT THIS TIME, though..
..It's not raining - it's VOMITING!!..
Good God... even the environment's sick of it all...

The Do-Not Press
Fiercely Independent Publishing

Keep in touch with what's happening at the cutting edge of independent British publishing.

Join The Do-Not Press Information Service and receive advance information of all our new titles, as well as news of events and launches in your area, and the occasional free gift and special offer.

Simply send your name and address to:
The Do-Not Press (Dept. RLI)
PO Box 4215, London SE23 2QD
or email us: thedonotpress@zoo.co.uk

There is no obligation to purchase and no salesman will call.

Visit our regularly-updated web site:

http://www.thedonotpress.co.uk

Mail Order

All our titles are available from good bookshops, or (in case of difficulty) direct from The Do-Not Press at the address above. There is no charge for post and packing. (NB: A postman may call.)